M000188958

Active Directory™
Bible

Active Directory™
Bible

Curt Simmons

IDG BOOKS
WORLDWIDE

IDG Books Worldwide, Inc.
An International Data Group Company

Foster City, CA ✦ Chicago, IL ✦ Indianapolis, IN ✦ New York, NY

Active Directory™ Bible

Published by
IDG Books Worldwide, Inc.
An International Data Group Company
919 E. Hillsdale Blvd., Suite 400
Foster City, CA 94404
www.idgbooks.com (IDG Books Worldwide Web site)

Copyright © 2001 IDG Books Worldwide, Inc. All rights reserved. No part of this book, including interior design, cover design, and icons, may be reproduced or transmitted in any form, by any means (electronic, photocopying, recording, or otherwise) without the prior written permission of the publisher.

ISBN: 0-7645-4762-3

Printed in the United States of America

10 9 8 7 6 5 4 3 2 1

1B/RU/RR/QQ/FC

Distributed in the United States by IDG Books Worldwide, Inc.

Distributed by CDG Books Canada Inc. for Canada; by Transworld Publishers Limited in the United Kingdom; by IDG Norge Books for Norway; by IDG Sweden Books for Sweden; by IDG Books Australia Publishing Corporation Pty. Ltd. for Australia and New Zealand; by TransQuest Publishers Pte Ltd. for Singapore, Malaysia, Thailand, Indonesia, and Hong Kong; by Gotop Information Inc. for Taiwan; by ICG Muse, Inc. for Japan; by Intersoft for South Africa; by Eyrolles for France; by International Thomson Publishing for Germany, Austria, and Switzerland; by Distribuidora Cuspide for Argentina; by LR International for Brazil; by Galileo Libros for Chile; by Ediciones ZETA S.C.R. Ltda. for Peru; by WS Computer Publishing Corporation, Inc., for the Philippines; by Contemporanea de Ediciones for Venezuela; by Express Computer Distributors for the Caribbean and West Indies; by Micronesia Media Distributor, Inc. for Micronesia; by Chips Computadoras S.A. de C.V. for Mexico; by Editorial Norma de Panama S.A. for Panama; by American Bookshops for Finland.

For general information on IDG Books Worldwide's books in the U.S., please call our Consumer Customer Service department at 800-762-2974. For reseller information, including discounts and premium sales, please call our Reseller Customer Service department at 800-434-3422.

For information on where to purchase IDG Books Worldwide's books outside the U.S., please contact our International Sales department at 317-572-3993 or fax 317-572-4002.

For consumer information on foreign language translations, please contact our Customer Service department at 800-434-3422, fax 317-572-4002, or e-mail rights@idgbooks.com.

For information on licensing foreign or domestic rights, please phone +1-650-653-7098.

For sales inquiries and special prices for bulk quantities, please contact our Order Services department at 800-434-3422 or write to the address above.

For information on using IDG Books Worldwide's books in the classroom or for ordering examination copies, please contact our Educational Sales department at 800-434-2086 or fax 317-572-4005.

For press review copies, author interviews, or other publicity information, please contact our Public Relations department at 650-653-7000 or fax 650-653-7500.

For authorization to photocopy items for corporate, personal, or educational use, please contact Copyright Clearance Center, 222 Rosewood Drive, Danvers, MA 01923, or fax 978-750-4470.

Library of Congress Cataloging-in-Publication Data

Simmons, Curt, 1968-
 Active directory bible / Curt Simmons.
  p. cm.
 ISBN 0-7645-4762-3 (alk. paper)
 1. Directory services (Computer network technology) 2. Microsoft Windows (Computer file) I. Title.
 TK5105.595 .S55 2000
 005.7'1369—dc21

 00-046159
 CIP

LIMIT OF LIABILITY/DISCLAIMER OF WARRANTY: THE PUBLISHER AND AUTHOR HAVE USED THEIR BEST EFFORTS IN PREPARING THIS BOOK. THE PUBLISHER AND AUTHOR MAKE NO REPRESENTATIONS OR WARRANTIES WITH RESPECT TO THE ACCURACY OR COMPLETENESS OF THE CONTENTS OF THIS BOOK AND SPECIFICALLY DISCLAIM ANY IMPLIED WARRANTIES OF MERCHANTABILITY OR FITNESS FOR A PARTICULAR PURPOSE. THERE ARE NO WARRANTIES WHICH EXTEND BEYOND THE DESCRIPTIONS CONTAINED IN THIS PARAGRAPH. NO WARRANTY MAY BE CREATED OR EXTENDED BY SALES REPRESENTATIVES OR WRITTEN SALES MATERIALS. THE ACCURACY AND COMPLETENESS OF THE INFORMATION PROVIDED HEREIN AND THE OPINIONS STATED HEREIN ARE NOT GUARANTEED OR WARRANTED TO PRODUCE ANY PARTICULAR RESULTS, AND THE ADVICE AND STRATEGIES CONTAINED HEREIN MAY NOT BE SUITABLE FOR EVERY INDIVIDUAL. NEITHER THE PUBLISHER NOR AUTHOR SHALL BE LIABLE FOR ANY LOSS OF PROFIT OR ANY OTHER COMMERCIAL DAMAGES, INCLUDING BUT NOT LIMITED TO SPECIAL, INCIDENTAL, CONSEQUENTIAL, OR OTHER DAMAGES.

Trademarks: All brand names and product names used in this book are trade names, service marks, trademarks, or registered trademarks of their respective owners. IDG Books Worldwide is not associated with any product or vendor mentioned in this book.

is a registered trademark or trademark under exclusive license to IDG Books Worldwide, Inc. from International Data Group, Inc. in the United States and/or other countries.

ABOUT IDG BOOKS WORLDWIDE

Welcome to the world of IDG Books Worldwide.

IDG Books Worldwide, Inc., is a subsidiary of International Data Group, the world's largest publisher of computer-related information and the leading global provider of information services on information technology. IDG was founded more than 30 years ago by Patrick J. McGovern and now employs more than 9,000 people worldwide. IDG publishes more than 290 computer publications in over 75 countries. More than 90 million people read one or more IDG publications each month.

Launched in 1990, IDG Books Worldwide is today the #1 publisher of best-selling computer books in the United States. We are proud to have received eight awards from the Computer Press Association in recognition of editorial excellence and three from Computer Currents' First Annual Readers' Choice Awards. Our best-selling ...*For Dummies*® series has more than 50 million copies in print with translations in 31 languages. IDG Books Worldwide, through a joint venture with IDG's Hi-Tech Beijing, became the first U.S. publisher to publish a computer book in the People's Republic of China. In record time, IDG Books Worldwide has become the first choice for millions of readers around the world who want to learn how to better manage their businesses.

Our mission is simple: Every one of our books is designed to bring extra value and skill-building instructions to the reader. Our books are written by experts who understand and care about our readers. The knowledge base of our editorial staff comes from years of experience in publishing, education, and journalism — experience we use to produce books to carry us into the new millennium. In short, we care about books, so we attract the best people. We devote special attention to details such as audience, interior design, use of icons, and illustrations. And because we use an efficient process of authoring, editing, and desktop publishing our books electronically, we can spend more time ensuring superior content and less time on the technicalities of making books.

You can count on our commitment to deliver high-quality books at competitive prices on topics you want to read about. At IDG Books Worldwide, we continue in the IDG tradition of delivering quality for more than 30 years. You'll find no better book on a subject than one from IDG Books Worldwide.

John Kilcullen
Chairman and CEO
IDG Books Worldwide, Inc.

*Eighth Annual
Computer Press
Awards 1992*

*Ninth Annual
Computer Press
Awards 1993*

*Tenth Annual
Computer Press
Awards 1994*

*Eleventh Annual
Computer Press
Awards 1995*

IDG is the world's leading IT media, research and exposition company. Founded in 1964, IDG had 1997 revenues of $2.05 billion and has more than 9,000 employees worldwide. IDG offers the widest range of media options that reach IT buyers in 75 countries representing 95% of worldwide IT spending. IDG's diverse product and services portfolio spans six key areas including print publishing, online publishing, expositions and conferences, market research, education and training, and global marketing services. More than 90 million people read one or more of IDG's 290 magazines and newspapers, including IDG's leading global brands — Computerworld, PC World, Network World, Macworld and the Channel World family of publications. IDG Books Worldwide is one of the fastest-growing computer book publishers in the world, with more than 700 titles in 36 languages. The "...For Dummies®" series alone has more than 50 million copies in print. IDG offers online users the largest network of technology-specific Web sites around the world through IDG.net (http://www.idg.net), which comprises more than 225 targeted Web sites in 55 countries worldwide. International Data Corporation (IDC) is the world's largest provider of information technology data, analysis and consulting, with research centers in over 41 countries and more than 400 research analysts worldwide. IDG World Expo is a leading producer of more than 168 globally branded conferences and expositions in 35 countries including E3 (Electronic Entertainment Expo), Macworld Expo, ComNet, Windows World Expo, ICE (Internet Commerce Expo), Agenda, DEMO, and Spotlight. IDG's training subsidiary, ExecuTrain, is the world's largest computer training company, with more than 230 locations worldwide and 785 training courses. IDG Marketing Services helps industry-leading IT companies build international brand recognition by developing global integrated marketing programs via IDG's print, online and exposition products worldwide. Further information about the company can be found at www.idg.com.   1/26/00

Credits

Acquisitions Editor
Judy Brief

Project Editor
Amanda Munz

Technical Editor
Jim Kelly

Copy Editor
Kevin Kent

Project Coordinator
Marcos Vergara

Graphics and Production Specialists
Bob Bihlmayer
Jude Levinson
Michael Lewis
Victor Pérez-Varela
Ramses Ramirez

Quality Control Technician
Dina F Quan

Permissions Editor
Carmen Krikorian

Media Development Specialists
Brock Bigard
Angela D. Denny

Media Development Coordinator
Marisa Pearman

Illustrators
Gabriele McCann
Shelley Norris
Karl Brandt

Proofreading and Indexing
York Production Services

Cover Illustration
Lawrence Huck

About the Author

Curt Simmons, MCSE, MCT, CTT, is a freelance author and technical trainer focusing on Microsoft operating systems and networking solutions. Curt is the author of almost a dozen high-level technical books on Microsoft products, including *Master Active Directory Visually* and *MCSE Windows 2000 Server For Dummies*. He has been working closely with Windows 2000 and the Active Directory since Beta 1. Curt lives with his wife and daughter in a small town outside of Dallas, Texas. You can reach him at curt_simmons@hotmail.com or at http://curtsimmons.hypermart.net.

Preface

The *Active Directory Bible* is your comprehensive resource for planning, installing, configuring, and managing the Microsoft Active Directory. The Active Directory, which is the core networking technology in Windows 2000, provides advanced directory service features that makes your network—regardless of its size—easier to manage and use.

Welcome to the World of Active Directory

You have heard plenty of things about the Active Directory. Some say the Active Directory is the best product Microsoft has ever produced—some say the Active Directory is still a baby that has a lot of maturing to do. No matter your position, we can all agree that the Active Directory is Microsoft's flagship product at the moment and that the Active Directory is here to stay.

The Active Directory is the foundational networking component in Windows 2000. The Active Directory completely revamps Microsoft networking from the days of NT and brings Windows networking to a hierarchical, directory service model. This model modernizes NT and paves the way for the future. With the Active Directory, you have more manageability, more support for network resources, standardized naming, and excellent query capabilities. In short, the Active Directory opens an entire new world for Windows.

Before I get too carried away with the details (which you can jump into in Chapter 1) and before I sound like I'm singing Microsoft's praises, let me just answer two questions I am asked quite frequently. The first is simply, "Do you like the Active Directory?" The answer is—yes, I do. Quite a bit, actually. The second question is, "Is the Active Directory perfect?" I usually smile and shake my head because you already know the answer. No—the Active Directory is not perfect, and there are some serious design issues Microsoft will need to address in the future. But in Microsoft's defense, I will say that the first release of the Active Directory is awfully good—and when you see the potential a live directory service can bring to a network, I think you will agree.

If you are reading this book, you are likely one of two people. First, you're a newcomer to Windows 2000. Perhaps you have joined the ranks of the technical professionals in search of a better career, and you know that Windows 2000 is a wise move. If that is you—you have come to right place. This book is all you need to learn all about the Active Directory and the technologies that make it tick.

Second, you may be a systems administrator — someone who has a place in designing an Active Directory implementation and in keeping everything running after it is in place. You have a lot of work to do, and you need a resource that helps you meet your goals quickly. You have come to the right place as well.

The *Active Directory Bible* is a comprehensive look at this new directory service. You'll learn how to plan, install, configure, manage, and integrate other technologies with the Active Directory with this book.

How to Read This Book (Don't Skip This Part!)

By now, I have read more than a few Active Directory books, white papers, and other Microsoft documentation. One of my biggest complaints with these resources is the problem with organization. The Active Directory is often difficult to explain because you need to know about points A, B, and C at the same time before understanding D. Likewise, you can't explain C without A, and you can't understand B without knowing about D ... you get the picture. The problem is that the Active Directory is built on a number of components that all play an equal role, so structuring a book or document so that it makes sense is not easy.

I have worked very hard on this book to present a logical, chapter-by-chapter approach to the Active Directory. If you are already familiar with the Active Directory, you can turn straight to the chapter you need and get started. If you are new to the Active Directory, read each chapter in order. I have tried to make the book as sequential as possible so all of this will be easier to understand.

Along the way, you'll find many useful step-by-step instructions and sidebars to give you additional explanations. Be sure to read these as you learn all about Active Directory.

A Little about This Book's Structure

This book is divided into four parts. The following sections give you an overview of what you will find in each part.

Part I: Planning an Active Directory Deployment

In Part I, you learn about the Active Directory technology and conceptual framework, and then you jump right into Active Directory planning. The planning process is extremely important, and this part teaches you all about the Active Directory namespace, constructing forests and trees, developing an OU plan, upgrading and migrating to the Active Directory, and planning Active Directory sites and replication.

Part II: Implementing the Active Directory

Once you have planned an Active Directory deployment, your next step is to implement your plan. This part shows you how to install the Active Directory in a number of scenarios; set up forests and trees; configure sites and trusts; set up users, computers, and groups; publish your resources; and deploy security.

Part III: Active Directory Management

Once your implementation is in place, you'll need to know how to manage and maintain the Active Directory. This part explores backup and recovery, various tools, defragmentation, replication management, and modification of the schema.

Part IV: Integrating Supporting Technologies

This part explores supporting technologies that work with the Active Directory. Here, you learn about IntelliMirror, Group Policy, Distributed File System, Indexing Service, Exchange Server and the Active Directory, and Domain Name System.

Appendixes

The book concludes with six helpful appendixes. You will find an MMC tutorial, an exploration of Resource Kit and AdminPak tools, a PDC and BDC upgrade tutorial, an exploration of Windows 2000 deployment strategies, a schema class and attribute reference, and an appendix discussing what's on the CD-ROM included with the book.

Icons Used in This Book

This book contains a few icons to help point out important information to you. As you see these, make sure you take note of them:

 This icon gives you information that could cause planning, implementation, or functionality problems. I use these only when necessary, so do pay attention to them.

 This icon points the way to useful information in other locations in the book.

This icon gives you some additional information about a subject at hand. You'll find these helpful as you read.

This icon tells you about a utility or product that is available on this book's CD-ROM.

This is a piece of friendly advice.

Acknowledgments

I would like to thank everyone at IDG Books for all their hard work on this book. Thanks to Judy Brief who made the initial offer and to Amanda Munz and Kevin Kent, my editors at IDG Books, who have made this book easier for you to read. Special thanks to Jim Kelly, my technical editor, who brought his expertise and content suggestions to this project. As always, thanks to my agent, Margot Maley, for taking care of my career. Finally, thanks to my wife, Dawn, and my daughter, Hannah, for always supporting me and giving me the "alone time" I need to write books.

Contents at a Glance

Contents

· ·

Part I: Planning an Active Directory Deployment   1

Chapter 1: Introduction to Active Directory Technology and Deployment Planning 3

Chapter 2: The Active Directory Namespace 19

Part III: Active Directory Management   233

Planning an Active Directory Deployment

An Active Directory implementation should always begin with a group of IT planners and several sharpened pencils. As with most technology rollouts, planning an Active Directory infrastructure is of the utmost importance. Most potential Active Directory problems and failures can be easily avoided through the use of proper, smart planning.

In this part of the book, you explore the technologies that make up the Active Directory. With this firm foundation, you then explore how to plan an Active Directory infrastructure. Topics found in this part are planning a domain name, planning a domain and OU structure, planning for sites and replication, and planning for upgrading and migrating to the Active Directory.

Armed with these planning tools and concepts, you can develop a highly effective Active Directory infrastructure plan that meets the needs of an organization's business model, capitalizes on the strengths of the network, and reduces networking and end user problems.

Introduction to Active Directory Technology and Deployment Planning

If you have been at all involved in the networking and computer scene during the past few years, you have certainly heard about the Active Directory. Perhaps you are facing an upcoming Active Directory implementation, or perhaps you are already waist deep in one. Maybe you want to tackle the Active Directory to further your career options. You have come to the right place. This book helps you make sense of the Active Directory — how to plan an implementation and how to configure it. Specifically, this chapter gets you started off by exploring Active Directory's architecture, concepts, and definitions. This chapter serves as an introduction — a starting place for the rest of the book. You can rest assured that the topics covered in this chapter are explored in other places in the book as well. With that said, let's jump into the Active Directory.

What Is a Directory?

You've heard all the marketing hoopla. You've heard the competitor's complaints. However, with all the excitement (and lack of excitement), I think I can safely say that the Active Directory is a permanent part of Windows 2000 (and beyond) networking. You have heard that directory services in computer networks will change the face of computing. Whether this is true or not I'll leave to your own opinion. Still, directory services certainly do change networking, and I believe you will find the change for the better. In order to begin talking about the Active Directory, the term *directory* should first be defined.

A *directory* is, at its most fundamental level, a collection of information that is organized in a particular way. The organizational method makes sorting through the information fast and easy so you can find the desired data. Directory services are often compared to a phone book. A phone book is a collection of data organized by last name, first name, phone number, city, and state. Because the information is organized in a particular way, you can quickly find a particular person and get his or her telephone number. Directories, of course, are nothing new — they have been used for about as long as books have been available; but in terms of networking, directories are still on the cutting edge of networking technology.

What Is a Directory Service?

The Active Directory is not the first directory service to hit the market. In fact, directory services have been around for some time now. However, the release of Windows 2000 and the Active Directory from Microsoft and the existence of NDS from Novell solidify the idea that networks should be directory based.

Only a few short years ago, networking was not as important as it is today. There were, of course, big businesses with big mainframes and a lot of data. But, it was not until the PC took hold that computing began to change and networks began to grow at an alarming rate. In most major networks today, every user has a computer, public and personal data, and many kinds of different computing needs. Because of sheer numbers, networks today can easily get out hand — too many servers, too many resources, too much mass confusion. In fact, finding needed information on the network can be a serious time-loss issue and a common complaint among users.

Enter directory services. The goal of directory services is to bring order to both big and small networks. Directory services provide a streamlined approach to network and resource discovery. With a directory, users can perform search queries and find network information quickly and easily. The Active Directory is Microsoft's answer to the directory services needs of today's networks.

What Does the Active Directory Do?

The Active Directory is a directory service — it provides a number of different services relating to the organized storage of network resources. The following points highlight some of the Active Directory's features:

✦ **Organized Approach** — The Active Directory brings order to your network by organizing network resources, such as user accounts, group accounts, shared folders, printers, and so on. With the Active Directory, users can quickly find information they need.

✦ **Ease of administration** — Windows 2000 networks no longer use primary domain controllers (PDCs) and backup domain controllers (BDCs). All domain controllers are simply peers, providing you a single point of administration and excellent fault tolerance.

✦ **Removes Topology from Users** — The Active Directory helps remove knowledge of the network topology from end users. End users do not have to know which server holds which resource and where it is located on the network. The Active Directory contains powerful query capabilities so users can perform full text searches to find what resources they need.

✦ **Reduction of NT Domains** — This is the part where all Windows NT network administrators cringe. A major goal of the Active Directory is to make large networks more manageable — and part of that lofty goal is to reduce the number of NT domains. The Active Directory does not have a domain user/group account limit (well, it does have one of about 1 million), and due to its design, many networks that currently have several existing NT domains now need only one Windows 2000 domain.

✦ **Growth Potential** — Two buzzwords thrown around about the Active Directory are *scalability* and *extensibility*. *Scalability* means that a service can grow with the needs of your network. The Active Directory is a scalable product because it can grow to meet the needs of your network. The Active Directory works on a network of a few hundred computers or on a network of thousands of computers. *Extensibility* means that service can be extended. The Active Directory can be extended in terms of its namespace and through resources it contains.

✦ **Standardization** — The Active Directory is completely built on networking and protocol standards that currently exist and are heavily used. In other words, there are no totally new standards that must be mastered. The Active Directory is built on a TCP/IP network, which is the networking protocol of choice these days, and it is completely integrated with Domain Name System (DNS) and Lightweight Directory Access Protocol (LDAP), both of which are explored in detail later in this book.

✦ **Network Control** — The Active Directory offers a very fine level of network management, both in terms of server management and desktop management. Through Windows 2000's Group Policy, you can manage network user desktop configurations much more easily and effectively. Through the Active Directory, you can finely control resource security and even delegate administrative tasks to other people through Delegation of Control.

✦ **Easier WAN Management**—Once you get Active Directory correctly set up, it manages its own replication topology. The Active Directory includes more internal services that help it manage and control its own processes, including replication. This feature keeps administrators out of such deathly details and enables software to take care of itself and replicate data between domain controllers and sites as needed.

Aside from these major points, the Active Directory also brings order and management options to larger networks, which was a major pitfall with Windows NT networks. NT networks functioned well, especially if the network did not get too large. However, the NT architecture was *flat* in that there were not different levels of administration and security. The larger NT networks became, the more domains were needed, which increased network traffic, trust relationship issues between domains, and administrative headaches. The Active Directory solves this problem because it is built on a hierarchy where information can be managed at different levels.

Active Directory Logical Structure

To begin the exploration of the Active Directory, I want to take a look at its logical structure. In order to effectively plan, implement, and administer the Active Directory, this logical structure will need to become second nature.

The Active Directory is built on the domain level. Before Windows 2000 was released, it was often rumored that domains were no longer going to be a part of Windows 2000. That is not all true, but domains have changed quite a bit because they can be bigger and do not have the restrictions found in NT domains. As a point of reference, a *domain* is a logical grouping of computers and users for both administrative and security purposes. In Windows NT, you found yourself working with and spending a lot of time troubleshooting domains. If you currently have an NT network of any size, you probably have quite a few domains. NT domains were so limited that they seemed to grow and multiply too rapidly, creating headaches and confusion for both users and administrators.

The Windows 2000 Active Directory domain model is different. Windows 2000 Active Directory domains are organized into *domain trees* that exist in a *forest.* When you first install the Active Directory, you create the first domain in a new forest. That new domain becomes the *root domain.* If you choose to install additional domains, they are created from the forest root.

Tip   You can create additional domain trees in a single forest. In other words, a forest can contain more than one domain tree. These issues are explored in detail in Chapters 2 and 3.

The Active Directory prefers a few domains (or even just one) with several *Organizational Units* (OUs). An OU is like a file folder—it holds important information.

OUs are containers designed to hold all kinds of Active Directory resources, such as users, computers, printers, and even other OUs. The great thing about OUs is you can set security, administrative control, and even policies at the OU level. In fact, many existing NT networks that have several domains can now be replaced with one domain and several OUs.

As I mentioned, an OU is designed to hold resources, such as users, computer accounts, printers, shared folders, and so on. These resources are called *objects*, and from this point on, I will refer to them as such. Figure 1-1 shows you a graphical representation of this model.

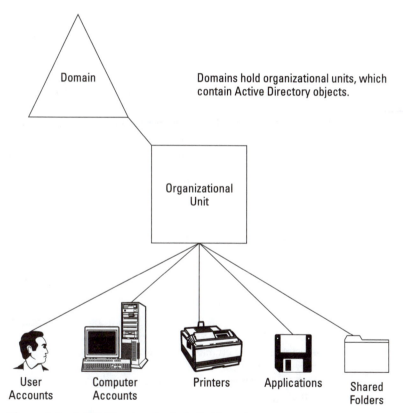

Figure 1-1: Active Directory logical structure

Each object that the Active Directory contains possesses *attributes*, shown in Figure 1-2. You can think of attributes as qualities of an object that help define it. For example, a user account has attributes such as user name, password, e-mail address, phone number, group memberships, and so on. These attributes define the object. Each object in the Active Directory contains predefined attributes.

If you think of the Active Directory as a database (which it is), think of an object as a database entry and the attributes as fields for the object.

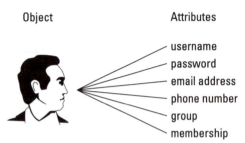

Object   Attributes

username
password
email address
phone number
group
membership

Figure 1-2: Objects and attributes

Consequently, in the logical structure, you have the domain, the OU, and the object, and each object has attributes that define it. The Active Directory also uses sites, but sites are not considered a part of the Active Directory logical structure, or *hierarchy*. Sites are maintained in the Active Directory for replication and traffic-control purposes only. A *site*, by definition, is a physical location of computers and users, contrasting to a domain, which is a logical grouping of computers and users. It is important to note that sites and domains are not interrelated — a site can contain several domains or a domain could span multiple sites. While a domain is a logical, administrative level of networking, a site is a physical level. In the Active Directory, sites are based on *well-connected* IP subnets, and they can be a point of planning and configuration confusion. Several of the following chapters address site configuration and replication traffic to help clear up this confusion.

Say Good-bye to Difficult Trust Relationships

If you have worked in a multiple domain NT network, you know a thing or two about trust relationships. Trust relationships enable a user in Domain A to access resources in Domain B. Trust relationships must be established to enable remote domain resource access, and in Windows NT, you had to configure each side of the trust — determining who was *trusted* and who was *trusting*. In complex environments, trust relationship became very complex and difficult to configure and manage.

Say good-bye to complex trust relationships in Windows 2000. In Windows 2000 environments that need more than one domain, automatic Kerberos transitive trusts are established when you create new domains in the forest tree. Kerberos is the security protocol in Windows 2000, replacing NTLM in Windows NT. Kerberos provides superior security technology and many new security features, like transitive trust relationships. A transitive trust simply means that if Domain A trusts Domain B, and Domain B trusts Domain C, then Domain A automatically trusts Domain C. The transitive trust relationships are automatically configured with all other domains and domain trees within the forest. The forest serves as your boundary, and all domains automatically trust each other — no configuration from you required!

DNS and LDAP

I mentioned earlier in the chapter that Active Directory is fully compatible with Domain Name System (DNS) and Lightweight Directory Access Protocol (LDAP). DNS is explored in several later chapters, so I'll approach it from an overview perspective here. DNS is a name resolution method that resolves host names to IP addresses. DNS is used on TCP/IP networks and is the name resolution system used on the entire Internet. DNS enables a host name like www.microsoft.com to be resolved to a TCP/IP address like 131.107.2.200. Computers communicate using an IP address. IP addresses are difficult for humans to remember because we are language-based creatures. DNS allows us to give friendly, language names, like microsoft.com, to hosts instead of having to remember its numerical IP address. DNS's job is to resolve the two. When a user requests www.microsoft.com, DNS uses several name servers to find the actual IP address of microsoft.com. Once it is found, the IP address is returned to the client so the client can use the IP address to contact microsoft.com. All of this is invisible to users and very fast.

So, what does all of this have to do with the Active Directory? DNS is a *namespace*, which means it is an area that can be resolved. A phone book is a namespace because it contains certain data that you resolve (name to phone number) in a certain way. Internet names, such as microsoft.com, yahoo.com, amazon.com, and so forth, all follow this naming scheme in order to be resolved. The Active Directory is built on DNS — in fact, Active Directory names are DNS names. In earlier versions of Windows, NetBIOS was used to provide friendly names to computers, and Windows Internet Name Service (WINS) was used for the locator service. In pure Windows 2000 networks, DNS is now used for the locator service.

 Note   WINS is still supported in Windows 2000 for backward compatibility, but Windows 2000 computers (Server and Professional) need only DNS.

It is important to note that the Active Directory namespace is not the DNS namespace. The DNS namespace is used on the Internet while the Active Directory namespace is used for private networks. However, the Active Directory namespace is based on DNS, and it connects into the DNS namespace. In other words, DNS is a global namespace that makes up the entire Internet, and the Active Directory namespace is built on the DNS hierarchical structure so that it connects into the DNS global namespace. For now, it is important to remember that you cannot implement the Active Directory without DNS, and all Active Directory names are DNS names.

The Active Directory is also a fully compliant LDAP directory service. To understand why this is important, you need to understand a few things about LDAP. LDAP is based on the Directory Access Protocol (DAP), which was an implementation of X.500 networks. X.500 is a very broad directory service that is built on a hierarchical structure, much like DNS. X.500 directories are searchable, and DAP is used in X.500 networks to query the database in order to locate directory information. The problem with DAP is that it places a lot of the processing burden on client computers and so gained the reputation of having a high overhead. LDAP was developed from DAP (RFC 1777), but it does not have the high overhead of DAP and does not require the X.500 network implementation. LDAP maintains the functionality of DAP without the X.500 overhead.

Since it was developed, LDAP has become an Internet standard. You use it in search engines and newsgroups. It works great, is a standard, and is used in the Active Directory for client queries. Let's say that a user performs a directory search to locate all "laser printers." LDAP uses the keywords to perform a search of objects and attributes to locate all laser printers. All access to Active Directory objects is performed through LDAP, and it is used when administrators modify Active Directory objects.

Tip   LDAP can be used in any attribute-based, hierarchical directory, which is why it works well with the Active Directory.

In order to provide the powerful query capabilities that make LDAP so popular, LDAP assigns Active Directory objects several different names. These different names provide information about the object that can be used for query matches.

First, LDAP gives objects a *distinguished name (DN)* and a *relative distinguished name (RDN)*. The DN shows the complete path to the object or where the object resides within the Active Directory. Remember that the Active Directory hierarchy begins at the domain level, then moves to the OU, and finally to the object level. The DN shows this complete path. The RDN provides the common name of the object. For example, the following line shows the DN and RDN of a user account.

```
Cn=ksmith,ou=namerica,dc=triton,dc=com
```

The RDN is ksmith, the common name for a user account. The DN provides the entire path to the user account, which exists in an Organizational Unit called "namerica," which in turn resides in the triton.com domain. (Remember that all Active Directory names are DNS names, so your domain names will be followed by .com or some other DNS first-level domain.) The RDN (cn) always appears first, followed by the DN (path to the object — dc stands for *domainDns object class*).

Here's another example:

```
Cn=HPDeskJet30,ou=resources,ou=acct,dc=triton,dc=com
```

In this example, the RDN is HPDeskJet30, a shared network printer that resides in the Resources OU, which resides in the Acct OU, which resides in the domain triton.com.

Note Neither administrators nor users see the DN information when working with the Active Directory, but you can view this information using various Active Directory administration tools found in the Windows 2000 Resource Kit. See Appendix C for more information.

In addition to the DN and RDN, LDAP also uses the *user principal name (UPN)* to locate objects. The UPN is a friendly name assigned to an object that is displayed as *objectname@domainname*. For example, a user account named ksmith in the triton.com domain appears as ksmith@triton.com. To LDAP, this is a local name on a local network. On the Internet, this same name is an e-mail address. The UPN is used both by LDAP and to make Windows logon much simpler. Administrators can generate UPN suffixes to make user logon more mainstream and less confusing.

Cross-Reference See Chapter 8 for more information on user principal names.

While on the subject of LDAP names, this is a good place to mention that each Active Directory object also has a *Globally Unique Identifier (GUID)*. The GUID is a 128-bit number that is assigned to the object when it is created. The GUID is worth mentioning here because it never changes for a particular object, unlike the DN or RDN, which can both change.

Note An object's GUID is actually an attribute of that object. The GUID, like other attributes, is required for every object. Depending on the object, some attributes are mandatory while others are optional. The GUID is always required for every object. Which attributes are required and which attributes are not required depend on the object itself. For example, when creating a user account, a GUID is assigned, and you also have a required attribute of user name. You can't create the account without a user name, so that attribute is required. Other attributes, such as e-mail address and phone number, are optional — you can include them if you want, but these are not required by the Active Directory.

Windows 2000 Domain Controllers

I mentioned earlier that Windows 2000 no longer uses PDCs or BDCs. That's enough to rattle the brain of any NT administrator, but to truly get into Active Directory mode, you'll have to lose a few sacred artifacts from the NT world. A couple of those are PDCs and BDCs.

Windows 2000 domain controllers function as peers. This means there is no single primary domain controller. All domain controllers are simply "domain controllers" and all of them are equal. Because you can use any domain controller to make changes to the Active Directory and fault tolerance is automatically built-in, this is an excellent management feature. If one domain controller crashes, no problem, the other domain controllers continue functioning as normal, and network activity functions as normal. In Windows NT networks, the PDC contains the writable copy of the database while BDCs all have a replicated copy from the PDC. In Windows 2000 networks, all domain controllers contain a writable copy of the database.

So, now that you know that all Windows 2000 domain controllers are peers, let me throw a little confusion into the mix. Although all Windows 2000 domain controllers are peers, some domain controllers have certain specialized roles assigned to them. These specialized roles exist because they do not work well functioning on all domain controllers. The following two sections examine these specialized roles.

Global catalog servers

Some domain controllers are global catalog servers. Depending on your network configuration, you may have several global catalog servers. Global catalog servers perform two major functions:

1. Global catalog servers contain a *full replica* of all Active Directory objects in their domain and a *partial replica* of all Active Directory objects in other domains in the forest. For example, let's say that Karen Anderson, a user in a domain called triton.com, needs to use a printer in the prod.triton.com domain. Karen searches for the printer. In order to fulfill Karen's request, a global catalog server is consulted because the global catalog server has a partial replica of all objects in the other domain. Using the global catalog server, Karen can find and connect to a desired printer (assuming she has appropriate permission to do so).

Tip

A *partial replica* simply means that the global catalog server is aware of the object and the most common attributes for that object. Since its job is to help with user queries, only the most common attributes that might be used in a search process are kept on global catalog server.

2. Global catalog servers are required for user logons. This may sound strange, but global catalog servers assist with user logons in that they provide information about Universal groups, a new type of group in Windows 2000, to a domain controller where the logon request initiated.

Cross-Reference

For more information on Universal groups, see Chapter 9.

Global catalog servers are necessary for user logons if the domain is running in native mode — not mixed mode – because Universal groups are only supported in Native mode. Mixed mode means that Windows NT BDCs are still in use while native mode means that only Windows 2000 servers are in use.

 Tip   Users cannot logon to the network if a global catalog server is not available when the domain is running in native mode. You can learn more about mixed mode and native mode in Chapter 8.

When installing the Active Directory for the first time, the first domain controller where you begin the installation becomes the global catalog server for the domain. You can change this role to another server if necessary.

Multimaster roles

Aside from the global catalog server, some domain controllers also run what is called *flexible single master operation (FSMO)* roles. In order to explain FSMO roles, I need to mention a few things about Windows 2000 replication (which is covered in detail in Chapters 5 and 13). Replication is the process of sending update information to other domain controllers. Windows 2000 uses *multimaster replication*. Just as with the absence of a PDC, there is no single master replicator. This means that changes to the database can occur from any domain controller and that then that domain controller is responsible for letting all other domain controllers know about database changes.

Imagine this scenario. Let's say you add a new user account to one domain controller. Remember that each domain controller maintains its own copy of the Active Directory database. If the domain controller does not let all other domain controllers know about the new user account, will the user be able to log on? No — not unless by some stroke of luck the user attempts authentication on the domain controller where the account was created. Now imagine if this happens over and over each day. Eventually, each domain controller will have a different database and a different view of the network because the domain controller would not know about database changes on all other domain controllers. Enter replication. Replication is a fairly complex process that sends changes to other domain controllers so that each domain controller can keep up with all the database changes made on different domain controllers. Without effective replication, the Active Directory would quickly become a hopeless mess of inaccurate data due to the peer domain controller design.

With all that said, turn your attention back to FSMO roles. Multimaster replication works great, but for some database changes, the process does not work well. In order to solve this problem, certain domain controllers hold certain FSMO roles. This means that only those domain controllers accept certain types of database changes and perform certain functions. There are five different FSMO roles that cover the replication exceptions and process handling exceptions of multimaster replication. Table 1-1 gives you a preliminary overview of these five roles.

Table 1-1 **FSMO Roles**	
FSMO Role	*Explanation*
Schema Master	The schema master role belongs to only one domain controller in the entire forest. The schema is simply a schematic, or blueprint, of all Active Directory objects and their attributes. The schema determines what kinds of objects can be stored in the directory and what attributes define those objects. Any modifications made to the schema must be made on the domain controller holding the schema master role.
Domain Naming Master	The domain naming master role belongs to only one domain controller in the forest. The domain naming master controls the addition and removal of domains in the forest.
Relative ID (RID) Master	The RID master manages the distribution of RID numbers to other domain controllers. When a domain controller generates a new security ID (SID) for a new user, computer, or group account, a domain security ID and a RID number are used. The RID master makes certain that no two domain controllers have the same or overlapping RID numbers. Each domain in the forest has one RID master.
PDC Emulator	Windows 2000 domains that have Windows NT BDCs still in operation (mixed mode) and Windows 2000 domains that have downlevel clients (such as 9x and NT) expect a PDC to be present on the network. The PDC Emulator role is played by one domain controller in each domain to "act like" a Window NT PDC.
Infrastructure Master	The Infrastructure master role, which is held by one domain controller in each domain, updates group members as necessary. For example, when the membership of a particular group changes, the Infrastructure master updates the group to ensure that changes are processed appropriately.

The Active Directory Schema

I've mentioned the Active Directory schema in Table 1-1. The Active Directory schema is a complete collection, or schematic, of Active Directory objects and attributes and the classes to which objects belong. The schema determines what can be stored in the Active Directory, where it belongs in the database, and what attributes belong to what objects. As a result, you can think of the schema as rules that determine what can be stored in the Active Directory.

Within the schema, objects belong to different classes. For example, user objects belong to the user class. Whenever you create new objects, the schema determines if the object can be created, and it determines what mandatory attributes and optional attributes belong with that class. Windows 2000 Active Directory ships with a default schema that is installed when you install the Active Directory. For most Active Directory implementations, the default schema is all you need for an effective implementation; however, you can extend the schema by adding new classes of objects and new attributes to define those objects. Extending the schema is a serious operation that can have devastating consequences on your enterprise implementation if performed incorrectly, so modification is something that requires careful planning. As a security precaution, schema modification can occur only on the domain controller holding the Schema master role.

Cross-Reference   Chapter 14 explores modification issues in more detail.

The schema exists on each domain controller in the Schema container. Upon installation, the first domain controller receives the schema and each domain controller thereafter. Like all Active Directory data, the schema is replicated among domain controllers to ensure accuracy in the event that a schema modification does occur. The schema is found on all domain controllers, along with the Active Directory database, in %systemroot%\system32\ntds.

Planning an Active Directory Deployment

The entire first part of this book is devoted to Active Directory deployment planning. This fact alone should tell you a thing or two. Like all complex networking technologies, the Active Directory requires a significant amount of planning in order to deploy the directory service in a way that will function from a networking view to an administrative view. I can't say enough here about how important deployment planning is to the success of your Active Directory implementation. It is always tempting to start with that installation CD, but you have some pencil-and-paper work to do before ever starting an installation.

The remaining chapters in this section explore planning your deployment — from your namespace to your domain and OU structure, your site structure, as well as upgrade and migration plans. Before getting into those technical issues, however, you have some up-front work to do.

As a starting place for your implementation, you and your company will first have to decide who will make the Active Directory implementation decisions. Under most circumstances, the best solution involves a number of people, including IT administrators, company managers, and possibly even team/division leads. Choose a mixture of people who can bring different perspectives to the table. As an administrator, it is easy for you to get caught up in the technical details, but when you are planning, gather information from all kinds of people on the network. The following are some questions to consider:

✦ What do your users need?

✦ What have been the previous problems?

✦ How can an Active Directory implementation meet the needs of users and solve existing problems?

✦ How can you plan for future growth and changes?

These are all complex questions, but ones that need to be addressed. After all, the Active Directory seeks to provide end users with a network environment that is basically invisible to them and helps them find the resources they need.

So, you'll need to decide who will be a part of the planning process. It is not unusual for an enterprise to include several people on a primary committee and a number of additional people on a review committee. This ensures that all issues, concerns, and potential problems are addressed.

Once the planning group is established, you have some preliminary actions to take before you begin designing your own Active Directory infrastructure. You can call this boring detective work. Nevertheless, this boring detective work will pay off as you begin planning. I've broken this action out into sections for quick review and reference.

Gather business data

The Active Directory is designed to help your network meet the needs of your business. Thus, Active Directory's structure and design allows business policy to become network policy and to assist in all business goals. Obviously, the purpose of networks is to exchange information so that companies can be more productive and lower the Total Cost of Ownership (TCO). The Active Directory can help you accomplish this goal, but you'll need to know a thing or two about your business to make the goal a reality. Aside from business goals and processes with your company, take a look at how your company management is structured. Businesses are either structured in a centralized or decentralized management structure (or a combination of the two). It is not unusual for a company to begin operations with a centralized management structure where there is one chain of command, but as companies grow, this structure usually becomes impractical. Therefore, most larger companies use a decentralized management structure where there are several chains of command. Of course, there is no right or wrong here, but you do need to find out how your business functions. A flowchart or schematic will help, so consider generating one as you gather data about your business.

Consider IT management structure

Your existing IT management structure may need some revamping, and an Active Directory implementation gives you a good reason to do so. Let's face the facts — networks grow and change and, due to growth and politics, IT administration can become complicated and redundant. This is a good opportunity to perform an analysis and make certain your IT structure is effective and logical.

Examine your physical locations

You should create a chart of your company's physical locations. This data includes geographic locations, city locations, buildings, and even locations within a particular building. Gather this information, chart it, and make sure it is accurate. Include any subsidiaries or alternate groups as well. You'll use this information as you consider your Active Directory deployment scope.

Examine employee distribution

Along with your physical locations, gather information about the number of employees at each physical location. For example, you may have one building that holds 1,200 employees while another office across town holds only 10. Gather this data and combine it with the physical locations chart you created. This will give you an accurate view of your network employee distribution.

Gather network topology data

The Active Directory will function only as well as the network it is built on. If you have network problems now, then you will have network problems when you implement the Active Directory (and maybe even more). During the planning process, you should carefully chart your network topology, noting any and all WAN links between sites and their speeds. This information will greatly impact your Active Directory design so make certain the data is accurate. As you gather network data, create a list of current network problems, especially problems with connectivity reliability and lack of bandwidth. As you consider these problems, it may be time to make some network upgrades in order to support the Active Directory.

Study network services

In an existing network, you no doubt have a number of different services that may be in operation. For the moment, take a look at how your network functions, considering the following questions:

- ✦ What are the services that are needed by your clients and are critical for your business operations?
- ✦ What about custom applications?

✦ Do you have applications that need to be tested before implementing Windows 2000?

Explore protocol usage

The Active Directory must be built on a TCP/IP network. If your existing network is not running TCP/IP, it must be converted and updated as necessary before you continue. Also, consider other protocols that may be in use. Will they be necessary once the Active Directory is in place? If not, begin removing those and streamlining your network.

Note   Of course, if you are building a new network from scratch, this issue and the following issue do not apply. However, you should continue reading and considering the information in this section because your design plans might still be impacted.

Consider computer hardware

If you are upgrading your Windows NT computers to Windows 2000 and upgrading your client computers to Windows 2000 Professional, you'll need to spend some time examining server and computer hardware. Windows 2000 is rather resource intensive, and the NT server that limped along okay will probably not be able to handle Windows 2000. Alas, hardware upgrades may be needed to get the performance satisfaction you need. The Windows 2000 Server and Professional documentation lists system requirements, but keep in mind these are bare minimums. The reality is your server and desktop systems will need more processing power and RAM to perform optimally, so consider these issues and potential upgrades as a part of your implementation plan.

The key point with all of these initial planning considerations is to gather information. As always, information is power. With more information, you will make wiser decisions as you prepare to implement the Active Directory.

Summary

This chapter gave you a technical overview of the Active Directory and explored a starting point for your Active Directory implementation planning. The Active Directory is a rich, extensible, and scalable directory service whose namespace is built on the DNS standard. The Active Directory is built on a TCP/IP network and is designed to make network management and user resource usage easier and less problematic. As you begin planning your Active Directory infrastructure, begin by collecting data about your business and your network. With this data, you can begin to create an Active Directory deployment that will meet your company's business plans and function in an appropriate manner on your physical network.

✦   ✦   ✦

The Active Directory Namespace

In Chapter 1, you learned that the Active Directory must be built on some specific technologies. For example, the Active Directory must be built on a TCP/IP network, and the Active Directory uses LDAP for database queries. You were also introduced to the fact that the Active Directory is built on the Domain Name System (DNS). In fact, DNS and the Active Directory are completely tied together, and you cannot even install the Active Directory without DNS. As a part of the planning process, you must design the Active Directory namespace before ever beginning an installation, and as you can probably guess, that namespace must follow DNS. In this chapter, I explore all you need to know about designing your namespace and give you plenty of examples along the way.

What Is a Namespace?

A *namespace* is simply a word that describes an "area" that can be resolved. It refers to a system of name resolution where a single computer can be found due to the namespace pattern. If you are new to the concept of namespace, it can be somewhat confusing. The concept of namespace is often compared to a telephone book or the U.S. mail system. For example, the U.S. mail system is essentially a namespace because letters and packages are addressed in a particular way in order to reach a destination. For example, a letter always contains a person's name, address, city, state, and zip code. Using these namespace components, a letter can be delivered to a single person in a single place in the United States. By the information on the letter, millions of people can be disregarded and the correct recipient located (at least, we hope).

The reason millions of people can be disregarded and the correct recipient located is that the letter follows addressing rules for the namespace. If some letters contained only a name and street address, or a name and a city or state, the postal system would never be able to deliver mail because it would not follow a particular namespace. In other words, the addressing information on the letter is *resolvable* to a particular person residing in a particular place.

The Active Directory namespace is the same. Following the DNS namespace, Active Directory names follow a particular namespace. This organized approach enables a computer in one domain to locate and communicate with a computer in another domain. The namespace enables one domain to be distinguished from another and permits clients both within the domain and outside of the domain to have a unique name that can be resolved. Just as a person has a unique postal address, domains and computers in an Active Directory network all have a unique DNS name that can be resolved.

Exploring the DNS Namespace

In order to fully understand the Active Directory namespace and begin planning your own Active Directory domain name, you first must take a look at the DNS hierarchy. The Active Directory is built on DNS, and all Active Directory names *are* DNS names — you cannot separate the two. Thus, once you understand the DNS hierarchy, you'll understand the Active Directory namespace hierarchy.

Note   You should note that although the DNS namespace and the Active Directory namespace are the same in terms of the hierarchy, they are not the same in terms of management. DNS is used to manage the Internet while the Active Directory *using* DNS is used to manage your private network. The two namespaces can interconnect, however, so that you have *both* an Internet presence and a private network.

As you learned in Chapter 1, DNS is a *name system* that enables domain names to be resolved to a unique TCP/IP address. For example, www.idgbooks.com is a domain name that can be resolved to an exact TCP/IP address assigned to IDG Books. Each fully qualified domain on the Internet has a unique IP address. DNS's job is to resolve the friendly name, such as www.idgbooks.com, to a not-so-friendly TCP/IP address, such as 131.107.2.200. Of course, you do not have to use a computer's domain name to communicate with it. You can bypass all of this resolution trouble by just remembering and using the computer's IP address. The problem is simply that we are language-based creatures who do not remember strings of numbers very well. In a large network or on the Internet, people would never be able to remember computers and Web sites without DNS.

So now that you know the virtues of DNS, why did Microsoft choose to implement DNS in Windows 2000? In previous versions of Windows and in Windows networking, NetBIOS names were used with Windows Internet Name Service (WINS) to perform the computer name–to–IP address resolution. What happened to WINS? Why DNS?

There are a couple of reasons. First, NetBIOS works fine (although many administrators will be more than happy to kiss it good-bye), but it doesn't provide an organized, network-wide approach to name resolution. WINS is not completely gone — yet. WINS is supported in Windows 2000 for backward compatibility with downlevel Windows computers, such as NT and 9x systems. However, Windows 2000 computers only need DNS for name resolution. In a pure Windows 2000 network, you don't need to implement WINS at all, and you can expect WINS to die a slow death in the next several years as NT and 9x clients are slowly retired to 2000 and beyond OS versions.

Microsoft chose DNS for a couple of important reasons, and I believe it was a wise choice. First, DNS is an *extensible* name resolution method. This means that DNS can be extended, or it can grow to meet the needs of your organization. If you have a small network of 500 computers, DNS will work fine for you. If you have a network of 10,000 computers, DNS will work just fine. What if you have a network of a million computers? No problem — after all, DNS makes up the entire Internet. Because of DNS's extensibility, there is no concern about limiting your network's size due to naming limitations.

Another reason Microsoft chose to use DNS is because of its common use on the Internet. Internet surfers use DNS all the time. They may not know it, but the system is very familiar in today's Internet age. Using DNS in private Active Directory networks makes the networks more familiar and more easily integrated with intranets and the Internet. For example, triton.com can be both an Internet web site and the name of a local network. Peggy_anderson@triton.com can be both an Internet e-mail address and a user name on the private network. This integration makes remembering information easier and begins to blur lines between traditional networks, the Internet, and e-commerce.

With all that said, then, you now understand that the Active Directory is built on the DNS namespace hierarchy. In order to build your own implementation, first consider how the DNS hierarchy works. The DNS hierarchy can be thought of as an upside-down tree structure. A DNS name is resolved from the root down through the branches of the tree structure until the actual host computer is located.

Returning to the postal example, suppose that John Smith has the following address:

John Smith
110 Apple Bird Lane
Anycity, Texas 75000

In order to resolve the postal address so that a letter actually reaches John Smith, the postal service works the address in reverse order. In other words, they begin at the root of the address in order to resolve it. Using the zip code and state, all other 49 states can be automatically ruled out. So far, the letter has been resolved from the entire United States to Texas. Next, the address is resolved further by locating the specific city, Anytown. Now the address has been further resolved from the entire state to only one city. Once the letter reaches the city, a postal carrier resolves Apple Bird Lane in order to rule out all other streets and then resolves 110 in order to rule out all other houses on that street. The postal carrier compares the street address with the owner, John Smith, to verify accurate delivery.

DNS resolves domain names in much the same way. Because a DNS address is made up of resolvable domain names, each domain can be resolved until the actual computer host is finally reached. The domains are as follows:

✦ **Root domain**—The very top of the inverted domain tree. The root domain is represented by a period. "."

✦ **First-level domains**—First-level domains, owned by the InterNIC, are major divisions of addresses. The following are common first-level domains:

- com—stands for commercial
- net—stands for network
- edu—stands for education
- gov—stands for government
- mil—stands for military
- org—stands for nonprofit organizations

✦ **Second-level domains**—Second-level domains represent private businesses, organizations, or groups. For example, microsoft, idgbooks, amazon, msn, yahoo, and so on, are all second-level domains.

✦ **Third-level domains**—Third-level domains can be a type of service, such as www or ftp, or they can further subdivide the second-level domain, such as acct.idgbooks.com.

✦ **Child domains**—You can have any additional domains beyond the third-level domain. These are called child domains and are further used to subdivide other domains. For example, in acct.corp.namerica.idgbooks.com, acct and corp would be considered child domains.

Beyond the final domain is the actual server or computer for which the address belongs. The full DNS address ending at a particular server or computer is called a Fully Qualified Domain Name (FQDN). As you can see in Figure 2-1, the DNS hierarchy begins at the root and branches from the root.

When DNS needs to resolve a name, it begins with the Internet root and works it way through each domain until it reaches the final *leaf* or *end node*, which is a computer. The computer can then answer the resolution with its IP address so that the FQDN is resolved to a single IP address.

Cross-Reference   You can learn more about the DNS resolution process in Chapter 18.

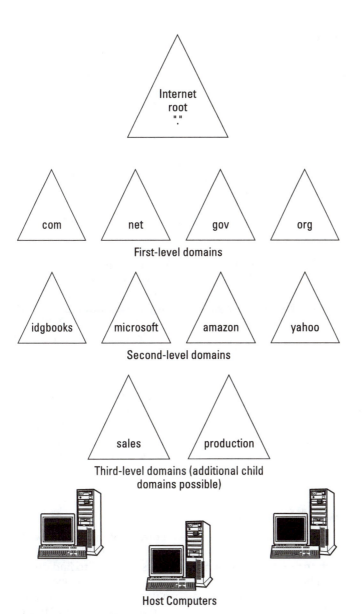

Figure 2-1: DNS hierarchy

Issues with DNS Planning

Chapter 18 explores DNS implementation, how to install it, and how to set it up on a Windows 2000 Server in great detail. However, while discussing the topic of name-space planning, it is a good time to mention DNS requirements. In an Active Directory implementation, as you have learned, DNS is required. The Active Directory naming structure is built on DNS, and the Active Directory simply will not work without DNS. In fact, when you install the Active Directory, the Active Directory Installation Wizard will search for a DNS server. If it does not find one, the wizard will prompt you to allow it to install DNS with the Active Directory. You can think of the Active Directory as interconnected and interdependent with the DNS.

Cross-Reference   You can find step-by-step installation information on DNS in Chapters 6 and 7.

So, when you are planning your Active Directory implementation, you need to stop and take a serious look at DNS. If you do not have a DNS implementation, your best approach is to use Microsoft DNS that installs automatically with the Active Directory. (DNS is a service that can be installed from your Windows 2000 CD-ROM like any other service.) This ensures complete compatibility and will avoid a world of problems. However, you may already have a DNS implementation in your network. You may have already spent a lot of money and configuration time on your imple-mentation, and it may not be Microsoft DNS. Now what can you do?

The Active Directory does *not* require that you implement Microsoft DNS, but it does require a DNS implementation that supports certain DNS features. If you have an existing DNS infrastructure and you want to keep it, then you need to spend some serious time investigating and testing that infrastructure to ensure compatibility with the Active Directory. There are some specific issues you should pay close attention to, and these are explored in the following sections.

Service Location Records

Service Location Records (SRV) are DNS resource records that map Windows 2000 servers that run the DNS service. Each server maintains a list of SRV records for the domain or zone in which the server resides. SRV records are used to find domain controllers, and they can be used in several ways. For example, if you want several servers to respond to a single domain name, you can use SRV records to configure this option. When client computers need to contact a domain controller, they do so through LDAP, which accesses the SRV record. In short, SRV records are *required* for an Active Directory implementation. If your current DNS implementation does not support SRV, you are going to have to upgrade to a version that does. Microsoft DNS supports SRV (naturally) and BIND 8.1.1 and higher also support SRV records. If you do not have these versions, you can delegate child domains to a DNS server that does support SRV. However, this solution is likely to cause you more headaches and poor performance. My best advice is to upgrade to a version of BIND that supports SRV, or preferably, to Microsoft DNS.

Dynamic Update Protocol

Dynamic Update Protocol (RFC 2136) enables the DNS server to dynamically update its records when the DNS name–to–IP address mappings change. This may not sound like much, but before RFC 2136, DNS was a static database that had to be manually updated by an administrator. Dynamic Update Protocol enables the DNS server to automatically update its database when it is notified of DNS name–to–IP address mapping changes (such as in the case of a new DHCP lease). RFC 2136 was a much needed improvement and helps administrators keep their hands off DNS HOSTS file manual configuration. Technically, the support of Dynamic Update Protocol is not required for an Active Directory implementation, but considering that your computer names are DNS names and that IP addresses can regularly change when DHCP is used, Dynamic Update is required for all practical purposes. Microsoft DNS supports Dynamic Update Protocol as does BIND 8.1.1 and higher.

Note   Before Dynamic Update Protocol, DNS was a static creature. DNS host names–to–IP address mappings were kept in a static text file called a HOSTS file. If a DNS host name–to–IP address mapping changed, an administrator had to open the text file and manually make the change. As you can imagine, this would be an impossible administrative feat in the Active Directory. Dynamic Update Protocol enables DNS host–to–IP mappings to be dynamic — they can automatically be updated as mappings are updated.

DHCP updates

In conjunction with the Dynamic Update Protocol, the Windows 2000 version of DHCP is designed to provide DNS with name–to–IP address mapping changes. As you can imagine, without this dynamic update feature, the DNS database would quickly become a hopeless mess of incorrect name–to–IP mappings. Not to sound like a commercial, but if you implement Microsoft DNS, you can be assured of compatibility between DHCP and DNS. If you use BIND or another DNS service, you should perform some testing to make certain that your DNS servers can receive dynamic updates from DHCP.

Incremental zone transfers

You can refer to Chapter 18 to learn more about DNS zones, but for now, let me just say that a zone is a contiguous portion of the DNS namespace that is segmented for management purposes. Within that zone, there is a primary DNS server that holds the *primary zone database file.* All other servers are provided for load balancing and contain a copy of the primary zone database file called the *secondary zone database file.* The primary zone database file is the only writable version, so all updates are made to the primary zone database file and replicated to the secondary zone database files through a process called *zone transfer.* Incremental zone transfers (RFC 1995) enable only the portions of the database that have changed to be sent to the secondary zone servers instead of the entire database. This feature, though not at all a requirement, you should consider important because it will help reduce network traffic.

The Active Directory Domain Hierarchy

In the previous section, you read about the DNS hierarchy, which consists of domains that can be resolved. DNS is built from the Internet root level up and can represent virtually an unlimited number of hosts on the Internet. Now, you can turn your attention to the Active Directory domain hierarchy, which for all practical purposes is exactly the same.

The Active Directory hierarchy, or namespace, begins with a root domain, which is actually the domain forest root for your entire enterprise. This root domain is a Windows 2000 domain of users, computers, and resources. From this single root domain, all other Windows 2000 domains can be created. Because the Active Directory uses DNS for its namespace design, the root domain serves as the building block for all other domains.

Consider this example. Triton, Inc. (a fictitious company I'm using as an example throughout the book) wants to install the Active Directory. They will have one major Windows 2000 domain and two child domains — one for production and one for development.

I'm keeping our domain discussion at a minimum here because the Active Directory domain hierarchy is addressed in detail in Chapter 3.

Triton, Inc., decides to create a root domain using their company name. The root domain name becomes triton.com. From this root domain, the company decides to create two child domains, having names of production.triton.com and development. triton.com, as you can see in Figure 2-2.

From this hierarchical structure, a contiguous namespace is created — an area in which all domains and computers within the domain can be resolved. Obviously, other child domains can be created from the root, or they can be created from existing child domains. For example, at any time, the company could add a domain from the root, such as europe.triton.com, or they could create a child of a child, such as europe.production.triton.com. In any case, the namespace created is contiguous, and it is resolvable.

There are all kinds of domain configuration options, problems, and perils, and all of those are explored in Chapter 3.

Designing the Root Domain

Before you ever sit down at a computer and begin the Active Directory installation, I strongly suggest that you sit down with a pencil and some paper and first design your Active Directory namespace, including your root domain name and all other domains. The remainder of this chapter focuses on the root domain name and several potential options and problems.

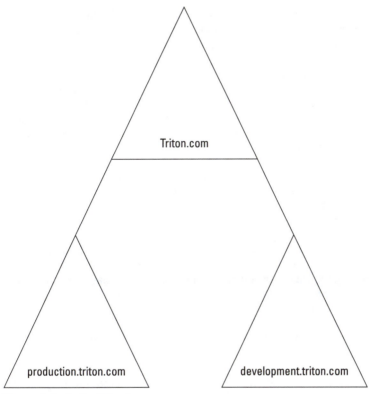

Figure 2-2: Active Directory namespace

Permanent considerations with the root domain

Why do I spend an entire chapter essentially focusing on the root domain name? After all, at first glance creating your root domain name does not appear that difficult. There are two major reasons for spending a considerable amount of time discussing and planning your root domain name:

✦ The Active Directory is not all forgiving with the root domain name. Once you install the Active Directory and assign a root domain name, you're stuck with it. *You cannot change the root domain name without reinstalling the Active Directory.*

✦ Things are never as simple as they appear. You have several things to think about before ever determining your root domain name. After all, what if your company name changes, or what if your company acquires another company? There are a number of possible issues.

Caution   It is very important that the root domain name is carefully planned and analyzed. The root domain affects all other names in your Active Directory forest, and it cannot be changed without starting completely over.

So with that in mind, you can begin to think about the Active Directory root domain. When you create your Active Directory root domain name, it is a permanent name that is used to generate all other DNS names in your Active Directory implementation. Think of this name as the root — all other names must come from the root. Consequently, you want your root domain to be something meaningful. In most cases, the domain root name will simply be the name of the company or organization. For example, Triton, Inc., has a single company name, so it makes sense for this company to use triton.com as their root domain name. All other names in their enterprise will be derived from this root. For that reason, your root domain name should be something meaningful and recognizable. After all, the purpose of DNS is to enable use of friendly names instead of IP addresses.

Once again this sounds very easy, but what do you do if your company's or organization's name isn't quite so simple? For example, suppose you have two companies that merge together, but each retains their own name. You want one Active Directory implementation (one forest) for the two companies. There can be only one root domain name, so what do you do? You obviously have to make some choices. You can use one of the company names, combine both names, or try to figure out an alternative name to represent the company as a whole. This brings up the next point.

Your root domain name should encompass your *entire* business or organization. This includes *all* offices, locations, child companies, subsidiaries, and so on. Think of your root domain name as an umbrella that must cover your entire enterprise. What name works best? This is a decision you will have to make, but the root domain must cover the entire business enterprise.

Consider an example of these two issues. Triton, Inc., purchases a company called Star Works. Triton, Inc., also has a number of subsidiary companies. When designing the Active Directory root domain, the company has to determine how to handle the different names used within the environment as a whole. After considering the subsidiary companies, management believes that triton.com encompasses the entire organization. The only problem is Star Works, which is a very recognizable name. The company thinks about combining the two names and using tritonstar.com, but this name doesn't accurately reflect their business. In the end, Triton, Inc., determines that triton.com is still the best root domain name. Later, they can create a child domain called starworks.triton.com if they so choose.

So, you should strive to create a root domain that is friendly, recognizable, and encompasses your entire business now and into the future. Unfortunately, however, there are more considerations, options, and potential issues you should evaluate before making a permanent decision.

What if My Company Name Changes After AD Implementation?

Here's a pitfall of the Active Directory. Suppose your company, Wilson Dog Collars (wilsondogcollars.com) changes its name to Wilson Pet Products. The company easily reserves the new name of Wilsonpetproducts.com on the Internet, but now wants to change the name of the Active Directory root to reflect the new company name. Sorry, no cigar.

You cannot change the root domain name without completely reinstalling the Active Directory—a process that is going to be seriously time-consuming and full of problems. While the Active Directory is a great directory service, the naming "lockdown" is a serious problem that needs to be addressed. In fact, I'll bet that Microsoft is going to address it, and you can look for a future tool to solve this problem.

Options and considerations with the Internet

Aside from the basic root domain name consideration issues, there are a number of other factors you must consider before making a permanent decision. These options and considerations are important because they may impact the way your company does business and how the Active Directory impacts your internal network and your potential e-commerce business. The following sections outline and explore these options and considerations with the Internet.

Integrating with the Internet

In the previous example, Triton, Inc., decided to use triton.com as their Active Directory root domain name. The company currently does not have a Web presence, but they intend to have one in the next few months. The administrators would like to use triton.com as the Internet presence as well to integrate their private network and the Internet. When the administrators attempt to register triton.com with a naming authority, such as Network Solutions, they discover that the name triton.com is already reserved. Due to this, the company cannot use triton.com as both their Active Directory name and their Internet name. They can, of course, attempt to buy the name from the current owner, or they can simply use triton.com for their Active Directory name and a different name, such as tritonservices.com, for their Internet name.

Here's the trick—the Active Directory is used on your private network. In a nutshell, you can use any name you want—you just can't use any name on the Internet. For example, you have a company named Micro Services National, and you name your Active Directory root msn.com. You can certainly do this, but you can't use msn.com on the Internet because that name belongs to Microsoft. As you can see, this can become a sticky issue and one that has major legal ramifications. The simple rule is to design a root domain name that works well for your business and is available on the Internet. This way, you're covered in both places. Your Active Directory implementation can connect to the Internet and serve Internet users under the same name, shown in Figure 2-3.

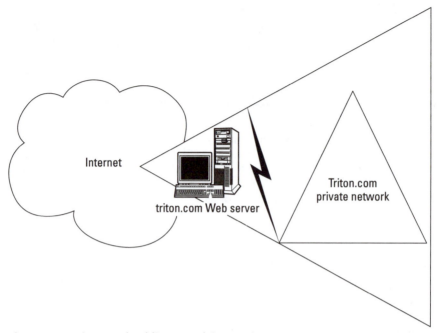

Figure 2-3: Private and public network integration

 Tip   You must use a root domain name that conforms to Internet rules. For example, you could not use the name triton@@!.com on the Internet, although you could for your private implementation. Just make sure your name conforms to DNS character set rules, which you can read about in RFC 1035. (If you use letters only, you have nothing to worry about.)

But ... I Don't Care about the Internet

When designing your Active Directory root domain, my suggestion is to use a name that is representative of and encompasses your entire company *and* one that is available for reservation on the Internet. Even if your company does not plan on having an Internet presence in the future, I still recommend that you pay the annual fee and reserve it anyway.

The Internet is still evolving and changing the way we do business. Just because a company does not need an Internet presence now does not mean it won't need one in the near future. If you do not reserve your name, someone else may reserve your name, which means your Internet name and Active Directory names will have to be different. So, my suggestion is to register the name. It's rather inexpensive and can avoid many potential issues and problems in the future.

Of course, the reverse side of this situation is also true. Suppose that Triton, Inc., already has an Internet presence called triton.com. When Triton, Inc., plans to implement the Active Directory, they can simply use triton.com — after all, it's friendly, encompasses their business, and they already own it in the public Internet arena.

However, using the same name on the Internet and on your private network does not come without a few disadvantages. First and foremost, you may need to take some additional security steps to keep Internet users out of your private Active Directory network. This may include the use of a proxy server or firewall hardware and software. For example, since triton.com is both an Internet presence and a private network presence, savvy Internet users can more easily compromise it. After all, you don't want Internet users wandering around your private network. The other disadvantage may just be simple confusion. In a business where a large Internet presence exists, general user confusion about what data belongs within the private network and what does not can occur. This can be especially true if the actual business itself is e-commerce. As I mentioned earlier, a goal of the Active Directory is to provide a more seamless structure to the private network and the Internet — but for some businesses, the division can be too seamless.

Overall, however, using your Internet presence name as your Active Directory name works well, and you will probably find that DNS configuration is much easier.

See Chapter 18 for implementing DNS.

Avoiding Internet integration

Integrating your Active Directory name with your Internet name may sound like the way to go, but for many companies, a definite distinction between the two is more desirable. There are a few different ways you can accomplish this goal, and this section points out the options you have.

First, and most obviously, you can simply use a root domain name that is different from your Internet presence. For example, suppose that Triton, Inc., already had an Internet presence of triton.com when they decided to implement the Active Directory. Because of security issues, the company does not want their root domain name to be triton.com. In this case, they simply have to choose another friendly name that encompasses their business. Possible examples are tritoninternal.com, tritonlocal.com, tritonad.com, or whatever name best meets their needs. This way, the existing Internet presence and the private network are kept completely separate.

There is another option, however, and one that is somewhat more complex. In order to explain the option, I'll have to spend a moment more back in the world of DNS. DNS zones are contiguous and discrete portions of the DNS namespace. For example, triton.com and prod.triton.com could be two different DNS zones because they each contain a different portion of the namespace. Zones are identified for administrative purposes. For example, suppose that triton.com exists in Dallas while prod.triton.com exists in San Francisco. You could use zones for each domain so administrators at each location could manage their own DNS zones — which makes life easier for the administrators. When you create zones, a DNS server holds the *primary zone database file* for that zone, and it is authoritative. This means that the DNS server has authority over the zone and serves its zone clients as well as lookup requests from clients out of the zone. Within the zone, you can also use secondary DNS servers that hold a *secondary zone database file*, which is just a copy of the primary zone database file. Changes to the DNS database are written only to the primary zone database file and all secondary zone database files receive the changes through a replication process called *zone transfer.*

With all that said, you can use DNS zones to create a child domain in order to keep your Active Directory implementation segmented from your Internet presence. Here's how it works, using Triton, Inc., once again for an example. Triton, Inc., wants to keep triton.com as its Internet presence, but they want their Active Directory implementation to connect with triton.com in order to make use of the DNS server already in use. The administrators create a new DNS zone on a new DNS server where the Active Directory domain will exist. They then install the Active Directory using a third-level domain, such as local.triton.com, private.triton.com, or corp.triton.com. This way, they get to use triton.com by beginning the Active Directory root at the third level. Then, they configure the triton.com DNS server with a delegation record to the new root, private.triton.com. This keeps triton.com in place and enables the Active Directory implementation to integrate with the Internet presence while keeping it separate, shown in Figure 2-4.

This design works well. You'll have additional DNS servers due to the additional zone, and a particular problem with this design is the third-level root. For example, private.triton.com is the root domain name for Triton, Inc. This means that all other names in the forest are derived from this root. Throw a few child or grandchild domains into the mix and a computer could theoretically have a DNS name of computer7.acct.namerica.private.triton.com — which is a little long for comfort. Yet, there is nothing technically wrong with this design; it just means that you may have long DNS names because the root is starting at the third-level DNS domain.

In the same manner, you can use the same domain name as your Internet presence and Active Directory root by using two different DNS zones and a firewall. The firewall keeps Internet traffic out of your private network and two DNS zones, containing a DNS server on each side of the firewall in order to keep public and private records separate. As you can imagine, this type of solution requires more configuration and presents more possible DNS communication problems. The advantage is the single domain name can be used on the Internet and in your Active Directory implementation, but the configuration of the zones and maintenance of the firewall may be prohibitive due to administrative costs.

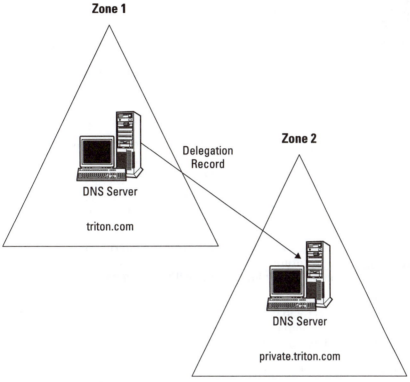

Figure 2-4: Zone divisions

Finally, there is one other option to keep your Active Directory implementation separate from the Internet. RFC 1918 defines the use of the .local first-level domain for private networks using DNS. With this implementation, a company would be named, for example, triton.local for the root domain. The .local domain is reserved by the InterNIC for private use, and you can think of it as the same as the 10.0.0.0 IP address range that is reserved for private use. The .local implementation is good for companies who have an Internet presence and who want to keep the Active Directory implementation completely separate. For example, Triton, Inc., can have triton.com for its Internet presence and triton.local for its Active Directory implementation. However, here's the problem: .local names cannot be resolved on the Internet, and you can never have an Internet presence using .local. If you later decide you want to have an Internet integrated implementation, you cannot change the .local first level on your Active Directory root without completely reinstalling the Active Directory. My advice — proceed with caution and planning before using this option. It is quite restrictive because it gives you no option to later use your network with the Internet.

Planning Summary

Well, I've spent quite a bit of time talking about one single planning aspect of the Active Directory—your domain root name. As you can see, you have a number of options, and you should carefully weigh them before deciding on an Active Directory root domain name.

With that said, here are some final reminders and thoughts:

✦ You cannot change your Active Directory root domain without completely reinstalling the Active Directory forest—which means reinstalling everything. Proceed with caution and plan your root name wisely.

✦ Your domain root name should encompass your entire business, and it should be a friendly, recognizable name. Make sure your name follows DNS Internet standards for Internet integration.

✦ Take a hard look at how your company uses the Internet or how it will use the Internet in the future. Find a plan that works best for your company—one that balances Internet integration with security needs.

✦ And here's the Bible statement for this chapter—Simplicity covers a multitude of sins. Keep your name and implementation design as simple as possible. Complex implementations with multiple DNS zones and firewalls, although effective, can cause you many problems. Examine your design and try to anticipate every problem that could possibly occur. Then examine how you would handle those problems.

Summary

This chapter introduced the Active Directory namespace and presented how that namespace is built on the DNS namespace. Active Directory names are DNS names. This feature provides an unlimited level of extensibility and possible integration with the Internet. As you plan your implementation, great care must be taken when designing your Active Directory forest root domain name since all other names in your environment are based on the root name. You should also remember that the root name cannot be changed at a later time without completely reinstalling the forest. Be certain to choose a friendly name that encompasses your entire business environment and to examine how you will integrate your name with the Internet and how you will secure your environment.

✦   ✦   ✦

Planning an Active Directory Structure

Once you have determined your Active Directory namespace and you understand the requirements for a DNS
implementation, you are ready to begin creating an Active
Directory structure in which you design a domain and forest
configuration for your network. This chapter explores this
process from the ground up, as if you were installing a new
Windows 2000 network. However, even if you are upgrading
to the Active Directory instead of installing from scratch, you
should carefully study this chapter for important planning
and implementation issues.

Active Directory Domains

If you have spent any time in an NT network, you are all too
familiar with domains. A domain is a method of network management. In other words, a domain is a way to partition a network for security and administrative purposes. Windows NT
introduced the domain concept, and Windows 2000 continues
using domains. However, Windows 2000 uses domains in a
different, more effective manner.

Domains under Windows NT

Windows NT domains are limited in terms of the number of
user and group accounts they can hold. Due to size limitation
and administrative needs, most NT networks of any size quickly
grow too many domains. Because of hardware and administration costs, this design is not desirable. Domains are expensive
in terms of hardware because you must have a primary domain

controller (PDC) and any number of backup domain controllers (BDCs) to manage each domain. The more domains you have, the more servers you are required to have. In terms of administration, domains are expensive because someone has to take care of all of those servers, solve problems, and ensure that network operations are functioning in a desirable manner. Therefore, a great number of domains in Windows NT networks can certainly be a problem.

On top of all of this, multiple domains can be very difficult to manage due to trust relationships. Consider this example: You have four NT domains. In order to access resources in any other domain, trust relationships must be established, or users cannot reach any resources outside of their own domain. Domain A might trust Domain B, but Domain B wouldn't necessarily have to trust Domain A. Domain B might trust domain C, and Domain C might trust both Domain A and B. Domain D might trust domain A, might not trust domain C, but might still be a trusting domain for Domain B. As you can tell, with only four domains, trust relationships can be a big mess. In Windows NT, you had the following trust relationship options:

✦ **One-way trust** — A single trust relationship between two domains, such as Domain A trusts Domain B.

✦ **Two-way trust** — Two domains trust each other, for example, Domain A trusts Domain B and Domain B trusts Domain A.

That sounds simple enough, but trust relationships in Windows NT are not transitive. This means that if Domain A trusts Domain B and Domain B trusts Domain C, Domain A *does not* trust Domain C. In order for Domain A to trust Domain C, a trust relationship between the two domains must be directly established.

I say all of this to make a point — administrators have to manually configure and administer these trust relationships along with all of the other problems associated with multiple domains, network traffic, and difficult resource access. This is not to say that NT networks aren't effective — they definitely are. In smaller networks, the model works just fine. But, I also do not mind saying that the directory service model in Windows 2000 is incredibly better.

Building domain trees

Active Directory domains are based on a hierarchical structure. When you install the first domain controller in the first domain of your Active Directory implementation, you create a new Active Directory forest and a new domain tree.

A forest is simply a collection of domain tree(s). When you begin installation, a forest is automatically created for your entire Active Directory implementation. Within that forest, you can create multiple trees if necessary, but you create only one forest. While it is true that forests can be connected together, you should not intentionally create an Active Directory implementation that uses multiple forests. Think of a forest as all encompassing for your implementation.

Within that forest, domain tree(s) are created. When you install the first domain controller in the first domain, you are creating the domain root. Think of the domain tree as an upside-down structure where all other domains *branch* from the root. As in an actual physical tree, the branches are all derived from the tree root — in other words, they all are connected together, and they all fit together.

 In Chapter 2, you explored the development of your root domain's name. This name becomes the root of your domain tree, and all other domains within the tree are derived from the domain root.

Consider how this works. As an example, suppose that Triton, Inc., installs its first domain and names it triton.com. Triton.com is now the domain root in Triton's forest, shown in Figure 3-1.

Triton Forest

Figure 3-1: Triton forest

Now, suppose that Triton, Inc., wants to add another domain to their existing domain tree. The domain tree forms a *contiguous* namespace. Contiguous means that the domains in the tree share a boundary or they are adjoining. In terms of DNS, the new domain is extended from the root domain. For example, suppose that Triton, Inc., wants to create a new domain called "production" in the domain tree. The new domain's name will be production.triton.com, as shown in Figure 3-2. The production domain becomes a child domain of triton.com and extends the namespace in a contiguous manner. If you attempted to name the new domain production.com, prod-tri.com, or some other DNS name, the name would be rejected because it would not be contiguous with triton.com — the root domain.

Continuing with the example, production.triton.com determines that it needs two child domains of its own, namerica and samerica, in order to manage administration and security in the two different areas. Since these domains will be child domains of production.triton.com (and grandchild domains of triton.com), the new domains, shown in Figure 3-3, will be named namerica.production.triton.com and samerica.production.triton.com in order to continue the contiguous namespace.

Triton Forest
triton.com
production.
triton.com

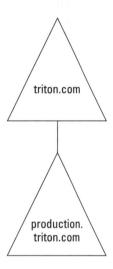

Figure 3-2: Child domain

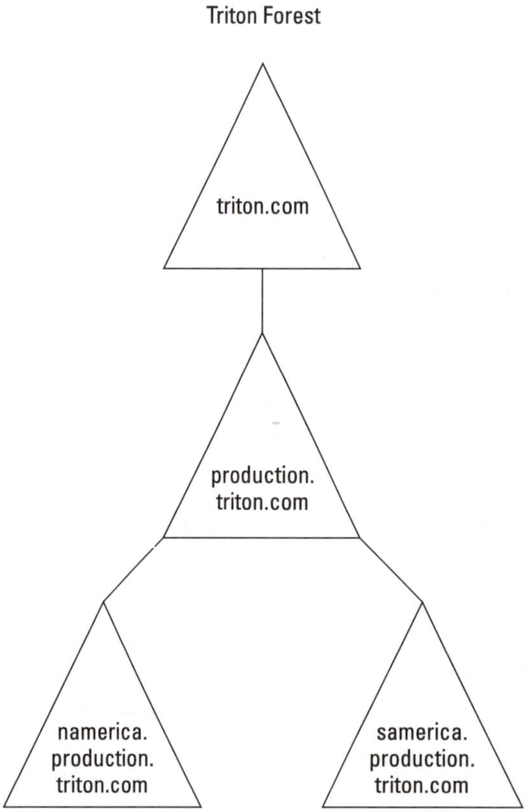

Triton Forest
triton.com
production.
triton.com
namerica.
production.
triton.com
samerica.
production.
triton.com

Figure 3-3: Additional child domains

As you can see, the domain tree can be logically built in this manner. However, suppose that the triton.com domain later determines that it needs another domain, japan.triton.com. Can this new domain be added? Yes. Japan.triton.com is simply a new child of triton.com. This does not interfere with production.triton.com, the existing child, as shown in Figure 3-4.

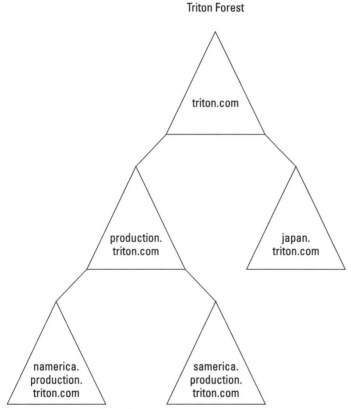

Triton Forest

Figure 3-4: New child domain

However, here is another pitfall of the Active Directory (with the first being that you cannot change the root domain name without a complete reinstallation): you cannot insert, or graft, domains into the domain tree. In other words, the domain tree has to be built one layer at a time—you cannot return and graft a domain between two existing domains.

Consider an example. Suppose that triton.com has installed the domain tree configuration shown in Figure 3-4. However, at a later date, Triton, Inc., reorganizes so that Production A owns the North and South America domains and Production B owns what will be a new domain in Europe. So under the production domain, they need to graft a proda.production.com and change the namerica and samerica domains so that they are child domains of ProdA. Installing ProdB as a child of production.triton.com so that it is a child is no problem. It's grafting ProdA and changing the existing child domains that is the problem, as shown in Figure 3-5.

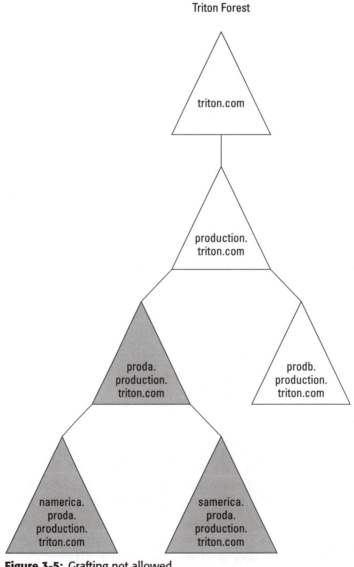

Triton Forest

Figure 3-5: Grafting not allowed

In fact, you just can't intuitively do this. In order to pull this configuration off, you have to uninstall the namerica and samerica domains, install the ProdA domain as a child of production.triton.com, and then reinstall the namerica and samerica domains as children of proda.production.triton.com. As you can see, this can become a big mess. Microsoft would tell you that you must carefully plan your domain tree structure so this does not happen. True enough, but such needs cannot always be foreseen.

Note   Hopefully, future releases of Active Directory will resolve this issue, especially considering the fact that Novell Directory Services can easily resolve such problems and have been able to for some time now.

Using multiple domain trees

In the previous section, you saw how a multiple domain tree is built — from the root domain up through various child domains. This single domain tree exists within your Active Directory forest — which encompasses your entire enterprise environment. For another example, suppose you install your domain tree, and then a year later, your company acquires another company. The acquired company will retain its own identity, IT administration, and security, but you want the two companies to share resources. Now what?

The answer in this case is very easy. You simply create a new domain tree within your existing forest. For example, suppose Triton, Inc., acquires a company called Acton Development. Triton, Inc., currently has a domain tree of triton.com. Triton, Inc., can install a new domain tree, which begins a new domain root of actondev.com. From this new root, Triton, Inc., can install additional child domains as needed. Suppose also that Acton Development needs two child domains — a Production domain and a Development domain. These domains become children of actondev.com called prod.actondev.com and dev.actondev.com.

Once you have two trees in the forest, they have the following characteristics, which are also shown in Figure 3-6:

✦ Obviously, triton.com and actondev.com do *not* share a contiguous namespace — and by design, two different trees do not. (If they did, they would have to be in the same tree.)

✦ Because the trees exist within a forest, they are still viewed as a single hierarchy. In other words, the Active Directory does not consider the two trees *two different* Active Directory implementations because DNS can resolve any of the names within the forest.

✦ Both trees share the same schema and configuration (because there is only one schema and configuration per forest).

✦ Both trees use the same global catalog. LDAP queries are limited to the domain tree, but the global catalog can resolve queries for the other domain tree.

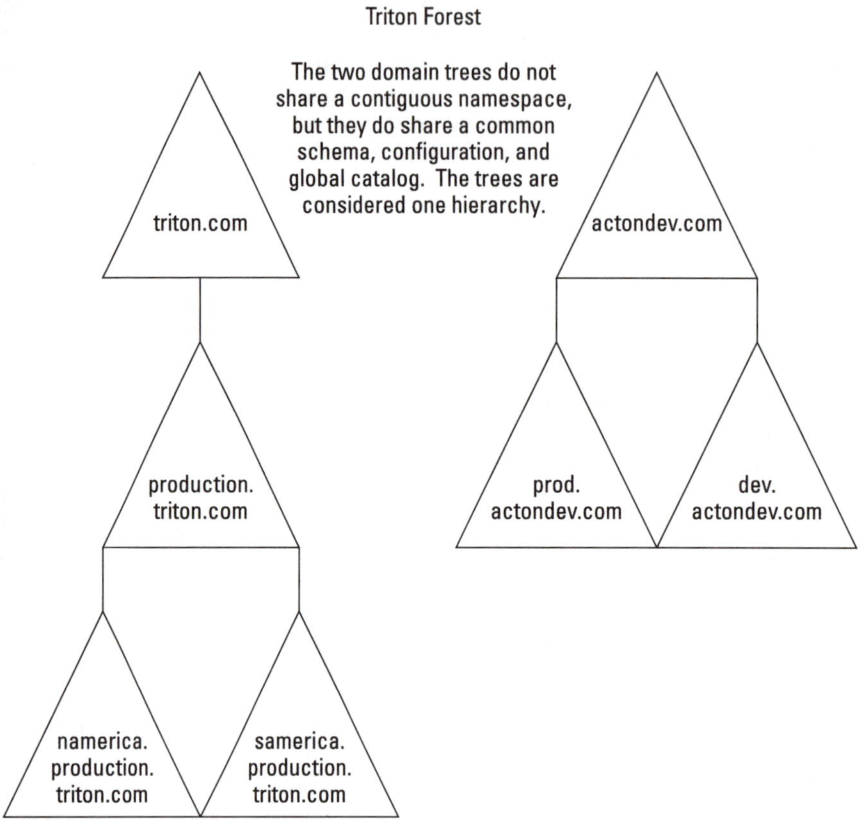

Triton Forest

The two domain trees do not
share a contiguous namespace,
but they do share a common
schema, configuration, and
global catalog. The trees are
considered one hierarchy.

triton.com

actondev.com

production.
triton.com

prod.
actondev.com

dev.
actondev.com

namerica.
production.
triton.com

samerica.
production.
triton.com

Figure 3-6: Two domain trees

The primary reason for implementing a multiple domain tree configuration is the
acquisition or merger of two companies. This configuration can be useful if one
company already has an Active Directory implementation and later acquires
another company that needs to maintain its own identity. You can use the multiple
domain tree configuration to maintain the two different companies while still providing a way for the two companies to share resources under one network.

Cross-Reference   Chapters 6 and 7 give you step-by-step instructions for installing domains and
domain trees.

Using multiple forests

I said earlier that the forest is all encompassing for your enterprise. That statement should be true under normal circumstances, but there are instances where two different Active Directory forests need to be connected. For example, suppose your company works with another company on a big project on a temporary forest. You could potentially join the two forests for a period of time in order to access resources in the other forest. This configuration is incidental — it is not one that you should intentionally plan to implement. Although there is no advantage to using multiple forests over a single forest configuration, there are plenty of disadvantages. First, you have to manually connect two forests together by connecting the domain roots in each forest through manual, one-way trust relationships. After this, you have the job of manually trying to manage the connection. Each forest has its own global catalog and schema — and simply put, accessing resources and trying to sort through effective permissions can be very difficult and troublesome. In such circumstances where two forests need to share information, there are often easier solutions, such as simply using Internet e-mail or setting up a private Web site for data transfer. The point here is that the multiple forest configuration is possible, but it should *never* be intentionally planned and implemented.

Understanding transitive trusts

In Chapter 1, I mentioned that Windows 2000 leaves the legacy of ridiculously confusing domain trust relationships behind with the implementation of Kerberos transitive trusts. Kerberos is the security protocol in Windows 2000, replacing Windows NT LAN Manager (NTLM), and Kerberos trusts are a tremendous improvement over the manual trust options in Windows NT. Kerberos trusts are two-way transitive trust relationships that are automatically created and configured by the Active Directory within a forest. The beauty of Kerberos trusts is they work well, and you, as the administrator, do not have to do anything to configure them (which is always a plus).

 Note NTLM is still supported in Windows 2000 for backward compatibility, but Kerberos is the primary and preferred security protocol.

As I said, Kerberos trusts are *always* transitive. That is, if Domain A trusts Domain B, then Domain B automatically trusts Domain A; or if Domain A trusts Domain B and Domain B trusts Domain C, then Domain A transitively trusts Domain C. Kerberos trusts are shown in Figure 3-7.

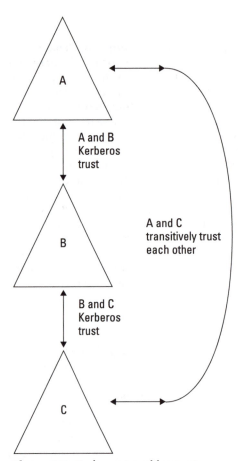

Figure 3-7: Kerberos transitive trust

The great thing about transitive trust relationships is that they reduce the number of relationships that must be established and maintained by the Active Directory. Due to the transitive nature of the Kerberos trusts, a domain needs to trust only one other domain to actually have access to all other domains in the forest. This is also true with multiple domain tree forests. When multiple forests are created, transitive trusts are automatically configured between the forest roots. For example, consider Figure 3-8.

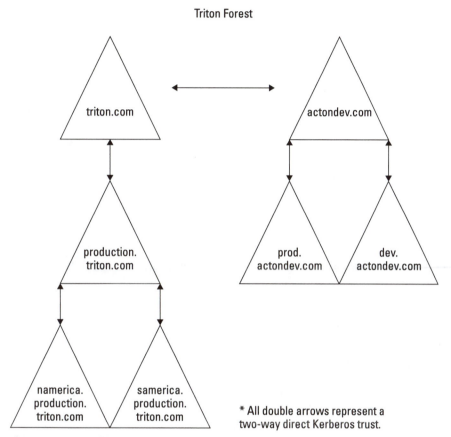

Figure 3-8: Transitive trusts

Suppose, for example, that a user in namerica.production.triton.com needs to access a resource in prod.actondev.com. There is no direct trust relationship between the two domains, but the user, assuming he or she has appropriate permissions for the resource, will still be able to transitively access the resource. This is all because namerica.production.triton.com transitively trusts triton.com through production. triton.com and triton.com transitively trusts prod.actondev.com through actondev. com, as you can see in Figure 3-9.

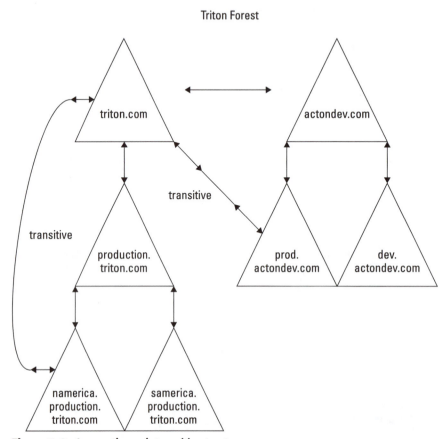

Figure 3-9: Access through transitive trusts

Consider one more example. A user in dev.actondev.com needs to access a resource in production.triton.com. There is no direct trust relationship between these two domains, but the user, with appropriate permissions, can still access the resource through the transitive trust. Dev.actondev.com transitively trusts triton.com through actondev.com. Since triton.com directly trusts production.triton.com, the resource can be accessed, as shown in Figure 3-10.

As you can see, any scenario I generate comes back to the same truth — if a domain in a tree trusts a domain in another tree, it can reach any domain in the forest through the transitive nature of Kerberos trusts.

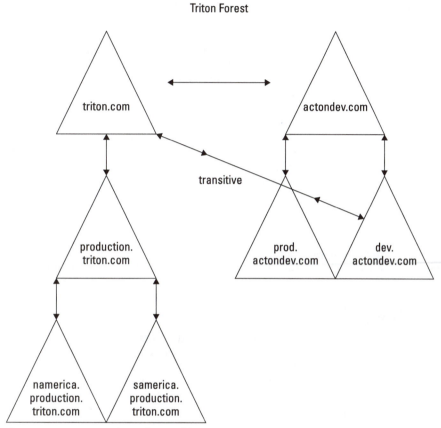

Figure 3-10: Access through transitive trust

As I mentioned earlier in this section, you do *not* have to manually create any Kerberos trusts in an Active Directory forest because they are automatically created with each new domain you install. However, you may need to connect some of your Windows 2000 domains to existing Windows NT domains. Windows NT does not support Kerberos, so you cannot configure transitive trusts between the two. You can, however, configure one-way trust relationships as necessary. The Active Directory still supports one-way trusts for backward compatibility purposes with NT style domains. You cannot create one-way trusts between Windows 2000 domains within a forest (and would never want to anyway), but this backward compatibility is provided to help you during transition to a total Windows 2000 network. You can use the Active Directory Domains and Trusts tool to manually configure one-way trusts as necessary.

See Chapter 8 to learn more about configuring domain trusts and sites.

There is one other type of trust relationship you may find useful in an Active Directory forest — the cross-link trust relationship. In complex Active Directory forests with several domains and more than one domain tree, you can create cross-link, or shortcut, trusts to speed resource access. Return to the example in Figure 3-9. Namerica.production.triton.com needs to access resources on a regular basis in the prod.actiondev.com domain due to a new project the two groups are jointly working on. Users can access resources in each other's domain due to the transitive trust, but you can improve network performance by manually creating a transitive cross-link trust between the two domains. This cross-link trust enables the two domains to bypass the transitive trust and communicate with each other on a one-on-one basis. This configuration can be helpful in large, complex environments where users in one domain must access resources frequently in another domain for which there is no direct trust relationship.

You can learn more about manually creating trust relationships in Chapter 8.

Revisiting domain controllers

Having explored the Active Directory forest and domain tree design, I want to revisit the issue of domain controllers, global catalog servers, and operations masters discussed in Chapter 1. This information is important, and you can expect me to discuss these issues in other relevant parts of the book as well.

Domain controllers

As you know, domain controllers in Windows 2000 are peers. Neither primary domain controllers (PDC) nor backup domain controllers (BDC) are used in a pure Active Directory domain.

Tip   You can use NT BDCs in your Windows 2000 domain during implementation. The Active Directory provides for backward compatibility to support NT BDCs until your network upgrade is complete. However, you cannot *install* a Windows 2000 PDC or BDC because they do not exist in 2000 networks.

Each domain controller holds the forest schema, and each domain controller maintains its own copy of the Active Directory database in %*systemroot*%\WINNT\ntds.dit. If you are or were heavily entrenched in the Windows NT PDC/BDC model, you may wonder where the Active Directory actually resides on the network. The answer is that it resides on *every* domain controller — there is no single master copy of the Active Directory database. This is a by-design feature of a peer domain controller network. Because all domain controllers hold the Active Directory database, you have built-in fault tolerance for your domains (if you have more than one domain controller in the domain—which you should). If one domain controller goes down, all other domain controllers hold copies of the database, so network operations continue as normal. When you bring the downed domain controller back online, its database can be updated automatically through replication with other domain controllers.

Cross-Reference   You can learn about fault tolerance and backup in Chapter 12 and replication in Chapters 5 and 13.

In addition to fault tolerance, you also gain ease of administration because you can make changes to the Active Directory database on any domain controller in the domain. Since there is no PDC, all peer copies of the database are *writable*. As a result, you can make changes from any location that will be replicated to other domain controllers in the domain.

So, if there is no single, master copy of the database, how are domain controllers installed? Consider the following process:

1. When you install the first domain controller, the Active Directory forest and root domains are created. This domain controller automatically becomes a global catalog server and holds all five FSMO roles. A default database is in place once installation is complete. At this point, you have a functioning Windows 2000 domain with a single domain controller. You can begin configuring user accounts and publishing other resources as needed. However, for fault tolerance and load balancing, you should have more than one domain controller in the domain.

2. You begin the Active Directory Installation Wizard on what will be the second domain controller in the root domain. The Installation Wizard will ask you to make a selection, and you choose the "additional domain controller option." When you choose this option, the Active Directory database, schema, and other files are copied to the domain controller from the first domain controller. This is a new "copy" of the Active Directory, yet one that is exactly the same and writable.

3. The process continues for as many domain controllers as you want to use in the new domain.

So, how many domain controllers do you need in a single domain? This is a question you must carefully answer and one to which I cannot give you an answer. The number of domain controllers you need in a single domain depends on the following:

✦ **Desired fault tolerance.** You need two or more for the domain to be fault tolerant against the failure of a single domain controller.

✦ **Load Balancing.** A domain with 10,000 users will obviously need more domain controllers than one with 500. Look at your network load and attempt to find a balance that works best for your network.

✦ **Services.** Depending on the additional services and functions of your domain controllers, you may need more in your domain to handle the usage demand.

✦ **Cost Tolerance.** In the real world, you have to balance what would be a "great" design with what you can actually afford. Your budget as well as your needs drive the number of domain controllers you have in your domain. However, it is important to note that too few domain controllers may slow response and service time due to client request overload.

You can use Windows 2000 member servers to run different services needed in the domain. This configuration helps remove some of the network load from domain controllers. For example, your DNS and DHCP servers do not need to be domain controllers. Any Windows 2000 Server that does not have the Active Directory installed is a member server.

Global catalog servers

Global catalog servers contain a full replica of Active Directory objects within their domain and a partial replica of Active Directory objects in other domains in the forest. As I mentioned in the previous section, when you install the root domain in a forest, the first domain controller becomes a global catalog server by default.

You can check out Chapter 1 for a complete overview of global catalog servers.

In order to plan the placement of global catalog servers in your implementation, you have to step away from the logical structure planning and examine your physical structure planning. Sites are maintained in the Active Directory to help control user and replication traffic over slower WAN links. For global catalogs, the best configuration is to have one global catalog server at each site. This will increase traffic somewhat, but users will experience the best query performance this way. As you are making notes and planning your deployment, make a note that a global catalog server should ideally reside in each physical site.

Chapter 5 explores Active Directory site configuration and planning.

FSMO roles

Chapter 1 introduced you to flexible single master operation (FSMO) roles, and in this section, I want to reiterate their placement within the Active Directory forest. First, let me note that you do not have to install FSMO roles. They are installed automatically and placed by default when you install the Active Directory. However, you should know where those roles belong to avoid possible configuration errors later. Here's the easiest way to remember it:

✦ **Forest wide** — The schema master and domain naming master exist on one domain controller in the entire forest. By default, the first domain controller installed in the root domain is assigned these roles.

✦ **Domain wide** — Each domain in the forest contains a RID master, PDC Emulator, and Infrastructure master. By default, these roles are assigned to the first domain controller installed in the child domain or in the root domain of a second forest domain tree.

To solidify these concepts, consider an example. Triton, Inc., installs triton.com, its root domain in the first domain tree. On the first domain controller, which installs triton.com, the following roles are assigned: schema master, domain naming master, RID master, PDC Emulator, and Infrastructure master (as well as the global catalog server). In each child domain that is installed from the triton.com root, the first domain controller in each child domain also receives the RID master, PDC Emulator, and Infrastructure master roles, since these are domain specific.

Next, when Triton, Inc., installs the new root domain of actondev.com in their forest, the first domain controller in this domain receives the roles of RID master and PDC Emulator. Any other child domain in the new tree receives these roles as well. Keep in mind that the schema master role and domain naming master role exist on one domain controller in the entire forest — do not confuse this with each domain root that might exist.

The logical question in this discussion might be, "Why examine these roles if they are installed by default anyway?" I bring all of this up in this chapter — while you are planning domains — to make certain you're up to speed with the technical concepts and also to assert these two points:

✦ Your first domain controller in your first root domain has all FSMO roles plus the global catalog server. Make certain this first domain controller is powerful enough to handle all of these roles, at least initially. The best advice is to use a server that has hardware that well exceeds the minimum requirements provided by Microsoft. That should put you in the clear.

✦ You can move operations master roles to different domain controllers. You may not want that first domain controller in the first root domain to shoulder all of the FSMO roles as well as the global catalog server. No problem — you can move them to a different server, and Chapter 7 shows you how.

As you continue planning the deployment, keep in mind how FSMO roles are automatically installed, where they are installed, and consider any needed plans to move those roles to different domain controllers as needed for load balancing purposes.

Planning Your Domain Structure

The previous section explored a number of possible domain structures in a Windows 2000 environment. Your enterprise will always begin with a single root domain and build other domains from the root. It is also possible to have more than one root domain in your forest, depending on the structure and needs of your company.

As you sit down and begin to plan your domain structure, you may spend some time scratching your head. After all, which domain structure is best? In the previous section, for example, you considered several domain structures involving child and even grandchild domains. Keep in mind that these configurations are provided to help you understand the hierarchical nature of the structure — not necessarily to recommend a particular configuration.

Here's what I mean: Domains are expensive, both in hardware and personnel costs, and they require more administrative maintenance to manage. As I have mentioned several times, one of Microsoft's major goals with the Active Directory is to help reduce the number of domains in Microsoft networks. This goal benefits us all and is one you should wholeheartedly consider. In Windows NT networks, you may have used multiple domains for a variety of reasons — with one of those being network size accommodation. Because of the Security Accounts Manager (SAM) database, NT domains had an object limit of about 40,000 objects. Remember that the Active Directory domain is virtually unlimited — it can hold a few hundred objects up to about a million (or even beyond). So, in an Active Directory network, you can implement domains based on real needs and *not* due to technology limitations.

Caution   You should never implement a domain structure based on concerns about domain size in the Active Directory. Windows 2000 domains are basically unlimited.

So, who needs multiple domains and who needs a single domain? The three questions you should ask yourself are as follows:

1. Do I have decentralized security needs?
2. Do I have decentralized administrative needs?
3. Do I have problems with network traffic?

Although simple questions, they are not always so simple to answer. Consider them in more detail. First, do you have decentralized security needs? This issue arises when one segment of the network has a completely different security policy than another segment. Consider an example. Suppose that Triton, Inc., has two divisions — a corporate division and a production division. The production environment is highly sensitive. Physical security is very tight, and network security is even tighter. The corporate division also has tight security, but nothing like the production division. The production division is planning on incorporating many of the security features in Windows 2000, including IP Security, while the corporate division is not. Different administrators handle security in each division. In this scenario, the two divisions have very different security needs, and different administrators manage each division. In this case, two domains would be best.

However, what if the two divisions had slightly different security needs, but nothing as dramatic as presented in the previous scenario? Suppose that one division has different permissions policies for resource access, but overall, the two are not that different. Keep in mind that you can use Organizational Units (OU) to effectively segment your network for moderate security needs, as well as administrative needs. In this situation, all you probably need is one domain with different OUs for each division.

The next question concerns administration. You may use multiple domains if you have very different administrative needs. In most cases, if you have decentralized security needs, you will also have decentralized administrative needs, which in turn calls for a multiple domain structure. However, what if you do not have decentralized security needs, but you do have decentralized administrative needs? While there are certainly scenarios where decentralized administrative needs can require multiple domains, now is a good time to throw up a red flag and spend some time studying your network administrative structure.

Networks are alive — they grow and change as companies grow and change. As companies grow, acquire other companies, and merge groups together within the company, the IT administrative structure is affected. It is not uncommon for this administrative structure to become complex and overly cumbersome. From simple structure issues to politics, your administrative structure can be too complex and unnecessary. Now is a time to take a look at that structure and determine why your administration is so decentralized that you are considering multiple domains. In the case where your decentralized administration needs are legitimate, a single domain with multiple OUs will still be your best choice.

NO PDC Limit Problems

While we're on the subject of NT domain limitations, a more serious limitation than the SAM database limit is the PDC. In Windows NT domains, only the PDC has a writable copy of the database — all BDCs have a read-only copy of the database. This causes two problems with domain size:

1. **Changes:** Only the PDC has a writable copy of the database. Changes must be made on the PDC, or on BDC that connects with the PDC and makes the changes to the PDC database. In a large domain spread over several different buildings or even cities, this design is impractical.

2. **Load:** The domain can grow only so large because the PDC has to handle the write load. This can quickly become too much for one machine to handle.

Windows 2000 leaves this legacy behind with peer domain controllers — all of which have a writable copy of the database and all of which can be used by administrators to make update changes. As the domain grows, you need only to add more domain controllers to scale the implementation with your growth, which solves a lot of potential problems!

Finally, think about network traffic. You can use the Active Directory to create sites to manage network traffic over slower WAN links, but domains can also help reduce network traffic.

Cross-Reference   See Chapter 5 for more information about sites and site planning.

Domains help control network traffic by keeping logon and query traffic local. In other words, the domain serves as a boundary for security and administration, but also for traffic. You can use a domain that spans multiple geographic locations, but consider how this design will affect network traffic between the locations and how capable your network is of handling the traffic.

Caution   As you plan your domain structure, keep in mind that grafting is not allowed. Once implemented, you can only add child domains to existing parents. You *cannot* generate a new parent for an existing domain. Keep your initial domain structure as simple as possible to prevent this Active Directory design limitation from becoming a serious issue.

So, when you consider these issues as you plan your own domain structure, you obviously have a number of things to think about. The key is to find the structure that works best for your company and supports your users in the best possible way. As you plan your domain structure, keep these points in mind (read them over and over!):

✦ A single domain is always your best choice. It is easier to manage and is less expensive.

✦ Keep in mind that Organizational Units (OUs) can provide security and administrative boundaries. A single domain with multiple OUs is always a better design choice than a multiple domain structure.

✦ Make sure your decentralized security and administrative needs are *real* needs. Analyze the need carefully. If the answer seems to be *"We've always done it that way,"* then this may be a good time to consider some restructuring.

✦ Administrative boundaries based on politics (or just mass confusion) need to be changed. An Active Directory implementation is an excellent time to change it, so study your administrative structure carefully.

✦ When designing your structure, if you begin using several child domains or grandchild domains, consider this a warning. You are probably trying to follow the NT model. Grandchild domains should be incidental domains used for specific enterprise purposes — not a structure you purposefully design. In other words, there is probably a more simple structure that will meet your needs.

✦ As I will say over and over throughout this book, simplicity is always best. Keep your domain structure as simple and generic as possible. Complicated domain structures are hard to manage and hard to change when the need arises.

✦ Never intentionally design a multiple forest structure.

If you are upgrading an existing NT network, you will probably need to do some domain restructuring in order to reduce the current number of domains. See Chapter 4 to learn more.

Understanding Organizational Unit Structure

In the previous sections in this chapter, I have referred to Organizational Units (OU) several times and even said that OUs can effectively replace domains so that you can have a single domain with multiple OUs. Think of an Organizational Unit like a file folder. The OU's job is to hold other Active Directory objects (including other OUs). The OU enables you to organize your Active Directory resources in an effective manner.

However, OUs are more powerful than simple containers. OUs can also serve as administrative and security boundaries. Different security standards can be placed on OUs, including different group policies. Administratively, an OU can be delegated so that a certain administrator or group controls it.

See Chapter 15 to learn more about group policy and Chapter 11 to learn more about delegation.

With an OU, you can set security for a subset of an existing domain, have different administrators manage, and place different policies on the OU—just like you would normally do for an NT domain. So, with all of that said, you can understand how important OUs are to an Active Directory design and how their effective use can greatly impact your Active Directory network. Before exploring the OU hierarchy, there are two important points about OUs that I want to mention here:

✦ OUs are invisible in terms of DNS. For example, suppose that computer5 is located in the Accounting OU of triton.com. The computer's DNS name is computer5.triton.com *not* computer5.accounting.triton.com.

✦ Second, OUs are specific to the domain and can contain only resources that are within the domain. *An OU cannot contain any resource that resides in another Active Directory domain.*

Understanding the OU hierarchy

As you might guess, there is a potential OU hierarchy that you can implement, just as there is a domain hierarchy. The OU hierarchy is rather simple. When you create a domain, you implement OUs at the domain level. For example, suppose that Triton, Inc., decides to implement three OUs in the triton.com domain. The three OUs are created and named Accounting, Production, and Marketing.

Cross-Reference You learn how to create OUs in Chapter 10.

These three OUs are called first-level OUs. They are OUs directly under triton.com. Now suppose that Accounting decides that it needs some OUs of its own. Within the Accounting OU, several child OUs are created to help manage resources. These child OUs are called second-level OUs. Continuing with the same example, suppose these second-level OUs are later subdivided into additional OUs. These new OUs would be called third-level OUs. This process is called *nesting*. Beyond the third level OU, the OUs are called *deeply nested OUs*. The hierarchy is presented in Figure 3-11.

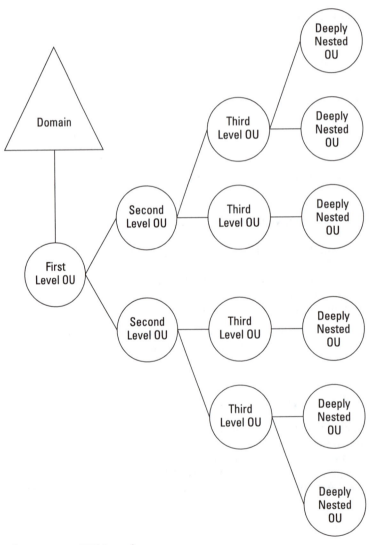

Figure 3-11: OU hierarchy

You can nest OUs to as many levels as necessary, but as you might guess, nesting can also cause you some problems. Before exploring those issues, however, you must understand the administrative function of OUs.

OU administrative functions

OUs are designed for administrators — not users. An OU structure should help you meet administrative needs and back up your existing administrative plan. With OUs, you can effectively group Active Directory objects and manage those objects both in terms of administration and security. When users browse the Active Directory, they can see your OU structure. For example, if users browse triton.com, they can see the Accounting OU, Marketing OU, and Production OU. Users can then browse those OUs and find resources. However, OUs are not designed to assist user browsing. The Active Directory provides powerful LDAP query services to users so they can find resources on the network. Browsing is not the preferred method of finding resources, and you should not design an OU structure with user browsing in mind. With that said, keep in mind that your OU structure should be built on your administrative plan.

Caution

It is very important that you plan your OU structure based on administration. OU structures not based on administrative need usually grow at an alarming rate and can make life difficult and very complicated for administrators.

Problems with nested OUs

As I mentioned previously, you can create an OU hierarchy that is uncomplicated and one that includes many nested OUs. However, deeply nested OUs are usually a sign of a faulty OU design. As a general rule of thumb, you should only use first- and second-level OUs. When you begin creating OUs at the third level and beyond, a warning light should come on in your head. Third-level OUs (and deeply nested OUs) are usually a sign that your OU structure is growing too much or that your hierarchical design is not broad enough.

This does not at all mean that third-level OUs and beyond should not be used. In fact, situations do arise where they are needed. But, the point I want to make here is simply that third-level OUs and beyond should cause you to pause and carefully examine your OU structure. Here's why:

✦ Deeply nested OUs can affect Group Policy. Group Policy is implemented at the site, domain, and OU levels. Deeply nested OUs may cause performance problems and user logon delays because of the filtering effect that must occur through the OU structure.

✦ Inheritance is in effect. This means that the parent OU passes its properties to the second-level OU, which passes its properties to the third-level OU, and so forth. With deeply nested and excessively complex OU structures, inheritance issues can be problematic both in terms of administration and performance.

✦ Active Directory resource discovery is slower in deeply nested OUs.

✦ To a point, complex OU structures cause more problems than they solve. Remember that an OU structure should support your administrative needs — not user browsing. Complex structures can cause more problems than they solve and tend to become more confusing than helpful.

Planning Your Organizational Unit Structure

Just as you should carefully plan your domain structure, you should carefully plan your OU structure. Due to the issues explored in the previous section, you should attempt to use the simplest OU structure possible, always focusing on administration. Just like your domain structure, simplicity is your best choice. Keep your OUs broad so they serve a general purpose. Highly specific OU structures grow at an alarming rate and can get completely out of hand, so keep things as simple as possible.

Your OU structure should also be relatively static. This means that your OUs should be based on network or business divisions that are not likely to change. OUs that are not built on static network or business divisions must be restructured or deleted, thus causing you to move Active Directory objects from one OU to another. This can be time consuming and frustrating, so keep your OUs as static as possible.

As you plan your OU structure, take a close look at your administrative model and your actual IT staff. Consider the following questions:

✦ How can my OU structure support and simplify my administrative model?

✦ How can my OU structure *fulfill* my administrative model?

✦ How will my IT staff manage OUs?

✦ How can my OU model be generated so that it makes effective use of my IT staff?

As you consider OUs, think about these issues so that you implement the best plan to support administration.

 Tip   When planning OUs, always keep your attention focused on your administrative model — do not begin to think about resources and user access to those resources based on browsing.

There is no single correct way to design an OU structure. Microsoft leaves that to you and your network/administrative needs. Since there is no single correct way, you have a few different options available to you, plus a mixture of these and possibly a design that you create yourself. The main point is that your OU structure should be simple, static, and should benefit administration.

With that said, consider a few possible OU structure designs. Remember that OUs are domain specific and dependent. In other words, they are used to contain resources within a specific domain. A domain may physically reside in one geographic area or a number of areas. If your domain resides in several geographic areas, then you may consider creating OUs for each location. For example, suppose that the triton.com domain resides in Houston, Dallas, and Austin. You could create three OUs for each location. Then, each location OU can contain resources specific to that location, and administrators in each location can manage the OU and the resources. Naturally, each location OU could contain other OUs to further subdivide the location for management purposes. This type of OU design is effective because administrators at each site can manage resources within the site, and the structure is generic enough to survive most internal company changes.

Another type of OU structure commonly used is the business division structure. For networks that use only one Active Directory domain, OUs can be used to further partition the domain by department. For example, you might have a corporate OU and a production OU to separate the two diverse business partitions within the domain. Second-level OUs can then be used in each top-level OU to further define resources and administration for that division. As you can imagine, this type of structure works well, but you must make certain that your structure is broad enough to survive changes. Avoid using OUs for smaller departments. Try to use a higher view of your business structure so that policies and security can be applied at a higher level. Remember — the more OUs you use, the more administrative time and administrative cost you may use.

Finally, some Active Directory environments focus their domain OUs on large groupings of resources. For example, you could have a Users OU, Computers OU, and Published Resources OU. This design can also be effective, particularly in environments where administrative delegation is not a major issue and diverse security or group policy settings are not required. This design enables you to delegate control of your users to a group of administrators while another group is responsible for published resources, and so forth.

As you might imagine, most environments use a combination of these three so they are tailored to meet the needs of the business. Once again, there is no right or wrong structure, just avoid too many OUs and deeply nested OUs and make certain your OU structure supports your administrative model.

Summary

This chapter explored the Active Directory domain structure and the OU structure and examined how to plan your domain and OU implementation. Active Directory domains are built on a DNS root domain for the forest. All domains within the root are derived from the root domain. An Active Directory forest can also contain additional trees with different root domain names. With this configuration, a contiguous namespace is not shared between the two trees, but they are considered one single resolvable area because of the forest. Like domains, OU structures are built in a hierarchical fashion and can nest to as many levels as desired. For both domain and OU structure development, simplicity is your best option. Complex domain and OU structures are expensive and problematic. Your best Active Directory design is a single domain that contains multiple OUs. This gives you the administrative and security control needed for different partitions of the network while lowering cost and the potential for problems.

✦   ✦   ✦

Upgrading and Migrating to the Active Directory

✦ ✦ ✦ ✦

In This Chapter

Planning domain
upgrades

Consolidating
NT domains

Migrating to the
Active Directory

✦ ✦ ✦ ✦

Designing an Active Directory infrastructure from scratch is the easiest possible implementation plan. After all, you can design your domain structure appropriately, create your own network wish list, and make certain all your computer hardware is up-to-speed. Unfortunately, most of us will be faced with either an Active Directory upgrade or a migration to the Active Directory from some other directory service. This proposition does not have to be a nightmare, but it can be without careful planning and consideration.

This chapter explores the upgrade process and migration issues. I'm going to take a little liberty with the terms *upgrade* and *migrate*. For this chapter, upgrade means to move to the Active Directory from a previous Windows network. Migrate means to move to the Active Directory from a different directory service, such as Novell's NDS. Additionally, I will refer to Windows NT 3.51 and NT 4.0 simply as NT, unless otherwise noted. That way, when I say Windows NT, you can be assured that I am talking about both NT 3.51 and NT 4.0.

Upgrading to the Active Directory

Microsoft networks using Windows NT and the NT networking model will need to upgrade to the Windows 2000 model in order to move to the Active Directory. This upgrade process includes many different factors to make the upgrade successful. When you think about upgrading, you can first think about the actual upgrade process. In other words, in a perfect world, consider the following questions:

✦ How would you like the upgrade process to work?

✦ What are your goals during the actual upgrade?

The possible answers vary wildly, but here are some common sentiments:

- ✦ **No network downtime!** In a production environment, the availability of servers and functionality of the network is considered mission critical. Network downtime costs companies money and delays productivity. An important upgrade goal is to perform the upgrade without losing any network availability or functionality.

- ✦ **Seamlessness.** This buzzword is used a lot today and rightfully so. The upgrade to Windows 2000 should be seamless. Users should be able to access the same servers and the same resources. User accounts and groups should be upgraded without interruption, and administrators should not have to visit every machine in the production environment to get everything working again (in other words, no "Sneaker Net").

- ✦ **No Security breaches.** A common and quite necessary need of the upgrade is the maintenance of security. An upgrade should not compromise any network security at any time.

Of course, other goals may be specific to your environment, such as application access and user profile maintenance. Regardless, you should know up front the specific needs of your network and the ways the upgrade will affect network performance. From this information, you can determine when to upgrade the network and at what time(s) of the day.

Upgrading NT to 2000

The actual process of upgrading refers to running the Windows 2000 Setup Wizard on a Windows NT Server and then installing the Active Directory. During installation, if a computer is a primary domain controller (PDC), the Active Directory Installation Wizard is immediately and automatically launched once Windows 2000 Server is installed.

Cross-Reference   See Appendix D for a PDC upgrade tutorial.

When you upgrade a Windows NT PDC to a Windows 2000 domain controller, the existing domain structure and all user and group accounts are moved to the Active Directory and maintained. In other words, a client that could log on before the upgrade will be able to log on immediately after the upgrade using the same user account and password. Once the PDC is upgraded to a Windows 2000 domain controller, the Active Directory immediately uses the PDC Emulator FSMO role to act like a PDC to existing backup domain controllers (BDCs) and downlevel clients (NT and 9*x*). At this point, the domain is operating in mixed mode because it supports NT BDCs. The new Windows 2000 domain controller acts like a PDC to the existing BDCs, and once the BDCs are upgraded to Windows 2000, they see the server as simply another domain controller. This backward compatibility is *very* effective because you can slowly upgrade your network without a loss of functionality. You can remain in a mixed mode for as long as you like. However, once the upgrade is complete and there are no longer any BDCs, you should change the domain to native mode in order to make the best use of Windows 2000 features.

Tip The new domain can still access your other NT domains because all trust relationships you have configured are preserved. See Chapter 8 to learn more about mixed and native modes.

Because of the nature of Windows 2000 setup and Active Directory setup, upgrading your PDC and later your BDCs to domain controllers and installing the Active Directory are not difficult tasks. As I mentioned, the good news is that you can perform this process in stages, and you do not have to get in a big hurry because mixed mode will still support your BDCs.

Getting ready to upgrade the PDC to 2000

There are several actions you should take prior to putting the installation CD into your NT PDC. These actions will ensure that your domain is ready to begin the upgrade to Windows 2000.

Tip Only Windows NT 3.51 and NT 4.0 servers can be directly upgraded to Windows 2000. Earlier versions of NT must be upgraded to at least 3.51 before they can be upgraded to 2000.

1. Force a synchronization of all BDCs in the domain to ensure that all have updated data.

2. Perform a complete data backup. This includes all of your user and group accounts as well as applications and other network data.

3. Plan how you will recovery data in the event of a serious error. How can you quickly recover your data so it is available?

What Does the PDC Emulator Do, Exactly?

The PDC Emulator performs processes that make it look like a PDC to Windows NT BDCs and like a logon server to downlevel client computers. The Active Directory is a hierarchical database, but NT BDCs have no concept of this hierarchy. The PDC Emulator displays directory data to BDCs as a flat store and replicates database changes to them using LAN Manager Replication Server. (Windows 2000 uses File Replication Service.)

Essentially, every job function a PDC performed, the PDC Emulator performs as well. However, to other Windows 2000 domain controllers, the PDC Emulator appears and functions as just another domain controller. You use the PDC Emulator just like any other domain controller to create, modify, or delete Active Directory objects. In fact, the PDC Emulator role is invisible to the administrator, who simply uses the server like any other Windows 2000 domain controller.

4. Consider taking one of your BDCs offline before performing the upgrade to Windows 2000. Promote the offline BDC to a PDC and verify your data. You can then keep this machine for online use in the case of a catastrophic upgrade failure (which is unlikely, but all things are possible).

Note   Naturally, you would need an extra BDC to keep one offline. You can consider installing an additional BDC and use it for the offline copy. Any domain should have at least one functioning, online BDC (and preferably more) in case of a PDC failure.

5. Check the PDC's hardware very carefully for Windows 2000 compatibility and minimal requirements. In fact, the minimal requirements are not enough. The PDC must have plenty of RAM and a fast processor to function satisfactorily. The PDC that is upgraded must also be a global catalog server and run all FSMO roles because it is the first Windows 2000 domain controller. Therefore, make sure the server is ready to handle the load!

6. Clean up the system, removing unnecessary files and applications as well as protocols and services that are no longer used.

Caution   These steps do not cover every action you need to take before beginning an upgrade process because this section focuses on only the actual machine upgrade. Read the entire chapter to gain a clear perspective of all planning that must be done.

Cross-Reference   You can see a complete walkthrough of a PDC upgrade to Windows 2000 and the Active Directory in Appendix D.

Using the Active Directory Sizer

While I'm on the subject of upgrading your computer to Windows 2000, I have an excellent opportunity to introduce you to the Active Directory Sizer Tool. The Active Directory Sizer is what Microsoft calls an evolving tool. As more input is gained from Active Directory deployments, Microsoft will continually add to the tool to make it work better for network environments.

What If I Don't Want to Use the PDC?

What if you have a PDC that is getting old? You do not want to replace the hardware, and after upgrading to Windows 2000, you want to use the old PDC as a simple Windows 2000 Server. What do you do? Because your PDC contains your user and group accounts (and related data), you need to upgrade to Windows 2000 domain controller in order to install the domain. This ensures that your user and group accounts remain intact.

Once you install several other Windows 2000 domain controllers in the domain and you ensure that replication has taken place, you can then remove the Active Directory from the old PDC so that it becomes a simple member server. Because of Active Directory's peer domain controller structure, all other domain controllers will have the user and group accounts from the old PDC due to replication.

Tip   The Active Directory Sizer is a free download from www.microsoft.com/
windows2000/downloads.

So what is the Active Directory Sizer? The Active Directory Sizer is a tool that
gathers information from you about your network and your computers and then
gives you a report that estimates the hardware you will need on your computers
to meet the workload demands of your environment. When you complete the wizard, the Sizer will provide you with an estimated list of server machines, number
of CPUs per machine and speed of CPUs, hard disk needs, memory needs, and
network bandwidth utilization.

Once you install the Sizer, shown in Figure 4-1, it appears in your Administrative
Tools folder and is an MMC snap-in.

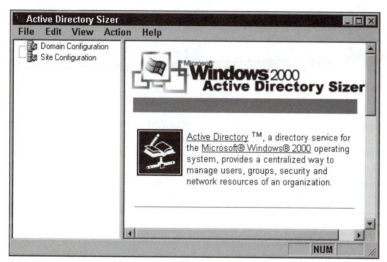

Figure 4-1: Active Directory Sizer

The Sizer is rather intuitive and easy to use. By using the Action menu, you can
begin a new wizard. As you can see in Figure 4-2, the wizard gathers information
from you about your domain, user accounts, computers, administration, Exchange
2000 use, and services. Using this information, the Sizer generates information
about your hardware needs. I'm not going to give any more details about the
Sizer since it is so straightforward, but do keep the Sizer in mind as you plan
your network upgrade and Active Directory implementation.

Considering domain consolidation

The act of upgrading NT Servers to Windows 2000 Servers is relatively simple. The
process of planning the path to that upgrade and determining what to do with your
existing NT domain structure is another story.

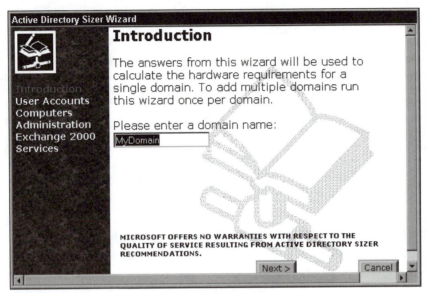

Figure 4-2: Sizer Wizard

As you have learned in the previous chapters, a major benefit of Windows 2000 networks is the reduction of domains. In Windows 2000, you are not limited by domain size, and you can effectively use organizational units (OUs) to replace domains so that you have a single domain with several OUs. Although there are many reasons to maintain several domains, you should be able to reduce the number of NT domains you currently maintain. In Windows NT, the maximum SAM database size was 40MB. Theoretically, this means a single domain could hold about 40,000 user accounts, but in practice this was not necessarily so. The result was excessive domains (a master domain and a number of resource domains) so you could store user and computer accounts separately. None of this is necessary in the Active Directory because there are no size limitations. A single Active Directory domain can hold more than a 1 million objects, so you don't need all of those domains you used in NT. By decommissioning existing domains, you can lower your Total Cost of Ownership (TCO) by lowering administrative time and headaches as well as domain controllers required for multiple domains.

The process of restructuring or consolidating domains essentially involves moving security principals from one domain to another, moving computers, and then decommissioning the domain. Windows 2000 (finally) provides the tools necessary to restructure your domain without using third-party tools (although some excellent ones are available that you may find easier to use).

With all of that said, *you* have to decide what you need to do with your domain structure during an upgrade. The options primarily consist of the following:

✦ **Nothing** — You can keep your NT domain structure just the way it is if you like. Think carefully, however, and make certain that some domain consolidation would not be beneficial before taking this path. If you are certain you want to maintain your structure, you simply upgrade the PDC in the master domain so that the PDC becomes the Active Directory root. Then, begin upgrading other domains as desired so they become child domains, as shown in Figure 4-3.

Cross-Reference

See Chapter 3 for more information about planning a forest structure.

✦ **Consolidate Domains** — You may be able to keep some domains as they are while consolidating other domains together, as shown in Figure 4-4. This typically occurs when you want to maintain your master domain and consolidate all resource domains together, or even consolidate the resource domain into a single domain with OUs to replace the resource domain.

✦ **Complete Restructure** — You may determine that your existing NT domain is, well, a mess. There are too many domains that never should have been created in the first place, resource access is complicated, you're sick and tired of dealing with it all, and you want to use the Active Directory to create a new forest and completely restructure your existing domains. The Active Directory enables you to perform this option while maintaining a production environment by creating a *pristine forest*, shown in Figure 4-5. A pristine forest is an ideal Active Directory forest containing the domain structure you want to implement. You create the pristine forest separately from the production environment and then move a test batch of users, computers, and groups into the pristine forest to determine the impact of the move. Once you have all of the bugs or issues worked out, you can begin to move all resources into the desired domains. Once complete, you decommission the old domains, and you are left with your desired implementation. Naturally, this process takes careful planning and testing along the way in order to avoid major disruption to the production environment.

Domain consolidation, regardless of which path you choose, can be tedious and difficult. You'll need to design the domain structure that you want, including your desired namespace, and then create a plan to transition your existing domain structure into the new domain structure.

Caution

Remember that you cannot change the root domain name or child domain names without reinstalling the Active Directory, so proceed with caution and plan carefully.

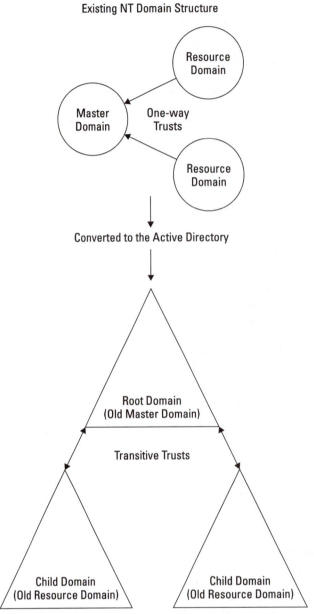

Figure 4-3: Conversion of existing domain structure to Active Directory

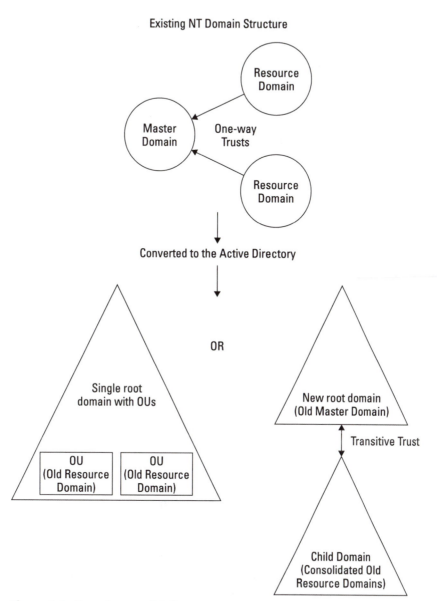

Figure 4-4: Domain consolidation

Existing NT Domain Structure

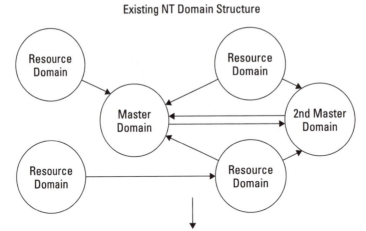

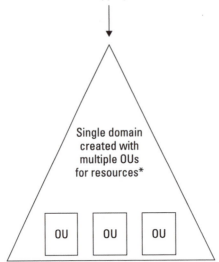

Desired pristine forest designed for migration of
resources into appropriate domains

Single domain
created with
multiple OUs
for resources*

OU   OU   OU

*Other options could have been used, such as
a domain tree with a single root and several
child domains, depending on the design
wishes of the company.

Figure 4-5: Pristine forest

Moving SIDS

As I mentioned previously, the major way you consolidate domains is to move all of the resources from one domain to the next, which includes moving users, groups, computers, and so on. In Windows NT, you could not natively move users from one domain to the next because you could not move the SID. The SID was domain specific, and the only way to move a user from one domain to the next was to re-create the user account in the target domain so it would have a new SID. This isn't exactly the best way to do things. Windows 2000 includes the capability to move SIDs from one domain to the next. Part of this process is due to a directory attribute called SID History (sIDHistory). An attribute of security principals, SID History stores the former SID of moved objects (users and security groups). This way, the old SID is maintained and can still be used when necessary.

SID History enables you to move security principals to a different domain while still maintaining access to resources available before the move. This feature helps prevent disruption of the production environment.

Caution   SID History is not the answer to all problems. Some NT 3.51 groups do not work well when moved to a new domain because of the way access tokens are generated, and both NT 3.51 and 4.0 may experience problems with profiles and policies due to the new SID assigned by Windows 2000. Just be aware of these issues and expect some possible problems to arise.

Fortunately, you are given some native tools you can use to move objects from domain to domain. First, there are some command-line utilities found in the Windows 2000 Resource Kit and AdminPak tools (see Appendix C for more information). For example, Movetree enables you to move objects such as OUs, groups, and user accounts among domains, and ClonePrincipal enables you to clone security principals. Additionally, other tools such as SIDWalker help you move and merge users and groups.

A primary tool you would want to consider using is the Active Directory Migration Tool (ADMT). ADMT enables you to perform cloning functions, but it also contains useful wizards to help you move users and groups between domains in a forest.

Note   ADMT is a free download from Microsoft, found at www.microsoft.com/
windows2000/downloads.

Once you install the ADMT, shown in Figure 4-6, it appears in your Administrative Tools folder, and as you might guess, it is an MMC snap-in.

If you select Active Directory Migration Tool in the console, as shown in Figure 4-6, you can see a list of the wizards provided by the tool, shown in Figure 4-7.

Figure 4-6: ADMT

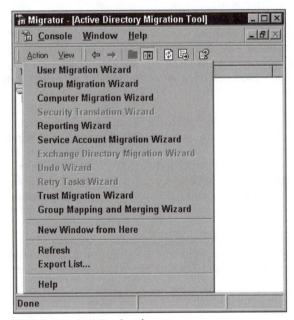

Figure 4-7: ADMT wizards

The ADMT wizards are rather easy to use and straightforward, so I'll not explore them all in this chapter. I do, however, want to walk you through one of them so you can see how they work. The following steps give you a tutorial of migrating a user account to a different domain.

1. In ADMT, select Active Directory Migration Tool and then click Action ⇨ User Migration Wizard.

2. Click Next on the Welcome Screen.

3. The ADMT allows you to test a migration or to choose to migrate now. The test feature can be very beneficial so you can see the potential problems before actually migrating any objects. Make a selection by clicking the appropriate radio button, shown in Figure 4-8, and then click Next.

4. On the Domain Selection page, shown in Figure 4-9, select a source domain and a target domain using the drop-down menus. Click Next.

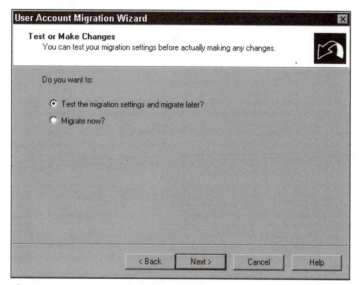

Figure 4-8: Test or Make Changes

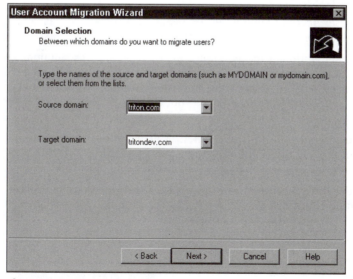

Figure 4-9: Domain Selection

5. In the User Selection window, click the Add button and select the user(s) you want to migrate. Then click OK. The users you selected now appear in the User Selection window, shown in Figure 4-10. Click Next.

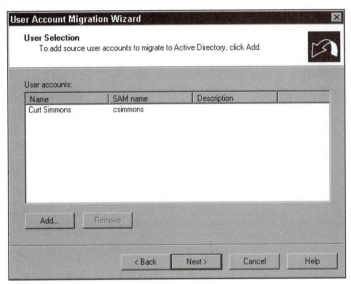

Figure 4-10: User Selection

6. In the Organizational Unit Selection window, click the Browse button to select the OU or container to which you want to move the user account in the target domain. Notice that the OU is displayed by its LDAP name, as shown in Figure 4-11. Click Next.

7. In the User Account window, enter a valid user name and password with administrative rights to the target domain and then click Next.

8. In the User Options window, shown in Figure 4-12, you see a number of check box options you can select. For example, you can choose to migrate roaming profiles, associated groups, and so forth. You can also choose to rename the migrated account if desired. Make your selections and then click Next.

9. In the Naming Conflicts window, the wizard asks you how you would like to handle group account name conflicts. You can choose to ignore the conflict and not migrate the account or to replace conflicting accounts by renaming them or removing them. Make your selection and click Next.

10. Click the Finish button. A window appears showing you the progress of the account migration. If you chose to test the account, you see any errors that might have occurred.

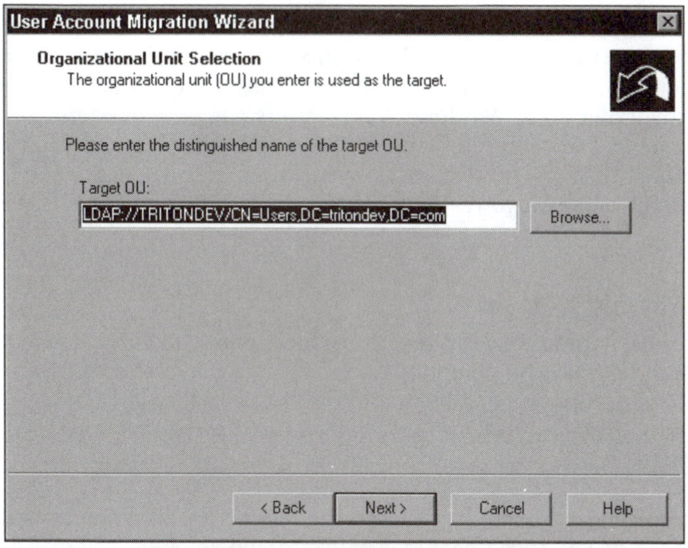

Figure 4-11: Organizational Unit Selection

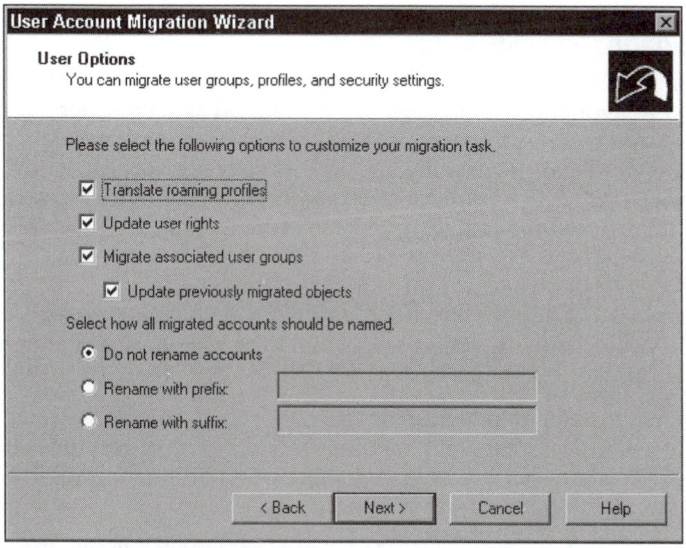

Figure 4-12: User Options

As you can tell, there are a number of wizards available in and things you can do with this tool. I would also like to point out that this tool contains a reports wizard that helps you analyze potential migrations and generate reports. This can help identify and solve potential migration problems before attempting the actual migration.

Moving computers

Moving accounts is your most difficult task of domain migration. Moving computers so they become domain members is not so difficult — assuming those computers are installed with Windows 2000. Windows 2000 servers can be moved from domain to domain without having to completely reinstall the operating system. You can use ADMT or the Netdom utility to create computer accounts in the new domain for NT computers. You can also use Movetree to move Windows 2000 accounts between domains.

Decommission the old domain

Once all users, groups, computers, and resources have been moved, you can finally decommission the old domain by demoting and removing the existing BDCs and finally the PDC. These computers can be recommissioned in the new domain (or another domain) and upgraded to Windows 2000 where they can be used as domain controllers or member servers.

Note   You'll have some cleanup work to do once the process of decommissioning is complete. Make sure you take a hard look at your group accounts. You may need to consolidate or even remove some to make the most of Windows 2000 features. See Chapter 9 to learn more.

Domain consolidation checklist

Consolidating domains is no fun task and a lot of planning has to go into the process so attempt to avoid problems. Even so, you should expect issues to arise and should be prepared to solve them as necessary. Depending on the existing structure of your network and the existing strength of your network structure, domain consolidation can move along somewhat smoothly. As a quick reference, just remember to think about the following issues before consolidating your domains:

✦ Consider your existing domain structure carefully. Do you need to restructure? If so, how can you restructure your domains into the Windows 2000 model using the least path of resistance?

✦ If you believe your existing domain structure needs to be completely revamped, plan to create a pristine forest and then to move your existing resources into the new forest. This process enables you to maintain a production environment while you are actually restructuring your network.

✦ Begin the upgrade to Windows 2000 in the domain that will become the root domain. You can then begin to merge existing domains into that domain and then consolidate resource domains into child domains or OUs. Complete the migration of that domain before beginning other domain upgrades. Once you are completely upgraded, you can change the domain mode to native.

Caution Native mode does not support Windows NT BDCs. You cannot use BDCs once you upgrade to native mode, and the upgrade to native mode cannot be changed back to mixed mode.

✦ Test your implementation at every step.

✦ Make certain you keep a current backup of data in case of problems.

Migrating to the Active Directory

As I mentioned in this chapter's introduction, I'm taking a few liberties with the terms upgrade and migrate. In this section of the chapter, I want to briefly address migrating to the Active Directory from another directory service. This section serves as introductory material to the migration process. The actual migration plan will vary according to your current directory service and migration needs, but this section gives you an overview of the tools you can use and where to go to find out more information.

Upgrading to Windows 2000 presents plenty of potential challenges, but migrating from another directory service can be difficult — at least in terms of preserving directory data. For example, suppose a network wants to migrate from Novell's NDS to the Active Directory. The company does not, obviously, want to re-create all their user and object data — they want to migrate it into the Active Directory.

In Services for NetWare V5, you will find a tool called Microsoft Directory Synchronization Service (MSDSS). MSDSS should help Novell networks migrate to the Active Directory, preserving accounts and even entire directory trees. You can purchase Services for NetWare V5 and read more about it at http://www. microsoft.com/windows2000/guide/server/solutions/netware.asp.

There are a number of third-party tools that can help you migrate and manage directory services. For example, BindView (formerly Entevo) offers a suite of tools called by-Admin for Windows 2000 that includes tools to migrate objects from other directory services into the Active Directory.

There are other third-party tools available as well, and you may find them useful for your own implementation plans.

Cross-Reference While I'm on the subject of connecting and synchronizing with the Active Directory, I should mention that Windows 2000 includes an Active Directory Connector (ADC) for connecting the Exchange Server 5.5 directory with the Active Directory. See Chapter 17 to learn more.

The previous tools I have mentioned are all graphical tools for administrators. However, if you have a head for programming, you can also use a few other tools to migrate objects between different directories. First, DirSync is a programming tool that gives developers a way to synchronize the information between two different directory services. In fact, MSDSS is based on DirSync so that LDAP-compliant directories can synchronize. You can learn more about DirSync on MSDN Web site at `http://msdn.microsoft.com/windows2000`.

Finally, you can use the Active Directory Services Interface (ADSI), available on the Windows 2000 Resource Kit to programmatically connect the Active Directory with other directory services using VBScript or any COM-enabled programming language. You can learn more about ADSI by visiting `http://msdn.microsoft.com/windows2000` and clicking the Active Directory link.

Cross-Reference   For more information on the Windows 2000 Resource Kit, see Appendix C.

Summary

This chapter explored upgrading and migrating to the Active Directory. Fortunately, upgrading your NT network to Windows 2000 does not have to be a difficult task. Do your homework, understand the possible issues and problems, and always back up your data in case of problems. If you need to restructure your Windows NT domains, Windows 2000 includes tools to help you move objects and user accounts in order to consolidate domains together. Finally, you can access some available tools, as well as third-party tools, to migrate to the Active Directory from other directory services. All of these processes require careful planning and testing before implementation.

✦   ✦   ✦

Planning Active Directory Sites

The creation and use of Active Directory sites is one of the most confusing aspects of planning an Active Directory deployment. In this chapter, I hope to help you understand how the Active Directory uses site information and how that information fits into the Active Directory's grand scheme of things. It is impossible to talk about Active Directory sites without mentioning some configuration information, and it is certainly impossible to talk about sites without also talking about replication. So, I approach this chapter from a planning perspective, but I also strongly urge you to study Chapter 8, which gives you all of the site configuration step-by-step information, and Chapter 13, which thoroughly explores replication and replication management.

What Is a Site?

An Active Directory site is a physical grouping of computers. A site, by definition, encompasses a certain geographic location in which all computers reside on one or more well-connected subnets. In reality, a site can be one specific geographic place, or it can span several geographic locations. The key to understanding sites in the Active Directory is to see sites in the same way the Active Directory sees them—in terms of connectivity. The Active Directory expects your sites to be based on well-connected TCP/IP subnets. The term *well-connected* is a soft term in that it does not mean one specific thing. Typically, a well-connected subnet has fast, reliable, inexpensive, and abundant bandwidth, such as in typical LAN connectivity. How you define well-connected will vary from one Active Directory planner to the next, but the key point—and it is a very important one—is to understand that the Active Directory *always* assumes a site has fast, reliable, inexpensive, and abundant bandwidth. In short, if your view of site definition is different from how the Active Directory sees sites, be sure to get on board with the Active Directory's definition before planning your own sites.

When a site is established, the Active Directory assumes that bandwidth is readily available, reliable, inexpensive, and fast. Because the Active Directory assumes these qualities, it plans replication traffic within the site based on these well-connected features. So, it is important that you build your sites based on the Active Directory's definition of a site.

Cross-Reference   You can learn all about intrasite and intersite replication in Chapter 13.

Sites and Domains

A site is physical grouping of computers based on TCP/IP connectivity, and a domain is a logical grouping of users, computers, and other Active Directory objects based on administrative and security needs. It is very important to keep the definitions and uses of domains and sites straight as you plan your own deployment. In previous planning chapters, you have learned that Active Directory domains are virtually unlimited in size and scope. You can have smaller domains as you did in NT networks, or you can have a single domain encompass an entire network. The decision is based on security and administrative focus. With that said, constantly keep in mind that domains and sites are not interconnected. Several domains can exist within a single site, or a single domain can span several sites. The domain structure is the logical view of your network while the site structure is the physical view of your network.

To solidify this concept, consider an example. Triton, Inc., has three domains: a root domain of triton.com and two child domains of prod.triton.com and dev.triton.com. The domain structure provides the logical view of the network. Each child domain is independently managed, and each child has its own security and administrative procedures, as shown in Figure 5-1.

In reality, Triton, Inc.'s, domains span several cities and two continents, as you can see in Figure 5-2.

As you can see, triton.com and dev.triton.com each reside in a site while prod. triton.com, a single domain, resides in two different sites.

As you are thinking about planning sites, it is important to keep sites and domains clear in your mind. This may seem like a simple task, but as you are planning an Active Directory design and deployment, issues such as these can become tricky and confusing. The following bullet list summarizes the differences between sites and domains:

✦ A domain is a logical grouping of users, computers, and other objects that function as an administrative and security boundary.

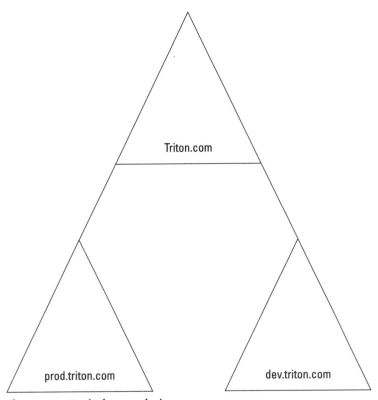

Figure 5-1: Logical network view

✦ A site is a physical grouping of computers based on well-connected subnet(s).

✦ Domains are a part of the DNS namespace and are used to build an Active Directory infrastructure.

✦ Sites are not a part of the DNS namespace but serve as a boundary for user logon traffic, user service/query requests, and replication traffic.

Note
If your network is built on a single LAN or combination of LANs with a high-speed backbone and you need only a single site, then there is nothing for you to plan or configure. When you install the first Active Directory domain (explained in Chapter 6), a default first site is automatically created. With only a single site, you're home free.

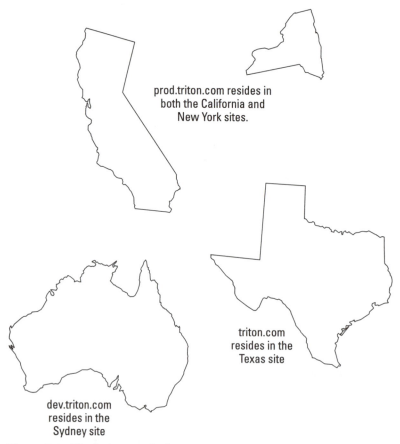

Figure 5-2: Physical network view

Why Are Sites Necessary?

The primary reasons the Active Directory maintains sites are for user logon/query/ service traffic and for intersite replication purposes. These sound simple enough, and in reality, these are the only reasons the Active Directory needs to maintain sites. For example, your network is spread out over several cities in North America and Canada. If the connectivity between your company's offices in the various cities were just as fast as the LAN connectivity within each office, you would have no need for multiple sites. But unfortunately, networking technology hasn't evolved to that point — yet, anyway. In most cases, your WAN connectivity is much slower, more expensive, and more unreliable than your LAN connectivity. Because of these expensive and slower WAN links, the Active Directory maintains sites to help you control user traffic and replication traffic. The following two sections examine both of these issues.

User traffic

It you're like me, you have a tendency to get so bogged down in networking concepts that you have a tendency to forget the fundamental purpose of networking. The primary reason for networking is to enable users to access resources and to provide server services to those users. After all, the basic purpose of the Active Directory is to provide a directory service that makes networking easy on end users as well as the administrators managing the network.

Because networking is based on user needs, it is only natural that users generate a lot of network traffic. Users must log on to a domain controller. Then users access various resources, such as shared folders, printers, and applications, and a variety of services that are offered by network servers. With any Active Directory environment, you also have the added component of user query traffic as users query the Active Directory to locate the resources they need. In a small network, this amount of traffic is not overwhelming, but in large enterprise networks, user traffic can greatly consume a network bandwidth. Because of user logon, service requests, and query traffic, the Active Directory must use sites to control this traffic. The Active Directory uses a site to contain user traffic — if at all possible. For example, suppose Susan Anderson is a user of an Active Directory site located in Seattle. Susan comes to work in the morning and logs on to the network, but her logon request is sent over a WAN link to a domain controller in the Dallas site. The domain controller in the Dallas site then has to authenticate Susan and send the authentication tickets back to her computer in Seattle. Now, imagine that each user in the Seattle site is being authenticated over WAN links to various remote sites. This is obviously not a situation that you want. For networking to be effective, you want a user within a particular site to be authenticated by a domain controller within that site. You do not want a user authenticated by a domain controller at a remote site, and you do not want a domain controller at a remote site to provide the user with services — unless absolutely necessary.

Consequently, a major purpose of site configuration is to control user traffic, as shown in Figure 5-3. Without site configuration, slower and expensive WAN links would become hopelessly saturated.

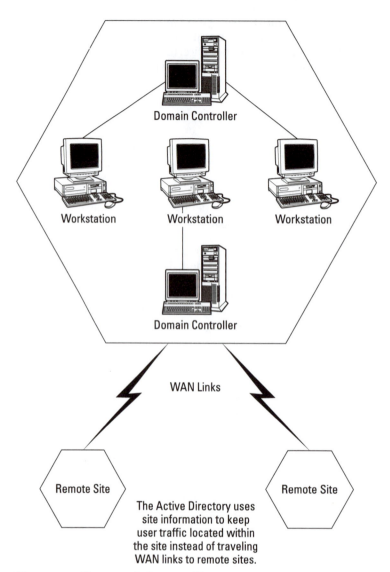

The Active Directory uses site information to keep user traffic located within the site instead of traveling WAN links to remote sites.

Figure 5-3: Site control of user traffic

Replication traffic

Aside from user traffic, the Active Directory also maintains sites for replication purposes. In this section, we'll examine the planning perspective of replication.

Cross-Reference Chapter 13 provides replication information in detail.

If you read the previous chapters in this part of the book, you are well aware that PDCs and BDCs are no longer used in Windows 2000 networks, and all domain controllers function as peers. The PDC and BDC model, although effective in many ways, caused a lot of problems in large distributed networks because the PDC was writable and the BDCs received copies of the data from the PDC. This design required that changes be made at the PDC. In Windows 2000 networks, all domain controllers have a writable copy of the Active Directory database. In other words, there is no one master domain controller or master database, but all domain controllers function as peers, maintaining their own copy of the Active Directory database. With this design, changes to the database can be made at any domain controller at any time. For example, an administrator can create a user account on one domain controller and later create another user account on a different domain controller. It does not matter which domain controller the administrator uses for configuration because any changes made to the database will be replicated to all other domain controllers.

Replication, then, is the process of sending and receiving update information to ensure that all domain controllers have an exact copy of the Active Directory database. Through replication, the integrity of the Active Directory database can be ensured. For example, when an administrator creates a new user account on a domain controller, that user account will be replicated to all other domain controllers in the domain. When the user logs on to the network, the user can then be authenticated by any domain controller. As you can imagine, without replication the Active Directory database would quickly become a hopeless collection of inaccurate data. In essence, as different administrators would make different database changes on different domain controllers, each domain controller would have a different view of the network and the contents of the database. In a short amount of time, no domain controller would have accurate data. Consequently, you can see how *very* important replication is to the integrity of data on a network.

The Active Directory defines two kinds of replication: intrasite and intersite. Intrasite replication occurs within a site, while intersite replication occurs between sites. Before you start worrying about massive replication configuration headaches, let me just put your mind at ease. The Active Directory configures its own replication topology, which is simply a series of connections, and enables database changes to reach one domain controller to the next. For intrasite replication, an Active Directory service called the Knowledge Consistency Checker (KCC) examines all of your domain controllers in a site and builds connections between them so that replication can occur automatically. In other words, you, as the administrator, do not have to configure anything. The Active Directory completely generates its own replication topology within a site and then configures how replication will work. The KCC constantly monitors the replication topology and changes it if a new domain controller is added to the domain or if one goes offline or is removed. For intrasite replication, shown in Figure 5-4, there's nothing for you to configure or manage—it is all automatic.

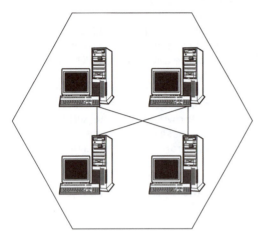

Within a site, the Active Directory automatically creates a replication topology so that each domain controller has at least two connections. This topology is automatically adjusted when domain controllers are down, removed, or added.

Figure 5-4: Intrasite replication

Tip
Although intrasite replication is automatically generated and managed, you can manually adjust the topology for certain specific reasons. Chapter 13 shows you how.

For intersite replication, or replication that occurs between sites—shown in Figure 5-5—the Active Directory automatically generates a replication topology after you configure your sites and define the communication links between them, which are called the site links. Once you have defined your sites and site links, the Active Directory, using the KCC, determines how to best manage replication data over the WAN.

So, the following are important points about Active Directory replication:

✦ It is quite capable and does a good job of managing replication. In other words, replication is not something you spend your time configuring as an administrator.

✦ It uses the information you give it about your sites and site links to configure replication between sites. Therefore, defining sites as well as the links that connect them appropriately is very important.

In the past few paragraphs, I have sung the praises of the Active Directory replication model and the automatic work of the KCC. The Active Directory does a good job of generating its own replication topology and managing replication on a daily basis. However, the Active Directory *only* does a good job if your network matches the Active Directory's own internal assumptions. In other words, the Active Directory assumes that your sites are based on well-connected IP subnets and that each site is connected by at least one site link. So, what do you do if your site is not based on well-connected subnets or if you have some serious connectivity problems within a particular site? The answer is not much. The KCC manages the replication topology and replication with the site. Intrasite replication is not scheduled, not compressed, and occurs often. In other words, the Active Directory assumes you have sufficient and available bandwidth within your site so that replication can occur frequently and without restraint. If this is not the case, there's not much you can do to change the Active Directory's behavior. This is why I say that the Active Directory functions great if it is built on a physical network that can support it. If it is not, I'm afraid you are going to have a lot of problems.

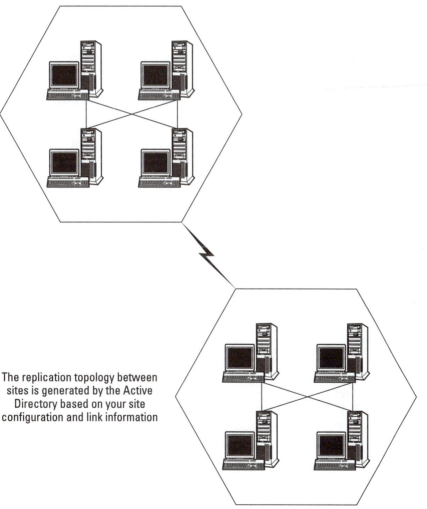

The replication topology between sites is generated by the Active Directory based on your site configuration and link information

Figure 5-5: Intersite replication

So, once again I make the point that it is *very* important that your physical network topology and your TCP/IP implementation is carefully examined and even upgraded if necessary before implementing the Active Directory. Careful exploration of your current network enables you to resolve connectivity issues and bandwidth problems *before* implementation, and doing so will help you avoid many serious problems with intrasite and intersite replication and connectivity.

Understanding Site Links

Now that you have a global understanding of Active Directory sites and why sites are needed due to a user traffic and database replication, I want to turn your attention to a very important part of site configuration, the site link. As I mentioned in the previous section, the Active Directory assumes that each site is connected to at least one other site through some kind of WAN connection. The good news is that the Active Directory does not assume those WAN connections are fast and inexpensive as it does with the intrasite topology. In fact, the Active Directory was designed so that you must input information about site links to help the Active Directory determine how to control replication data.

In a perfect world, every network would have nice, inexpensive WAN links between sites so that user or replication traffic would never be a problem. In reality, even many large networks have some WAN links that are fast and have much bandwidth while others are slow and unreliable. In Figure 5-6, you see a site sketch showing the bandwidth between each site. As you can see, this company has everything from a T1 link to a 56 Kbps connection — a situation that is not uncommon for many networks spanning multiple geographic areas. As companies change and grow and acquire other companies, a mixture of WAN technologies is often used. This is why the Active Directory needs you to get information about the links between your sites.

In order to accommodate a wide variety of WAN technologies, you create site links to give the Active Directory information to help configure replication.

 Chapter 8 shows you how to create site links and configure the properties that help the Active Directory make decisions based on your input.

The following sections explore the three items that help the Active Directory determine how replication should occur over the site link: cost, frequency, and schedule.

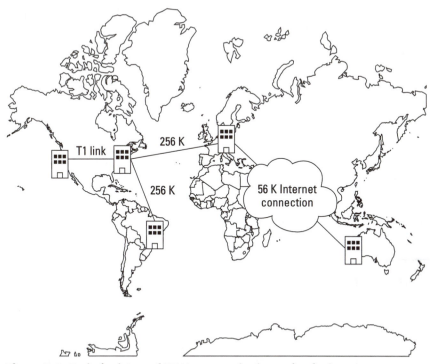

Figure 5-6: Typical mixture of WAN communication technologies

Cost

In order to determine how to use site links, the Active Directory enables you to assign a cost to the link. This cost is considered a logical cost in that it defines bandwidth usage. For example, a T1 link would have a much lower cost than a 56 Kbps dial-up connection because the T1 link has much more bandwidth available. So, in terms of the Active Directory the cost of a link is based on the amount of available bandwidth. Low-cost links are defined as those that have a higher amount of bandwidth and are more reliable. High-costs links have less bandwidth and, perhaps, lower reliability. The Active Directory uses the cost information to determine which links to favor. For example, suppose you have two sites, one in Seattle and one in Tampa. Between those sites, you have a 1.54 Mbps connection and also a 256 Kbps connection. The 1.54 Mbps connection should have a lower cost than the 256 Kbps connection because more bandwidth is readily available. So, when you create these two site links, you assign a low cost to the T1 connection, such as a cost of "10," while you assign a higher cost to the 256 Kbps connection, such as "100." With these cost factors, the Active Directory will always attempt to use the T1 connection over the 256 Kbps connection. If the T1 connection is unavailable, only then will the 256 Kbps connection be used.

Note   You are not required to have multiple site links between sites, but providing at least two site links, such as a primary link and a backup link, gives you fault tolerance in case the primary link fails.

Aside from bandwidth, you can also base cost on other factors. For example, let's say you have two 256 Kbps site links between two sites. Each link has the same available bandwidth, but one link is less reliable than the other. You can use cost to favor the link that is more reliable over the link that is less reliable. Consequently, a number of cost issues could come into play. The point to remember is that the cost you assign to a link enables you to tell the Active Directory to use certain site links first, and others second. This is one way you help the Active Directory determine how to use site link information.

Frequency

When you create a site link, you can determine how often replication should occur over the link. For example, you can tell the Active Directory to replicate over the link every 15 minutes, every hour, every three hours, and so forth. In reality, the Active Directory uses pull replication, which simply means that domain controllers *pull* replication data from other domain controllers instead of having it forced on them through push replication.

Cross-Reference   For more information on pull and push replication go to Chapter 13.

The frequency interval you input determines how often a domain controller can poll another domain controller over the site link for replication updates. If you have ever worked with replication in a WAN environment, you know that it is a juggling act of sorts. You want replication to occur as frequently as possible to reduce the amount of time when domain controller databases are out of sync due to database changes (called latency). However, you should consider the following questions about your WAN connection:

✦ How much traffic can it handle?

✦ How often is it available?

✦ Is the WAN connection costing your company money each time it is used?

You must weigh all of these factors and determine a frequency value that is right for your network and, ultimately, your users. The good news is that the frequency of a site link is easy to configure and easy to change, so you may have to do some experimenting to determine what works best for your network.

Schedule

Intrasite replication occurs without a schedule because the Active Directory assumes you have fast, inexpensive, and available bandwidth within the site. However, replication between sites can be scheduled to avoid peak traffic hours. For example, suppose a particular site link always experiences a lot of traffic from 10:00 a.m. to 2:00 p.m. You can use the site link's schedule to block replication so that it cannot occur during those hours. Of course, the more time you block, the longer replication will take due to the delays, so again, you are faced with the proverbial juggling act to find what works best for your company and network.

Understanding the Bridgehead Server

When you create an Active Directory site, the Active Directory automatically assigns the role of bridgehead server to one domain controller. A bridgehead server sends and receives replication data for an Active Directory site. When the bridgehead server receives data from a remote site, it replicates that data to all other domain controllers throughout the site. In other words, domain controllers do not directly replicate data to domain controllers in other sites, but all exchange of information is performed through the bridgehead server, as shown in Figure 5-7.

As you can see in Figure 5-7, the bridgehead server is considered the preeminent server for exchanging directory information between sites. As I mentioned, the Active Directory automatically assigns a bridgehead server when you create a new site, but you can change the bridgehead server to a different domain controller if desired. You may have a server with more system resources or a server who does not have as much user load that you prefer to use as the bridgehead server. At any rate, the bridgehead server should be a domain controller that has adequate system resources to handle the additional processing load placed on the bridgehead.

 Tip
An easy way to establish the bridgehead server is simply to use the domain controller in a site that has the best bandwidth and system resources, such as RAM and processor.

Additionally, you can also specify additional bridgehead servers. At any given time, only one bridgehead server is used per site, but you specify additional bridgehead servers for backup purposes. For example, suppose your bridgehead server has a hard disk failure and goes down. The Active Directory will automatically select a new domain controller to be the bridgehead server, but you can control this automatic behavior by specifying additional bridgehead servers. This way, if the primary bridgehead server goes down, you have already preselected which domain controller should function as the replacement.

 Cross-Reference
You can learn how to select bridgehead servers in Chapter 8.

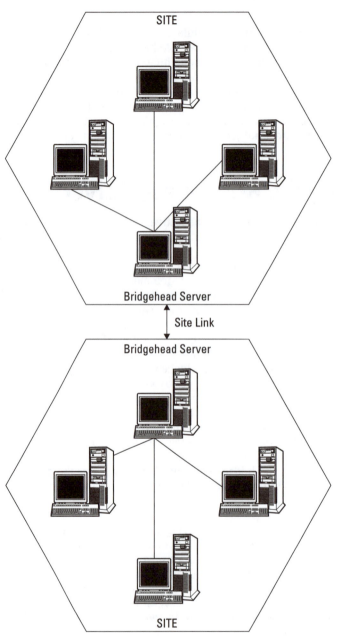

Figure 5-7: Bridgehead server

Understanding Site Link Bridges

Replication between the Active Directory occurs through the use of Internet Protocol (IP) or Simple Mail Transport Protocol (SMTP). Protocol usage and replication is thoroughly explained in Chapter 13, so I'm not going to repeat that discussion here. However, do understand that in most cases, IP is used to send replication traffic. With that said, we move to a discussion about site link bridges. When you create various site links in the Active Directory, the Active Directory automatically bridges those site links together if they use the same protocol (such as IP). Site link bridges are provided so that transitive connections can be made to other sites. For example, in Figure 5-8 you have an Atlanta site, a London site, and a Sydney site. Atlanta and London are connected by a site link, and London and Sydney are connected by a site link. Through the site link bridge, Atlanta and Sydney are transitively connected to each other through a logical link. To generate a cost of this logical link, the KCC adds the cost of the two links that connect the sites together. For example, in Figure 5-8, you can see that the site link between Atlanta and London has a cost of 1 while the link between London and Sydney has a cost of 10. So, the cost of the transitive site link is 11. The Active Directory configures the transitive link this way so that the actual, physical site links always have a lower cost than the transitive link. This feature ensures that traffic routing is always performed in an appropriate manner between physical and logical site links.

Tip   You can think of a site link bridge as a router in an IP network.

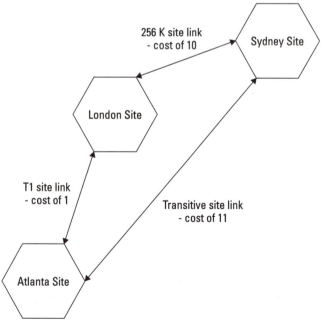

Figure 5-8: Site link bridge

As I mentioned, the Active Directory automatically generates site link bridges, so in a fully routed IP network, this is not something you have to configure. However, if your network is not fully routed or you have an excessive number of sites, you can turn off this automatic site link bridge configuration feature and create them yourself.

Chapter 8 addresses this implementation issue in more detail.

Sites and Server Placement

As you are planning your Active Directory site implementation, you will also need to think about server placement, such as domain controllers, global catalog servers, and DNS servers. Remember that sites and domains are not dependent on each other, so you could have a domain that spans two sites so that one site does not have any servers at all. As you might guess, this is not a wise configuration because one of the major purposes of creating a site is to restrict user traffic to the site—a task that requires servers. With that in mind, the following bulleted list tells you the best server placement decisions for your sites:

✦ Each site should have at least one domain controller. In reality, depending on the size of the site, you'll need more, and to maintain fault tolerance, you will need at least two. The domain controllers within the site can process user logon authentication and service requests in order to keep user traffic off the WAN link.

✦ Each site should have a global catalog server. Global catalog server access is required for user logon (in multiple domain implementations) because the global catalog server determines universal group memberships for users in a native mode domain and processes user logon requests when a user principal name (UPN) is used. Also, the global catalog server processes user object location queries for the entire forest, so your best performance option is to have a global catalog server in each site.

Although the best performance option is to have a global catalog server in each site, global catalog servers increase replication because they must maintain a partial database replica for the objects in each domain. If at all possible, have only one global catalog server in each site—the more global catalog servers per site the more replication traffic you will have.

✦ Under most circumstances, you will see the best performance if you have at least one DNS server in each site to process DNS queries. Make sure your clients within the site are configured to contact the DNS server(s) existing within the site.

Make sure the DNS server in the site is authoritative for the name locator records for the domain(s) that exist in the site. This prevents clients from having to query remote DNS servers to locate the DNS server(s) in their own site.

Final Planning Considerations

The greatest trick in planning an Active Directory site configuration is making certain you understand the Active Directory's definition and approach to the use of sites. Once you are certain you are ready to begin the actual planning process, consider using the following planning steps to assist you:

1. Site planning always begins with your physical network. You will need to carefully examine your IP subnets that are connected by a high-speed backbone and then consider subnets that are connected by slower, more expensive WAN technologies. You need a careful and very accurate view of your physical IP network, so you may need to employ the help of several administrators or network engineers to make certain you gain a total and accurate view.

2. Create a site where there is fast, inexpensive, reliable, and readily available connectivity (well-connected subnets). You must make certain your site definition is based on well-connected subnets because the KCC will assume this is true and configure intrasite replication accordingly.

3. As you begin planning your sites, think about replication and try to make site decisions with replication in mind. Consider how your LANs are connected with WAN technologies and what bearing these connections will have on the Active Directory.

4. Any physical location that is not directly connected to your network, such as one that uses SMTP mail or a virtual private network (VPN), for communication with your network should be configured as a site.

5. When you think you have your site structure in mind, create a chart that shows each site, the IP subnet(s) contained in each site, and the existing WAN technologies that connect any of the sites together.

6. Examine the WAN links and how those will become site links in the Active Directory. Consider site link cost, replication frequency, and potential schedules. You may consider creating a chart to help you in the planning process. Attempt to find a balance between bandwidth usage, scheduling, and the replication delays that will occur between sites. There is no formula for this, but you will have to determine what combination works best for your network.

7. Determine if you will need to manually create site link bridges or if you can allow the Active Directory to configure them for you by default. If you do not have a fully routed IP network or if you have excessive numbers of sites, you may need to manually configure site link bridges to see the best performance.

8. Examine how you will place domain controllers, global catalog server(s), and DNS server(s) within the site. Also, examine the domain controllers that will be placed in the site and determine which domain controllers(s) should be designated as preferred bridgehead servers for the site.

Summary

This chapter explored Active Directory sites in terms of conceptual content and site planning. Planning your Active Directory sites does not have to be a difficult task, but it is imperative that you thoroughly explore your current network TCP/IP implementation so that you can accurately define your well-connected subnets and site links. Through the effective configuration and use of sites, the Active Directory can control user traffic and replication traffic in order to make the most of your WAN bandwidth and connectivity expense.

✦   ✦   ✦

Implementing the Active Directory

Once you have planned an Active Directory infrastructure and reexamined that plan carefully, you are ready to begin installing and deploying the Active Directory. In this part of the book, you learn how to implement the Active Directory by first installing it. You examine how to install root domains, child domains, and new domain trees and how to remove the Active Directory.

Next, you learn how to install Organizational Units, printer objects, shared folders, and related Active Directory resources. You also learn how to configure domains and domain controllers and how to create Active Directory sites and related components.

You also explore user, group, and computer account creation, as well as the security features of the Active Directory. Once you study this portion of the book, you will be able to effectively use the Active Directory tools to implement and manage an Active Directory infrastructure.

Installing the Root Domain

◆ ◆ ◆ ◆

In This Chapter

Examining domain
controllers

Understanding the
root domain

Exploring installation
requirements

Installing the root
domain

◆ ◆ ◆ ◆

You have planned an Active Directory implementation,
and now it is time to begin the actual implementation of
the Active Directory. Fortunately, compared to the planning
process, the installation of the domain root and all other
Active Directory domain controllers or domains after the root
is rather easy. As with many tasks in Windows 2000, you are
provided with a handy wizard to walk you through the installation; in fact, you *must* use the wizard to install the Active
Directory. The wizard ensures that setup collects all the necessary information from you in order to install the directory
service.

In this chapter, you explore the domain root installation. As
with all installations, however, there are a few last minute
planning and consideration options that you need to address.

Examining Domain Controllers

Remember, all domain controllers run the Active Directory.
You *cannot* have a domain controller that does not run the
Active Directory. When you install Windows 2000 Server, you
install either a member server for an existing Windows 2000
domain or a standalone server. In Windows 2000, there are
only three server roles: domain controller, member server,
and standalone server. In order to get into the Windows 2000
mode of thinking, you have to forget about a few things close
to your NT heart, such as primary domain controllers (PDCs)
and backup domain controllers (BDCs).

In Windows 2000, all domain controllers run the Active
Directory, and all domain controllers function as peers. This
multimaster approach to networking solves many problems
and shortcomings of the NT network and makes your job as
administrator much easier. With a peer-to-peer approach, you

can use any domain controller to manage the Active Directory and make configuration changes. Once those changes are made, the changes are replicated to all other domain controllers. If another change is made on a different domain controller, the same process occurs. There is no master domain controller in Windows 2000, and you benefit from this design with easier administration and built-in fault tolerance. If one domain controller goes offline, you do not have a problem. The other domain controllers continue to function normally, and clients are not hindered from gaining access to resources. Once the domain controller comes back online, it catches up to the database changes through replication.

So, if there are no PDCs and BDCs in Windows 2000 networks, how many domain controllers do you need per domain? At a minimum, you need two. Without two domain controllers in a domain:

✦ Your Active Directory database is not fault tolerant.

✦ Clients are not protected against the failure of the domain controller.

For example, suppose that a server, ADSER1, is the only domain controller in a domain called AD. Clients access the server to log on to the network and use the Active Directory. In a small domain, the single server may be able to handle the logon and service requests of the hardware (depending on domain size and server hardware), but what happens if the server suddenly has an internal error and locks up? What happens if the server's motor fan burns out, and its insides slowly cook? Unfortunately, if the server cannot be rebooted and the operating system regained, the answer is that all of the Active Directory data is lost, and you end up with a bunch of clients connected to the network. Clients cannot be authenticated, and no Active Directory services are available.

Caution   Under no circumstances should you configure a domain with only one domain controller.

Consider this same scenario with a second domain controller. With a second domain controller, both servers act as peers. Through replication they have the exact same Active Directory information. When ADSER1 goes down, the second sever continues functioning normally, authenticating clients and providing services. When ADSER1 is repaired, it can be brought back online and even reinstalled if necessary. The remaining server can update ADSER1's Active Directory database through replication. No harm done, and as far as clients are concerned, the event never happened (which in the end is the goal anyway).

Note   It is important to note that this scenario refers to Active Directory data. Multiple domain controllers provide fault tolerance for the Active Directory database. Other data on your server and other server configurations are *not* protected by this design. Domain controller fault tolerance is in no way a replacement for a solid backup and disk fault tolerance plan.

Practically speaking, you will probably need several domain controllers per domain. Multiple domain controllers provide not only fault tolerance, but also load balancing. Also, you may have other services running on your domain controllers that you must take into account.

So, the final word is simply this — upgrading a member server to the Active Directory makes that member server a domain controller. Uninstalling the Active Directory from a domain controller demotes the domain controller to a member server. (You do not have to reinstall Windows 2000 Server, however, as you did with Windows NT Server 4.0.)

How Do I Install the Root Domain?

Installation of the root domain sounds like a complicated task, but it really is not. Installation of the root domain occurs when you install the first domain controller in what will be the new domain. From that point, all other domain controllers you install in the domain receive a copy of the initial installation. So, you create the domain root by installing the first domain controller.

We need to make two distinctions here. When you install the root domain, you will either be creating a new root domain on a new network, or you will be upgrading from an NT network to a Windows 2000 network. If you are creating a new network, you first need to choose a server that will be the first domain controller. If you are upgrading from NT, you begin with your primary domain controller. When you install Windows 2000 on the primary domain controller, setup detects that the machine is a PDC. Once Windows 2000 Server installation is complete, setup automatically prompts you to begin the Active Directory Installation Wizard to move the former PDC to a Windows 2000 domain controller. In the process, all of your NT accounts are preserved and migrated to the Active Directory.

In the previous section, we explored the fact that domain controllers are peers in a Windows 2000 domain. Now I am going to contradict myself a little. Although domain controllers are peers, that statement isn't entirely true because there are certain server roles that are played by certain domain controllers only. These sever roles, called *single master operation* roles, fulfill network requirements that simply do not function well in a multimaster setting. We explored these in Part One of the book, but they are important for our discussion here. The following list reviews the master operation roles functioning in an Active Directory environment:

✦ **Schema Master** — The schema master is a domain controller that manages any changes that are made to the Active Directory schema. There is only one schema master in an Active Directory forest.

✦ **Domain Naming Master** — The domain naming master domain controller manages the addition or removal of domains from the Active Directory forest. There can be only one domain naming master per forest.

✦ **Relative ID (RID) Master** — The RID master manages the allocation of RIDs to domain controllers in the domain. The RID master manages object security IDs and RIDs for the domain. There is one RID master per domain in the forest.

✦ **PDC Emulator** — The PDC Emulator role allows a Windows 2000 domain controller to act like a PDC to Windows NT servers and clients. Since NT is not aware of the peer-to-peer relationship, the PDC Emulator role allows the Windows 2000 domain controller to act like a PDC — it emulates the PDC role. This feature allows you to use Windows NT Servers and Windows 2000 Servers in the same domain (called mixed mode). There can be only one PDC Emulator in a domain at a time in the forest.

✦ **Infrastructure Master** — The Infrastructure master role updates group-to-user references. In other words, the Infrastructure master keeps track of what users belong to what groups and in what domains. There is only one Infrastructure master in each domain in the forest.

✦ **Global Catalog** — In addition to the standard master operation roles, there are also global catalog servers. Global catalog servers hold a partial replica for all objects in all domains. Global catalog servers are used for network logons by providing universal group membership information to a domain controller when a logon occurs. Global catalogs also assist user object queries.

Cross-Reference You can learn more about Windows 2000 universal groups in Chapter 9.

So, why review all of this again and what does this have to do with installing the root domain? The answer is simply this: When you install the root domain by installing the first domain controller, that domain controller will be assigned all of these roles because it is the first one. You can move these roles around to different domain controllers, which you can learn about in Chapter 7, but upon your initial installation, your first domain controller will hold all of the single master operation roles. With that said, you should wisely choose which server will be the first domain controller in the root domain.

Installation Requirements

Technically, if you have installed Windows 2000 Server on a computer, you can upgrade the member server to the Active Directory. However, as with server installation, you should carefully examine the server to see if its hardware can meet the needs of your network. Your domain controllers should have fast processors and plenty of RAM (256 or higher is good). So, examine the server hardware and choose a domain controller for the initial installation that has plenty of storage space, plenty of processing power, and plenty of RAM.

Next, all domain controllers must have an NTFS volume in order to install the Active Directory. Simply put, the Active Directory does not install on FAT or FAT32.

The Skinny on File Systems

A file system is a like a file folder in a filing cabinet. The file system provides a way for your operating system to store data in a logical, organized manner. Without a file system, your computer would not be able to logically write and read data on a hard disk. Windows 2000 supports FAT, FAT32, and NTFS.

FAT (File Allocation Table) is an older file system. FAT was around when hard disks were rather small. In fact, FAT should not be used on disks larger than 511MB. (When was the last time you saw a drive that small?) You can use it on drives up to 4GB, but FAT does not make good use of storage space once you move away from the 511MB ceiling. As you can guess, FAT is provided in Windows 2000 for backward compatibility.

FAT32 was designed to solve the size limitations of FAT, and it was first supported in Windows 95 OSR2 and then in Windows 98. FAT32 can make good use of space on larger hard drives; however, you do not have any of the security features of NTFS, and many Windows 2000 services and options will not work on FAT or FAT32. Like FAT, FAT32 is provided in Windows 2000 for backward compatibility.

Finally, the new NTFS with Windows 2000 makes excellent use of storage space and supports all of the features provided by the Kerberos security protocol. NTFS is the file system of choice in Windows 2000 and is required for an Active Directory installation.

Tip　Unless you are dual-booting Windows 2000 Server with Windows 95 or 98 (which you are probably not), then there is no reason to use FAT or FAT32 volumes on your server. FAT and FAT32 are provided for backward compatibility in Windows 2000 and do not support many of Windows 2000's disk and security features.

If you have not set up your Windows 2000 Server with an NTFS volume, you'll need to do so before attempting the installation of the Active Directory. You have two options: format a volume with NTFS or convert the drive to NTFS. First, you can format a volume with NTFS. Formatting erases all of the data on the volume and formats the volume with NTFS. If you have data existing on the volume that you want to keep, you will need to convert the volume to NTFS rather than format it. To format a volume with NTFS, follow these steps:

Caution　The formatting process will erase any data currently residing on the volume. The erased data cannot be recovered.

1. Click Start ⇨ Programs ⇨ Administrative Tools ⇨ Computer Management.

2. In the left pane, expand Storage and click Disk Management. The Disk Management console, shown in Figure 6-1, appears in the right pane.

Figure 6-1: The Disk Management console

3. To format the volume, right-click it in Disk Management and click Format.

4. In the Format window that appears, select NTFS from the File System drop-down menu and then click OK. You can also choose to perform a quick format.

5. The disk will be formatted with NTFS. You do not need to reboot your server.

The second option to set up an NTFS volume is to convert the drive to NTFS, if you have data on a particular FAT or FAT32 volume that you do not want to lose. The conversion process preserves your FAT or FAT32 data, but once you convert to NTFS, you cannot return to FAT or FAT32 without reformatting the disk. To convert a drive to NTFS, follow these steps:

1. Click Start ➪ Run and then type **CMD** in the dialog box. Press OK.

2. At the command prompt, type **convert *drive_letter*: /fs:ntfs** and press Enter.

Once you have an NTFS volume for installation, you should verify that TCP/IP is installed on your server. Typically, you should have TCP/IP installed as a default option, and your network must use TCP/IP in order for the Active Directory to function. You can still check your system for the protocol, however, by right-clicking My Network Places and clicking Properties. In the Network and Dial-up Connections window, right-click your Local Area Connection and click Properties. You see a components list used by the LAN connection, and you should see Internet Protocol (TCP/IP), as shown in Figure 6-2.

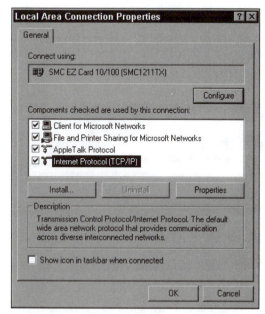

Figure 6-2: TCP/IP appears in the Local Area Connection Properties sheet.

Tip

If TCP/IP is not installed, click the Install button on the Local Area Connection Properties sheet. Click Protocol and then click the Add button. Select TCP/IP from the list and click OK. You may need your Windows 2000 Server installation CD-ROM.

Finally, DNS must be installed on your network to install the Active Directory. As you learned in the first part of the book, DNS is required for an Active Directory implementation. If DNS is not configured, the wizard will prompt you to allow the operating system to automatically configure DNS on the domain controller. It's your choice — you can install and configure DNS on a different Windows 2000 Server, or you can allow the Active Directory installation to automatically set up and configure DNS.

Finally, you'll need to make certain you are ready to begin the installation. Review all of your implementation plans carefully and make certain you have a desired domain name. Once you install the domain root, you cannot change the domain name without reinstalling the Active Directory — which is not something you will want to do during your implementation. Also, before installing any new software, always perform a full backup to protect your data in the event of a setup failure.

Installing the Root Domain

Once you have checked the installation requirements and have determined which server to select for your Active Directory root domain installation (in an NT upgrade, you use the PDC), logon to the server with an administrative account. You can start the Active Directory installation in one of two ways. First, Windows 2000 provides a Configure Your Server tool that gives you a graphical interface for starting the Active Directory Installation Wizard, shown in Figure 6-3.

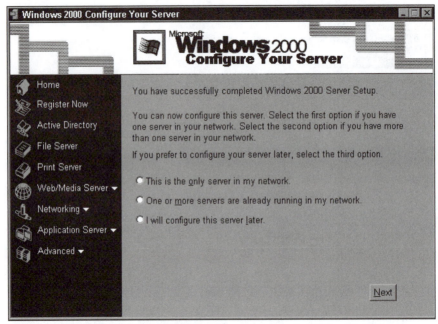

Figure 6-3: You can use Configure Your Server to start the Active Directory Installation Wizard.

You can access the Configure Your Server tool by clicking Start ➪ Programs ➪ Administrative Tools ➪ Configure Your Server. The Configure Your Server tool works like a Web page. The left pane contains links to other portions of the tool, and you'll notice links within the description pane where you can get additional information about various Windows 2000 technologies. If you click the Active Directory link in the left pane, the Active Directory information window appears in the left pane, giving you information about Active Directory installation, shown in Figure 6-4. If you scroll down the page, you will see a Start link. Click the Start link to begin the installation.

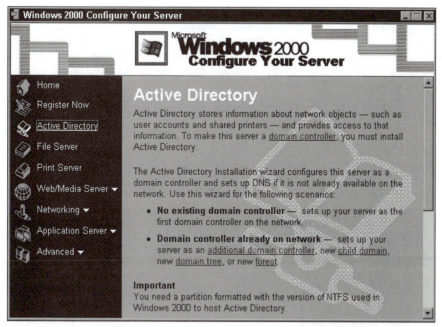

Figure 6-4: You can start an Active Directory installation from this window.

New Feature

Configure Your Server is a simple tool that helps you install various Windows 2000 components. It is designed to help you master the new Windows 2000 learning curve by providing an easy way to configure your system. You can perform the options provided in Configure Your Server in other places in the operating system as well, such as Add/Remove Programs – Add/Remove Windows Components.

You can also start the Active Directory Installation Wizard by clicking Start ➪ Run and by then typing **dcpromo** in the dialog box. Click OK, and the wizard opens.

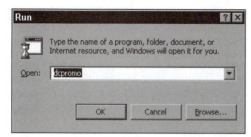

Figure 6-5: Type **dcpromo** in the Run dialog box to start the wizard.

You can start the Installation Wizard either way—just choose which method you like best. Once you start the Installation Wizard, you simply answer the questions that setup needs to know to create the new root domain. The following step-by-step instructions show you exactly what to do in order to install the root domain. You'll also see all of the wizard's screens here to make sure you are on track. Use this section as a handy reference tool.

1. You see a Welcome screen, shown in Figure 6-6. As the window tells you, once you install the Active Directory on your member server, the server will become a domain controller. Click Next to continue.

Figure 6-6: Click Next on the Welcome screen.

2. You see a window, shown in Figure 6-7, with two radio button options. You can install the domain controller either for a new domain or for an existing Active Directory domain. Since you are creating the domain root, click the "Domain controller for a new domain" radio button and then click the Next button.

3. Another two radio button window appears. In this window, you can select to create a new domain tree or a new child domain in an existing tree. Since this is the domain root, click the new domain tree radio button, shown in Figure 6-8, and then click the Next button.

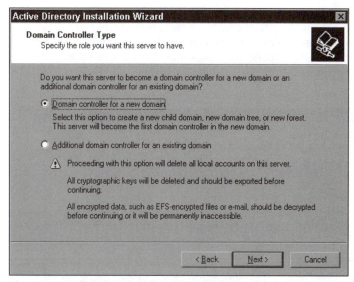

Figure 6-7: Click the new domain radio button and click Next.

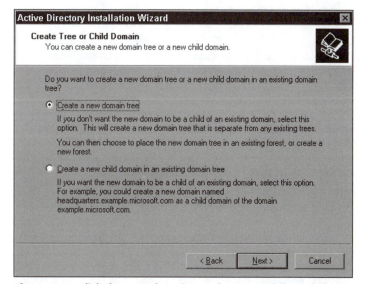

Figure 6-8: Click the new domain tree button and then click Next.

4. You see two radio button options in the next window, shown in Figure 6-9. You have the option to either create a new forest of trees or join your new tree to an existing forest. This step-by-step assumes you do not currently have other Active Directory forests, so choose the "Create a new forest of domain trees" radio button and then click the Next button.

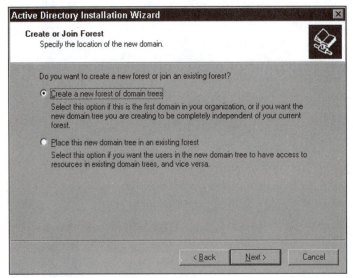

Figure 6-9: Click the create a new forest radio button and then click Next.

5. The domain name window appears, shown in Figure 6-10. Enter the desired DNS name of your Active Directory root in this window. Throughout the rest of the book, my example root domain is triton.com, a fictitious company. Type the name into the box and click the Next button.

6. The NetBIOS name window appears, shown in Figure 6-11. Your NetBIOS name of the domain is shown. The NetBIOS name is taken from your root domain name, but you can change it by typing a new name in the dialog box. The NetBIOS name is the name downlevel clients see when logging onto Windows 2000. For example, in the domain triton.com, Windows 9x or NT clients simply see the domain name as TRITON. NetBIOS naming is unnecessary in pure Windows 2000 networks because DNS is used, but the NetBIOS name is maintained for backward compatibility. Click the Next button.

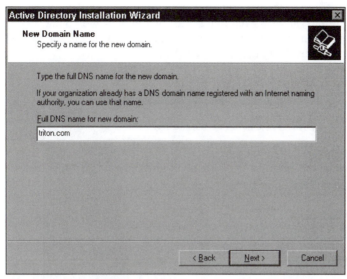

Figure 6-10: Enter the root domain name and click Next.

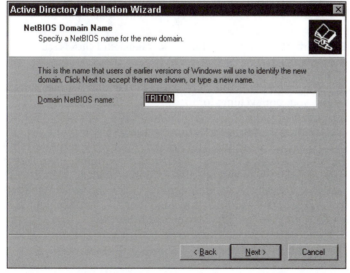

Figure 6-11: Accept or change the NetBIOS name and click Next.

7. Next, as shown in Figure 6-12, you see a window with default storage locations for the Active Directory database and the log files, which is C:\WINNT\NTDS by default. You can change this default location by using the browse button. Make any desired changes and click Next.

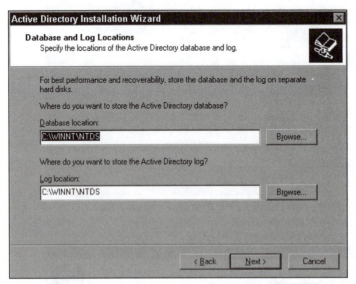

Figure 6-12: Adjust database and log file locations and click Next.

Microsoft recommends that you store the database and log files on a hard disk separate from your boot volume for maximum performance.

8. You must decide on a storage location for the SYSVOL folder, which is C:\WINNT\SYSVOL by default. All Windows 2000 servers have a SYSVOL folder, but domain controllers' SYSVOL folder contains Active Directory information. As with database and log files, you may want to store the SYSVOL on a different volume, but the volume must be formatted with Windows 2000's version of NTFS. In the window shown in Figure 6-13, make your selection and click Next.

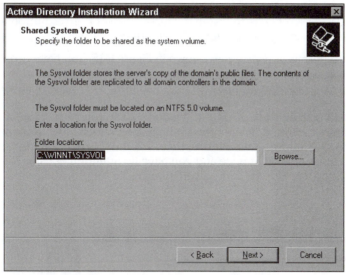

Figure 6-13: Choose a SYSVOL location and click Next.

 You can learn more about the SYSVOL folder in Chapter 12.

9. If you did not configure DNS on another Windows 2000 Server, then a message appears telling you that a DNS server could not be contacted, as shown in Figure 6-14. If a DNS Server could be contacted, the Active Directory Installation Wizard would query the DNS Server to make certain that it supports dynamic updates. By clicking OK to the message, you tell Windows 2000 to install and configure DNS automatically with the Active Directory on this domain controller. Click OK to continue.

Figure 6-14: Click OK to automatically install DNS.

10. The next window allows you either to let the Active Directory automatically set up DNS or to choose to install it yourself. Select the Yes button to allow the Active Directory to configure DNS and then click Next.

11. You see a permissions window, shown in Figure 6-15. You have two options. You can choose to use either permissions compatible with Windows NT Server or permissions compatible with Windows 2000 Servers in Windows 2000 domains only. If you use Windows NT permissions, you are using weaker permissions than those offered in Windows 2000, specifically in that anonymous users can see domain information if anonymous logon is allowed. If your upgrade to Windows 2000 will take time, use the NT permissions options. If you are upgrading all at once and you have no intention of using NT Servers in the future, choose the 2000 permissions radio button. Make your selection and click the Next button.

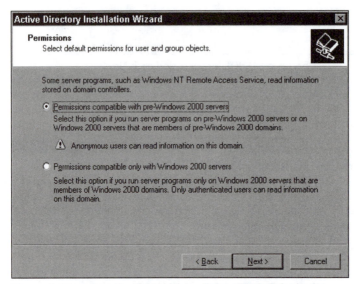

Figure 6-15: Select the desired permissions and click Next.

12. The Active Directory contains a Restore Mode option that allows you to restore Active Directory data when a domain controller failure occurs. The use of Restore Mode is password protected as a security measure. The Restore Mode window asks you to enter a Restore Mode password and confirm the password. You will need this password if you ever have to use Restore Mode. Enter a password, confirm it, and then click the Next button.

13. A summary window appears, as shown in Figure 6-16. Review your selections and use the Back button if you need to change anything. If the information is correct, click the Next button.

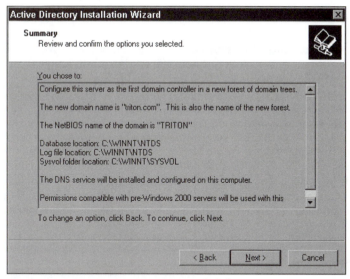

Figure 6-16: Review your settings and click Next.

14. Setup begins configuring the Active Directory, as shown in Figure 6-17. Configuration may take several minutes. Once the installation is complete, you are prompted to reboot the server. Once the reboot takes place, the installation is complete, and your former member server is now an Active Directory domain controller for the root domain.

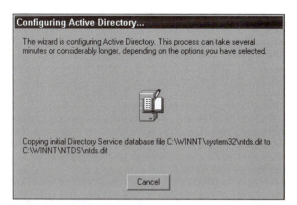

Figure 6-17: Configuration of the Active Directory

Summary

In this chapter, we examined the issues and installation of the Active Directory root domain. Active Directory installation is not difficult due to the Active Directory Installation Wizard, which is available by using the Configure Your Server tool or by using the `dcpromo` command. Before beginning the installation of the root domain, you should make certain that you have an understanding of domain controller functions, including the use of master operation roles in the Active Directory. Also, before installing the Active Directory in a new domain on a new server, make certain the server's hardware can support the demands of the Active Directory and the master operation roles assigned to the first domain controller in the root domain. In the case of an upgrade from NT, begin with the PDC in the old Windows NT domain so that your accounts are migrated to the Active Directory. Install Windows 2000 Server on the PDC first and then continue with the installation to begin the domain upgrade.

✦   ✦   ✦

Setting Up Resources

The installation of the first domain controller in your first Windows 2000 domain creates a new forest and the domain root for the first tree. From this domain root, all other domains within that tree are built. Once you have installed your first domain controller and have established your root domain, you can then begin the process of implementing the rest of your Active Directory network.

That implementation task may involve several different actions, including adding new domain controllers to an existing domain, creating new child and grandchild domains, creating new trees, or possibly even uninstalling the Active Directory. This chapter also addresses Active Directory operations master locations and how to move master roles to different computers.

As with all aspects of an Active Directory implementation, continue to proceed carefully and cautiously, testing your Active Directory implementation along the way.

Installing Additional Domain Controllers

In Chapter 6, I examined the issue of domain controllers (DCs). Active Directory domain controllers are peers within a domain. There is no primary domain controller (PDC) or backup domain controller (BDC) in an Active Directory domain. Once you install the root domain, you have one domain controller in that domain. While technically, one domain controller is all you need to create the root domain, you need to install additional domain controllers for load balancing and fault tolerance. Depending on the size of your domain, you may need a few more domain controllers or possibly a large number in enterprise networks. Regardless, additional domain controllers can be used to load balance user logon and service requests and provide fault tolerance. When several domain controllers are used, an Active Directory domain is protected against the failure of a domain controller because all domain controllers maintain an exact copy of the Active Directory database through replication.

So, when you create the root domain, your next order of business — and one you should get to right away — is the installation of additional domain controllers in the new domain. If you are upgrading your network from Windows NT to Windows 2000, you have already converted the PDC to a Windows 2000 domain controller. Your next task is to install Windows 2000 Server on your BDCs and upgrade to the Active Directory.

Cross-Reference You can find a step-by-step reference for installing Windows 2000 Server and the Active Directory on PDCs and BDCs in Appendix D.

In new networks, or even in existing NT networks, you may also choose to install Windows 2000 Server and the Active Directory on new servers. Regardless of whether you are upgrading your current machines or installing Windows 2000 on new machines, the Active Directory installation functions the same.

Before upgrading a member server or BDC to an additional domain controller for a domain, take note of a few warnings:

✦ All local accounts on the server will be deleted. The local users and groups feature of member servers is disabled on domain controllers.

✦ All cryptographic keys will be deleted. You should export any cryptographic keys to another server before performing the upgrade.

✦ All encrypted data, such as that encrypted with Encrypting File System (EFS), will become inaccessible after the upgrade. Encrypted data should be decrypted first.

After installing Windows 2000 Server on the machines, follow these steps to upgrade the member server to an additional domain controller for an existing domain:

1. In Configure Your Server, click the Active Directory link in the left pane, then click the Start link in the right window or click Start ➪ Run. Then type **dcpromo** in the dialog box and click OK.

Note If you are upgrading a former BDC, Windows 2000 will automatically prompt you to begin the Active Directory installation when the Server installation portion is complete.

2. The Active Directory Installation Wizard presents you with a Welcome screen. Click the Next button.

3. In the Domain Controller Type window, click the "Additional domain controller" radio button, as shown in Figure 7-1 and then click the Next button.

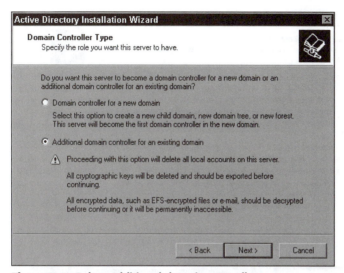

Figure 7-1: Select additional domain controller.

4. Enter a valid administrative account, password, and domain name, as shown in Figure 7-2. This action authenticates you to complete the action of installing a new domain controller.

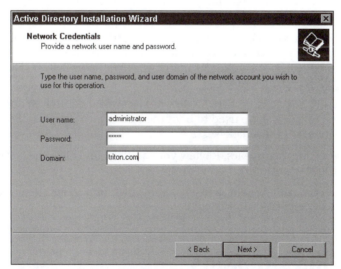

Figure 7-2: Enter an administrative account and password.

5. In the Additional Domain Controller window, enter the full DNS name of the domain for which this computer will become an additional DC, as shown in Figure 7-3. Enter the name and click the Next button.

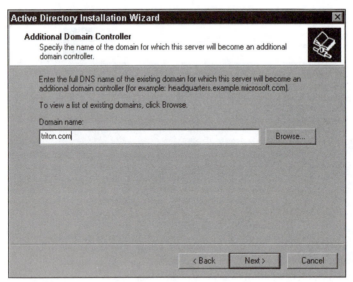

Figure 7-3: Enter the full DNS name of the domain.

6. The default database and log file locations window appears. By default, these files are stored in C:\WINNT\NTDS. You can change the location by using the Browse buttons, and Microsoft recommends that you place these files on a separate hard disk for maximum performance. Make your selection and click the Next button.

7. Next, the default SYSVOL location is presented (C:\WINNT\SYSVOL). You can also change the SYSVOL location using the Browse button, but SYSVOL *must* be located on a disk or volume formatted with Windows 2000 NTFS. Make your selection and click Next.

8. The Directory Services Restore Mode window appears. Enter an administrative password that can be used to boot the server into Directory Services Restore Mode and then click Next.

9. A summary window appears. Review your settings and click the Next button to begin the installation.

10. Once the installation is complete, click the Finish button and then reboot your server.

Creating Child Domains

Once you have a root domain established, you can install child domains as necessary. In Part I of the book, you learned about child domains, also called subdomains. For our discussion, I prefer to use the term *child* because it more accurately reflects the relationship of the domain to its *parent*. The child domain is a subordinate domain of the root domain, and the child domain follows a few particular rules:

✦ A child domain is built on the root domain namespace. It is contiguous in nature because the root domain and child domain share a boundary. For example, if the root domain (parent, in this case) is triton.com, a child domain must follow the triton.com namespace. If there is child domain named namerica, then the child domain's name is namerica.triton.com. Child domains are built on the root domain namespace, and the Active Directory Installation Wizard will not allow you to build them in another manner.

✦ The child domain is a part of the root domain's tree. Because it is a portion of the tree, the child domain shares the same Active Directory schema, configuration, and replication information.

✦ Child domains are automatically connected to the root domain through a transitive trust relationship. Transitive trusts are two-way trust relationships and allow all domains in a tree to trust each other automatically. Because the trust is *transitive*, if Domain 1 trusts Domain 2 and Domain 2 trusts Domain 3, then Domain 1 automatically trusts Domain 3 through the transitive nature of the trust.

To install a new child domain, begin with the server or Windows NT PDC for that domain. Installing a child domain is just like creating a root domain in terms of the server. If you are converting an existing Windows NT domain to the Active Directory, you begin with the PDC. If you are installing a new domain, begin with the server that will be the first domain controller for that domain.

As with other Active Directory configurations, you use the Active Directory Installation Wizard to begin the installation. The following steps show you how to install a child domain:

1. Start the Active Directory Installation Wizard by using the Configure Your Server tool. Click Active Directory in the left pane and then click the Start link that appears in the right window. Or, simply click Start ➪ Run and then type **dcpromo** in the dialog box and click OK.

2. The Active Directory Installation Wizard begins and presents you with a Welcome screen. Click the Next button.

3. In the Domain Controller Type window, click the "Domain controller for a new domain" radio button, as shown in Figure 7-4, and then click the Next button.

4. In the Create Tree or Child Domain window, click the "Create a new child domain in an existing tree" radio button, shown in Figure 7-5, and then click the Next button.

5. Enter a valid administrative account, password, and domain name and then click the Next button.

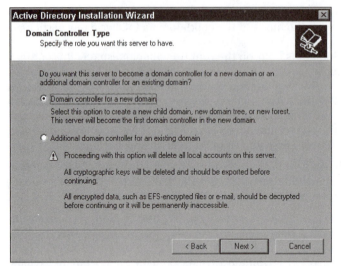

Figure 7-4: Click the "Domain controller for a new domain" radio button.

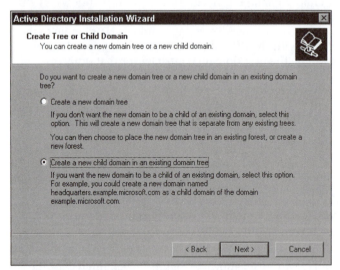

Figure 7-5: Click the "Create a new child domain in an existing domain tree" radio button.

6. In the Child Domain Installation window, enter the DNS name of the parent domain in the first dialog box and the name of the child domain in the second dialog box. For example, in Figure 7-6, you see the parent domain is triton.com and the name of the child domain is namerica. The complete DNS name of the new child domain is displayed automatically, in this case, namerica.triton.com. Enter the desired name and click the Next button.

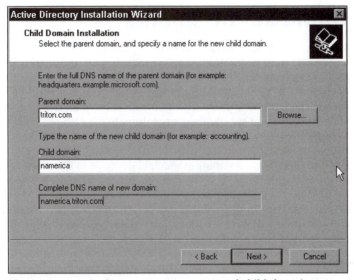

Figure 7-6: Enter the DNS parent name and child domain name.

7. The NetBIOS name of the child domain appears. You can accept the default name or change it if you like. The NetBIOS name is the name seen by down-level Windows clients for logon purposes. Make your selection and click the Next button.

8. The default database and log file locations window appears. By default, these files are stored in C:\WINNT\NTDS. You can change the location by using the Browse buttons, and Microsoft recommends that you place these files on a separate hard disk for maximum performance. Make your selection and click the Next button.

9. Next, the default SYSVOL location is presented (C:\WINNT\SYSVOL). You can also change the SYSVOL location using the Browse button, but SYSVOL must be located on a disk or volume formatted with Windows 2000 NTFS. Make your selection and click the Next button.

10. The Directory Services Restore Mode window appears. Enter an administrative password that can be used to boot the server into Directory Services Restore Mode and then click Next.

11. A summary window appears. Review your settings and click Next to begin the installation.

12. Once the installation is complete, click the Finish button and then reboot your server.

Creating Grandchild Domains

Grandchild domains are subdomains of an existing child domain. For example, if triton.com is a root domain and namerica.triton.com is a child domain, a grandchild domain is production.namerica.triton.com. Grandchild domains are a further division of a child domain. In our example, namerica is a child domain, and production further subdivides the namerica domain. In many circumstances, grandchild domains may be necessary to subdivide a large domain for different security or administrative purposes.

Cross-Reference You can learn more about designing grandchild domains in Chapter 3.

In terms of Active Directory configuration, a grandchild domain is no different than a child domain—it is simply an extension of an existing DNS namespace that has its own security and administrative boundary.

To install a grandchild domain, begin with the server or existing PDC in the domain that will become the new grandchild domain. Start the Active Directory Installation Wizard using either the Configure Your Server tool or dcpromo. The installation steps are the same as installing a child domain, so I'll not repeat them here. However, when you reach the Child Domain Installation window, you simply enter the full name of the child domain and then the name of the new grandchild domain. For example, in Figure 7-7, you see the child domain is namerica.triton.com and the name of the new grandchild domain is production. Therefore, the full DNS name of the new grandchild domain is production.namerica.triton.com.

Active Directory Installation Wizard ✕

Child Domain Installation
Select the parent domain, and specify a name for the new child domain.

Enter the full DNS name of the parent domain (for example: headquarters.example.microsoft.com).

Parent domain:

    namerica.triton.com   Browse...

Type the name of the new child domain (for example: accounting).

Child domain:

    production

Complete DNS name of new domain:

    production.namerica.triton.com

    < Back   Next >   Cancel

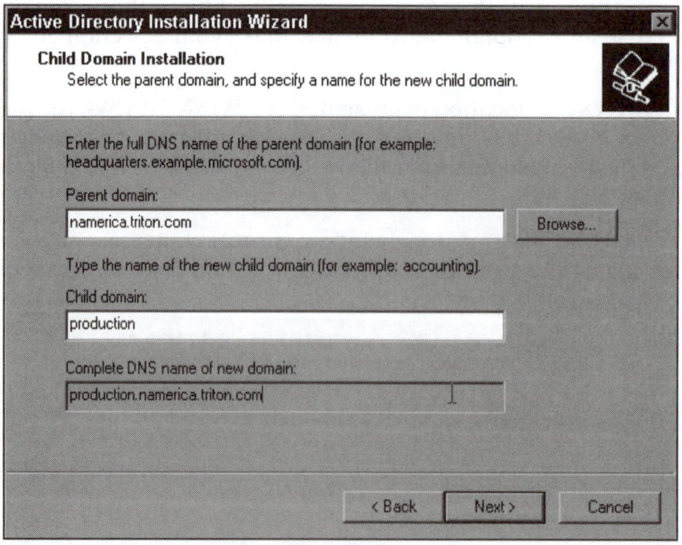

Figure 7-7: New grandchild domain

Creating a New Tree in an Existing Forest

The final installation option you have, with the exception of creating a new root domain in a new forest, is the creation of a new domain tree in an existing forest. When you created your first root domain, you created the root domain and a new forest in which that domain resides. You can also create a new domain tree within that forest. A new domain tree shares a common schema and global catalog with the existing tree, but the new domain tree does not share a contiguous namespace.

Cross-Reference　For more information on creating a new root domain in a new forest, see Chapter 6.

Consider an example. Assume that Triton, Inc., acquires another company, Angle Development. This company already has an Internet presence, angledev.com, and the company has existing administrative and security needs. Triton does not want to change all of this, but they do want Angle Development to be a part of the Active Directory environment. The solution? Create a new domain tree in the existing forest. A transitive trust relationship between triton.com and angledev.com will be established, and the two companies can share information with each other.

To create the new tree in an existing forest, begin in what will be the root domain of the new tree. Begin with the desired server that will be the first domain controller, or the PDC in case of an NT upgrade, and use either Configure Your Server or dcpromo.exe to start the Active Directory Wizard. Then, follow these steps:

1. As the Welcome screen window tells you, once you install the Active Directory on your member server, the server will become a domain controller. Click Next to continue.

2. In the window with two radio button options, you can either install the domain controller for a new domain or for an existing Active Directory domain. Since you are creating a new domain root in an existing forest, click the "Domain controller for a new domain" radio button and then click the Next button.

3. Another window with two radio buttons appears. In this window, you can select to create a new domain tree or a new child domain in an existing tree. Since this is the domain root, click the new domain tree radio button and then click the Next button.

4. In the next window, you should see two radio buttons. You have the option to either create a new forest of trees or join your new tree to an existing forest, as shown in Figure 7-8. Click the "Place this new domain tree in an existing forest" option and then click the Next button.

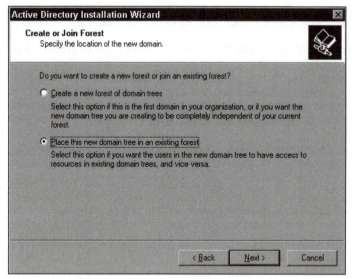

Figure 7-8: Choose to place the new domain in an existing forest.

5. The Network Credentials window appears. Enter a valid administrative user name, password, and domain and then click the Next button.

6. The domain name window appears. Enter the desired DNS name of your Active Directory root in this window and then click the Next button.

7. The NetBIOS name window appears. The NetBIOS name of the domain is shown. The NetBIOS name is taken from your root domain name, but you can change by typing a new name in the dialog box. The NetBIOS name is the name downlevel clients see when logging onto Windows 2000. Click the Next button.

8. You see a window with default storage locations for the Active Directory database and the log files, which is C:\WINNT\NTDS by default. You can change this default location by using the Browse button. Make any desired changes and click Next.

Tip   Microsoft recommends that you store the database and log files on a hard disk separate from your boot volume for maximum performance.

9. You must decide on a storage location for the SYSVOL folder, which is C:\WINNT\SYSVOL by default. All Windows 2000 servers have a SYSVOL folder, but domain controllers' SYSVOL folder contains Active Directory information. As with database and log files, you may want to store the SYSVOL on a different volume, but the volume must be formatted with Windows 2000's version of NTFS. Make your selection and click Next.

10. If you did not configure DNS on another Windows 2000 server, then a message appears telling you that a DNS server could not be contacted. If a DNS server could be contacted, the Active Directory Wizard would query the DNS server to make certain that it supports dynamic updates. By clicking OK to the message, you tell Windows 2000 to install and configure DNS automatically with the Active Directory on this domain controller. Click OK to continue.

11. The next window allows you either to let the Active Directory automatically set up DNS or to choose to install it yourself. Select the Yes button to allow the Active Directory to configure DNS and then click Next.

12. You now see a permissions window. You have two options. You can choose to use either permissions compatible with Windows NT Server or permissions compatible with Windows 2000 servers in Windows 2000 domains only. If you use Windows NT permissions, you are using weaker permissions than those offered in Windows 2000, specifically in that anonymous users can read domain information if anonymous logon is allowed. If your upgrade to Windows 2000 will take time, use the NT permissions options. If you are upgrading all at once and you have no intention of using NT servers in the future, choose the Windows 2000 permissions radio button. Make your selection and click the Next button.

13. The Active Directory contains a Restore Mode option that allows you to restore Active Directory data when a domain controller failure occurs. The use of Restore Mode is password protected as a security measure. The Restore Mode window asks you to enter a Restore Mode password and confirm the password. You will need this password if you ever have to use Restore Mode. Enter a password, confirm it, and then click the Next button.

14. A summary window appears. Review your selections and use the Back button if you need to change anything. If the information is correct, click the Next button.

15. Setup begins configuring the Active Directory. Configuration may take several minutes. Once the installation is complete, you are prompted to reboot the server. Once the reboot takes place, the installation is complete, and your former member server is now an Active Directory domain controller for the root domain.

Because the new domain is a member of the Active Directory forest, an automatic, transitive trust relationship is configured between domains. As you can see in Figure 7-9, triton.com and angledev.com share a tree root, transitive trust relationship.

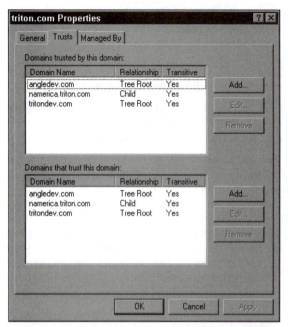

Figure 7-9: Tree root transitive trusts are automatic.

You can learn more about Windows 2000 transitive trust relationships in Chapter 8.

Operations Master Placement

I want to focus attention on how to manage operations masters, and specifically, how to move those master operations roles among domain controllers.

For more information on the concept of operations masters, see Chapters 1 and 6.

Master operations roles are installed by default when you install Active Directory forest, trees, and domains. In an Active Directory forest, there is one schema master and one domain naming master per forest, and there is one potentially one RID master, PDC Emulator, Infrastructure master, and global catalog server per domain. Those roles are assigned by default to the first domain controller in the first domain in the forest, and the domain specific roles are assigned to the first domain controller in the additional domains. This default behavior, however, may not be best. Depending on the structure of your environment, you may need to move master operations roles so they reside on other domain controllers in order to distribute the workload. Fortunately, moving master operations roles is not a difficult task The following section explores the movement of master operations roles to different domains controllers and provides you with the steps to accomplish these movements.

Note   All single master operations roles are examined in this section, except the schema master role, which is explored in Chapter 14. Because of the seriousness of the schema master and the use of the Schema Manager MMC snap-in, this operation is explored in conjunction with schema modifications.

Global catalog server

Before you send me an e-mail, I know that global catalog servers are not technically classified as single master operations roles. However, the global catalog always seems to fit into this discussion, so I am including it here. Global catalogs can be moved from server to server. In essence, a particular domain controller plays the role of a global catalog server. A global catalog server is required for successful logon attempts because the global catalog server determines group memberships during the logon process. In addition to this task, the global catalog server contains a partial replica of all Active Directory objects in the forest. In short, your clients must be able to contact a global catalog server, so your placement of global catalog servers is critical.

A general implementation rule to follow is to place a global catalog server at each site. Although it greatly helps query performance, this action, however, will increase replication traffic.

Caution   Categorically, I can say the more global catalog servers you have on your network, the more replication traffic you will experience. The trick is to find the balance that works best for your environment.

A final note about global catalog server placement: In a domain that has more than one domain controller (which they all should), do *not* place the global catalog server role on the same domain controller that holds the Infrastructure master role. The Infrastructure master finds data that is out-of-date and then requests updated data from the global catalog server. As you can see, if both roles reside on the same domain controller, then the Infrastructure master will not be able to function because it will never find any out-of-date data since the global catalog is always up-to-date.

You may think, "So what?" The problem is that the Infrastructure master replicates its out-of-date and update findings from the global catalog server to other domain controllers. Think of it this way—global catalog servers replicate data with one another regularly so that object data is always up-to-date. The Infrastructure master compares its object references in its domain and other domains by consulting the global catalog. Updates are made, and then the changes are replicated to other domain controllers. However, if the Infrastructure master and global catalog server are on the same domain controller, there will never be any updates because the Infrastructure master role cannot detect changes. Therefore, those updates will never be sent to the other domain controller.

Of course, if all domain controllers are global catalog servers, then the Infrastructure master is not necessary since replication among all of the global catalogs takes care of any outdated information. However, unless you have a lot of excessive bandwidth you would like to eat up, you should certainly never implement such a configuration.

The key point — do *not* put the Infrastructure master and global catalog server roles on the same domain controller.

With all that said, I want to consider how you enable and disable the global catalog server role from one domain controller to another. The following steps show you how to perform this task:

1. Once you choose a domain controller you want to enable as a global catalog server, click Start ➪ Programs ➪ Administrative Tools ➪ Active Directory Sites and Services.

2. Expand the Sites container, expand the desired site, and then expand the Servers container, as shown in Figure 7-10. Select the desired server, and then in the right pane, right-click NTDS Settings. Then click Properties.

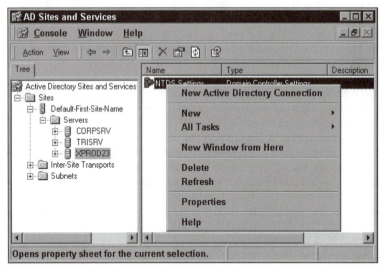

Figure 7-10: Right-click the desired server in the desired site and click Properties.

3. On the General tab, click the Global Catalog check box to enable the server as a global catalog server or clear the check box to disable the domain controller from being a global catalog server, as shown in Figure 7-11.

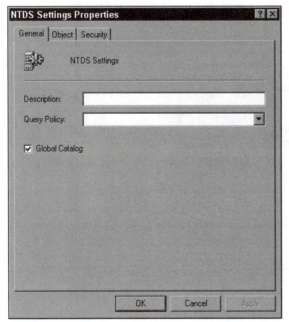

Figure 7-11: Click or clear the Global Catalog check box.

Make certain you have carefully analyzed your needs before enabling more than one global catalog server in a site. Typically, most sites need only a single global catalog server.

Domain naming master

There is one domain naming master per forest. The domain naming master role controls the addition or removal of domains to and from the forest. You can move the domain naming master role from domain controller to domain controller. However, there can only be one domain naming master at any given time in a forest, and that domain controller must be a global catalog server.

To transfer the domain naming master role to a different domain controller in the forest, follow these steps:

1. Click Start ➪ Programs ➪ Administrative Tools ➪ Active Directory Domains and Trusts.

2. In the console tree, right-click Active Directory Domains and Trusts and click Operations Master, as shown in Figure 7-12.

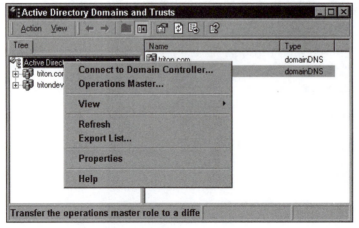

Figure 7-12: Click Operations Master.

3. The Active Directory presents a Change Operations Master window with the name of an alternate domain controller, shown in Figure 7-13. To change the domain naming master to that computer, click the Change button.

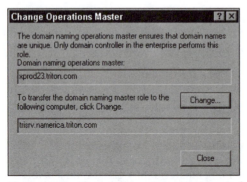

Figure 7-13: Change Operations Master window

You can also use the command-line utility ntdsutil to change the domain naming master role instead of the GUI interface provided in the Domains and Trusts console. To use ntdsutil for this purpose, follow these steps:

1. Type Start ⇨ Run and type **ntdsutil** in the dialog box and click OK.

2. Type **roles** and press Enter. Then type **connections** and press Enter.

3. Type **connect to server new_server_name**. For example, if a server is named XTRI23 and I want to transfer the domain naming master role to that server, I would type **connect to server XTRI23**. Press Enter.

4. Type **quit** and press Enter.

5. Type **transfer domain naming master** and press Enter. Choose Yes when the dialog box appears.

6. Type **quit** and press Enter. (Typing **quit** brings you to the previous level, so you may have to type **quit** several times to completely exit out of ntdsutil.)

Finally, concerning the domain naming master role, what do you do if the domain controller assigned to the role goes down? There is only one domain naming master role per forest, and to transfer the role, the domain naming master must be available.

If there is a catastrophic failure of the domain naming master domain controller, such as one that will require a complete operating system reinstall, you can perform an operation called "seizing the domain naming master role." This allows you to authoritatively seize the role and assign it to another domain controller.

 You should perform this action only if the existing domain naming master will *never* be available again. You should not transfer the role if the existing domain naming master will come back online or be used again.

To seize the domain naming master role, you use ntdsutil. Follow these steps:

1. Type Start ⇨ Run, type **ntdsutil** in the dialog box, and click OK.

2. Type **roles** and press Enter. Then type **connections** and press Enter.

3. Type **connect to server new_server_name**. For example, if a server is named XTRI23 and I want to transfer the domain naming master role to that server, I would type **connect to server XTRI23**. Press Enter.

4. Type **quit** and press Enter.

5. Type **seize domain naming master** and press Enter.

6. Type **quit** and press Enter. (You may have to type **quit** several times to completely exit out of ntdsutil.)

Infrastructure master

The Infrastructure master manages updates for group-to-user references whenever the members of groups are changed. In other words, the Infrastructure master keeps track of which users belong to which groups in the domain. There can be only one Infrastructure master in the domain at any given time. When group-to-user changes are made, the Infrastructure master replicates those changes to other domain controllers in the domain through multimaster replication.

You can move the Infrastructure master role among domain controllers within a domain, but you should not move the Infrastructure master role to a global catalog server. However, the Infrastructure master should be well connected to a global catalog server for the best performance.

To transfer the Infrastructure master role to another domain controller in the domain, follow these steps:

1. Click Start ➪ Programs ➪ Administrative Tools ➪ Active Directory Users and Computers.

2. Right-click Active Directory Users and Computers and then click Connect to Domain.

3. Type the domain name or click Browse and select the domain from the list. Then click OK.

4. Right-click Active Directory Users and Computers and then click Operations Master.

5. Click the Infrastructure tab and click Change, as shown in Figure 7-14.

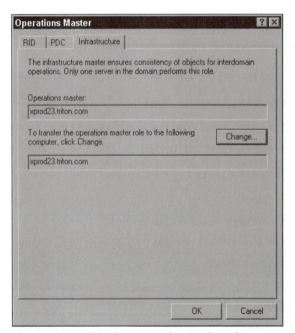

Figure 7-14: Click Change to change the role.

You can also change the Infrastructure master role by using ntdsutil. To change the Infrastructure Master role using ntdsutil, follow these steps:

1. Type Start ➪ Run, type **ntdsutil** in the dialog box and click OK.

2. Type **roles** and press Enter. Then type **connections** and press Enter.

3. Type **connect to server new_server_name**. For example, if a server is named XTRI23 and I want to transfer the Infrastructure master role to that server, I would type **connect to server XTRI23**. Press Enter.

4. Type **quit** and press Enter.

5. Type **transfer infrastructure master** and press Enter.

6. Type **quit** and press Enter. (You may have to type **quit** several times to completely exit out of ntdsutil.)

RID master

The relative ID (RID) master provides sequences of relative identifiers to domain controllers in the domain. The relative IDs are then used by the domain controllers to assign to new user, group, or computer objects. There is only one RID master in each domain. As with the Infrastructure master, you can transfer this role to another domain controller in the domain, but not to a global catalog server.

To transfer the RID master using the Active Directory Users and Computers console, follow these steps:

1. Click Start ⇨ Programs ⇨ Administrative Tools ⇨ Active Directory Users and Computers.

2. Right-click Active Directory Users and Computers and then click Connect to Domain.

3. Type the domain name or click Browse and select the domain from the list. Then click OK.

4. Right-click Active Directory Users and Computers and then click Operations Master.

5. Click the RID tab and click Change, as shown in Figure 7-15.

You can also change the RID master role by using ntdsutil. To change the RID master role using ntdsutil, follow these steps:

1. Type Start ⇨ Run and type **ntdsutil** in the dialog box and click OK.

2. Type **roles** and press Enter. Then type **connections** and press Enter.

3. Type **connect to server new_server_name**. For example, if a server is named XTRI23 and I want to transfer the RID master role to that server, I would type **connect to server XTRI23**. Press Enter.

4. Type **quit** and press Enter.

5. Type **transfer rid master** and press Enter.

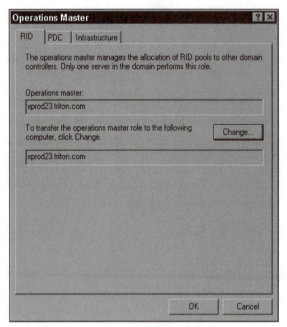

Figure 7-15: Click the Change button.

6. Type **quit** and press Enter. (You may have to type **quit** several times to completely exit out of `ntdsutil`.)

PDC Emulator

Finally, only one domain controller in an Active Directory domain can function as the PDC Emulator. The PDC Emulator acts like a primary domain controller to downlevel servers and clients (Windows NT). In mixed networks, where both Windows 2000 Server and Windows NT Server are used, the PDC Emulator role is necessary to make one of the Windows 2000 domain controllers appear as a PDC.

You can easily move the PDC Emulator role between Windows 2000 domain controllers using the Active Directory Users and Computers tool. Follow these steps:

1. Click Start ➪ Programs ➪ Administrative Tools ➪ Active Directory Users and Computers.

2. Right-click Active Directory Users and Computers and then click Connect to Domain.

3. Type the domain name or click Browse and select the domain from the list. Then click OK.

4. Right-click Active Directory Users and Computers and then click Operations Master.

5. Click the PDC tab and click Change, as shown in Figure 7-16.

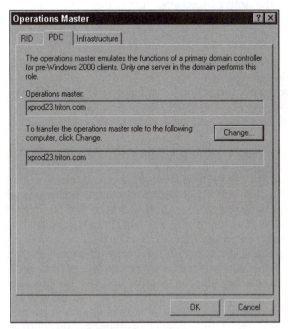

Figure 7-16: Click the Change button.

You can also change the PDC Emulator role by using `ntdsutil`. To change the PDC Emulator role using `ntdsutil`, follow these steps:

1. Type Start ⇨ Run and type **ntdsutil** in the dialog box and click OK.

2. Type **roles** and press Enter. Then type **connections** and press Enter.

3. Type **connect to server new_server_name**. For example, if a server is named XTRI23 and I want to transfer the PDC Emulator role to that server, I would type **connect to server XTRI23**. Press Enter.

4. Type **quit** and press Enter.

5. Type **transfer pdc** and press Enter.

6. Type **quit** and press Enter. (You may have to type **quit** several times to completely exit out of `ntdsutil`.)

Uninstalling the Active Directory

What! Uninstall the Active Directory? In reality, there are several reasons why you may need to uninstall the Active Directory, some being more serious than others. Fortunately, uninstalling the Active Directory is performed with a wizard and is typically not an earth-shattering task that leaves the server in shambles. For the most part, uninstalling the Active Directory is straightforward and problem free.

New Feature   If you were a former "NT Head" like me, getting used to the Windows 2000 Server role changes requires a slight learning curve. Keep in mind that you can move from member server to domain controller and vice versa without having to completely reinstall Windows 2000. The promotion or demotion occurs with the installation or removal of the Active Directory.

There are a few reasons for uninstalling the Active Directory. First, remember that each domain controller in a domain has the Active Directory installed. Those domain controllers in the domain all work as peers; there is no one domain controller that is the master for the domain. Being an Active Directory administrator, you will certainly remove the Active Directory from a domain controller from time to time. The primary reason for the uninstallation is to remove the domain controller from DC status. For example, you have a domain controller that needs to be decommissioned because of its age or hardware, or perhaps you have a domain controller that simply has some hardware problems. By uninstalling the Active Directory, you remove the domain controller from DC status, and then you can simply remove it from the network. This brings up an interesting point — why not just unplug it? Remember that the domain controllers in a domain use multimaster replication to communicate with each other. All domain controllers are aware of the existence of other domain controllers. If you simply remove the domain controller from the network, the other domain controllers believe the missing domain controller is just offline and expect it to come back online at any time. Although this may not cause you any real problems, it is better to let the other domain controllers know that you are removing a peer from service. This allows the other domain controllers to adjust their replication topology to exclude the old domain controller. This feature keeps order in the Active Directory universe, so if you want to uninstall a domain controller, do use the wizard and perform a complete uninstall.

Tip   Because all domain controllers in a domain function as peers, the removal of a domain controller does not damage the Active Directory database because each peer has an exact copy. You can uninstall old domain controllers and install new domain controllers at any time necessary.

Aside from removing a domain controller from a domain, another possible reason for uninstalling the Active Directory is the removal of a child or grandchild domain (or even the removal of the root domain if you are uninstalling the Active Directory altogether). Uninstalling a domain is easy — you simply run the uninstallation wizard on each domain controller until all of the domain controllers have been removed from the domain. When you remove the last domain controller, the wizard will ask if the domain controller "is the last DC in the domain." If it is, all Active Directory data is lost, and the domain is disconnected from its parent. Any Active Directory data you had in the domain is gone, unless you have made some plans to move those users accounts and other data to another domain. Specifically, when you remove a domain, the following happens:

✦ The domain controllers become standalone servers — the domain no longer exists.

✦ No users can logon to the domain, and all user accounts for the domain are lost.

✦ Users cannot access any domain resources that were previously provided by the Active Directory.

✦ All cryptographic keys, such as those used in a Certificate Services implementation, are deleted.

✦ Any data stored using Encrypting File System (EFS) or other cryptographic data must be unencrypted, or it becomes permanently inaccessible.

Under most circumstances, you will not be removing domains. With careful Active Directory planning, your domain structure should be able to accommodate growth and changes in the organization for several years.

Caution   Removing a domain is a serious task and one that should be planned carefully to ensure that no desirable data is lost.

As you can see, the removal of the Active Directory, whether you are simply removing a single domain controller or an entire domain/forest structure, occurs with each domain controller. Because the Active Directory is built on a domain controller peer structure, you cannot run one wizard or press one button that wipes out an entire Active Directory implementation. Instead, removal of the Active Directory occurs on a domain controller by domain controller basis.

So, how do you do it? The answer is simple. When you installed the Active Directory, you used either the Configure Your Server tool or dcpromo.exe. To uninstall the Active Directory, you can only use dcpromo.exe. This action starts the Active Directory Wizard, which helps you with the uninstallation. Use the following steps:

1. Click Start ➪ Run. Then type **dcpromo** in the dialog box and click OK.

2. The Welcome screen appears, shown in Figure 7-17. Notice that the message tells you the server is already a domain controller, and running this wizard will remove the Active Directory. After this is complete, the domain controller will become a normal member server. Click the Next button to continue.

Figure 7-17: Removal of the Active Directory will demote this DC to a member server.

3. If the domain controller you want to remove is a global catalog server, you will receive a message, shown in Figure 7-18, telling you that other global catalog servers must be available in the domain to process user logons. If you are removing a single domain controller in a domain and get this message, STOP the uninstallation and do not proceed. You need to transfer the global catalog server role to another domain controller before proceeding. If you are removing an entire domain, then you can ignore this message.

Cross-Reference
See the "Operations Master Placement" section earlier in this chapter for instructions for transferring the global catalog server role to another domain controller in the domain.

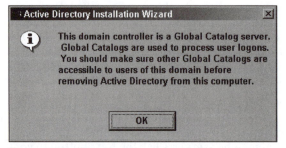

Figure 7-18: You must move the global catalog server role before proceeding.

4. The next window provides you with a single check box, as shown in Figure 7-19. If the domain controller you are uninstalling is the last domain controller in the domain, check this box. You should see a list of warnings about removing the last domain controller. If you are simply decommissioning a single domain controller in a domain, leave this check box unchecked.

Caution

Make certain you understand the ramifications of removing the last domain controller from a domain before proceeding. All untransferred data will be lost if you continue.

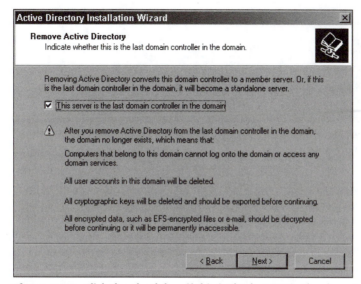

Figure 7-19: Click the check box if this is the last DC in the domain.

5. As a security precaution, the Active Directory cannot be removed without Enterprise Administrator account permissions for the forest. This window, shown in Figure 7-20, asks you to enter the user name and password of an Enterprise Admin account. You cannot proceed without a valid user name and password. Enter this information and click the Next button.

Cross-Reference

You can learn more about the Enterprise Admin group and other group and user accounts in Chapter 9.

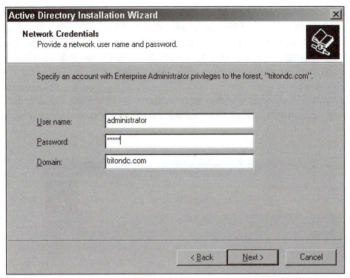

Figure 7-20: Enter a user name and password with Enterprise Admin privileges.

6. A window appears, shown in Figure 7-21, where you enter the administrator account password for the local machine. When the Active Directory is removed, you no longer use an Enterprise Admin account, but a local administrator account since the computer will become a member server. Enter and confirm the desired administrator password. Then click the Next button.

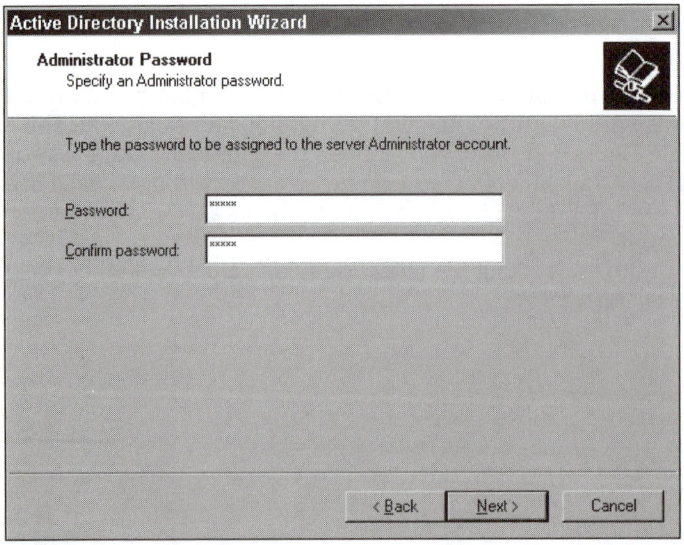

Figure 7-21: Enter and confirm an administrator account password.

7. A summary window of your choices appears. Review your choices, then click Next to begin the uninstallation. When uninstallation is complete, click the Finish button and reboot your server. When the server is rebooted, it will be a simple member server in the domain, or if you have removed the domain, the server will be a standalone server.

Summary

This chapter explored creating child and grandchild domains, creating new domains in the same forest, placing operations masters, and uninstalling the Active Directory. Due to the Active Directory installation, the installation tasks are not difficult, but they do require planning to ensure that you implement an Active Directory domain and forest structure that is right for your environment. Likewise, operations master placement is configured by default when you install the Active Directory. However, you may need to move these roles to other domain controllers using the Active Directory GUI tools or using `ntdsutil`. Either way, you should plan and examine your implementation before changing single master operations roles.

✦   ✦   ✦

Configuring Active Directory Domains and Sites

This chapter explores two implementation issues — Active Directory domains and site configuration. Once your Active Directory domains are configured, you can use the Domains and Trusts snap-in to manage the domains and trust relationships as needed. Active Directory sites define physical locations on your network. They help the Active Directory understand that a portion or portions of your network are in remote areas and that communication to those remote areas may involve slower, expensive, and possibly even unreliable bandwidth. This chapter tells you all about sites and site components and offers many step-by-step instructions to help you configure domains, sites, and related information.

 You can learn all about site and replication planning in Chapter 5.

Configuring Domains and Trusts

You create a domain by installing the first domain controller and specifying the new domain and domain name using the Active Directory Installation Wizard. Once your domains are installed, you can then use the Active Directory Domains and Trusts tool to configure the domains. In reality, you don't need to perform a lot of configuration with this tool, and many of the configuration options are a one-time thing. The following sections explore the configuration tasks and issues.

Managing a domain

The Active Directory Domains and Trusts MMC snap-in, shown in Figure 8-1, provides you with a list of all domains in your enterprise. With this snap-in, you can easily manage your domains from one simple interface.

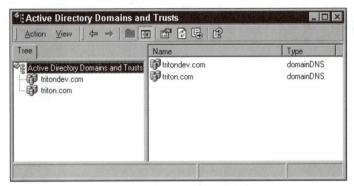

Figure 8-1: Active Directory Domains and Trusts

If you select a desired domain in the left pane, you can then choose the Action menu and select Manage. This action opens the Active Directory Users and Computers console for that domain. You can then create objects, such as user accounts, group accounts, printer objects, and so forth. Although this is an easy task, it is one I wanted to point out to you as an Active Directory administrator. When you need to configure objects in multiple domains, you can choose to open a Users and Computers console and to manually load the various domains into one console, or you can use the Domains and Trusts console to easily access them all.

Changing from mixed to native mode

When you install an Active Directory domain, it is installed in mixed mode by default. Mixed mode is maintained for backward compatibility with Windows NT. Suppose you have an existing Windows NT domain, and you decide to upgrade that domain to Windows 2000. During the upgrade process, you begin with the PDC. Once the PDC has been upgraded, you can then move to your BDCs and then to your client computers as desired. Mixed mode enables you to take your time with the conversion because it permits Windows NT BDCs to function within the new Active Directory domain. This is because the upgraded PDC (now a Windows 2000 domain controller) still acts as PDC through the PDC Emulator FSMO role. The PDC Emulator handles all password and replication changes for BDCs. In essence, the BDCs believe the new Windows 2000 domain controller is still a PDC—even though PDCs do not technically exist in Windows 2000 domains.

You can learn more about flexible single master operation (FSMO) roles in Chapter 3.

Windows 2000 mixed mode is a great design because you can upgrade your PDC and spend some time testing and playing around with the upgrade before ever moving to your backup domain controllers. In other words, your domain doesn't go down while you are upgrading. In fact, your domain can remain in mixed mode as long as you want, but there are some drawbacks:

✦ Windows 2000 domain controllers must support legacy services in order to support the NT BDCs.

✦ You can't use Universal groups, Domain Local groups, or nested groups. In mixed mode, the Universal group option is not available when you configure and create groups (see Chapter 9).

✦ If you upgrade only the PDC and you do not upgrade any other BDCs or install new, additional domain controllers for the domain, then you do not have any inherent fault tolerance for your domain or Active Directory database for that domain.

Mixed mode is a very important function of Windows 2000, but it is designed to support Windows NT BDCs only until you upgrade them to Windows 2000. Although you can remain in mixed mode indefinitely, you should move to native mode as soon as possible to get the most from your Windows 2000 domain. Native mode simply means that all domain controllers are Windows 2000 domain controllers, and Windows NT BDCs are not supported.

Native mode refers to domain controllers. After the change to native mode, down-level clients can still log on to access a Windows 2000 domain. Native mode simply means that NT 4.0 BDCs are no longer supported. You can, however, still use Windows NT member servers—just not BDCs.

Once you change to native mode, your domain:

✦ Will not support NT BDCs.

✦ Can use Universal, Domain Local, and nested groups.

✦ Removes the Netlogon Replication service and replaces it with File Replication Service (FRS). (Netlogon Replication is supplied for backward compatibility and is not needed in a pure Windows 2000 domain.)

✦ Will use true multimaster replication. In other words, you can make database changes at any domain controller.

So, the overall point is mixed mode is important to your deployment. Use mixed mode as long as necessary, but move to native mode as soon as possible to take full advantage of all Windows 2000 has to offer.

Caution Here's an important point to remember. The change from mixed mode to native mode is one-way. You cannot change back to mixed mode once you have changed to native mode. This means that the domain will never be able to support any Windows NT BDCs again. Thus, make certain you are ready for the move to native mode before proceeding.

Changing to native mode is very easy. In fact, it is just the click of a single button. To change a domain to native mode, follow these steps:

1. Click Start ➪ Programs ➪ Administrative Tools ➪ Active Directory Domains and Trusts.

2. Select the domain that you want to move to native mode, and then click Action ➪ Properties.

3. On the General tab, you see a Change Mode button in the lower half of the window, as shown in Figure 8-2. To change the mode, click the Change Mode button. Note the warning that the change to native mode cannot be reversed. Click the Yes button to continue.

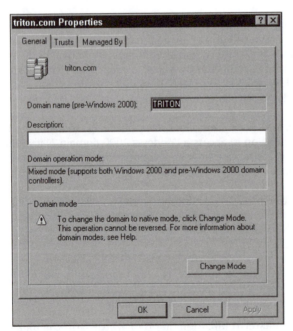

Figure 8-2: Change to native mode

4. The domain is changed and the General tab now displays native mode, as shown in Figure 8-3.

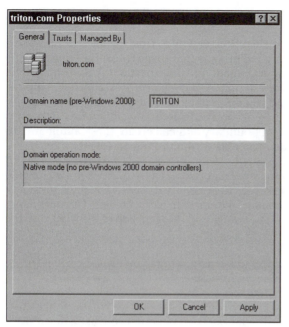

Figure 8-3: Native mode

Trust relationships

If you have spent any time in a complex Windows NT environment with many domains, you know how complicated trust relationships can be. In fact, configuring and managing trust relationships were and still are a major problem for administrators in NT networks. Thank goodness, Windows 2000 leaves all of that behind because automatic transitive trust relationships between domains in a forest are created.

Note I talked about trust relationships in Chapter 5, where you learned about planning trusts, sites, and replication.

Remember that a trust relationship is simply a method to enable users in one domain to access resources in another domain. This was not an easy configuration in Windows NT, but in Windows 2000, all domains in a forest have automatic, transitive trust relationships configured when the domains are installed. Transitive trust relationships are two-way relationships. In NT, you might have a situation where Domain A trusts Domain B, but Domain B does not trust Domain A, but does trust Domain C, which trusts Domain A but not Domain B. In environments with many domains, this process could become extremely confusing and difficult to manage. Transitive trusts are always two-way; if Domain A trusts Domain B, then Domain B trusts Domain A. In addition, transitive trusts are, well, transitive. This means that if Domain A trusts Domain B and Domain B trusts Domain C, then Domain A also trusts Domain C (and, in reality, Domain C also trusts Domain A because of the two-way relationship). The good news is that these transitive trusts are *automatically* configured in a forest or domain tree. As a part of the domain installation, the trust relationship for the new domain is *automatically* established with the existing domains in the forest — and you don't have to do anything! This process works because the Active Directory tree or forest is essentially a boundary. The Active Directory understands the forest boundary and can create these automatic transitive trust relationships between domains within the tree or forest.

However, you cannot create transitive trusts between two forests or two downlevel NT domains. Nevertheless, you can create one-way trust relationships to connect two Active Directory forests or to connect a domain to a downlevel NT domain. These one-way trust relationships *must* be configured on each side of the trust, and they are not transitive.

Windows 2000 also supports cross-link trusts, where you bridge certain trust relationships in the forest to increase performance.

So, the Active Directory automatically configures transitive trusts within the tree or forest, but you can also establish one-way trusts in order to trust a downlevel NT domain or to connect two forests. In Active Directory Domains and Trusts, select the desired domain and then click Action ➭ Properties. Click the Trusts tab, shown in Figure 8-4.

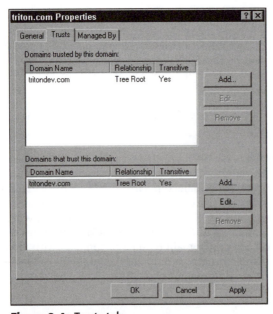

Figure 8-4: Trusts tab

You can see in Figure 8-4 that there are two domain trees in this forest, tritondev. com trusts and is trusted by triton.com. The two domain trees are shown as a Tree Root relationship and are connected together with a transitive trust. If a child domain existed, such as prod.triton.com, that domain would be shown as a child relationship and have a transitive trust as well.

If you select a desired trust relationship, you can click the Edit button to learn more about it. As you can see in Figure 8-5, this tab gives you information about the transitive trust and provides you with a Verify button. You will be prompted to provide an enterprise administrative user name and password. The Verify option is a good way to troubleshoot suspected trust relationship problems.

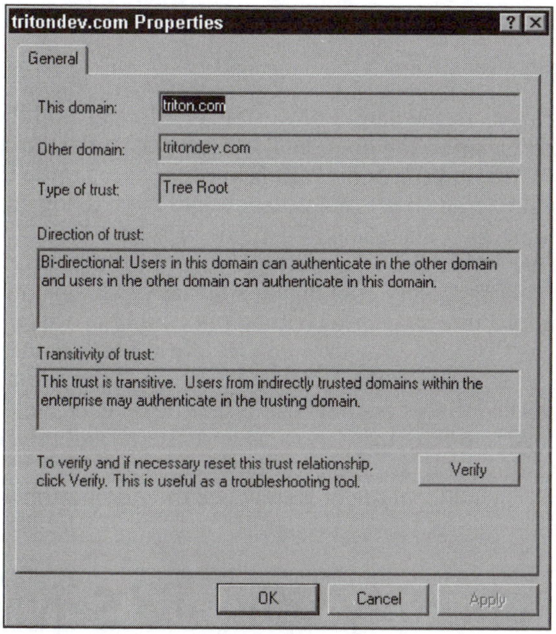

tritondev.com Properties ? ✕

General

This domain: triton.com

Other domain: tritondev.com

Type of trust: Tree Root

Direction of trust:

Bi-directional: Users in this domain can authenticate in the other domain and users in the other domain can authenticate in this domain.

Transitivity of trust:

This trust is transitive. Users from indirectly trusted domains within the enterprise may authenticate in the trusting domain.

To verify and if necessary reset this trust relationship, click Verify. This is useful as a troubleshooting tool.   Verify

OK   Cancel   Apply

Figure 8-5: Trust properties

In order to create a one-way trust relationship, click the Add button on the Trusts tab. A dialog box appears, shown in Figure 8-6. Enter the name of the trusted (or trusting) domain, enter an appropriate password, and click OK.

You must also configure the trust relationship on the other side of the trust. In other words, one domain must be the trusting domain while the other is the trusted domain. Once you have configured the trust, it appears on the Trusts tab and is displayed as a nontransitive trust.

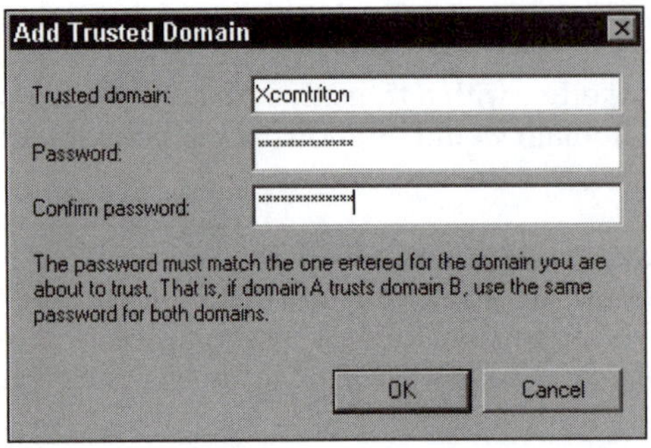

Figure 8-6: Add Trusted Domain dialog box

Adding UPN suffixes

User principal name (UPN) suffixes are the names of the current domain and the root domain. Users use UPNs to log on to the domain. For example, janderson@triton.com combines the user name and the domain UPN in order to log on to the domain. However, in more complex tree structures, a user might have to log on as janderson@prod.namerica.triton.com. This longer DNS name may be difficult for some users to remember in order to logon. You can simplify this UPN using the Active Directory Domains and Trusts tool by creating an alternative UPN name so that logons are easier. For example, prod.namerica.triton.com could have an alternate suffix of simply "triton.com." This way, the user can simply logon to janderson@triton.com and does not have to be aware of the full DNS structure of the actual domain — which makes life easier for users and makes for less headaches for administrators. In the console, select Active Directory Domains and Trusts, and then click Action ⇨ Properties. The UPN Suffixes tab appears, as shown in Figure 8-7. To add an alternative UPN suffix, just type the suffix in the box and click the Add button.

Configuring Active Directory Sites and Services

A site, in terms of the Active Directory, defines your physical network and helps establish boundaries within the Active Directory. In the Active Directory, sites are not a part of the DNS namespace, but they are maintained for traffic and replication flow purposes. The Active Directory assumes that within your sites connectivity is as fast and inexpensive as a typical LAN, and it assumes that bandwidth is readily available and reliable. The Active Directory also assumes that connectivity between sites is more costly, slower, and possibly unreliable. The Active Directory uses the information you enter with the Active Directory Sites and Services tool to configure replication and control traffic flow. Specifically, site definitions help control user logon traffic, service request traffic, and replication traffic. The point is to keep as much traffic as possible within the site, not traveling over expensive WAN links to remote sites.

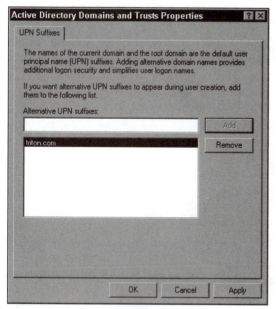

Figure 8-7: UPN Suffixes tab

 Note Don't confuse sites and domains. A site can contain several domains, or a single domain can span multiple sites.

As a part of your Active Directory implementation process, you'll need to define your sites and the communication links that enable them to communicate. The following sections explore site and related site component configuration.

Creating a new site

When you install the Active Directory, a default site called Default-First-Site-Name is created. You can see it in the Active Directory Sites and Services console, shown in Figure 8-8.

To change the name of Default-First-Site-Name, just right-click the site icon in the left console and click Rename. Then type a new name for the first site.

To create a new site(s), follow these steps:

1. Click Start ➪ Programs ➪ Administrative Tools ➪ Active Directory Sites and Services.

2. Select the Sites container in the left pane, and then click Action ➪ New Site.

3. In the New Object — Site window that appears, shown in Figure 8-9, enter a name for the new site and select a site link object. (You can select the DEFAULTIPSITELINK option for now.) Click the OK button.

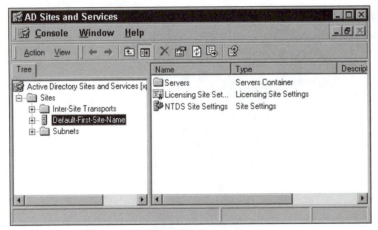

Figure 8-8: Default-First-Site-Name

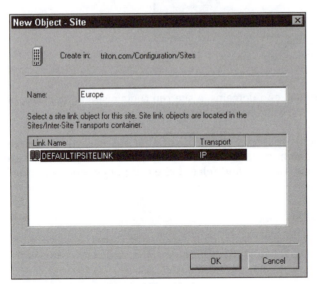

Figure 8-9: New Object — Site window

4. A message appears, shown in Figure 8-10, telling you the additional actions you need to take to complete the site configuration. Click OK.

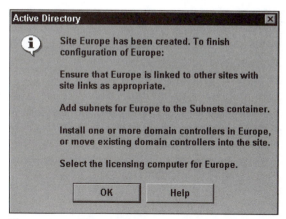

Figure 8-10: Site message

 Note   You can learn about the items listed in Figure 8-10 later in this chapter.

5. The new site now appears in the console.

Defining a site subnet

Once you create a site object, you need to define one or more subnets for the site. The Active Directory uses this information for replication and traffic flow processes, so you are essentially telling the Active Directory which IP subnets belong to which site.

To define a subnet(s) for a site, follow these steps:

1. In Active Directory Sites and Services, expand the Sites container and select the Subnets container.

2. Click Action ➪ New Subnet. The New Object — Subnet window appears, as shown in Figure 8-11. Enter the subnet and the mask for the subnet. The console automatically translates this information in a subnet name in the form of network/bits-masked. Select the site to which this subnet physically belongs, and then click the OK button.

 Note   Keep in mind that the subnet and mask information you enter should accurately reflect the subnet(s) physically existing in the site. The Active Directory uses this information for network communication purposes.

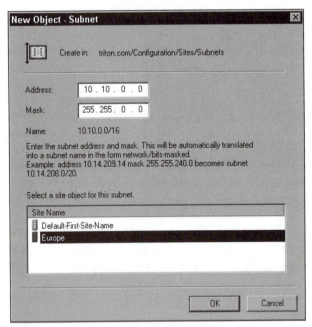

Figure 8-11: New Object—Subnet window

Moving domain controllers into a site

A site is a physical representation not directly associated with domains. However, each site needs one or more domain controllers. For example, suppose that one domain stretches from New York to Mexico City. You decide to implement a New York site and a Mexico City site. Technically, all domain controllers could reside in New York, but in a site configuration, Mexico City needs domain controllers for logon and service fulfillment to client computers so that all logon and service requests do not have to travel across a WAN link to New York. So, once you create a new site, you need either to install domain controllers into that site or to move existing domain controllers into the site.

To move a domain controller into a different site, simply locate the desired domain controller in the Sites and Services console, right-click the server icon, and click Move. In the window that appears, select the site that should contain the domain controller and then click OK.

Selecting a licensing computer for a site

Each Active Directory site must have a licensing computer that handles licenses for the site. When you create a site, the Active Directory will automatically assign a computer the task of licensing, or when you add a domain controller to the site, it will become the default licensing computer. The licensing computer for the site should actually reside within the site, but it does not have to be a domain controller. To change the licensing computer for a site, follow these steps:

1. In Active Directory Sites and Services, expand the Sites container and select the desired site. The Licensing Site Settings object appears in the right pane, as shown in Figure 8-12.

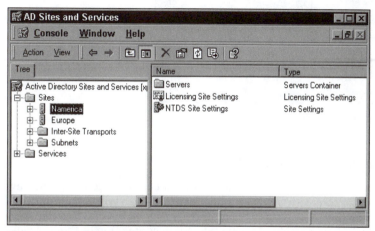

Figure 8-12: Licensing Site Settings object

2. Select Licensing Site Settings in the right console, and then click Action ⇨ Properties.

3. On the Licensing Settings tab, shown in Figure 8-13, you see the current licensing computer for the site. To change the licensing computer, click the Change button.

4. In the list that appears, select the desired computer and click OK.

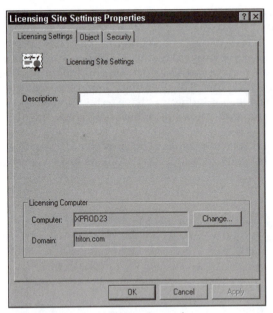

Figure 8-13: Licensing Settings tab

Configuring site links

Within your environment, your sites are connected to each other through some form of WAN connectivity. This connectivity enables your computers in different sites to communicate with each other. This may include fast, available bandwidth, such as a T3 link, or a simple dial-up 56 Kbps connection to the Internet. When you define various sites within the Active Directory Sites and Services tool, you enable the Knowledge Consistency Checker (KCC) and other Active Directory services to know that your enterprise contains remote sites. The KCC also knows that those sites are connected by WAN communication links or site links. When you define information about those site links, then the Active Directory can make decisions about how to best use the bandwidth available.

Cross-Reference   You can learn more about the KCC and site replication topology in Chapter 13.

Once you create sites in the Active Directory Sites and Services console, you then need to create site links to connect them together. The site links you create in this console should best define the type of connectivity you actually have between your sites. Specifically, you use the Active Directory Sites and Services tool to create site links and then define schedules and costs for those links. The Active Directory then uses this information to configure replication between the sites. Without site links, the Active Directory cannot replicate data between sites, so it is very important that you configure site links effectively for your environment.

Note The Active Directory can use RPC/IP (Remote Procedure Calls over Internet Protocol) or SMTP (Simple Mail Transport Protocol) to send replication data between sites. SMTP can be used for low-bandwidth links or links that use the Internet. You can learn more about site link protocol usage in Chapter 13.

Caution Once again, you must manually configure site links in order for the Active Directory to configure site replication. The Active Directory *cannot* automatically generate site links for you.

To create a site link, follow these steps:

1. In Active Directory Sites and Services, expand the Sites container in the left pane, expand the Inter-Site Transports container, and then select either IP or SMTP, depending on the type of inter-site transport you want to use.

2. Click Action ➪ New Site Link.

3. The New Object — Site Link window appears, as shown in Figure 8-14. Select the sites that are connected by this link and then click the Add button to move them to the "Sites in this site link" dialog box. For example, in Figure 8-14, you see that two sites are connected together by this link, Namerica and Samerica. Click OK when you are done.

Tip Because a site link connects two sites, you must have at least two sites in the "Sites in this site link" dialog box.

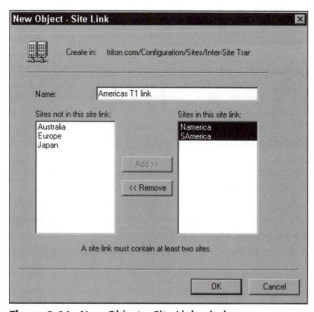

Figure 8-14: New Object — Site Link window

Configuring replication cost/frequency

Once you have created the site link, you can configure two options that help the Active Directory determine how replication traffic should be sent over the site link—cost and schedule. The cost of a site link is a logical cost that you and the Active Directory use to determine how links should be used. For example, suppose you have two sites—Namerica and Samerica. You have a T1 link connecting the two sites, and you also have a 56 Kbps Internet connection as a backup. Obviously, you want all traffic to use the T1 link as long as it is available. If the T1 link becomes unavailable, then the 56 Kbps connection can be used. To grasp the concept of cost, you have to think in terms of bandwidth expense. For example, a T1 link would have a much lower bandwidth expense than would a 56 Kbps connection because a T1 link has much more bandwidth available that can be used by traffic. So, to ensure that the Active Directory always favors the T1 link over the 56 Kbps connection, you could assign a cost of "10" to the T1 link and a cost of "100" to the 56 Kbps connection. The Active Directory will always use the lower cost link (which is the T1) over the high cost link (which is the 56 Kbps connection).

> **Tip**   Always remember, high bandwidth equals low cost—low bandwidth equals high cost. The Active Directory will always use lower cost links first.

You can additionally consider the cost option in terms of the actual expense, availability, and so forth. For example, if you have two site links that are very similar in bandwidth, you can further define their Active Directory cost based on physical expense, how often the links are available for use, and so forth. The end result should be that the Active Directory uses the lowest cost links before using more expensive links. You define this information, so consider all of the possible factors before assigning site link costs.

> **Tip**   Your method for defining site link costs should be consistent throughout the enterprise. In other words, a site link cost between two sites should be based on the same criteria as a site link cost between two other sites. This ensures consistency in how the Active Directory uses cost information in your network. Consider creating a network plan for cost determination so that all administrators judge site link costs based on the same criteria.

To configure a site link's cost, follow these steps:

1. In Active Directory Sites and Services, expand the Sites container and then expand the Inter-Site Transports container.

2. Select either the IP or SMTP container that contains the desired site link. The site link(s) for the container appear in the right pane. Select the desired site link and then click Action ➪ Properties.

3. On the site link's properties General tab, shown in Figure 8-15, enter a desired cost for the site link in the Cost dialog box and then click OK.

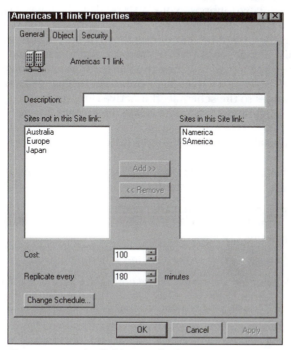

Figure 8-15: Site link General tab

Just below the Cost dialog box in Figure 8-15, you also see a "Replicate every" dialog box. This number tells the Active Directory how often, in minutes, to replicate data. The default is 180 minutes, or every 3 hours. You can change this default behavior so that replication occurs more frequently or less frequently, depending on your needs. Once again, you are faced with the trade-off between replication latency and your available bandwidth. Often, administrators want a "magic" number for the replication frequency, but the frequency of replication depends on the site link bandwidth, physical cost, availability of the connection, and the urgency of the need of data replication in your network. At the most fundamental level, you simply have to take a look at what you have and what you want and consider how to make the two meet in the middle as best you can.

Configuring the site link schedule

By default, the Active Directory configures the site link so that replication is always available for use. However, this may not be the best configuration, depending on the link and the bandwidth available. Suppose your WAN tends to be heavily saturated during the hours of 10:00 a.m. and 3:00 p.m. You can configure the replication schedule so that replication traffic cannot be sent during those hours. Of course, how you should schedule your site link depends on many factors, and you may have to experiment with the schedule some to find the correct balance for your organization. Fortunately, the schedule is *very* easy to configure and can be changed at any time. Whenever you make changes to the schedule, the Active Directory automatically adjusts its replication configuration to accommodate the change.

To change a site link's availability schedule, follow these steps:

1. In Active Directory Sites and Services, expand the Sites container, and then expand the Inter-Site Transports container.

2. Select either the IP or SMTP container that contains the desired site link. The site link(s) for the container appear in the right pane. Select the desired site link and then click Action ➪ Properties.

3. On the site link's General tab, click the Change Schedule button.

4. You see a Schedule window with grids representing the hour of each day. When the grid block is blue, that hour is available for replication. When the grid block is white, the hour is not available for replication. Use the radio buttons to adjust the schedule to meet your needs. As you can see in Figure 8-16, replication is available every hour of the week except on Mondays and Tuesdays between 10:00 a.m. and 3:00 p.m.

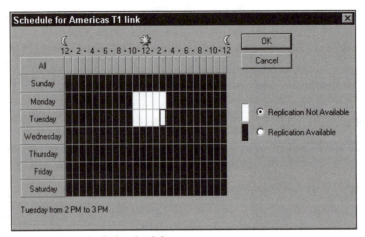

Figure 8-16: Site link schedule

Assigning a bridgehead server

Within each site, the Active Directory automatically configures a domain controller to be a bridgehead server. The bridgehead server sends and receives replication data from remote sites. In other words, all replication traffic in and out of a particular site must flow through the bridgehead server in order for replication data to reach remote sites. The bridgehead server receives replication data and makes certain it is replicated throughout the site. The bridgehead server also sends replication data to bridgehead servers at other sites. Although the Active Directory automatically assigns the bridgehead server role to a domain controller in a site, you may want to change this default configuration so that the role of bridgehead server is placed on the domain controller that has the best system resources (CPU, RAM, and so on) to handle the extra load.

You can assign the role of bridgehead server to several domain controllers if you like, but only one bridgehead server is used at a time. If the primary bridgehead server should go offline, then the next bridgehead server is selected. This provides you with fault tolerance for the bridgehead server role. However, if you do not specify any additional bridgehead servers, the Active Directory will automatically select one for you should the primary bridgehead server fail. If you select it, however, you can determine which domain controller will be the next bridgehead server instead of relying on the Active Directory's random selection.

Tip If your site uses a firewall, your proxy server must be designated as the bridgehead server for the replication traffic to flow through the firewall.

To assign the bridgehead server role to a desired domain controller, follow these steps:

1. In Active Directory Sites and Services, expand the Sites container in the left pane and then expand the desired site. Select the Servers container. The site's servers appear in the right pane.

2. Select the desired server in the left pane and then click Action ⇨ Properties.

3. On the Server tab, shown in Figure 8-17, select the inter-site transport for which the server will function as the bridgehead server (IP, SMTP, or both) and then click the Add button to move the transport to the "This server is a preferred bridgehead server for the following transports" dialog box. Click OK when you're done.

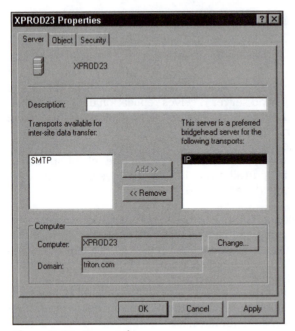

Figure 8-17: Server tab

Configuring site link bridges

Site link bridges create transitive connections between site links that use the same transport protocol. For example, suppose that you have a site link between Dallas and London and a site link between London and Sydney. Both site links use the IP transport. The Active Directory automatically configures a site link bridge between Dallas and Sydney. This bridge is transitive because Dallas and Sydney are not directly connected, but are connected through the London site link bridge. If all of your site links use a common transport, such as IP, you do not have to configure any site link bridges because the Active Directory automatically creates them for you. However, if your network is not fully routed, then you can turn off this automatic bridging feature and configure site link bridges yourself.

Tip   Site link bridge cost is automatically configured by the Active Directory by adding the cost of the two site links that form the bridge. For example, if one site link has a cost of 5 and the second has a cost of 10, then the site link bridge cost is 15. This ensures that that site link bridges always have a higher cost over the primary site links.

If your network is not fully routed, follow these steps to turn off the automatic transitive feature of site link bridges for the Active Directory:

1. In Active Directory Sites and Services, expand the Sites container, expand the Inter-Site Transports container, and then select the desired transport.

2. Click Action ⇨ Properties.

3. On the General tab, shown in Figure 8-18, clear the "Bridge all site links" check box and then click the OK button.

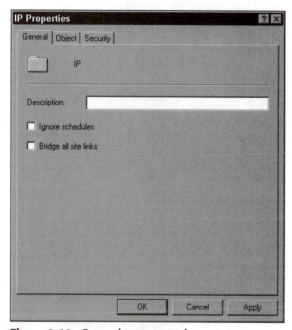

Figure 8-18: General transport tab

To manually configure a site link bridge, follow these steps:

1. In Active Directory Sites and Services, expand the Sites container, expand the Inter-Site Transports container, and then select the desired transport.

2. Click Action ⇨ New Site Link Bridge.

3. The New Object — Site Link Bridge window appears, as shown in Figure 8-19. A list of the current site links appears in the left dialog box. Select the site links you want to bridge and use the Add button to move them to the "Site links in this site link bridge" dialog box. Click OK when you are done.

Tip   You must have at least two site links to create a site link bridge.

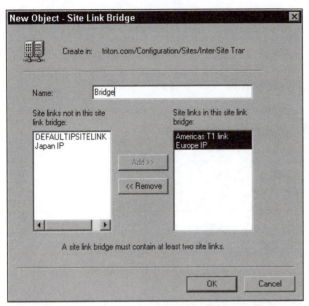

Figure 8-19: New Object—Site Link Bridge window

Summary

This chapter explored the actual configuration and management of Active Directory domains and trusts as well as sites and related site components. You use the Active Directory Domains and Trusts tool to manage various domains in your network, change the domain mode, or configure one-way trust relationships. The Active Directory Sites and Services tool enables you to configure Active Directory sites and related site components, such as site links and site link bridges. Using these two consoles, you can easily administer and configure these components, yet you should always carefully plan before using these tools to configure your enterprise.

✦   ✦   ✦

Setting Up Users, Groups, and Computers

✦ ✦ ✦ ✦

In This Chapter

Creating and managing user accounts

Creating and managing group accounts

Examining computer accounts

✦ ✦ ✦ ✦

One of your major administrative tasks is the creation and management of user, group, and computer accounts. In a Windows 2000 network, all creation and management of user, group, and computer accounts is performed in the Active Directory Users and Computers MMC snap-in. You'll spend a lot of time working with this tool in an Active Directory network, and this chapter shows you how to create and manage users, groups, and computers in your network. You'll find a lot of information in this chapter explaining Windows 2000's perspective of users, groups, and computers, and hopefully you'll learn plenty of tips and tricks that will help you along the way.

Creating and Managing User Accounts

At its core, the purpose of a user account is to allow a certain person to log on to a computer or a network. The user account enables the user to enter a user name and password to prove the user's identity. User accounts give users access to network resources and are used to determine group membership and resource access rights on a network. In a nutshell, a user account is designed to authenticate a user. In Windows 2000 networks, users are authenticated both at the local machine and by a domain controller.

While we're on the topic of authentication, now is a good time to point out that Windows 2000 supports three different authentication protocols. First, the primary authentication protocol in Windows 2000 is the Kerberos V5 security protocol. Kerberos is an Internet standard authentication protocol, and it provides much faster service and more powerful security features than NTLM, the authentication protocol in Windows NT, does. Kerberos V5 is the default protocol among Windows computers (Server and Professional) within an Active Directory forest. Second, Windows 2000 supports Windows NT LAN Manager (NTLM) for backward compatibility. With NTLM, downlevel clients and servers, such as NT and 9x, can log on to a Windows 2000 Server.

Note   NTLM is available only when a domain is operating in mixed mode — not native mode. You can learn more about native and mixed modes in Chapter 8.

Finally, Windows 2000 also supports Secure Sockets Layer/Transport Layer Security (SSL/TLS), which is a protocol used to authenticate Web clients to Web servers. Windows 2000 can use SSL/TLS to authenticate users on the Internet on a Windows 2000 Server, and this protocol is used in conjunction with Windows 2000's certificate services.

For our discussion, I'll focus on Kerberos V5 since Kerberos is the new technology and the one natively used by Windows 2000 computers. Kerberos brings a lot of security features to the Windows 2000 table, but one of the best features is the single logon for user accounts. Single logon simply means that a user need only be authenticated one time by a domain controller in order to gain access to network-wide resources (assuming proper permissions are in place).

Consider this Kerberos authentication process for logging onto a domain. At a Windows 2000 computer, the user presses Ctrl+Alt+Del and enters a user name, password, and domain name. The local Windows 2000 computer takes this information and converts the user's password into an encryption key so that timestamp information for the logon can be processed. The computer then sends the user name and encrypted timestamp information to a domain controller. The domain controller unencrypts the password and checks the Active Directory for the validity of the user name and password. If the user name and password are valid against the now encrypted timestamp, the domain controller makes two Kerberos V5 tickets using the user's password as an encryption key and then sends the two tickets back to the local computer where the user initiated the logon attempt. The two tickets are the following:

✦ **Logon Session Key** — This ticket contains the permissions that enable the user to have a logon session in the domain.

✦ **Ticket-Granting Ticket** — This ticket is used to obtain additional access tickets so the user can access resources on the network.

This entire process is very secure, very fast, and completely invisible to the user. Figure 9-1 gives you a graphical representation of this process.

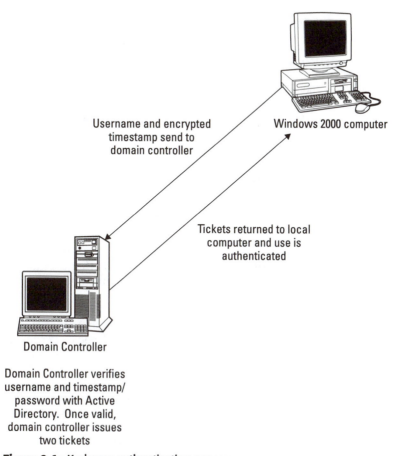

Username and encrypted
timestamp send to
domain controller

Windows 2000 computer

Tickets returned to local
computer and use is
authenticated

Domain Controller

Domain Controller verifies
username and timestamp/
password with Active
Directory. Once valid,
domain controller issues
two tickets

Figure 9-1: Kerberos authentication process

Concerning access to network resources, the process works in much the same way. If the user attempts to access a network resource, the local Windows 2000 computer sends a Kerberos Ticket-Granting Ticket to a domain controller along with the user's name, timestamp, and the resource the user wants to access. The domain controller then processes this information and sends a service request session key to the Windows 2000 computer. The computer then sends the session key to the server that holds the resource for which the user wants access. The server checks the session key against the access control list for the resource to see if the user has permission to access the resource. If the user does, access is granted. As you can imagine, all of this is invisible and seems very fast (thank goodness) to users. But this model provides a highly secure single sign-on or user authentication method both on the domain and for domain resources.

Creating user accounts

You create user accounts using the Active Directory Users and Computers MMC snap-in. Account creation is a very easy and fast process, but before walking you through the steps, I should mention a few related items. First, there are two built-in accounts in Windows 2000 computers — administrator and guest. The administrator account gives the user full rights to the local machine and, on a domain controller, rights to administer the domain. The administrator account is very powerful and one that should be carefully protected with a complex password. You can also rename the administrator account to help hide it, but you *cannot* delete it or remove it from the Administrators Local group. The guest account is also built-in, although it is disabled by default. You can enable it, however, and use the guest account for limited network access and resource permission. The guest account does not require the use of a password, and the administrator account password is created upon installation of Windows 2000.

Next, be aware of the user account creation rules. User account names can be from one to twenty characters in length and must be unique to all other user names on the network. Also, you can use any combination of letters, numbers, and symbols, except "/\{};:|=,+*?<>

Tip   Most networks employ the use of standardized user names that generally contain a combination of the user's first and last name or an employee ID of some kind. This is, of course, not required, but is something you may want to consider to reduce administrative headaches.

Concerning passwords, you as the administrator can assign passwords, or you can assign a default password and then have your users change it. The second option is most popular because handling all user passwords can be a serious administrative headache. You may, however, want to require certain password lengths or passwords that combine letters and numbers. Keep in mind that longer and more complex passwords are much more difficult to breach than simple passwords.

With all that said, open the Users and Computers tool by clicking Start ➪ Programs ➪ Administrative Tools ➪ Active Directory Users and Computers, as shown in Figure 9-2.

Notice there is a default Users container in the left console pane. This is the default storage location for user accounts, but you can move and create them in any desired location, such as in various OUs (which you will probably want to do in larger environments).

Cross-Reference   If you are not familiar with the Microsoft Management Console, see Appendix B for a tutorial.

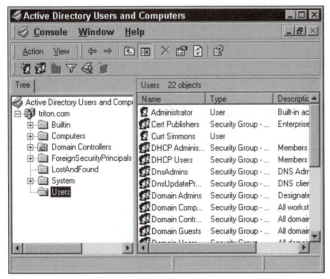

Figure 9-2: Active Directory Users and Computers

To create a user account, follow these steps:

1. Select the Users container or the OU or container where you want to create a new user account. Click Action ➪ New ➪ User. The New Object — User window appears, as shown in Figure 9-3.

Figure 9-3: New Object — User window

2. Enter the user's name and desired logon name in the appropriate dialog boxes. Notice that the downlevel logon name is automatically displayed. When the information is entered, click the Next button.

3. Enter and confirm the user's password in the provided dialog boxes, shown in Figure 9-4. You also have four check box options, which are as follows:

- User must change password at next logon—The user logs on with a default password, but then is forced to change it.

- User cannot change password—This option prevents the user from creating a new password or altering the existing one.

- Password never expires—This option does not put a time restriction on the life of the password.

- Account is disabled—This feature locks the account so it cannot be used to logon to the network.

Tip

You don't have to enter a password. In other words, you can use a blank password and require the user to create a new one at the next logon.

Make your desired selections and then click the Next button.

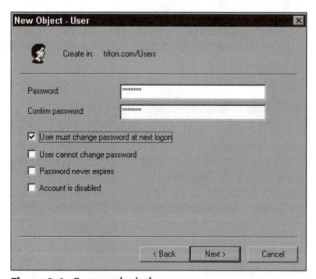

Figure 9-4: Password window

4. A summary window appears. Review your settings and click the Finish button. The new user account now appears in the desired container or OU and is ready for use.

Creating Bulk Accounts

You can easily create new user accounts with the Active Directory Users and Computers tool. But what if you need to create one thousand of them, or what if you need to import a bunch of accounts? Windows 2000 provides two command-line utilities (which are automatically installed on Windows 2000 Server) for this purpose. The two utilities can create information in either comma-delimited or comma-separated value text formats.

The first utility is Comma Separated Value (CSVDE), which you can use to add objects to the Active Directory using a text file that can be imported to the Active Directory. However, you can only create accounts with CSVDE—not delete or change them.

The second utility is Lightweight Directory Access Protocol Interchange Format (LDIFDE), which enables to you to create, delete, and manage bulk import accounts.

To learn more about either utility, just type **CSVDE** or **LDIFDE** at the command prompt and press enter.

Configuring user account properties

Once you create a user account, you can further configure the account by accessing its properties sheets. You can access the properties sheets by selecting the user account icon in the right console window and then clicking Action ⇨ Properties, or you can just right-click the user account icon in the right console pane and click Properties. Either way, the user account's properties sheet, which contains a number of important tabs, appears. The following sections explore the configuration options on each tab.

General

The General tab, shown in Figure 9-5, provides you a place to enter additional information about the user. You can enter a description, office location, telephone numbers, e-mail address, and even Web pages. For telephone and Web pages, you can make a desired entry, but you can also click the More button to enter additional telephone numbers and Web pages.

Caution

As you are configuring the General tab, it is important to remember that Active Directory users can view this information. Therefore, make sure you do not enter any data that should not be made public.

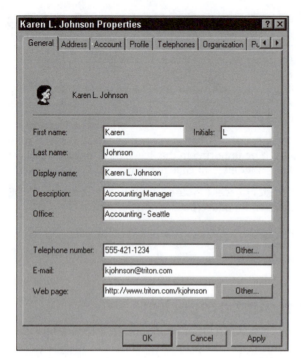

Figure 9-5: General tab

Address

The Address tab, shown in Figure 9-6, is similar to the General tab in that it simply provides you a place to put address information about the user. You can enter a physical address on this tab. As with the General tab, it is important to remember that Active Directory users can view any information you input here. As a result, be certain that you do not enter information that should not be made public.

Account

The Account tab, shown in Figure 9-7, provides you a place to configure a number of account options. This is an important tab, and we'll consider each part of it.

First, at the top of the tab you see the User logon name section, which contains the user's logon name and the automatic downlevel logon name. If you need to change the user account logon name, make the change in the dialog box provided. Notice that any changes made are automatically made to the downlevel name as well.

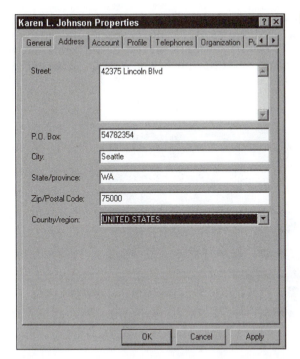

Figure 9-6: Address tab

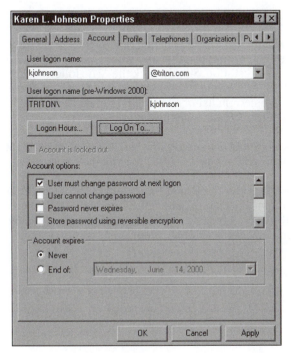

Figure 9-7: Account tab

Next, you see two buttons. First, the Logon Hours button opens the Logon Hours window for the user, as shown in Figure 9-8. By default, the user is permitted to log on to the network at all hours. However, you can select the desired grids and click the Logon Denied button to change this default behavior. As you can see in Figure 9-8, this user can log on 24 hours a day Monday–Saturday, but is not permitted to log on Sundays.

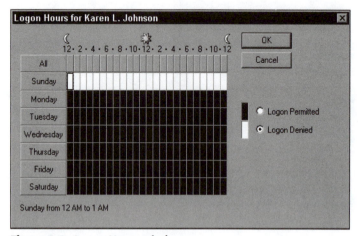

Figure 9-8: Logon Hours window

Next, if you click the Log On To button on the Account tab, the Logon Workstations window appears, as shown in Figure 9-9. Use this dialog box to enter workstation restrictions for the user. For example, suppose that you want a particular user to be able to log on only to a certain workstation. Simply click the "The following computers" radio button, then the NetBIOS name of the computer, and then click the Add button. If the user can log on to a certain list of computers, repeat the process. You can use the Edit and Remove buttons to manage the list.

Note   Logon Workstations uses the NetBIOS protocol, so when you enter the computer name, use the NetBIOS name and not the full DNS name for the computer.

Next, on the Account tab directly under the Logon Hours and Log On To buttons, you see an "Account is locked out" check box (which is grayed out). If the account becomes locked, such as in the case of too many failed logon attempts, this check box will be selected. To unlock the user's account, simply access this tab and clear the check box.

Figure 9-9: Logon Workstations window

In the middle of the Account tab window, you see a check box list where you can select several different account options. Some of these were made available to you when you first created the user account, but you can make additional configurations here or make changes as necessary. The following list explains each check box option:

✦ **User must change password at next logon** — When this option is selected, the user is required to create a new password for the account at the next logon attempt.

✦ **User cannot change password** — When this option is selected, the user cannot change the default password.

✦ **Password never expires** — When this option is selected, the password has no timestamp and will never expire.

✦ **Store password using reversible encryption** — When this option is selected, reversible encryption is used to store the password. This is an additional security feature primarily designed to support Apple computers, so use this reversible encryption option if the user is logging on from an Apple computer, such as a Macintosh.

✦ **Account is disabled** — When this option is selected, the account cannot be used to log on to the domain.

✦ **Smart card is required for interactive logon** — Smart cards are somewhat like credit cards in that the user uses a smart card reader and PIN to log on instead of using a user name and password. Select this option if your network uses smart cards.

✦ **Account is trusted for delegation** — When this option is selected, the user has the right to delegate administrative rights to other users.

Cross-Reference

You can learn more about delegation of control in Chapter 11.

✦ **Account is sensitive and cannot be delegated** — When this option is selected, delegation cannot be used with this user account.

✦ **Use DES encryption types for this account** — When selected, this option enables you to use DES encryption for this account instead of standard Kerberos encryption.

✦ **Do not require Kerberos preauthentication** — When this option is selected, the user can log on from a computer that supports Kerberos, but does not support the preauthentication feature of Kerberos.

Finally, at the bottom of the Account tab, you can select a date for the account to expire. Use the Never radio button to not set an account expiration or click the End Of radio button and select a desired date.

Profile

The Profile tab, shown in Figure 9-10, enables you to specify locations for a user profile and home folder. In the Profile path dialog box, enter the location for the profile, or if left blank, the default location is used, which is C:\Documents and Settings*username*. You can also enter a location for a logon script if in use, as well as the location of a home folder. Logon scripts are stored in the NETLOGON folder on domain controllers and are, by default, found in the SYSVOL folder on all domain controllers in the domain.

Telephones

The Telephones tab, shown in Figure 9-11, is like the Address tab — it is a location where you can enter detailed telephone contact information for the user. This information is made available to Active Directory users, so do not enter any numbers that should not be made public.

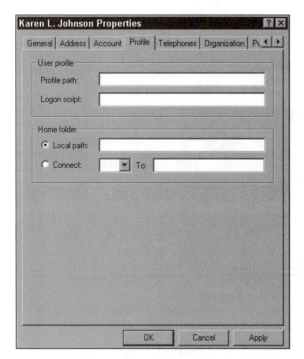

Figure 9-10: Profile tab

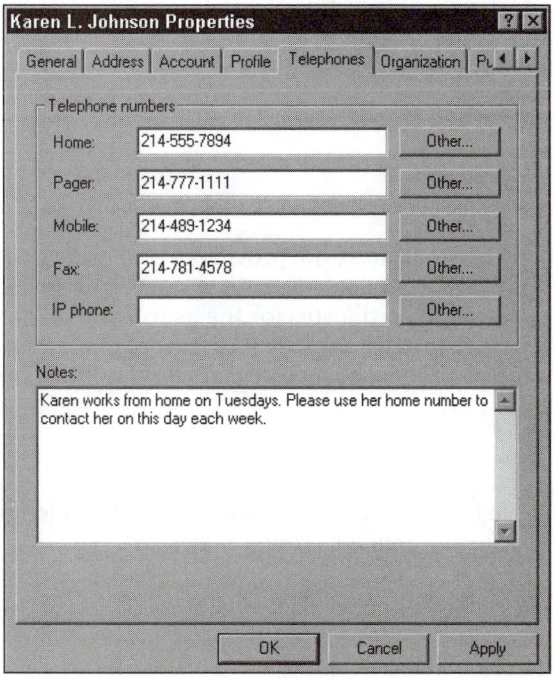

Figure 9-11: Telephones tab

Organization

The Organization tab, shown in Figure 9-12, provides you a place to enter information about the user's relationship to the organization, such as the user's title, department, manager, and so forth. This information is visible to Active Directory users.

Figure 9-12: Organization tab

Published Certificates

The Published Certificates tab, shown in Figure 9-13, provides you a place to add or remove X.509 certificates to the user's account. If certificate services are used in your network, use this tab to manage the certificates for the user. If you do not see a Published Certificates tab, then in the Active Directory Users and Computers console, click View ➪ Advanced to turn on advanced features. The tab will then become visible.

Member Of

The Member Of tab lists the Active Directory groups to which the user belongs. Use the Add and Remove buttons to select or remove groups as desired.

Cross-Reference   You can learn more about group accounts later in this chapter.

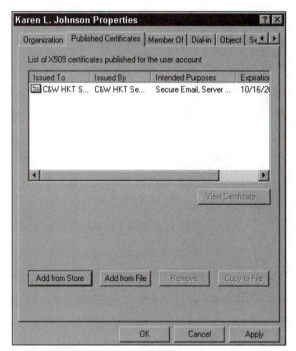

Figure 9-13: Published Certificates tab

You also see a Set Primary Group button. This feature is provided for Macintosh and/or POSIX client applications. You do not need to set a primary group if you are not using Macintosh- or POSIX-compliant applications.

Dial-in

The Dial-in tab, shown in Figure 9-14, enables you to configure the user account for use with Remote Access Services (RAS) for either dial-in or virtual private network (VPN) access. In the top part of the window, you can choose to either allow or deny remote access by clicking the desired radio button, or you can choose to control access through remote access policy. You can also choose to verify the caller's ID. In the middle of the window, you see callback options. This feature enables the server to call the user back as a security feature. Your three radio button options are No Callback, Set by Caller, or Always Callback to, an option where you enter a desired phone number. Finally, you see IP address and route check boxes that enable you to define a static IP address and a default route.

Note Remote access is a complicated topic, and Windows 2000 provides you a number of important options. Although RAS is not discussed in this book, you should certainly spend some time studying RAS before implementing a RAS plan for your environment. You can learn more about RAS in the Windows 2000 Help files or in the Windows 2000 Resource Kit.

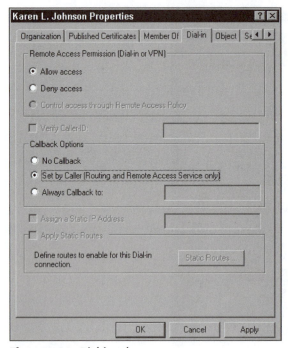

Figure 9-14: Dial-in tab

Object

The object tab provides you information about the user account object in the Active Directory. The fully qualified domain name of the object is displayed along with the date of contraction, last modification, and original and current Update Sequence Number (USN). There isn't anything you can configure on this tab, but it is provided for informational purposes only. If you can't see the tab in Active Directory Users and Computers, click View ➪ Advanced, and the tab will appear.

Cross-Reference You can learn more about objects and USNs in Chapter 14.

Security

The Security tab for the object functions like all other Security tabs for objects in the Active Directory. The Security and your configuration options for object security are covered in detail in Chapter 11.

Note Additional tabs may also be available, such as Environment, Sessions, Remote Control, and Terminal Services Profile, if Terminal Services are configured for your domain.

Other user account management options

Aside from configuring the user account properties, there are also a number of other management tasks you can perform. Simply select the user account in the Users and Computers console and then click the Action menu to see a list of management options (or just right-click the user account icon to see the same list). The following bulleted list points out the management actions you can take:

✦ **Copy** — The copy option enables you to copy a user account so you can create a new user account for a different user. This feature enables you to configure user account settings as desired in the form of a template and then just copy this standardized account so you can create a lot of users more quickly.

✦ **Add members to a group** — This option enables you to quickly add the user account to a specified group.

✦ **Name mappings** — This option enables you to configure security identity mappings for X.509 certificates and Kerberos names. You don't normally need to configure this option unless you want to map specific X.509 certificates to the user's account or you want to map users from a trusted nonWindows Kerberos realm to the user account.

✦ **Disable account** — This option prevents the account from being used.

✦ **Reset Password** — This option enables you to give the user account a new password. This option is used when a user forgets a password, and you need to reset the password to a default option so the user can access the account and create a new password.

✦ **Move** — This option enables you to move the user account to a different container or OU.

✦ **Open home page** — If a home page has been configured in the user account properties, you can use this option to quickly access the page.

✦ **Send mail** — If an e-mail address has been configured for the user account, use this option to easily send an e-mail message to the user.

✦ **Delete** — This option deletes the user account.

✦ **Rename** — This option renames the user account.

✦ **Refresh** — This option refreshes the account so you can see the latest changes.

✦ **Help** — This option opens the Windows 2000 Help files.

Creating and Managing Group Accounts

The purpose of groups in a Windows 2000 network is to manage and control user accounts and what permissions users have. Users can be grouped by similar permissions or job functions and managed as an entire group. This greatly simplifies your work as an Active Directory administrator because you can manage users at a group level instead of at an individual user level.

Before getting into the creation and management of group accounts in the Active Directory, I want to spend a few moments focusing on some group account technologies in the Active Directory. First, each group is one of three different kinds of groups, called Group Scopes. Table 9-1 presents these three Group Scopes and defines them for you.

Table 9-1 Windows 2000 Group Scopes	
Group Scope	*Explanation*
Built-in Local	Built-in (Domain) local groups are used to assign permissions to resources. Built-in local groups can contain users from the local domain or from Global or Universal groups in the forest.
Global	A Global group is used to organize domain users with similar permission needs. Global groups are then made members of built-in local groups so that users can access certain resources. A Global group can contain user accounts and other Global groups from within its domain only.
Universal	Universal groups are like Global groups, but Universal groups are used to organize similar users from multiple domains in the forest. Universal groups can contain user accounts, Global groups, and other Universal groups from any domain in the forest.

If you worked at all with Windows NT, you are certainly familiar with local and Global groups. Local groups are used to set permissions on resources, and then Global groups are used to organize users and place them in local groups so they can access resources. This approach enables you to easily manage many users. Universal groups are new in Windows 2000, and they essentially break the domain boundaries of Global groups. In a nutshell, your Universal groups can contain any user account, Global group, or other Universal group in your domain. However, Universal groups are available only if your domain is operating in native mode — not mixed mode.

See Chapter 8 to learn more about native and mixed mode.

Also, you do have to be careful with Universal groups. Excessive numbers of Universal groups can cause a lot of replication traffic, and the permissions for Universal groups can get complicated very easily. So, as with all aspects of the Active Directory, planning is of key importance.

Aside from understanding the group scopes available, there are two other terms, called Group Types, you should understand:

✦ **Security** — Security groups are used to organize users for permission purposes, which is the primary reason for local, Global, and Universal groups.

✦ **Distribution** — Distribution groups are new in Windows 2000 and provide you a way to organize users for nonsecurity purposes. You can expect to see more development with Distribution groups and other BackOffice products, such as Exchange Server.

Now turn your attention to the built-in group accounts that are automatically created by the Active Directory. You need to understand the purpose of each of these in order to design and implement groups effectively.

The following built-in local groups are created when the Active Directory is installed:

✦ **Account Operators** — Members can create, delete, and modify domain user and group accounts in the domain. Account Operators *cannot* change the Administrator account or the Administrators, Account Operators, Backup Operators, Print Operators, or Server Operators groups.

✦ **Administrators** — Members have full administrative rights to manage all domain objects.

✦ **Backup Operators** — Members can back up and restore all files on domain controllers in the domain.

✦ **Guests** — No rights or permissions are assigned by default.

✦ **Pre-Windows Compatible Access** — Members have read permission for domain user and group objects in the domain. This group enables Windows NT 4.0 users to log on to the Windows 2000 domain.

✦ **Print Operators** — Members can manage printers within the domain.

✦ **Replicator** — Members can manage replication on Windows NT. 4.0. This group is provided for backward compatibility.

✦ **Server Operators** — Members can share folders on domain controllers in the domain as well as back up and restore files and folders.

✦ **Users** — Members of this group do not have any default permissions or rights. New user accounts are automatically made members of this group.

There are also a number of Global and Universal built-in groups, which you can view in the Users container in the Active Directory Users and Computers console. The following bulleted list gives you a brief definition of each:

✦ **Cert Publishers** — Members create Enterprise-wide certificates and renewals.

✦ **DNS Update Proxy** — Contains DNS clients who are permitted to perform dynamic updates.

✦ **Domain Admins** — Contains administrators for the domain.

✦ **Domain Computers** — Contains domain computer accounts.

✦ **Domain Controllers** — Contains domain controllers.

✦ **Domain Guests** — Contains all domain guests.

✦ **Domain Users** — Contains all domain user accounts.

✦ **Enterprise Admins** — Contains enterprise administrative accounts. These accounts have permission to perform all Active Directory management and configuration tasks in the forest.

✦ **Group Policy Creator Owners** — Members can modify Group Policy objects.

✦ **Schema Admins** — Members can make configuration changes to the Active Directory schema.

Creating a new group account

You can easily create new group accounts in Windows 2000, but you should plan new group accounts carefully and determine how you will use them. To create a new group account, log on with an administrative account, access the Active Directory Users and Computers console, and then follow these steps:

1. Select the container or OU where you want to store the new group account and then click Action ⇨ New ⇨ Group.

2. The New Object — Group window appears, as shown in Figure 9-15. Enter a group name. The pre-Windows 2000 group name appears automatically, but you can change it if desired. Select a desired group scope and group type by clicking the appropriate radio button and then click the OK button.

Note   If the Universal group option is grayed out, then your domain is running in mixed mode. See Chapter 8 to learn more about mixed mode.

3. The new group now appears in the desired container or OU.

Figure 9-15: New Object — Group

Configuring group account properties

You can configure any group account by accessing its properties sheets. Select the group in Active Directory Users and Computers and then click Action ➪ Properties, or just right-click the group account icon in the console and click Properties. The following sections show you what configuration options are available on each tab.

General

The General tab provides you the same options you configured when creating the account. You can change the group name, and you see the group scope and type listed. The only other configuration options you have on this tab are to enter a description for the group, a group e-mail address, and any notes you would like to make about the group.

Members

The Members tab, shown in Figure 9-16, lists the Active Directory user accounts that are members of the group account and the Active Directory folder in which the user accounts reside. Use the Add button to add new members to the group and the Remove button to take members out of the group.

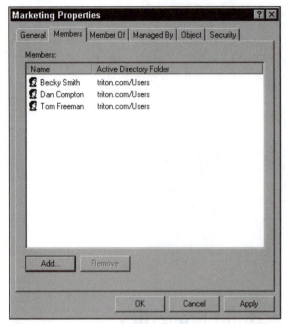

Figure 9-16: Members tab

Member Of

The Member Of tab, which looks almost identical to the Members tab shown in Figure 9-16, lists the groups to which this group is a member. Use the Add and Remove buttons to manage the group memberships as desired.

Managed By

The Managed By tab, shown in Figure 9-17, enables you to select a user from the Active Directory and make that user a manager of the group. Click the Change button and select a manager from the Active Directory. If additional information, such as office, street, phone numbers, and so on, is taken from the user account and placed on this tab, Active Directory users can see this information.

Note   The manager's contact information, such as office, street, phone, and so on, is taken directly from the user account. You cannot manually enter them here. If the user account does not have this information configured, then no information will be displayed.

Object and Security

The Object tab gives you information about the group object. You cannot configure anything on this tab. The Security tab functions like all other Security tabs in the Active Directory.

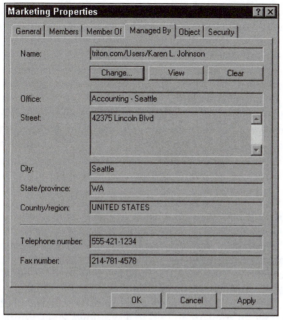

Figure 9-17: Managed By tab

Cross-Reference You can learn more about objects in Chapter 14, and you can learn more about the Security tab in Chapter 11.

Other management tasks

As you can with user accounts, you can select the group account object in the Users and Computers console and then click the Action menu or right-click the group icon to see other available management options. You can use this feature to move the group account, send e-mail to the group account, delete the account, rename it, refresh, or get help.

Examining Computer Accounts

All computers that are members of a Windows 2000 domain have a computer account configured in the Active Directory. These computer accounts are automatically generated when an administrator joins a computer to a domain. Windows 2000 computers and Windows NT computers can be members of a domain. Windows 9x computers cannot be domain members because they do not support the advanced security features of the Active Directory, but they can log on to a Windows 2000 domain and access resources within that domain. You can enable Windows 9x computers to use the Active Directory by installing the Active Directory client software found in the Clients folder of your Windows 2000 Server installation CD-ROM.

Tip You can also manually create the computer account by selecting the desired container or OU and then clicking Action ➪ New ➪ Computer.

You can use the Active Directory Users and Computers tool to access computer account properties, just as you would access a user or group. You have the same generic tabs on the properties sheets as you have seen earlier in this chapter, such as General, Member Of, Managed By, and so forth.

Summary

This chapter explored the creation and configuration of user and group accounts in the Active Directory using Active Directory Users and Computers. User and group accounts are not difficult to configure, but you should perform some planning actions before creating group accounts for your environment. Finally, this chapter explored computer accounts. Windows 2000 and NT computers automatically have a computer account generated when they are joined to a Windows 2000. Windows 9x computers cannot be domain members because they do support the advanced security features of the Active Directory, but they can log on and use domain resources if the appropriate client software is installed.

✦   ✦   ✦

Publishing Resources

With a new Active Directory implementation, one of your initial jobs is setting up your Organizational Unit (OU) structure and all of the resources you plan on offering to clients through the Active Directory. After a lot of planning and the initial installation, now is a great time to stop and remind yourself that the purpose of the Active Directory is to bring unity to the network and to enable users to more easily locate and use network objects. This goal alone makes the work environment more productive.

With that thought in mind, setting up your OUs and resource objects will be an ongoing task. In this chapter, you explore all of the Active Directory object resources and how to implement and configure them.

Setting Up Organizational Units

I like to think of Organizational Units (OUs) as file folders in a filing cabinet. The Active Directory is the file cabinet, and each OU, or file folder, serves as an organizational boundary. Within each OU, you can place any Active Directory resource, including other OUs. Like a file folder, an OU does not have any functionality on its own, but it is designed to hold other resources.

OUs are used in the Active Directory as an administrative and security boundary, as well as a Group Policy boundary. They can effectively take the place of Windows NT resource domains. In fact, NT networks with several domains can effectively upgrade to the Active Directory model and become one domain with several OUs.

Cross-Reference   Chapter 3 explores the purpose and nature of and design issues with OUs.

The importance of planning your OU structure before implementation cannot be understated. You can build multiple levels of OUs (nesting), and you can build as many top-level OUs as you like. However, an OU structure that is carefully planned should be simple and easy to use and administer. If the OU structure is not carefully planned, it can quickly get out of control with many unnecessary and deeply nested OUs.

Caution   Make certain you have studied the principles concerning OU structure design in Chapter 3 *before* beginning an implementation.

With all of that said, this section shows you how to set up and manage the properties of OUs for your Active Directory implementation.

Creating a new OU

As with user, group, and computer objects, OUs are created and configured using the Active Directory Users and Computers tool. To create a new OU, follow these steps:

1. Click Start ➪ Programs ➪ Administrative Tools ➪ Active Directory Users and Computers.

2. Select the desired domain in the left console pane and then click Action ➪ New ➪ Organizational Unit.

Note   If you need to connect to a different domain than what you see in the console tree, click Action ➪ Connect to Domain, then enter the domain name (or browse), and then click OK.

3. The New Object—Organizational Unit window appears, as shown in Figure 10-1. Enter the name of the new OU and click the OK button.

Once you have created the OU, you can see it in the Users and Computers console. At this point, you can be moving resources into the OU as necessary. You repeat the previous steps to create additional OUs and sub-OUs. To create a sub-OU, simply select the OU in which you want to create the new OU and then click Action ➪ New ➪ Organizational Unit. Then, repeat the process. Continue creating OUs until you have built the desired OU structure for the domains. As you can see in Figure 10-2, there are several OUs and sub-OUs for this domain.

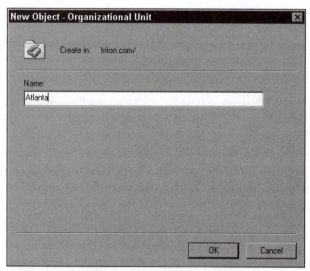

Figure 10-1: New Object — Organizational Unit

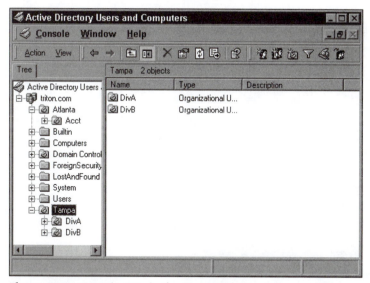

Figure 10-2: Domain OUs in the Users and Computers console

Configuring OU properties

Each OU has its own properties sheets where you have a few items that you can configure. The OU properties provide both configuration and general information about the OU and may be used differently from organization to organization. You can access an OU's properties by selecting the OU in the console and clicking Action ⇨ Properties or by just right-clicking the OU and clicking Properties. The following sections examine what is available on each properties tab.

General tab

The General tab enables you to input information about the OU. Depending on the structure of your domain, OUs may be physically grouped and located in different geographic areas. The General tab enables you to enter contact information for the OU location. For example, in Figure 10-3, you see an example OU called "Atlanta." This OU makes up part of the domain that includes a physical site called Atlanta. The General tab provides physical contact information for the Atlanta office — since the OU is an object representation of that location. Depending on your network, you may not even need to use this tab, but it is provided in the Active Directory so you can enter information as necessary and appropriate.

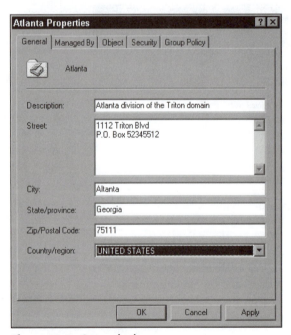

Figure 10-3: General tab

Managed By tab

The Managed By tab, shown in Figure 10-4, provides two functions: You can assign a manager to the OU and provide contact information about that manager. Essentially, the manager is the person who manages the group of users or resources residing in that OU. Once a manager is assigned, contact information is automatically entered from the manager's user account in the Active Directory. If no contact information is entered in the user's account, then no contact information will appear on Managed By tab; you cannot manually enter the information. Active Directory users can locate this contact information in the Active Directory in order to contact the OU manager.

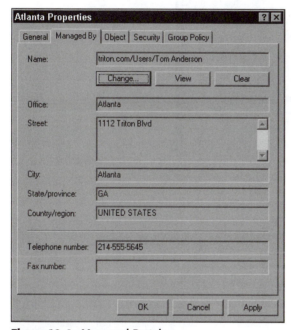

Figure 10-4: Managed By tab

Object tab

The Object tab does not have anything you can configure, but it provides object information about the OU, as shown in Figure 10-5. Using the Object tab, you can note the object class, when the OU object was created, when the object was last modified, the original USN, and the current USN. USNs (Update Sequence Numbers) are used in Active Directory replication.

Cross-Reference   You can learn more about USNs in Chapter 13.

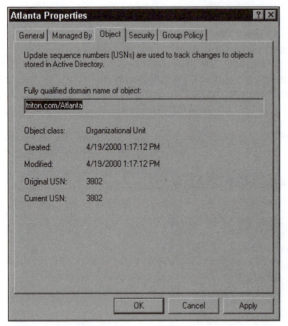

Figure 10-5: Object tab

Security tab

The Security tab for OUs functions like all other Security tabs in Windows 2000. Use the Security tab to configure access security for the OU.

 The Security tab is explored in detail in Chapter 11.

Group Policy

Group Policy is applied at the site, domain, or OU level, so you will see an OU tab where you can configure a particular Group Policy to apply to a particular OU.

 Group Policy configuration and application is explored in Chapter 15.

Publishing Contact Objects

Organizations and businesses are not static entities, and the needs of one organization or business vary greatly from another. Some networks are used strictly by sanctioned employees while others have a number of contractors and other individuals who are a part of the business as well.

Contact Examples

Since the contact object can be configured in a variety of ways, consider these two contact usage examples:

Triton.com uses a number of contractors in their business. These contractors range from individuals from other companies to independent freelancers. Triton.com has significant security needs. Therefore, contractors are never given a user account or allowed inside of the network infrastructure. However, these contractors are very important to Triton's business, and users must be able to contact them readily. The answer? Triton configures a contact for each contractor for the Active Directory. The contractor's contact information is available to users to search and find, but the contractors themselves never have access to the network.

Tritondev.com is another division of Triton, Inc. Tritondev uses several contractors on a regular basis, often for six months at a time. These contractors act as though they are Tritondev employees. Tritondev creates a contact object for each contractor, but in order to perform their jobs, each contractor is also given a user account and assigned membership in the Contractors group. This configuration gives the contractors access to the resources they need.

As you can see, each configuration is quite different, but each meets the desired outcomes and goals of the company.

Active Directory contacts allow you a loose way to include such individuals in your network. A contact is much like a business card; it contains information about a person or even a company that can be stored in the Active Directory. When a user searches for the person or company, the Active Directory can recall the person or company's contact information. However, because contacts can also have a user account and be members of groups within your organization, the line between a contact and a user can get obscured. The point is simply that the contact object provides you a way to include people and businesses in your Active Directory even though those people or businesses are not directly a part of your network. Beyond that, how you choose to use contacts is up to your business needs and model as well as your security needs.

Creating a contact

You can create contacts in any OU or container using the Active Directory Users and Computers console. To create a new contact, follow these steps:

1. Select the OU or container where you want to create the contact and then click Action ➪ New ➪ Contact.

2. Enter the contact's name and display name as desired, shown in Figure 10-6. Then, click the OK button.

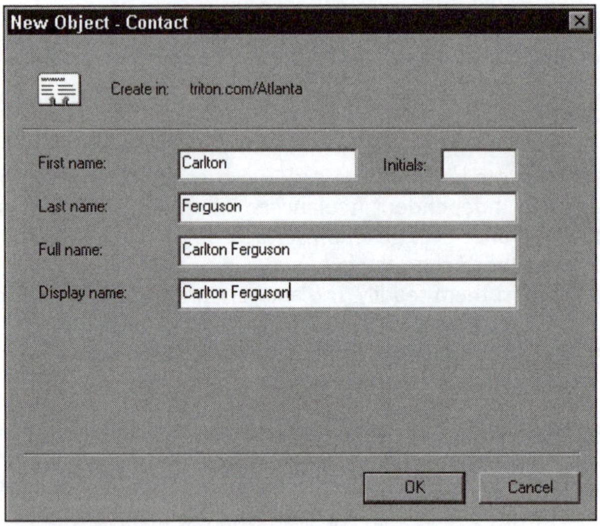

New Object - Contact

Create in: triton.com/Atlanta

First name: Carlton   Initials:

Last name: Ferguson

Full name: Carlton Ferguson

Display name: Carlton Ferguson

OK   Cancel

Figure 10-6: Contact object

Configuring contact properties

As previously explained, the contact can be a sort of "catch all" to meet the needs of certain business associates or contractors. Because of this, the properties sheets for the contact object contain several different tabs that enable you to configure the contact as desired. The following sections explore the configuration options presented to you on these tabs.

Note   The contact object has an Object tab and a Security tab, just as an OU and many other Active Directory objects. See the "Setting Up Organizational Units" section earlier in this chapter for more information about these tabs.

General tab

The General tab for contact objects is much like the General tab for user objects. The General tab, shown in Figure 10-7, is a place where you can enter standard information about the contact, such as name, description, phone numbers, and so on. Notice that next to the Telephone number dialog box and Web page dialog box you have an Other button. Click this button to enter additional phone or Web page information.

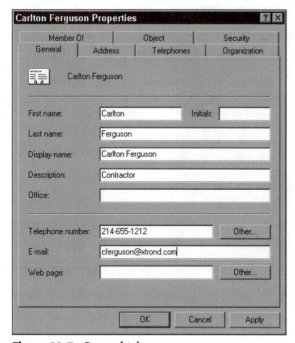

Figure 10-7: General tab

Address tab

The Address tab, as you might guess, provides you a place to enter the postal address information for the contact.

 Caution It is important to remember that any information you put on the General and Address tabs will be viewable to Active Directory users. Do not enter information you do not want made public on these tabs.

Telephones tab

The Telephones tab, shown in Figure 10-8, provides you a place to enter a variety of telephone numbers, such as home, pager, mobile, fax, and IP Phone. As with the General tab, you can use the Other buttons to enter additional phone numbers as needed. You also have a Notes dialog box where you can enter information related to the contact's telephone numbers. Again, remember that all of this information can be viewed by Active Directory users.

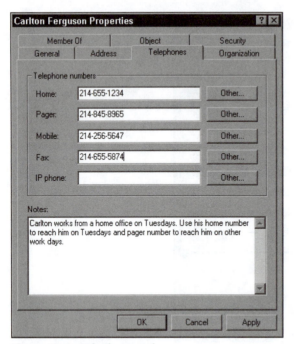

Figure 10-8: Telephones tab

Organization tab

The Organization tab enables you to enter information about the contact's organization, such as the contact's title, department, company, and the manager's name. The Manager information is taken from the Active Directory. Therefore, in this instance, the manager refers to someone within the Active Directory organization who manages the contact. Again, any information entered on this tab is made available to Active Directory users.

Member Of tab

The Member Of tab enables you to add the contact to various Active Directory groups. Depending on the relationship of the contact with the organization, the contact may have a user account and be able to log on to the Active Directory network. The Member Of tab enables you to configure group memberships as appropriate for the contact. As you can see in Figure 10-9, this contact is a member of the Guests group. You can use the Add and Remove buttons on this window to add the contact to more groups or remove previously configured group memberships.

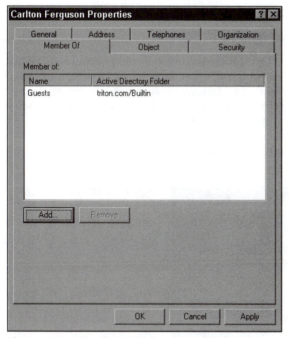

Figure 10-9: Member Of tab

Publishing Printer Objects

A very important resource you can publish in the Active Directory is printers. In networking environments, a common source of complaint from end users is connecting to and using various printers within an organization. The Active Directory *greatly* simplifies the use of printers through the Active Directory, particularly for Windows 2000 clients.

With the Active Directory, users can search for particular kinds of printers, directly connect to them, have the appropriate drivers automatically downloaded, and use the printer. The user does not have to know which server the printer is connected to or doesn't need to know anything about the network topology in order to use the printer.

You can publish printer objects in the Active Directory connected to either Windows 2000 computers or downlevel computers, such as NT and 9*x*. However, the publication method for Windows 2000 and downlevel computers is different. The following two sections examine how to publish each.

Publishing printers connected to Windows 2000 computers

Windows 2000 computers can automatically publish shared printers in the Active Directory without configuration from the Active Directory administrator, which is a big time-saver for administrators. In Windows 2000 computers (either Server or Professional), you have the option to automatically list the printer in the Active Directory when you share the printer. As shown in Figure 10-10, click the check box to list the printer in the directory. Once you click OK, the printer information is sent to a domain controller for publication in the Active Directory.

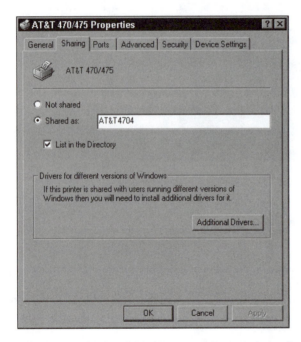

Figure 10-10: Printers can be automatically published using the List in the Directory check box.

Windows 2000 computers also have the capability of supporting downlevel clients by including the drivers for those clients. For example, suppose your network is primarily composed of Windows 2000 Professional computers and Windows 98 computers. When you share a printer from a Windows 2000 computer, you can also install the drivers for Windows 98 computers. This information is sent to the directory. Thus, when a Windows 98 client attempts to connect to the Windows 2000 computer, the drivers for the Windows 98 computer can be automatically downloaded so the Windows 98 client can use the printer.

To install additional drivers, click the Additional Drivers button. You see a list of operating systems, shown in Figure 10-11. Click the operating systems you want to install drivers for and then click OK. You will need your Windows 2000 installation CD-ROM and possibly a driver CD or disk, depending on your printer model.

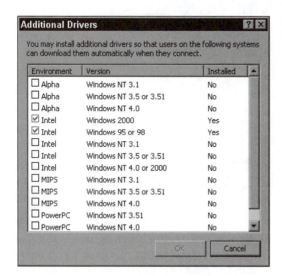

Figure 10-11: Click the check boxes to install additional drivers.

Publishing printers from downlevel computers

Downlevel computers, such as Windows NT or 9x, can also publish shared printers in the Active Directory so that other users can locate and access them; however, downlevel computers cannot automatically publish the printer. For downlevel shared printers, an administrator must manually add the printer object to the Active Directory.

To manually add a printer to the Active Directory, follow these steps:

1. In Active Directory Users and Computers, select the OU or container where you want to store the printer object. Then, click Action ➪ New ➪ Printer.

2. In the New Object — Printer window, shown in Figure 10-12, enter the UNC path to the shared printer, such as \\server_name\share_name and then click the OK button.

Note Once you click OK, the Active Directory checks for the network share and adds the printer object to the directory if it is available. If the printer is not available or is not shared, you receive an error message telling you the printer does not exist.

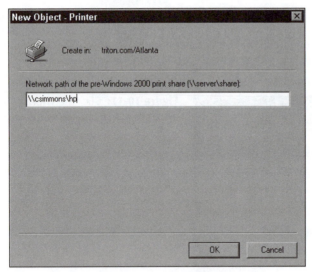

Figure 10-12: New Object — Printer window

It is important to note here that the Active Directory stores only information about the printer, such as the network location and some additional property information you can enter, which you learn about in the next section. However, the Active Directory does not manage the printer. The Active Directory acts as a pointer to the printer object. When a user searches for a printer, discovers a desired printer, and then connects to the printer, the Active Directory simply redirects the request to the computer that holds the share. This process is invisible to the end user, who is not directly aware of the server or computer that actually manages the printer. This feature enables users to access network resources without having to know which server or computer holds the shared printer. To the user, all of the shared printers are simply in the Active Directory.

Configuring printer properties

Once a printer object is placed in the Active Directory, you can select the printer object and then click Action ➪ Properties to access its properties sheets. As discussed in the previous paragraph, the properties sheets pertain only to Active Directory listing data. You cannot directly configure the printer from these properties sheets, but rather you configure the actual printer on the server or computer where the shared printer actually resides. With that said, you have four configuration tabs for printer properties: General, Managed By, Object, and Security.

Note   The Object and Security tabs are the same as all Object and Security tabs in other Active Directory objects. You can learn about the Security tab features in Chapter 11.

General tab

The printer object General properties tab enables you to enter additional information about the printer that is listed in the directory, as shown in Figure 10-13. You can enter the printer's physical location and use some check boxes and dialog boxes to enter additional information, such as whether or not the printer prints in color, whether or not it staples documents, and so forth. You are not required to enter information on this tab, but the information you do enter is stored in the directory. For example, suppose you have a color printer. If you check the Color check box, that data is stored. When a user searches for a "color printer," this printer will be returned as a search match. So, always use this tab and enter any applicable information to assist in user searches.

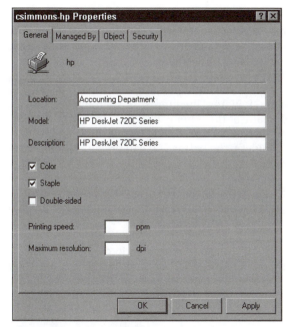

Figure 10-13: General tab

Managed By tab

The Managed By tab functions like all other object Managed By tabs. By clicking the Change button, you can select the printer's manager from the Active Directory. Any contact information configured in the manager's user account will also appear on this page as well. This information is available in the directory as well so that users can contact the person who manages the actual printer.

Publishing Shared Folders

Shared folders function in the Active Directory the same way as printers in terms of Active Directory objects. When you publish a shared folder, you are simply publishing pointer information that redirects a user to the computer that holds the shared folder. Just as a printer share redirects the user to the server or computer where the shared printer is attached, shared folders redirect the user to the computer that actually houses the shared folder. The Active Directory does not physically contain shared folders and resources, but simply points to those shared folders and resources. Just as a phone book does not actually contain people, but rather a number so you can contact a desired person, the Active Directory holds the network path to the shared folder that a user wants to access.

So, why publish shared folders? Always remember that at its basic level, the Active Directory is simply a directory — a place where users can find information. Users can search for shared folders using keywords and locate the folders they need, which contain the actual resources they need to use.

From an administrative point of view, you and your administrative team may need to devise a plan to manage shared folders. The number of shared folders on a network can get out of hand, with many of them being unnecessary. Also, shared folders cannot be automatically published, so the administrative load can be difficult in large networks. With shared folders, the better you can organize them, the easier users can search and locate them.

Before you publish a shared folder to the Active Directory, the folder must be shared and its permissions configured as desired on the computer that holds the share. Then, it can be published in the Active Directory.

Caution   All configuration and security for a shared folder is performed on the computer that physically holds the share. The Active Directory does not provide any security for any shared folder, but simply redirects user requests for access to the computer that holds the share.

Publishing a shared folder

You can easily publish a shared folder using the Active Directory Users and Computers console. To publish a shared folder, follow these steps:

1. In Active Directory Users and Computers, select the OU or container where you want to place the shared folder object and then click Action ➪ New ➪ Shared Folder.

2. In the New Object — Shared Folder window, shown in Figure 10-14, enter a name for the shared folder and the UNC path to the shared folder, such as \\computer_name\share_name.

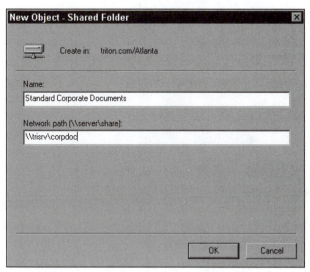

Figure 10-14: New Object — Shared Folder window

Tip The name that you enter for the shared folder is what Active Directory users will see and what will be accessed during searches. For example, the folder name Standard Corporate Documents indicates shared company documents. Users who search for *documents* or *corporate documents* would get this folder as a search return. In short, use the most descriptive name possible when naming the share. The actual share name can be anything desired, however, such as "corpdoc" in Figure 10-14.

Configuring shared folder properties

As with printer objects, you can enter share information on the General tab. The information you enter on General tab enables you to define the shared folder object in more detail and enables users to more accurately locate the shared folder they want to use. As you see in Figure 10-15, you can enter a description of the shared folder. You should be as specific as possible with the description so that users can locate the shared folder that holds the desired resources.

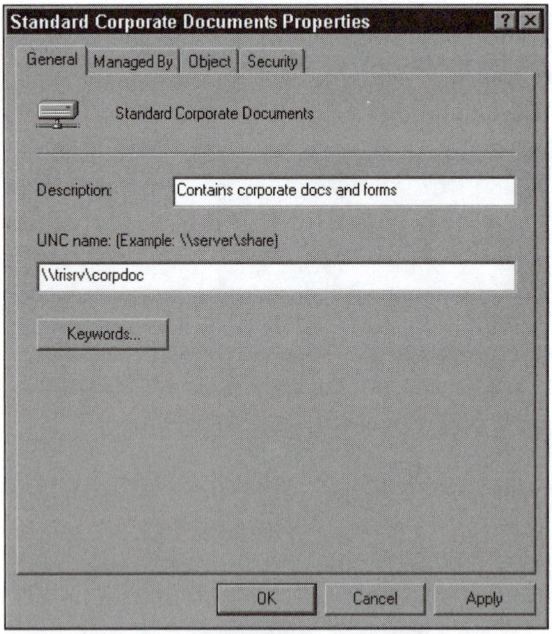

Figure 10-15: Shared folder General tab

A very important part of the General tab is the Keywords button. If you click the button, you see a simple dialog box where you can enter a list of keywords. Use the Add button to enter the keywords and create the list and use the Edit and Remove buttons to make changes to the list, as shown in Figure 10-16.

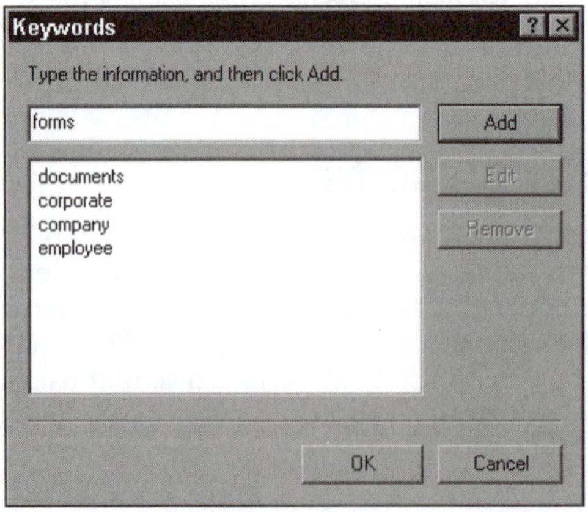

Figure 10-16: Keywords

Keywords are used to attempt to match the shared folder to user queries. For example, for the shared folder "Company Documents," I have entered the keywords of *documents*, *corporate*, *company*, *employee*, and *forms*. I have brainstormed the list and feel that if an employee is looking for a folder containing company documents, he or she is most likely to use one or more of these words. By entering these keywords, I am attempting to guess how users will search and help them find the desired folder. Your keywords are *very* important, and they should be descriptive of the contents of the shared folder.

Note   The Managed By, Object, and Security tabs are the same as those on all other objects. Refer to the sections earlier in this chapter to learn more about these tabs.

Summary

Publishing Active Directory resources is not a difficult task. Once your Active Directory installation is in place, you can begin adding OUs, contacts, printer objects, and shared folder objects. It is important to keep in mind that all of these objects give the Active Directory its administrative structure and provide end users with the needed resources. By design, the Active Directory contains powerful query capabilities so that users can locate contacts, printer objects, and shared folder objects easily and without having to know the network topology.

✦   ✦   ✦

Implementing Active Directory Security Features

The importance of security cannot be understated. As networks have become more complex and the data stored on those networks has become just as complex and confidential, security is an area of great concern for most networking environments.

The concept of Active Directory security is hazy at best. The Active Directory fully integrates with all security features of Windows 2000 Server—of which there are many. However, some security features do apply specifically to the Active Directory and Active Directory data. Aside from the Enterprise Admin group and other secure accounts, you can secure the Active Directory primarily through Windows security, delegation, or through object and attribute security. This chapter examines these issues and points out how you can make the most of them.

Security Overview

As you implement and configure the Active Directory, it is important to always keep in mind that the Active Directory is simply a database of information. Objects are stored in the database, and each object has attributes that are like database fields. The Active Directory provides tight security by providing security from as high as the domain level all the way down to the attribute level of an individual object. In other words, you, as the administrator, can set security for an entire domain, and you can set security for a single attribute of a particular Active Directory object. The end result is a database that allows you to finely control security.

Cross-Reference   You can learn more about attributes in Chapters 1 and 14.

In order to accomplish this fine level of security, the Active Directory is built on three different security components, which are as follows:

✦ **Security Principals** — Security Principals are users, groups, or computers. Security Principals are Active Directory objects that can access other Active Directory objects. Security Principals are automatically assigned a Security Identifier once they are created.

✦ **Security Identifiers (SID)** — A SID is a unique number that identifies a user, group, or computer account. Each user, group, or computer account in the Active Directory has a unique SID. Although we see user, group, and computer accounts in terms of a name, the internal processes in Windows 2000 see these objects in terms of their unique SIDs. SIDs are always unique and are never reused, even if an object is deleted.

✦ **Security Descriptor** — A Security Descriptor *describes* the permissions that have been assigned for an object. For example, a shared folder contains a Security Descriptor that defines the access permissions that have been configured for that object. The Security Descriptor also defines the owner of the object and who is allowed to set permissions for that object. The Security Descriptor is technically made up of two Access Control Lists — the Discretionary Access Control List (DACL) and the System Access Control List (SACL), which are defined as follows:

• **Discretionary Access Control List (DACL)** — The DACL holds the access control entries (ACEs) for a particular object and the object's attributes. The DACL holds the permissions configured for an object. For example, if Jane Smith is given Full Control over a particular printer object, that information is stored in the DACL.

• **System Access Control List (SACL)** — The SACL determines what events can be audited for a particular object. For example, you can audit a printer object and determine which users are accessing the printer and how they are accessing it. The SACL contains the entries that enable you to audit these events.

Cross-Reference   You can learn more about auditing in the next section.

Windows Security

If you have worked with Windows 2000 Server and the Active Directory at all, you are well aware that all objects and user accounts have a Security tab in their properties sheets. Other Windows items, such as shared folders, also have the same Security tab. In short, the Security tab works the same for all Active Directory objects or all Windows items, which is a good streamlining feature of Windows 2000.

Tip   If none of your objects in Active Directory Users and Computers has a Security tab on the Properties sheets, then you need to enable advanced features of the console by clicking View ⇨ Advanced Features. The Security tabs will appear once you have enabled the feature.

The Security tab, shown in Figure 11-1, provides a standard interface to determine which users or groups can access a particular resource and what rights or permissions those users or groups have for the resource.

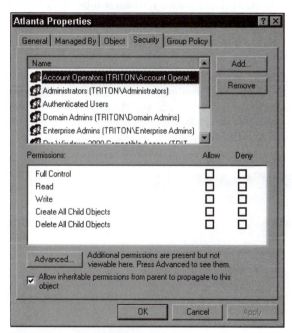

Figure 11-1: Security tab

The top part of the Window lists the current users or groups that have permissions for the particular object. You can select any of the users or groups and click the Remove button to remove them from the permissions list, or you can click the Add button and select other users or groups from the Active Directory to add to the list. By selecting a user or group, you can then manipulate the permissions by clicking either the Allow or Deny check boxes as desired. This design makes configuring permissions very easy and the same for all Windows and Active Directory objects and items.

Note   The permissions that appear in the list, such as Full Control, Read, Write, and so on, vary depending on the type of object. For example, Printer objects and OU objects have different check box options.

Notice the check box at the bottom of the Security tab. This check box allows inheritable permissions from the object's parent to propagate to the object. In other words, the check box allows the object to inherit permissions from its parent. For example, suppose I have an OU called Production within an OU called Atlanta. Permissions are configured on Atlanta. If I keep the check box selected on the Production Security tab, all permissions configured on Atlanta will be inherited by Production. This inheritance behavior is an excellent Windows 2000 design. By carefully creating your OU structure and storing items in appropriate OUs, you can simply configure security settings at the first-level OUs as needed. Then, those settings will be inherited by all other child objects. With careful organization and grouping, the inheritance feature is an excellent administrative tool.

However, there may be circumstances where you need to block inheritance. Suppose you have a printer residing in a particular OU. You want the printer object to be used only by administrators. You can configure the option by opening the printer object's properties, clicking the Security tab, and then clearing the "Allow inheritable permissions from parent to propagate to this object" check box. When you clear the check box, a Security window appears, shown in Figure 11-2.

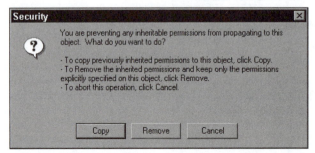

Figure 11-2: Security window

The Security window enables you to do one of three actions:

✦ To copy previously inherited permissions to the object

✦ To remove inherited permissions (Then you can manually specify the permission you want to keep.)

✦ To abort the operation

Normally, you will choose to just remove the inherited permissions. This removes any inherited permissions and blocks the object from receiving future inherited permissions. You can then configure the object's permissions as you desire.

Caution Inheritance is a design feature of Windows 2000 that reduces administrative burden. You should use the block inheritance feature only in rare cases. If you find yourself needing to block inheritance regularly, this is usually a sign that your OU structure and object organization need some work. Review Chapter 3 for important tips about designing an OU structure.

Finally, you also see an Advanced button near the bottom of the Security tab. The Advanced button enables you to configure advanced permissions, auditing, and ownership. The following sections examine each of these features.

Advanced permissions

The Permissions tab, shown in Figure 11-3, appears when you click the Advanced button on the Security tab. This tab lists the permission entries for the object. In other words, you see the users and groups and the permissions they have. You can use the Add and Remove buttons to manage the list, and you also see the "Allow inheritable permissions from parent to propagate to this object" check box.

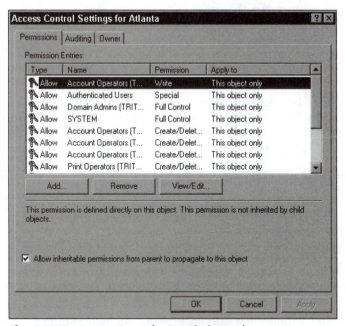

Figure 11-3: Access Control — Permissions tab

You can select a user or group and click the View/Edit button. This action opens a Permission Entry window, shown in Figure 11-4, that shows all of the permission objects for that user or group.

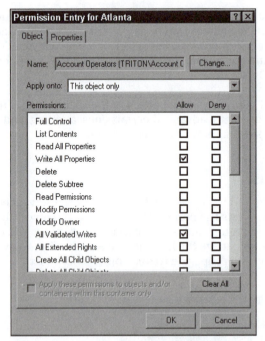

Figure 11-4: Permission Entry window

As you can see in Figure 11-4, there are many special permissions options that you can configure. Notice first the "Apply onto" drop-down menu. By default, the special permissions apply only to this object, but you can use the drop-down menu to have the special permissions apply to the following as well:

✦ **This object and all child objects** — Applies the settings to the current object and all child objects under the parent.

✦ **Child objects only** — Applies the settings to the child objects of the parent only.

✦ **aCSResourceLimits objects** — Applies the settings to Windows Quality of Service components.

✦ **certificationAuthority objects** — Applies the settings to Windows certification objects.

✦ **Computer objects** — Applies the settings to computer objects only.

✦ **Connection objects** — Applies the settings to connection objects only, as in site connection objects.

✦ **Contact objects** — Applies the settings to AD contact objects.

✦ **Group objects** — Applies the settings to AD group objects.

✦ **groupPolicyContainer objects** — Applies the settings to Group Policy container objects.

✦ **IntelliMirror Group objects**—Applies the settings to IntelliMirror groups.

✦ **IntelliMirror Service objects**—Applies the settings to IntelliMirror services.

✦ **MSMQ Configuration objects**—Applies the settings to Microsoft Message Queuing configuration objects.

✦ **Organizational Unit objects**—Applies the settings to OUs.

✦ **Printer objects**—Applies the settings to all printer objects.

✦ **Shared Folder objects**—Applies the settings to all shared folders.

✦ **Site objects**—Applies the settings to all sites.

✦ **Site Link Bridge objects**—Applies the settings to all site link bridges.

✦ **Site Setting objects**—Applies the settings to all site setting objects.

✦ **Site Container objects**—Applies the settings to site containers.

✦ **Subnet objects**—Applies the settings to all subnets.

✦ **Subnet Container objects**—Applies the settings to all subnet containers.

✦ **Trusted Domain objects**—Applies the settings to all trusted domains.

✦ **User objects**—Applies the settings to all users.

As you can see, you have several options, but they basically fall into two categories. You can have your advanced permissions for the user or group apply to the object or the object and all child objects, or you can specify the settings to apply to certain types of objects, such as user objects, printer objects, and so forth. These settings make up the bulk of your list options. This tab can be useful in a number of ways. For example, suppose you want to give a particular group certain advanced permissions for a shared folder. Instead of having to configure those advanced permissions on each folder object, you can simply use the "Apply onto Shared Folder objects" option to have the settings apply to all shared folders for which this group has permission.

Next, you see a long list of special permissions you can choose to apply or deny. The permissions list will vary, depending on the type of object, but the point of the advanced permissions is to give you, the administrator, a very fine level of control over objects as needed. For example, in Figure 11-4, you see advanced permissions for an OU. I can allow or deny many permissions to the users or groups, so I can finely control what the users and groups can do with that OU.

Note
Advanced permissions are just that—advanced options you can choose to implement in support of your environment. In most cases, you do not need to configure advanced permissions; the default options are all you need. However, Windows 2000 provides the advanced permission options so you can finely control security as needed.

If you click the Properties tab on the Permission Entry window, you see a similar window appear, which includes the "Apply onto" drop-down menu and a list of permissions you can configure. This window enables you to define what permissions a user or group has for the object's properties sheets, such as "read all properties, write all properties" and so forth.

Auditing

The Access Control Settings also enable you to audit objects both within the Active Directory and on the local machine by clicking the Advanced button on the Security tab and then clicking the Auditing tab. The Auditing tab works the same as the Permissions tab. You see a group name, Everyone by default, and you can use the Add, Remove, and View/Edit buttons to manage the list. You also see the same inheritance check box at the bottom of the window, shown in Figure 11-5.

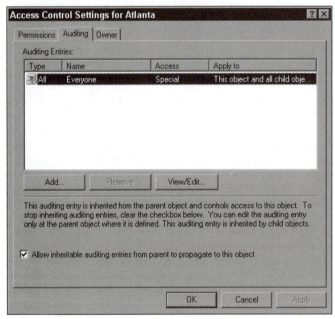

Figure 11-5: Auditing tab

Auditing is the process of tracking the activity that occurs on a certain resource or object. For example, you can choose to audit a printer object so you can see which users are accessing the printer and how frequently. Auditing is most commonly used to examine user work habits and possibly resource abuse. You can audit any object in the Active Directory as well as any other resource on your network. By clicking the View/Edit button, you can manage the auditing entry list for the user or group. This interface is the same as the permission entries interface, so refer to the previous section for more specific information.

Owner

Finally, the Owner tab is the last tab of the Access Control Settings dialog box, which you can access by clicking the Advanced button on the Security tab and clicking the Owner tab.

The Owner tab, shown in Figure 11-6, gives you a single interface. You are presented with the current owner of the object and then a possible list is provided of potential owners, which are the administrative groups or accounts in the directory. To change the owner of an object, just select the new owner in the list and click the OK button.

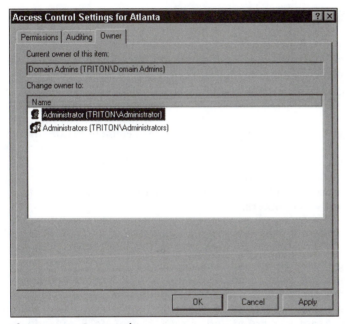

Figure 11-6: Owner tab

Every object in the Active Directory and on any NTFS volume has an owner. When an object is created, such as a new user account or a shared folder, for example, the person creating the object becomes the owner of the object. The owner can determine how permissions are granted for the object and who can access the object and under what permissions.

There are two ways ownership can be transferred to another person or group:

✦ An administrator can take ownership of any object under his or her administrative control. This feature is by design and allows an administrator to get control of an object from an employee who is no longer responsible for the object or who has left the company.

✦ The owner can transfer membership to a new owner by granting the Take Ownership right to the object. The new owner can then take ownership at any time once the permission has been granted.

New Feature

An exception to this rule is administrative ownership. Suppose that an administrator takes control of an object. Once the administrator forcibly takes ownership, the administrator cannot transfer ownership to another user. This is a security feature that prevents administrators from taking ownership of objects and randomly assigning them to other users.

Delegation of Control

Delegation of Control is a new feature in Windows 2000 that is designed for use with Active Directory. Delegation of Control allows you, as the administrator, to delegate Active Directory duties to other administrators or users. Delegation of Control enables you to finely delegate certain administrative responsibilities while denying others.

At first glace, Delegation of Control may seem like a management feature more than a security feature. In a certain respect, Delegation of Control is a management feature, but it is a security feature because you can safely delegate responsibilities while maintaining the desired level of control over Active Directory objects. You can maintain the desired level of control, but you can reduce your administrative burden by delegating tasks to others.

Consider an example. Suppose you are a senior administrator for an organization. You have an OU called Accounts where all user, group, and computer accounts are stored. The creating of user, group, and computer accounts is not a difficult task in terms of configuration, but it does tend to take up a lot of administrative time. You want to use Delegation of Control to delegate the administrative duties of creating user, group, and computer accounts to a new administrative trainee. You want the trainee to be able to create user, group, and computer accounts, but you do not want the trainee to have the right to delete any of the accounts. Can this be done? Yes — with delegation you give the delegate the right to create the accounts but no rights to delete any accounts. With Delegation of Control, you can keep your "administrative hand" over the tasks while delegating easier tasks to other people.

Tip

Delegation of Control is an excellent way to ease new or inexperienced administrators into an Active Directory environment. With Delegation of Control, you can limit the tasks an administrator can perform until he or she is technically capable of handling more complex tasks.

You can use Delegation of Control in many different ways, and you basically have to understand how delegation can fit into your administrative model. In most cases, you should delegate tasks at the OU level and allow inheritance to take effect for all objects within that OU. This way, you keep your delegation structure at the first-level OU instead of trying to delegate child and grandchild OUs.

Caution As with the "block inheritance" feature, you should not, as a practice, delegate control of child and grandchild OUs. Although the need may arise on a case-by-case basis, if you begin delegating child and grandchild OUs, this is a warning sign to stop and reconsider your delegation plan. You should delegate at the top-level OU and allow inheritance to take effect for all objects and child OUs within the top-level OU.

To delegate control, Windows 2000 provides you with a Delegation of Control Wizard. You use the Active Directory Users and Computers MMC snap-in tool to delegate control. The following steps show you how to use the wizard.

 Tip You can also delegate control using the dsacls.exe command-line utility, which you can learn about in Appendix C.

1. In Active Directory Users and Computers, select the domain or OU for which you want to delegate control and then click Action ➪ Delegate Control.

2. The Delegation of Control Wizard begins with a Welcome screen, shown in Figure 11-7. Click the Next button.

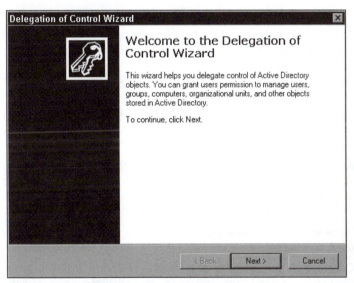

Figure 11-7: Delegation of Control Welcome screen

3. The Users or Groups window appears, shown in Figure 11-8. Click the Add button and select the user(s) or group(s) in the Active Directory to which you want to delegate control. Use the Remove button if you need to remove a user or group from the list. Click the Next button.

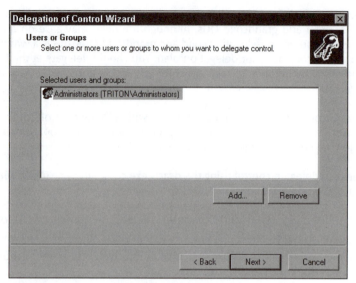

Figure 11-8: Users or Groups window

4. The Tasks to Delegate window appears, shown in Figure 11-9. You have two
   radio button options. Either you can choose to delegate control of a common
   tasks list, in which you select the desired options, or you can choose to delegate a custom task that you create. If you choose the common tasks option,
   you have the following check box list from which to select:

   - **Create, delete, and manage user accounts**—Delegation of this option
     allows the user or group the right to create, delete, and configure user
     accounts.

   - **Reset passwords on user accounts**—Delegation of this option permits
     the resetting of passwords only. Use this delegation to permit a particu-
     lar user or group the right to reset passwords when users forget their
     passwords or need to be assigned a new password.

   - **Read all user information**—This option enables the delegate to read all
     user information.

   - **Create, delete, and manage groups**—Delegation of this option permits
     the user or group to create, delete, and configure group accounts.

   - **Modify the membership of a group**—Delegation of this option allows
     the user or group to modify the membership of an existing group. Use
     this delegation to allow a particular user or group to manage group
     memberships, but not to create, delete, or configure group accounts.

   - **Manage Group Policy links**—Delegation of this option allows the user
     or group to mange Group Policy links and make changes to them.

If you want to delegate a common task, click the check box next to the desired task(s), click the Next button, and then click the Finish button. If you want to create custom tasks, click the "Create a custom task to delegate" radio button and then click the Next button.

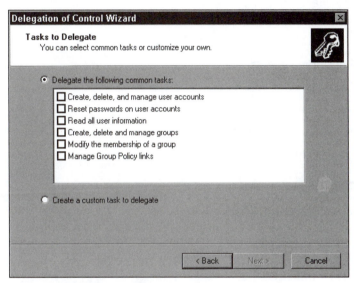

Figure 11-9: Tasks to Delegate window

5. If you chose to create custom tasks, the Active Directory Object Type window appears, shown in Figure 11-10. You have two radio button options. You can choose to delegate control of the folder, the objects in the folder, and the creation of new objects in the folder. Essentially, when you choose this option, you are delegating full control for the folder (OU or container) and to all inheritable objects. Your second option is to delegate certain objects in the folder, and you have the following objects from which to choose:

- aCSResourceLimits objects
- certificationAuthority objects
- Computer objects
- Connection objects
- Contact objects
- Group objects
- groupPolicyContainer objects
- intellimirrorGroup objects
- intellimirrorSCP objects
- MSMQ Configuration objects

- Organizational Unit objects
- Printer objects
- Shared Folder objects
- Site objects
- Site Link objects
- Site Link Bridge objects
- Site Setting objects
- Sites Container objects
- Subnet objects
- Subnets Container objects
- Trusted Domain objects
- User objects

As you can see, you have quite a bit of control of your Active Directory objects through this delegation option. For example, for a particular OU, you could delegate the control of printer objects or shared folder objects to a particular person or group. This allows one person or group to manage certain objects. Make your desired selections and then click Next.

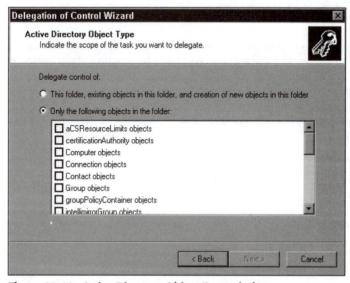

Figure 11-10: Active Directory Object Type window

6. The Permissions window appears. For the option(s) you chose on the preceding window, you now configure the desired permissions, shown in Figure 11-11. You have three check boxes that allow you to show various levels of permissions that you may want to assign. The three levels are General, Property-specific, and Creation/deletion of specific child objects. You can select any or all of the three types, and the permissions appear in the window. Make your selection and then choose the permissions you want to assign. The following bulleted lists present each of the options. Click the Next button.

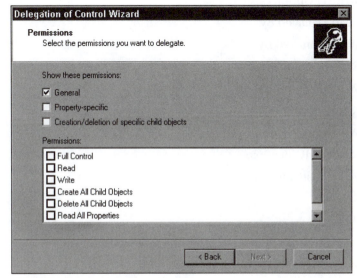

Figure 11-11: Permissions window

General:

- Full Control
- Read
- Write
- Create All Child Objects
- Delete All Child Objects
- Read All Properties
- Write All Properties

Property-specific:

- Read adminDescription
- Write adminDescription
- Read adminDisplayName

- Write adminDisplayName
- Read countryCode
- Write countryCode
- Read gPLink
- Write gPLink
- Read gPOptions
- Write gPOptions
- Read Managed By
- Write Managed By
- Read postalAddress
- Write postalAddress
- Read postalCode
- Write postalCode
- Read postOfficeBox
- Write postOfficeBox
- Read st
- Write st
- Read Street
- Write Street
- Read uPNSuffixes
- Write uPNSuffixes

Creation/deletion of specific child objects:

- Create Computer objects
- Delete Computer objects
- Create Contact objects
- Delete Contact objects
- Create Group objects
- Delete Group objects
- Create groupPolicyContainer objects
- Delete groupPolicyContainer objects
- Create IntelliMirror Group objects
- Delete IntelliMirror Group objects
- Create IntelliMirror Service objects

- Delete IntelliMirror Service objects
- Create Organizational Unit objects
- Delete Organizational Unit objects
- Create Printer objects
- Delete Printer objects
- Create Shared Folder objects
- Delete Shared Folder objects
- Create User objects
- Delete Users objects

7. A summary page appears. The summary page, shown in Figure 11-12, tells you what you have delegated, to whom, and the permissions that were assigned. Review the summary page, then click the Finish button if it is accurate. If it is not accurate, use the Back button to make changes.

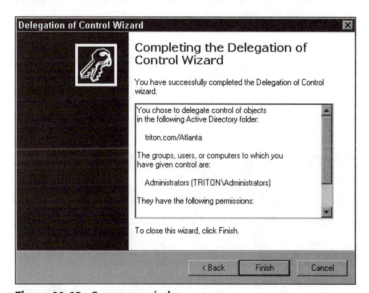

Figure 11-12: Summary window

Configuring Class and Attribute Security

Objects within the Active Directory are divided into different classes. Each object in the Active Directory contains a predefined set of attributes. Attributes define the object in terms of the Active Directory. For example, a user account object can have attributes, such as user name, e-mail address, phone number, and so forth. The

Active Directory allows you to set security both on classes of objects and attributes of objects themselves. Use the object's Security tab and use Advanced permissions to configure attribute security (see the first section in this chapter). With this option, you have a very fine level of control over permissions to Active Directory classes and attributes. For example, you could choose to grant a group of users permission to view a user account object, but you could deny the group the right to view the e-mail address attribute. This way, users could read the user account object, but not the e-mail address.

Obviously, this fine level of control requires some planning on your part to determine if setting special security on classes is desirable or necessary for your implementation. The point is that you can control security this finely and circumstances may present themselves where you need this fine level of control.

Installing the AdminPak

In order to set security on classes, you must install the Active Directory Schema Manager, which is a part of the AdminPak Tools found on your Windows 2000 installation CD-ROM. To install the AdminPak, follow these steps:

1. Log on with an administrator account.

2. Insert your Windows 2000 Server installation CD-ROM into your CD-ROM drive and choose the "Browse this CD" option when the splash screen appears.

3. Open the I386 folder and scroll down until you locate the AdminPak icon, shown in Figure 11-13.

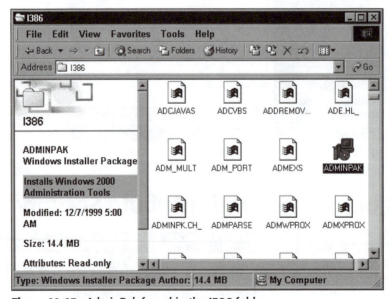

Figure 11-13: AdminPak found in the I386 folder

4. A Welcome screen appears. Click the Next button. The system installs the tools. Click the Finish button.

Once the AdminPak is installed, you can then manually load the Active Directory Schema Manager snap-in.

Caution

The Schema Manager has the capacity to alter your Active Directory, a very serious operation that can result in failure of the Active Directory and the need for reinstallation in some cases. You can learn more about the Schema Manager and the issues with schema modification in Chapter 14.

Opening the Schema Manager

To load the Schema Manager snap-in, follow these steps:

1. Click Start ⇨ Run and type **mmc** in the dialog box. Then click OK.

2. Click Console ⇨ Add/Remove Snap-in, as shown in Figure 11-14.

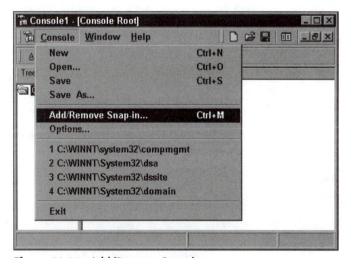

Figure 11-14: Add/Remove Snap-in

3. The Add/Remove Snap-in window appears. Click the Add button.

4. From the list of snap-ins that appears, select Active Directory Schema, shown in Figure 11-15, click the Add button, and then click the Close button.

5. Click the OK button. The Schema Manager appears in the console.

Figure 11-15: Select Active Directory Schema

Setting class security

You can set security for a class by selecting the class container and then double-clicking the desired class that appears in the right pane. Once again, be careful when using the Schema Manager. Incorrect changes are saved immediately and replicated to other domain controllers.

Right-click the desired class, shown in Figure 11-16, and then click Properties.

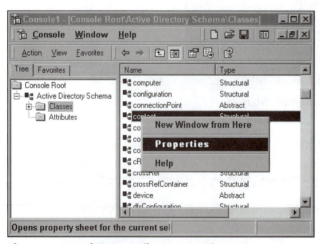

Figure 11-16: Class or attribute properties

On the properties sheet that appears, click the Security tab. The Security tab for classes looks and functions the same as all other Security tabs in Windows 2000. See the first section in this chapter for more information about using the Security tab.

Summary

This chapter explored the standard security features of the Active Directory. First, the Active Directory enables you to set permissions on objects and object attributes by accessing the Security tab on each object's properties sheets. With the Advanced options, you have a fine level of security control available to you. Next, the Active Directory provides for delegation of administration through the Delegation of Control Wizard. Use this wizard to decentralize your administrative demands while maintaining administrative control. Finally, the Active Directory Schema Manager also enables you to set security on individual classes of Active Directory attributes. All of these options create a secure database that can be configured to meet the security needs of your organization.

✦   ✦   ✦

Active Directory Management

Once the Active Directory is implemented, your job as an IT professional is to manage the Active Directory daily. Management is a broad term that includes not only daily tasks, such as user, group, and computer account management, but also a number of other items that keep the Active Directory functioning at its peak.

In this part of the book, you explore Active Directory management by examining fault tolerance, backup, restoration, and a number of related management features. You also explore Active Directory replication and how to manage and control replication traffic between Active Directory sites.

Finally, this portion of the book allows you to explore the Active Directory schema, a listing of definitions that provides the Active Directory with functionality. You learn how the schema works, how it can be modified, and when the schema should be modified to meet the needs of an organization.

Maintaining the Active Directory

The importance of effectively preserving data in the case of a catastrophic system failure cannot be understated. In fact, large companies spend a lot of time and money studying redundancy and how to make certain that data can be recovered in the event of a failure. In the same manner, databases must be maintained so they contain accurate data. Both of these issues are included in our discussion of maintaining the Active Directory. Fortunately, the Active Directory does a good job of taking care of itself, so you will not be overwhelmed with necessary maintenance tasks. However, there are a few items you need to know about, and this chapter explores these issues.

Backing Up the Active Directory

As with any data, the Active Directory can be backed up using Windows Backup (or third-party solutions) and can be restored in the event of a hard disk failure. Before discussing the backup process and technologies in Windows 2000, it is important to remember that the Active Directory uses multimaster replication. Each domain controller contains a copy of the Active Directory database, and that database is kept synchronized between the domain controllers through multimaster replication. Because of this feature, the Active Directory database is inherently fault tolerant. There is no one single master replicator or a master copy of the Active Directory database that must be protected. Each domain controller is a peer, and each domain controller maintains an exact copy of the database. The more domain controllers in a domain, the safer the data is from loss. For example in a domain that has four domain controllers, all four domain controllers would have to have hard disk failures simultaneously to actually "lose" the domain and all of your data—an event that is highly unlikely.

You can learn more about the replication process in Chapter 13.

So, if the Active Directory database is inherently fault tolerant, why bother backing it up? As a part of an effective backup plan, you should back up the database so you can restore a domain controller to its pre-fault state. The backup procedure enables you to return the domain controller to its exact state with the Active Directory database from the time of the last backup. Of course, the database will be outdated by the time you repair and restore the domain controller, but normal replication with other domain controllers will update the old database so that it is current. Another important reason to use an effective backup plan is catastrophic disaster. What if there is a fire or earthquake that destroys all of the servers? With an effective backup, you can restore the Active Directory implementation and network data on new servers.

As mentioned, this is all part of an effective backup plan that should be implemented not only for the Active Directory database, but also for all of your critical data. The following two sections examine some important fault-tolerant issues and a later section shows you how to back up the Active Directory.

Windows disk fault-tolerant solutions

The term *fault tolerance* simply means that a system has the capability to *tolerate* a system failure, or fault. In other words, the system has the capability to continue functioning even through part of it has failed. For example, the use of uninterruptible power supply (UPS) is a fault-tolerant solution. With a UPS, a server can tolerate an electrical failure and run from the UPS battery for a short period of time. This feature prevents data loss and allows the administrator to shut down the server in an orderly fashion.

Windows 2000 has two built-in fault-tolerant features for fixed hard disks. In the event of a hard disk failure, the system can recover the data so it is not lost.

It is important to note that disk fault-tolerant solutions are not a replacement for an effective backup plan. Although very effective and useful, you should use disk fault tolerance in conjunction with a backup plan.

Disk fault-tolerant solutions require you to have two or more hard disks, depending on the type of fault tolerance you want to configure. There are two supported types, but you can gain additional types using third-party software. The following bulleted list explains the two types of hard disk fault-tolerant solutions supported in Windows 2000:

✦ **Mirrored Volumes (called Mirror Sets in NT 4.0)** — A mirrored volume creates an exact copy of a Windows 2000 volume on a separate hard disk. When you make changes to the mirrored volume, both the primary volume and the mirror are written so that the mirror is always, well, a mirror. If either the primary or mirror fail, your system can continue functioning using the other disk. Two advantages to a mirrored volume are read and write speed and performance. Write speed is faster than using a RAID-5 volume, and the mirrored volume has better performance. In the event of a disk failure, your system automatically begins using the mirror as though nothing has happened. In other words, you can continue working until you can conveniently repair the disk. The disadvantage of a mirrored volume is the cost. Since a complete copy of the volume is generated on a different disk, you have a 50 percent megabyte cost. In other words, it takes twice as much storage space to store the same data.

✦ **RAID-5 Volumes (called Stripe Sets with Parity in NT 4.0)** — RAID-5 volumes require at least three hard disks in order to create the volume. RAID-5 uses a redundancy technology that writes data in an array across the three hard disks. A parity bit is used in the write technology. If a single disk in the array fails, Windows 2000 can use the parity bit to generate the lost data. Parity data is written to all disks in the array so that a block of data on one disk has a parity block on another disk. This feature enables you to read and write data that is stored across three different disks and is always fault tolerant. RAID-5 volumes have better read performance than mirrored volumes, but in the event of a disk failure, performance is greatly hindered until you stop, replace the failed disk, and regenerate the lost data onto the new disk. However, RAID-5 volumes are not expensive in terms of megabyte cost. In other words, the RAID-5 volume makes much better use of storage space than the mirrored volume.

In terms of Active Directory redundancy, you can use either of these solutions to back up your System State Data (discussed later in this chapter). When you installed the Active Directory, you could choose to place the Active Directory logs and the SYSVOL folder on different hard disks. As with any other data, you can mirror or RAID-5 the volume that contains your Active Directory data so that it is protected in the event of a single hard disk failure. It is important to once again note that disk fault-tolerant solutions protect you only from a single disk failure — this is not a replacement for an effective backup plan. Because a number of events, such as fire or theft, can occur that can cause the loss of an entire system and all hard disks, an effective backup plan is a must.

Windows backup strategies

Windows 2000 includes a built-in Backup utility found by clicking Start ➪ Programs ➪ Accessories ➪ System Tools ➪ Backup. The Windows Backup tool is rather easy to use and allows you to back up your data to all kinds of media devices, including tape drives, Zip and Jaz drives, or even a remote computer's hard disk. With Windows Backup, you can develop an effective backup plan, perform periodic backups, and then store your back media in safe places so it can be accessed and used in the event of catastrophic failure. Windows 2000 supports several different types of backup that you can perform. The following bulleted list explains these types:

✦ **Normal backup**—A normal backup copies all selected files to the backup media and marks each file as having been backed up by clearing the files' archive attribute.

✦ **Incremental backup**—An incremental backup backs up the changes that have occurred in the files since the last normal or incremental backup. For example, suppose you have a backup set that includes 50 documents. Three of those documents have been edited since the last normal backup. During an incremental backup, only the changes to those three documents will be written to the backup media. An incremental backup marks the files as having been backed up. Incremental backups are used with normal backups, so during a restoration, you will need to use both normal and incremental backup media to accurately restore the data.

✦ **Differential backup**—A differential backup copies files that have been created or have been changed since the last normal or incremental backup. It does not mark the files as having been backed up. That the file is not marked as having been backed up means that the archive attribute of the file is not cleared. As with an incremental backup, you must use differential backup jobs in conjunction with a normal backup in order to accurately recover the data, although a differential backup uses less media when restoring than an incremental backup.

✦ **Daily backup**—A daily backup copies all selected files that have changed that day. The backed up files are not marked as having been backed up. That the file is not marked as having been backed up means that the archive attribute of the file is not cleared. Daily backups are an effective way to selectively backup important files on a daily basis.

✦ **Copy backup**—A copy backup copies all files that you select but does not mark the file as having been backed up. That the file is not marked as having been backed up means that the archive attribute of the file is not cleared. A copy backup is a quick and easy way to back up files between normal and incremental backups because it does not interfere with the markers from the other backup jobs.

As an administrator, the question you have to consider is how to use these backup options to create a backup strategy that is effective for your network. Though it is beyond the scope of this book to thoroughly explore backup strategies, most environments use a combination of normal and incremental/differential backups. For example, you perform a normal backup on Monday and incremental backups Tuesday–Friday. This is an effective plan that keeps backup time to minimum, although it can take you longer to restore your data. For example, if you have a failure on Friday morning, you will need Monday's normal backup job and Tuesday's, Wednesday's, and Thursday's incremental backup jobs to accurately regain the data. This can be quite time-consuming, but most administrators consider the speed of backup more important than the speed of the restore since, hopefully, a restore will be a rare event. The trick is to find the right backup plan that provides you with current backups and doesn't take up too much administrative time. You can learn more about backup strategies from the Windows 2000 Resource Kit or from an IT book that explores these options.

Understanding System State Data

When you back up the Active Directory, you back up System State Data. System State Data is defined as a collection of system specific data that you back up as a collection. System State Data is made up of several components, but you cannot back up those components individually due to dependencies among the data. Every Windows 2000 computer contains System State Data, and when you perform a backup for the Active Directory, you simply choose to back up System State Data on the domain controller. For all Windows 2000 operating systems except domain controllers, System State Data contains the following:

✦ Registry

✦ COM+ Class Registration database

✦ System boot files

Tip   You can back up System State Data only on your local server. You cannot back up System State Data on a remote computer, regardless of your rights. So, to back up the Active Directory on a domain controller, the process has to be done at the actual domain controller.

For Windows 2000 domain controllers, System State Data contains the following:

✦ Registry

✦ COM+ Class Registration database

✦ System boot files

✦ Active Directory Services database

✦ SYSVOL directory

Note   Windows 2000 servers (including domain controllers) that are certificate servers
will also contain the Certificate Services database in the System State Data, and if
the server is a part of a cluster server, System State will also contain Cluster Service
information.

Performing a Backup

Now that you understand System State Data, you can use Windows Backup to back
up the Active Directory. The Windows Backup utility provides you with a wizard
to perform this task, or you can manually create the backup job. I want to first consider how to create a backup job using the Backup Wizard. The following steps walk
you through this process:

1. On a domain controller, log on with an administrative account and click
Start ⇨ Programs ⇨ Accessories ⇨ System Tools ⇨ Backup. The Backup
utility appears, shown in Figure 12-1.

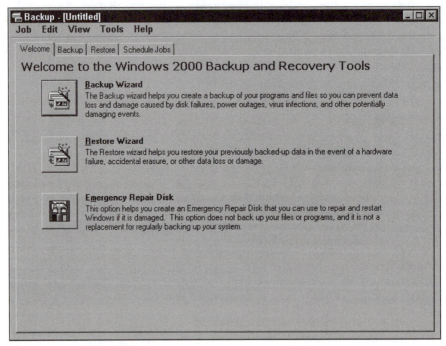

Figure 12-1: Windows Backup

2. Click the Backup Wizard button to start the wizard and then click Next on the Welcome screen.

3. On the What to Back Up window, you have three backup options. By default, "Back up everything on my computer" is selected. If you want to back up only System State data, click the "Only back up the System State data" radio button, shown in Figure 12-2, and then click the Next button.

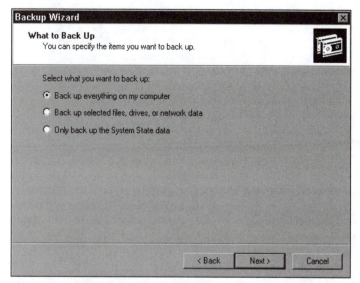

Figure 12-2: What to Back Up window

4. The Where to Store the Backup window appears, shown in Figure 12-3. Use the Browse button to select the device drive and name for the media. Backup jobs are stored as .bkf files (Windows Backup) with a default name of Backup.bkf. Select the appropriate location and name and then click the Next button.

5. The Completion window appears. Before clicking the Finish button, click the Advanced button located on this window.

6. The Type of Backup window appears, shown in Figure 12-4. Use the drop-down menu to select normal, incremental, differential, daily, or copy backups. Also, you have the option to back up files that have been migrated to remote storage. Since you are backing up only System State Data, you do not need to be concerned with this option. Make your selection and click the Next button.

Figure 12-3: Where to Store the Backup window

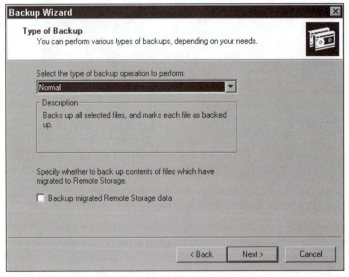

Figure 12-4: Type of Backup window

7. The How to Back Up window appears. You have two check box options. First, you can choose to verify data after backup. Selecting this check box enables the system to verify the backup job to make certain it is not corrupt. This option causes the backup job to take more time, but it does assure you of a good backup. Next, you can use hardware compression if it is available on your system. Selecting this check box enables your system to use hardware compression technology to compress the contents in order to conserve storage space. However, if you use this option, only drives that support compression can be used to restore the data. Make your selections and click the Next button.

Note If hardware compression is not supported on your system, this option will be grayed out.

8. The Media Options window appears. This window, shown in Figure 12-5, provides two radio buttons that enable you to determine whether to overwrite an existing backup job or to append this backup job to existing media. In the case of a full backup, you should choose to overwrite the data. Make your selection and click the Next Button.

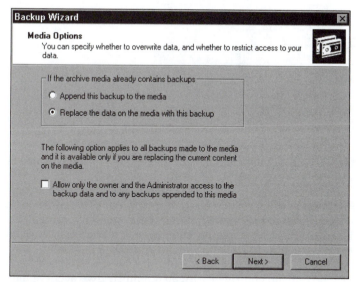

Figure 12-5: Media Options window

9. The Backup Label window appears. In this window, you can specify a label for the backup job and the media. For the backup job, the default label is "Set created on *date* at *time*." The date and time values are automatically filled in. The default label for the media is "Media created on *date* at *time*." You can change these default labels by clicking the dialog box to erase them and typing your new desired labels. Make your selections and click the Next button.

10. The When to Back Up window appears. You can choose either the Now or Later radio button. If you choose Later, enter a job name and a start date for the backup to occur. You can also click the Set Schedule button to create a backup schedule. For now, choose Now and click the Next button.

11. A summary window appears. Review your settings and then click the Finish button to begin the backup job. A progress window appears, shown in Figure 12-6.

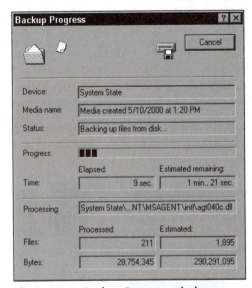

Figure 12-6: Backup Progress window

12. Once the backup is complete, click the Close button. You can also click the Report button to read a report about the backup job.

The Backup Wizard provides you a step-by-step approach to performing backup jobs. However, once you are savvy with the process, you will probably choose to manually create the jobs. In my opinion, the manual creation is a lot faster. The following steps show you how to back up System State Data manually.

1. Log on to the domain controller with an administrative account and click Start ➪ Programs ➪ Accessories ➪ System Tools ➪ Backup. The Backup utility opens.

2. Click the Backup tab, shown in Figure 12-7. In this window, select System State in the folder list and use the Browse button at the bottom of the window to select your desired backup media. Then, click the Start Backup button.

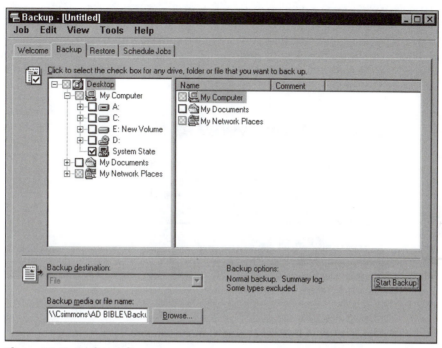

Figure 12-7: Backup tab

3. A Backup Job Information window appears, as shown in Figure 12-8. Make changes to this window as desired, such as the backup job and media label and whether to append or replace existing media.

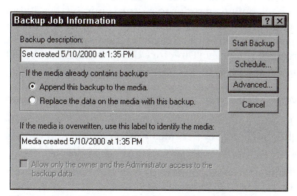

Figure 12-8: Backup Job Information window

You can also click the Schedule button to create a schedule, and you can click the Advanced button to open the Advanced Backup Options, shown in Figure 12-9. On this window, you can make some standard selections and also choose the type of backup to perform. Make your selections in the Advanced Backup Options window and click OK. Then, click the Start Backup button when you are ready.

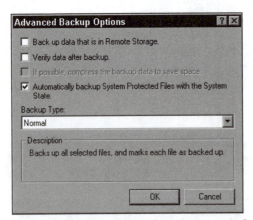

Figure 12-9: Advanced Backup Options window

Restoring Active Directory Data

In the event of a domain controller failure, you can use your System State backup job to restore your Active Directory database and SYSVOL folder. Of course, this data will be outdated, but replication with other domain controllers will update the data once the domain controller is back online. In order to restore your System State Data, you must first repair the domain controller and ensure that it is in working order. Then you must reboot your server into Directory Services Restore Mode. This Safe Mode option enables you to restore the Active Directory database and the SYSVOL directory. To perform a restoration on a domain controller, follow these steps:

1. Reboot your server. At POST, hold down the F8 key on your keyboard.

2. The Windows 2000 Advanced Options menu appears. Use your keyboard arrow keys to highlight Directory Services Restore Mode and then press Enter twice. Windows 2000 boots into Directory Services Restore Mode.

3. Log on with an administrative account and then click OK to the Safe Mode message that appears.

4. Click Start ➪ Programs ➪ Accessories ➪ System Tools ➪ Backup.

5. Click the Restore Wizard button on the Welcome tab and then click Next on the Welcome screen.

6. In the What to Restore window, select the desired media that you want to use to restore the System State Data, as shown in Figure 12-10. You may need to expand the categories to reach the backup job. Click Next.

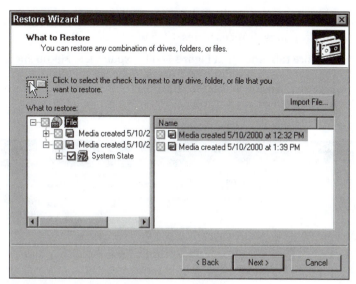

Figure 12-10: What to Restore window

7. The Completion window appears. Before clicking Finish, click the Advanced button.

8. The Where to Restore window appears. You see a drop-down menu that enables you to select the original location, an alternate location, or a single folder. Make your selection and then click Next.

9. In the How to Restore window, you can choose from three radio buttons concerning files that already exist. Your options are as follows:

   • Do not replace the file on my disk (recommended).

   • Replace the file on disk if it is older than the backup copy.

   • Always replace the file on the disk.

   Make your selection and then click the Next button.

10. In the Advanced Restore Options window, you can select three check boxes that may be available to you (depending on your configuration). They are Restore security, Restore Removable Storage database, and Restore junction points. Make your selections (if necessary) and click the Next button.

11. Click the Finish button and then click OK. The restore job begins and you see a Restore progress indicator. Once the restoration is complete, click Close.

Just as you can perform a backup job without the wizard, you can also restore a backup job without the wizard. As with backup, you will probably find this option faster. The following steps show you how to perform a restore job without using the Restore Wizard.

1. In Directory Services Restore Mode and when logged on as an administrator, click Start ➪ Programs ➪ Accessories ➪ System Tools ➪ Backup.

2. Click the Restore tab, shown in Figure 12-11. Expand the Media and select your System State Data backup job. You can also use the drop-down menu at the bottom of the window to restore the files to the original or alternate location. Click the Start Restore button.

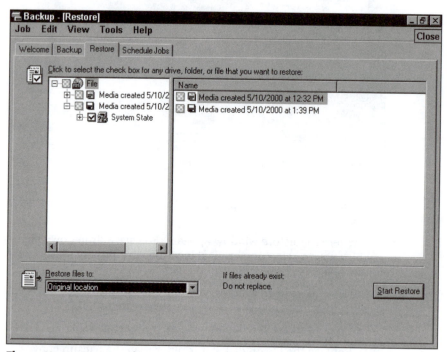

Figure 12-11: Restore tab

3. The Confirm Restore window appears, shown in Figure 12-12.

If you want to configure advanced restore options, click the Advanced button. This action opens a single window, shown in Figure 12-13, where you can select a few check boxes if desired. These are the same options presented to you when using the wizard. Click OK and then click OK again to start the restore. You see a status window as the restore occurs. Click the Close button when the restore is complete.

Figure 12-12: Confirm Restore window

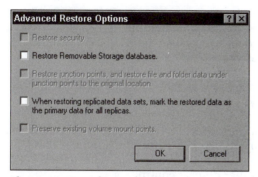

Figure 12-13: Advanced Restore Options window

Once you complete the restore job, you see a message telling you that you need to reboot your computer. Once you bring your domain controller back online, your Active Directory database will be updated through replication with other domain controllers.

Performing an Authoritative Restore

An important reason for backing up your Active Directory database is the possibility of the need for an authoritative restore. An authoritative restore enables you to restore an Active Directory backup and to prevent the restored changes from being overwritten due to domain controller replication. In fact, an authoritative restore marks the restore job as *authoritative* and its data is replicated to other domain controllers, overwriting their existing data.

Consider an example. Suppose you have a container that holds all of the printer objects on your network. You accidentally delete the entire container and all of the objects, and before you can do anything about it, the change is replicated to all domain controllers. Now, no domain controller holds this container or any of your printer objects. Fortunately, however you back up your System State Data each day. You restore your container and printer objects and bring your domain controller back online. However, you notice that in a short time, the container and objects are gone again. Why? Your restore job is older than the current Active Directory database residing on online domain controllers. You can restore the container and objects, but each time you bring the domain controller back online, replication will overwrite the older copy and delete the container and objects again. As you can see, this could be a hopeless situation. This is the purpose of an authoritative restore. You can restore your last backup job that will replace your container and printer objects and then use an authoritative restore so that your restored objects are replicated to the other domain controllers.

To use an authoritative restore, boot your server into Directory Service Restore Mode and then perform the restore with the Backup utility as described in the previous section. Then, before rebooting, you use the NTDSUTIL command-line utility to perform an authoritative restore.

Caution   You must perform the authoritative restore after you restore your data with the backup utility and before you reboot your server.

When you use NTDSUTIL, you mark which Active Directory objects are authoritative. When you do this, the objects' Update Sequence Numbers (USNs) are changed so they are higher than all other USNs. This ensures that the data is considered "new" and is replicated to all other domain controllers.

Cross-Reference   You can learn more about USNs in Chapter 13.

In order to use NTDSUTIL, you must install the AdminPak tools found in the I386 folder on your installation CD-ROM. For specific steps, see Appendix C. Once the AdminPak has been installed on your system, click Start ➪ Run and type **ntdsutil.exe** in the dialog box and click OK.

At the command prompt, type **authoritative restore**. At the prompt, type **?** to see a list of help commands available in performing the restore. You have the following options:

✦ **Restore database** — Restores the entire database.

✦ **Restore database verinc %d** — Restores the entire database and overrides version increase.

✦ **Restore subtree %s** — Restores a subtree.

✦ **Restore subtree %s verinc %d** — Restores a subtree and overrides version increase.

These are your standard options. To perform the restore, type one of the above options and enter the LDAP information. For example:

```
Ntdsutil: authoritative restore:
Restore Subtree OU=Acct, DC=triton, DC=com
```

As you can see, I have instructed NTDSUTIL to authoritatively restore an OU called Acct in the triton.com domain. You can also authoritatively restore specific objects using the CN or DN. To restore the entire database, just type the following:

```
Ntdsutil: authoritative restore:
Restore database
```

Once you have completed the authoritative restore, type **quit** then reboot your computer. When the server comes back online, the authoritative objects will be replicated to all other domain controllers.

 Caution   It is important to note here that an authoritative restore is designed to get you out of a jam — it's something that should be done carefully and only in specific circumstances.

Using the Recovery Console

While not used in recovering Active Directory data specifically, the Recovery Console in Windows 2000 is an excellent command-line tool that provides you with some powerful options when you're faced with a system that will not start. With the Recovery Console, you can format drives, stop and start services, read and write data on local drives, copy files to your system from the CD-ROM, and perform a number of other administrative tasks. As you can imagine, the Recovery Console can be dangerous and should be used only by experienced administrators.

There are two ways to use the Recovery Console. First, you can install it on your system so that it becomes a boot menu option. When installed, you can boot your computer, hold down the F8 key, and then select the Recovery Console from the list. Also, you can boot your system from your Windows 2000 installation CD-ROM (if your system supports booting from your CD-ROM).

You can install or access the Recovery Console at the command prompt. Insert your installation CD-ROM into your CD-ROM drive, and then at the command prompt, change to your CD-ROM drive and type the following:

```
\i386\winnt32.exe/cmdcons
```

A message appears asking if you want to install the Recovery Console (which requires 7MB of disk space). Click Yes if you want to install it and then follow the instructions that appear on your screen. Once the Recovery Console is installed, you can then access it by restarting your server and holding down the F8 key to get the boot menu.

If you do not want to install the Recovery Console on your computer, but you need to use it, restart your computer and allow it to boot off your CD-ROM drive. Your system will load a number of files, which will take several minutes. When prompted, choose the option to repair a Windows 2000 installation and then select the Recovery Console.

As mentioned, there are a lot of administrative functions you can perform with the Recovery Console. Table 12-1 lists the commands available and gives you a description of each. Also, be aware that additional parameters exist for many of the commands, so you can use the "?" feature to review parameters when you are using the console.

Table 12-1
Recovery Console Commands

Command	Explanation
Attrib	Used to change file or directory attributes.
Batch	Runs commands in a text file.
Chdir (CD)	Displays the current directory; used to change directories or folders.
Chkdsk	Checks the disk and gives you a status report.
Cls	Clears the screen.
Copy	Copies a single file to a specified location.
Delete (Del)	Deletes a single specified file.
Dir	Displays the contents in a directory.
Disable	Used to disable a service or device driver.
Diskpart	Creates and deletes hard disk partitions.
Enable	Enables a service or device driver.
Exit	Closes the Recovery Console.
Expand	Extracts a file from a compressed file, such as a .cab file.
Fixboot	Writes a new partition boot sector to the system partition.
Fixmbr	Writes a new master boot record to the hard drive.
Format	Formats a specified hard drive.
Help	Provides help files.
Listof	Provides a list of Recovery Console commands.
Listsvc	Lists services and drivers on the computer.

Command	Explanation
Logon	Logs you on to an installation of Windows 2000.
Map	Shows you the mapping of drive letters to physical device names.
Mkdir (md)	Creates a directory or subdirectory.
More	Shows you the contents of a text file.
Rename (ren)	Changes the name of a single file.
Rmdir (rd)	Deletes a directory.
Set	Displays and sets Recovery Console environment variables.
Systemroot	Sets the current directory to the systemroot.
Type	Displays the contents of a text file.

Common Maintenance Issues

Databases, the Active Directory included, are always changing. In large environments, data in the Active Directory database is changed and updated almost constantly, and those changes are replicated among domain controllers. Fortunately, the Active Directory does a very good job of taking care of its own maintenance needs, so as an administrator, you should not be faced with a regular onslaught of maintenance tasks. However, there are a few items I would like to mention in this section.

Before examining those issues, I want to spend a few moments examining how the Active Directory works in terms of storing data and managing the database file and transaction log file. The Active Directory is based on the Extensible Storage Engine (ESE) database and is considered a fault-tolerant, transaction-based database. This feature enables the Active Directory to totally manage and track its own data. There are two basic components of the Active Directory—the database file that contains all of the Active Directory objects and the transaction log files that provide the fault tolerance to the database.

The Active Directory database file contains all objects in the Active Directory and their metadata.

Tip

Metadata is defined as "data about data." Each Active Directory object contains attributes, which are characteristics about that object. For example, a user object may have attributes of user name, e-mail address, password, group membership, and so on. This metadata helps define the user object by providing data about data. You can learn more about metadata and object attributes in Chapter 13.

Each domain controller contains the Active Directory database file, which is called Ntds.dit (directory information tree) and is found, by default, in system\NTDS directory. Replication among domain controllers ensures that each domain controller's copy of the database file is accurate and up-to-date with all other domain controllers' database files. The database file stores information in three different tables:

✦ **Object table** — Contains objects and object attributes.

✦ **Link table** — Contains links or relationship information between the objects and attributes in the Object table.

✦ **Schema table** — Contains the definitions of all the possible objects that can be created in the Active Directory.

The transaction log files record transactions that occur within the database. In actuality, when a process needs to occur, the process is written to the transaction log files, and then the transaction is carried out in the database file. This feature provides fault tolerance because a written set of instructions is created before the action ever occurs. If something should happen, such as a server failure or power outage during the write process, the Active Directory uses the log files to reconstruct the data that had not been written to the database when the failure occurred.

Aside from the actual database file and the transaction log files, there are three other files used by the Active Directory:

✦ **Checkpoint files** — Checkpoint files hold pointers to transactions that have already been written to the database file.

✦ **Reserved log files** — Reserved log files are used as backups in the case of low disk space.

✦ **Patch files** — Patch files are used to manage data during an online backup.

The current transaction log file is named Edb.log and is stored in the same directory as the database file. The Edb.log file has a fixed size of about 10MB. When the Edb.log file fills to its capacity, a new log file is created and the old log file is renamed edb*xxxxxx*.log where *xxxxxx* is a hexadecimal character to indicate it is an old log file. Once all of the transactions in the old log file have been performed, the old transaction log is deleted.

You can change this default behavior by enabling circular logging. Circular logging does not create new transaction log files, but rather overwrites the old one when it fills. In essence, it uses the same log file over and over by overwriting unneeded information. Circular logging enables the Active Directory to maintain fewer transaction logs, but for the best data recoverability, you should not use circular logging. However, if you believe that circular logging may improve the performance of your server, you can enable it by opening the Registry Editor and accessing the following:

```
HKEY_LOCAL_MACHINE\CurrentControlSet\Services\NTDS\Paramters\CircularLogging
```

Enter a **1** to enable circular logging (**0** to disable it).

Caution   As always, here's the obligatory warning about editing the registry. Incorrect editing of the registry can cause system-wide failures and a boot failure, so edit with great care.

Checking the LostAndFound container

The LostAndFound container, shown in Figure 12-14, is a hidden container found in the Active Directory Users and Computers console. To see the container, click View ⇨ Advanced, and you will see LostAndFound appear in the left console pane.

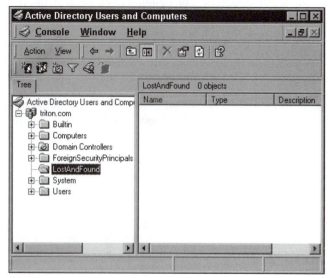

Figure 12-14: LostAndFound container

The LostAndFound container holds "orphaned" objects. An orphaned object is one that replication cannot determine where to place. When this occurs, the orphaned object is put into the LostAndFound container. Consider an example. Suppose that Administrator A wants to create a new printer object in a container called Mkt Printers. However, at the same time, Administrator B moves all of the existing printers from this container and deletes the container. The new object created by Administrator A has nowhere to go because its target container has been deleted. So, the Active Directory determines that this is an orphaned object and puts it in the LostAndFound container.

You don't need to spend your time worrying about orphaned objects because they rarely occur. However, as an Active Directory administrator, you should check the LostAndFound container from time to time. If objects are present, you can move them to an appropriate location or delete them if they are not needed.

Online and offline defragmentation

You're familiar with hard disk fragmentation, where your data is stored in noncontiguous pieces. In a likewise manner, databases become fragmented over time and become cluttered with "junk" and unused objects. The Active Directory performs its own routine maintenance by automatically deleting unused objects and files to recover usable space, and the Active Directory automatically defragments itself in order to optimize the data storage.

The automatic cleanup process, called Garbage Collection, occurs every twelve hours. During Garbage Collection, old transaction logs are deleted, and unneeded objects are deleted from the Active Directory. The deletion of objects occurs by a process called *tombstoning*. Suppose you delete a printer object from the Active Directory. During Garbage Collection, the printer object is tagged with a tombstone, which is not visible to clients. Once an object is tombstoned, it appears as though it has been deleted, when in reality the tombstone is kept for a default period of 60 days, called the Tombstone Lifetime. The process occurs to ensure that the tombstone has enough time to be replicated to all domain controllers in the forest so that the object can be deleted from all domain controller databases. If the tombstoning process did not occur, some domain controller databases would still contain the object while it would be deleted from others. Once the Tombstone Lifetime passes, the object is actually deleted from the database. Finally, the last part of Garbage Collection is online defragmentation of the database. This process rearranges objects to make the best and most logical use of space. Online defragmentation does not actually reduce the size of the database, but it does keep the database organized.

You can perform an offline, or manual database defragmentation, which organizes data and may actually reduce the size of the database. In order to perform an offline defragmentation, you must boot your server into Directory Services Repair Mode and use NTDSUTIL to create a second, defragmented version of the database. Then you begin using a new database. Microsoft strongly recommends that you perform this process with a test database to see if offline defragmentation will actually help you reduce the size of the database. If it does not, there is no benefit to performing an offline defragmentation.

 Caution Under most circumstances, you should not need to perform an offline defragmentation. Make sure you study your situation and need carefully before performing this action.

Removing ghost objects

A final maintenance issue I want to mention is ghost objects, also called phantom objects. Ghost objects are actually errors that occur within the database and occur when an object has been deleted, but some kind of error has prevented the object from actually being removed. You end up with a ghost object that appears in the directory although the object is not actually available. The same problem can possibly occur when you remove a domain. When the last domain controller is removed, you should select the "this is the last domain controller in the domain" check box. If you do not, the domain still appears in the Active Directory even though it does not actually exist.

Fortunately, ghost objects or domains can be easily removed. For objects, take note of the full object path, such as cn=object, cn=OU, dc=domain, dc=com and then boot the server into Directory Services Repair Mode. Run NTDSUTIL, type **Files**, and enter the full path of the object. Then run a header and integrity check in order to remove the ghost.

In the case of a ghosted domain, use NTDSUTIL and follow these steps:

1. Type **metadata cleanup** and press Enter.

2. Type **connections** and press Enter.

3. Type **connect to server domainnamingmasterserver** and press Enter.

4. Type **quit** and press Enter.

5. Type **select operation target** and press Enter.

6. Type **list domains** and press Enter.

7. Type **select domain number**, where **number** is the number of the domain, and press Enter.

8. Type **quit** and press Enter.

9. Type **remove selected domain** and press Enter.

Summary

This chapter explored a number of Active Directory maintenance issues. First, you can back up the Active Directory database on a domain controller using Windows Backup. In order to back up the Active Directory database, you choose to back up System State Data. In the case of a failure, the database can be recovered by booting the server into Directory Services Repair Mode and then using Windows Backup to restore the database. In some cases, you may need to perform an authoritative restore, which marks an entire database or certain objects as authoritative for replication purposes. This process is performed using NTDSUTIL and before you reboot the server. You can also use the Windows 2000 Recovery Console, which can be installed or run from the installation CD-ROM to perform a number of administrative tasks. Finally, you can maintain the Active Directory by checking the LostAndFound container, using manual defragmentation (if necessary), and removing ghost objects as needed. Overall, Active Directory maintenance is quite easy for administrators because the Active Directory takes care of most of its maintenance needs.

✦   ✦   ✦

Managing Active Directory Replication

As a technical instructor, I always hated to teach the topic of replication in the NT world. It was difficult, confusing, and often just irritating to students. Replication in Windows 2000 for intrasite and intersite Active Directory traffic is certainly no picnic either, but there have been a number of changes to the process that make replication more effective and certainly more *hands-off* for Active Directory administrators. Unfortunately, the process is still quite complex, and the information from Microsoft about managing intersite traffic is hazy at best. In this chapter, I am going to explore how replication works in a Windows 2000 network. Then I'll explore some practical solutions for managing replication traffic between your Active Directory sites.

How Replication Works

In terms of the Active Directory, replication can be examined in two major categories—intrasite and intersite. *Intrasite replication* is replication that occurs within an Active Directory site. *Intersite replication* is replication that occurs between different Active Directory sites. Before jumping into the details of replication, I first want to review Active Directory's replication model.

Replication is the process of synchronizing data on several computers. The purpose of replication is to ensure that each computer has the same data—in other words, to ensure that a change in data made on one computer is copied to all of the other computers to ensure data integrity.

The Active Directory functions by using multimaster replication. Multimaster replication means that there is no single master replicator computer in the environment, but all domain controllers are responsible for initiating and participating in replication as needed. This peer-to-peer approach is quite powerful because you can make configuration changes to the Active Directory on any domain controller and be assured that those changes will be replicated to all other domain controllers. Remember that each domain controller contains a copy, or replica, of the Active Directory database. The replica is writable, so each domain controller can update its copy when it receives changes through replication. In a large environment with several Active Directory administrators making configuration changes at different domain controllers, the data integrity among domain controllers would be quickly lost without effective replication.

Note　In Windows NT, only the PDC is writable—BDCs have a copy that is replicated from the PDC. So, all changes must be made on the writable copy—which is found only on the PDC. As you can see, the multimaster approach leaves this legacy behind.

So, replication is necessary to ensure that each domain controller's database replica is the same, and the Active Directory uses multimaster replication so that all domain controllers participate in and are responsible for the replication process. Now that I have covered the basics, I want to consider how replication actually works.

Replication concepts

You may be tempted to skip over this section, or you may be bracing for "techno-overload." However, I'll use this section to carefully explain how replication works. Once you have a handle on the design, this will help you understand the big picture of replication. The following sections examine some important conceptual information. Then I'll explore an example of replication and show you how it works in a step-by-step format.

Replication partitions

Active Directory replication functions at three levels, or partitions, of replication. These are the schema partition, configuration partition, and domain partition. The schema partition contains objects and object attributes. The Active Directory schema defines what objects and object attributes can belong to the Active Directory, and this schema is *enterprise* in nature. In an Active Directory environment, all domains and sites in the forest contain the same schema, and all schema replication is forest-wide. Next, replication functions on the configuration partition level. Configuration information contains the physical structure of the Active Directory, such as where sites are located, what domains are contained in what sites, and so forth. Configuration information is replicated to all domains in an Active Directory forest. Finally, there is a domain partition. The domain partition replicates information about Active Directory objects to all domain controllers within the domain. Then, a partial replica is also replicated to global catalog servers so that changes to domain objects are accurately reflected on global catalog servers. So, in terms of partitions, think of the schema and configuration partitions as forest-wide and the domain partition as domain restricted.

Attribute replication

To understand replication, it is important to first understand that the replication in the Active Directory is based on objects and object attributes. As you know, Active Directory objects are basically any Active Directory resource, such as users, printers, OUs, shared folders, and so forth. Each object contains attributes, which are descriptors for objects. Think of attributes as fields in a database. For example, suppose you have a user account object. Attributes for that object, such as user name, password, e-mail address, and so on define the object. Now, suppose you change a user's password. That password change must be replicated to all other domain controllers. However, the Active Directory does not have to replicate the entire user object — it has to replicate only the password change for the object because replication is based on the attribute level, as shown in Figure 13-1. Only changed attributes need be replicated — not entire objects. This design helps reduce network bandwidth usage because replication occurs at the smallest level.

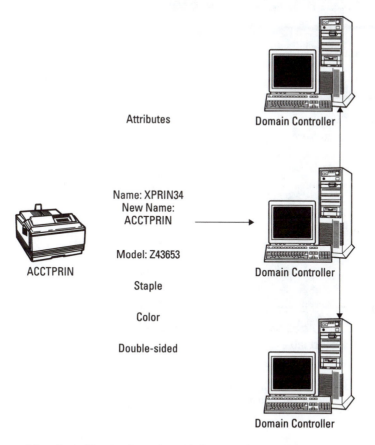

The name of the printer object has been changed. Due to attribute replication, only the name change needs to be replicated to all other domain controllers, not the entire object and all of its other attributes.

Figure 13-1: Attribute replication

Update Sequence Numbers (USNs)

Another concept you need to understand is Update Sequence Numbers (USNs). The Active Directory uses USNs, which are 64-bit numbers, in order to keep track of changes that occur to objects in the Active Directory. When an object is changed, its USN is updated so that all other domain controllers have an outdated USN for that object. By using USNs and updating them when database changes occur, domain controllers know they must receive replication data in order to update their databases. Each domain controller maintains a USN table that lists all of the USN numbers. When replication occurs, the USN table is checked for outdated USNs. Only the highest USN is stored to ensure that only the most current data is saved in the database. When you examine an Active Directory object's properties, such as a user account, you can click the Object tab and see the original USN and the current USN for the object, as shown in Figure 13-2.

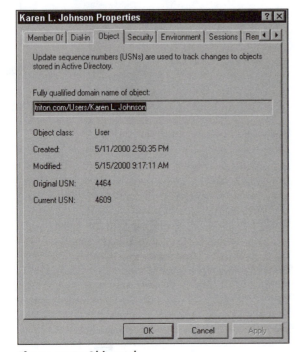

Figure 13-2: Object tab

    Tip   If you do not see an Object tab, then in the Active Directory Users and Computers tool, click View ➪ Advanced. The Object tab will appear.

Because of USNs, timestamps, which often made directory replication difficult due to time synchronization, are no longer necessary. However, the Active Directory still maintains timestamps for tiebreaking purposes using the W32Time service in Windows 2000. For example, suppose that two different administrators working on two different domain controllers change the same attribute of an object at almost exactly the same time (which is rather unlikely). Now you have two USN updates for the same object. The Active Directory can use the timestamp to determine which update is the latest. The latest update always wins the tiebreaker.

Store and forward, replication partners, and topology

Active Directory replication uses a process called *store and forward*. This simply means that replication changes are not directly sent to every domain controller. Instead, changes made on one domain controller are replicated to that domain controller's replication partners, who then send the replicated data to their replication partners, and so forth until the replicated data reaches all domain controllers. Fortunately for us, the Active Directory internally determines which domain controllers will be partners. This is accomplished through an automatic replication topology generation through the Windows 2000 Knowledge Consistency Checker (KCC) service. The KCC is built in to every Windows 2000 domain controller and runs every 15 minutes by default.

Within an Active Directory site, the Active Directory creates its own topology using the KCC to determine which domain controller will replicate to another domain controller. This partner approach ensures that each domain controller receives replicated data through a partner and reduces network traffic because each domain controller doesn't have to replicate with every other domain controller when a database change occurs. The KCC is used to create dynamic connection objects between domain controllers. Replication partners can be either direct or transitive, and a connection object is defined as a potential direct replication partner. Connection objects directly replicate with one another and all other partners transitively receive the replicated data. Again, this process reduces great bursts of network traffic because a single domain controller does not need to communicate directly with all other domain controllers for replication to occur.

By default, connection objects form a bidirectional ring based on information you provide about sites and cost of connections. Within the site, this bidirectional ring is constructed by the KCC so that the average number of hops a directory change will have to make is three or less. When a change is made on one domain controller that needs to be replicated, the process begins by waiting for a replication interval to occur, which is every 5 minutes. After this, data is replicated around the ring directly among connection objects and transitively to transitive partners. In a site, a complete replication cycle should take 15 minutes or less.

The KCC monitors this intrasite and intersite topology to ensure integrity. If one domain controller should fail or be taken offline, the KCC automatically adjusts the topology to account for the lost domain controller. The KCC automatically builds the replication topology in each site and then, based on your site link information, also builds a replication topology between sites.

Cross-Reference See Chapters 5 and 8 to learn more about sites and site links.

Once again, the KCC handles all of this automatically and in the background. You do not have to configure a replication topology manually; the Active Directory generates one for you based on information about your sites and site links.

Note You can manually alter the KCC's automatic replication topology if necessary. This issue is explored later in the chapter.

Replication protocols

Intrasite and intersite replication each use different transport protocols in order to effectively delivery Active Directory replication data. Intrasite replication uses Remote Procedure Calls (RPC) over Internet Protocol (IP). The RPC/IP communication within a site is considered *synchronous*. In other words, after a domain controller sends a request for Active Directory data replication to the originating domain controller, it waits for a reply before requesting data from any other originating domain controller. The synchronous request is *synchronized* in that the domain controller requests data in a "one at a time" fashion. Synchronous RPC/IP is used due to fast delivery nature of intrasite replication. It is also important to note that intrasite replication is uncompressed. Due to the fast nature of delivery and available bandwidth, compression is unnecessary within a site.

Intersite replication supports the use of two transport protocols. As with intrasite replication, intersite replication supports synchronous RPC/IP (compressed). However, intersite replication also supports Simple Mail Transport Protocol (SMTP) for directory replication. The major difference between using RPC/IP and SMTP is that RPC/IP is synchronous while SMTP is asynchronous, which simply means that a domain controller does not wait for a reply from an originating domain controller before making a replication request to another domain controller. SMTP is used for replication between the schema and configuration partitions (as well as the global catalog), but not for the domain partition. The purpose of SMTP transport for directory replication is due to the nature of WAN links or transport across the Internet. RPC/IP often cannot be used over these links, so the Active Directory uses SMTP, which enables "e-mail like" transmissions between sites. SMTP ignores replication schedules and configured replication availability.

The key point to remember about intersite transports is simply this: Use RPC/IP whenever possible. If you have well connected sites, use RPC/IP because there is lower latency, or delay of replication data delivery, than that of SMTP. Use SMTP when you have unreliable site links.

Note It is also important to remember that RPC/IP is synchronous. For slower WAN links, synchronous communication is often undesirable because you are essentially forcing a communication event to complete before another can begin. While it is true that SMTP is slower than RPC/IP, attempting to use RPC/IP over links that cannot handle the bandwidth needs of synchronous communication may produce even slower results (and a whole bunch of RPC time-outs).

The Replication process

Now that I have examined some fundamental concepts of Active Directory replication, it's time to consider how the process actually works. The Active Directory uses *pull* replication. This means that database changes are pulled from a source domain controller where the changes are made to direct replication partners. Replication can also be accomplished via *push* replication where a domain controller pushes unsolicited changes to other domain controllers, but pull replication works best and avoids potential repetitive problems. So, when a change is made on a domain controller, that domain controller issues a *change notification* telling the other domain controllers that it has changes to the Active Directory database. The change notification occurs after an originating update has occurred. An originating update occurs when an LDAP change is made to an Active Directory object or an object has been created. Specifically, an originating update occurs when:

✦ an object is added to the directory

✦ an objected is modified (such as an attribute modification)

✦ an object is moved

✦ an object is deleted

Replication partners respond to the change notification by pulling the originating update from the source domain controller. The USN table is examined on each domain controller, and they find that the USN for the change is outdated in their databases. The domain controllers accept the originating update and then update their databases and USN tables so they are accurate. Once the originating update has been accepted by the domain controllers, it is referred to as a replicated update.

Solving replication problems

Much to our advantage, the Active Directory does a good job of configuring its own replication topology and solving replication problems as they occur. The following sections point out the most common replication problems and show you how the Active Directory resolves these issues.

Resolving collisions

Because of the Active Directory's use of multimaster replication, the potential for replication collisions is present. Because of multimaster replication, two administrators could alter the same object attribute at the same time on different domain controllers. If this occurs, then a replication collision happens. The Active Directory avoids collisions first by attribute replication. For example, if one administrator changes the name of a user account while another changes the password, a collision does not occur because replication changes occur on an attribute level, not the entire object level. However, in the event that a collision does occur, the Active Directory examines the timestamps of the objects to determine which object is the latest. The latest timestamp wins the tiebreaker. In the unlikely event that the timestamps are the same, the Active Directory then examines the Globally Unique Identifier (GUID) of the directory system agent (DSA) to determine which change wins in order to resolve the collision.

Note   As you can see, the odds of two administrators making the same attribute change on the same object at the same time is small, but the Active Directory has this system in place to resolve any and all collisions that occur.

Propagation dampening

As mentioned previously, the Active Directory maintains a bidirectional ring for replication purposes. However, a potential problem that could occur with this design is unnecessary replication traffic. Because of the loop, one domain controller could be sent the same replication traffic more than once. The Active Directory prevents this potential problem through a process called *propagation dampening*. Propagation dampening enables domain controllers to detect when replication traffic has already reached a domain controller. If the replication traffic has reached the domain controller, then the sending domain controller kills the replication traffic so that it is not sent twice to the receiving domain controllers.

This process is accomplished through the use of two vectors called the Up-to-date vector and the High Watermark vector. The Up-to-date vector is a value that a domain controller maintains in order to track all originating updates that have been received. When a domain controller requests a pull change from another domain controller, it sends its Up-to-date vector. The resource domain controller examines the Up-to-date vector to determine if the domain controller in fact needs the update. The second vector used is the High Watermark vector. The High Watermark vector is maintained on a domain controller to determine the latest change for a specific object that was received from the source domain controller. Like the Up-to-date vector, the domain controller sends its High Watermark vector to the source domain controller for examination. The High Watermark vector prevents the same object changes from being sent twice.

Tip   The major difference between the Up-to-date and High Watermark vectors is that the High Watermark vector maintains values for domain controllers from which it requests changes, while the Up-to-date vector is maintained for every domain controller that has ever issued an originating update.

As you can see, the Up-to-date and High Watermark vectors are complementary and are used to filter replication data so the unnecessary replication traffic does not occur.

Examining Intrasite Replication

Now that I have taken a look at some important replication concepts, I want to turn my attention to intrasite replication. Intrasite replication is replication that occurs within an Active Directory site. An Active Directory site is loosely defined as one or more IP subnets that exist where bandwidth is fast and inexpensive. This "fast and inexpensive" definition leaves the final determination up to you, the network architect, but the point is that the Active Directory assumes a site has fast and inexpensive connections, such as a typical LAN or comparable topology.

Cross-Reference   The importance of understanding Active Directory sites and designing sites appropriately cannot be understated. You can learn more about Active Directory sites in Chapters 5 and 8.

Because the Active Directory assumes you have defined your sites in an appropriate manner, intrasite replication occurs in certain ways that make the best use of bandwidth that is fast and inexpensive:

✦ Replication occurs over synchronous RPC/IP.

✦ Replication data is uncompressed.

✦ Replication occurs automatically, without a schedule.

✦ Replication occurs frequently.

Because within your site configuration, the Active Directory assumes that fast, available, and inexpensive bandwidth is present, replication occurs without any schedules, and it happens often. Due to this low cost and availability of bandwidth, the Active Directory maximizes the use of replication to get database changes to other domain controllers as quickly as possible.

As you learned earlier in the chapter, the KCC automatically generates a replication topology within a site so that each domain controller has two connections in the replication ring. The KCC automatically monitors this replication topology and makes changes to it as domain controllers are added and removed. The nature of site replication is automatically configured.

So, within a site, what do you do if you want to manually change the replication topology? In truth — not a lot. Intrasite replication and the replication topology are designed to function without any human intervention. If your sites are configured in an appropriate manner, this is a good thing. The Active Directory handles the topology, replication occurs automatically, and as an administrator, you have one less problem to worry about. However, if you have not designed your sites carefully and if you have sites that do not have effective LAN bandwidth, then you're going to have problems. The key point here is that you *must* carefully design your Active Directory infrastructure and plan your sites carefully before installation. Careful and effective planning solves many, many problems before they ever occur.

Cross-Reference You can learn all about planning an infrastructure in the first part of this book, and you can learn specifically about site planning in Chapter 5.

You can alter the replication topology by manually creating connection points between domain controllers. However, the Active Directory, under certain circumstances, will overwrite your changes anyway, and in reality, there is seldom a situation where altering the automatic replication topology has any actual benefit. You cannot alter the RPC/IP protocol use, you cannot change the noncompression nature of the replication data, and you cannot create any schedules or reduce replication within a site. In short, the default configuration for a site is automatically in place, and there is precious little you can do to change it. So, as you can see, the importance of carefully defining sites and examining your available bandwidth and reliability of your LAN topology is extremely important.

Examining Intersite Replication

Intrasite replication is quite easy because the topology is automatically generated and doesn't work on a schedule. Replication occurs frequently in order to replicate database changes as quickly as possible. Intersite replication is an entirely different animal — a place where you must help the Active Directory determine how to replicate data and where you most likely will have to perform a balancing act on a thin tightrope.

Replication is always a trade-off in terms of data accuracy and time. When a database change occurs that needs to be replicated among sites, you're faced with the balancing act of getting that change to other sites as quickly as possible, given the amount of bandwidth available or speed in which the change can occur. This issue, called latency, is the amount of time that domain controllers' databases are not synchronized after a change has occurred. So, your job as an Active Directory administrator is to take a hard look at WAN connections between your sites and the bandwidth that is available on those connections and determine how to configure replication so that you move data across the WAN connections as fast as possible. Of course, there is no one single answer because the WAN connection speeds and the needs of your network will vary from other networks. The trick is simply to find what works best for your network, making your decision from your data needs and the available WAN connections you have to work with.

So, the process of managing replication between Active Directory sites begins with the site link. Each Active Directory site in an enterprise must be connected to another Active Directory site with a site link. The Active Directory automatically generates a replication topology and connection objects, but you must give the Active Directory information about site links in order for the KCC to generate a replication topology and connection objects between different Active Directory sites. Based on the site link information you configure in the Active Directory Sites and Services tool, the KCC determines how to use the site links for replication data. You can also adjust the schedule for replication and force replication to occur only during low site link bandwidth time periods.

Cross-Reference   Chapter 8 thoroughly covers the creation and configuration of sites, site links, site link bridges, and so forth. Armed with the knowledge of site configuration and replication from Chapter 8 and this chapter, you can configure an effective replication strategy.

So, considering that replication between sites is based on site links in terms of transmission and scheduling, here are some important planning tips:

✦ Always assign low costs to fast WAN connections or backbones and assign high cost to backup connections or slow connections. For example, suppose that between two sites, there is a T1 link and a 64 Kbps backup link. The T1 link should have a low cost and the backup link should have a high cost. This ensures that the T1 link is always used (if possible) over the 64 Kbps link.

✦ Create a schedule that balances your replication needs, user needs, and network bandwidth needs so that replication occurs as often as possible over the site link but does not jam the site link with traffic during peak hours. Try to make these schedules match between all sites and site links. This helps replication to occur at all sites and over all site links at the same time which helps reduce latency between sites. Keep in mind that RPC/IP replication can be scheduled but SMTP replication cannot. When creating the schedule, think carefully about replication latency and how much latency is acceptable for your network.

✦ Between sites, use bridgehead servers if possible.

✦ Between sites, use site link bridges and bridge all site links if possible.

A key question when defining replication within an enterprise is always, "How much time will replication between sites take?" There is not a specific, definite answer because there are too many factors that come into play. However, a general answer (using RPC/IP) is that replication within a site takes about 15 minutes or less. Then you must add the time of transport to the next site and then add about 15 minutes for that site to replicate. Then you consider again the time of transport to the next site and so on. Of course, the speed of data transfer over the WAN links and the network congestion between the WAN links affects this estimate. So, you're left with experimenting with replication between sites and finding solutions that work best for your enterprise network.

Aside from creating your site links and assigning effective costs to those links so that the KCC can generate appropriate connection objects and replication topology, there are a few other tasks you should know about. The following sections point out those tasks to you and show you how to perform them.

Forcing replication

You can force replication to occur between domain controllers. Under most circumstances, there is no need to manually force replication to occur; however, the Active Directory gives you this option to override configured schedules so that extremely important data changes can be made more quickly. To manually force replication to occur, follow these steps:

1. Click Start ➪ Programs ➪ Active Directory Sites and Services.

2. Expand the Sites container, expand the desired site, then expand the desired server, and select NTDS Settings, shown in Figure 13-3.

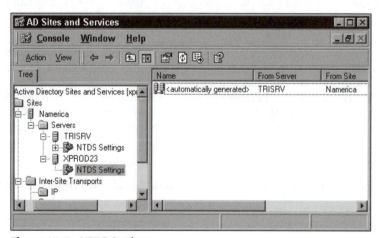

Figure 13-3: NTDS Settings

3. In the right console pane, right-click the connection and then click Replicate Now, shown in Figure 13-4.

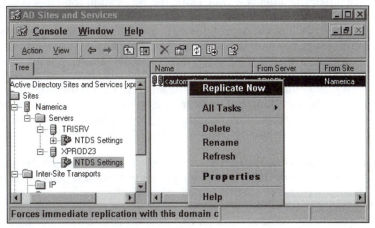

Figure 13-4: Replicate Now option

Manual connection creation

As I have noted a few times in this chapter, the KCC automatically generates connection objects between domain controllers and a replication topology within a site. Then it also automatically creates connection objects and a replication topology between sites, using your site configuration information from Active Directory Sites and Services. However, you can manually create additional connection objects.

Before manually creating any connection objects, you should carefully evaluate the need for manually created connection objects and remember these important warnings:

✦ The KCC does a good job of creating and maintaining connection objects. As an administrator, manually created objects should occur only in specific circumstances where a specific outcome is desired. The KCC does not overwrite manually created connection objects.

✦ The more manually created connection objects, the less effectively the KCC can manage your replication topology. With manually created objects, the KCC has less topology configuration options.

✦ Manually creating connection objects does not necessarily help replication latency. You should carefully evaluate manually created connection objects to determine if they are in fact assisting your replication process. If you are having latency problems within a site, the replication topology is almost never to blame. In fact, intrasite latency problems are usually caused by too much network congestion or too few domain controllers to handle the network load. In other words, replication is affected because the domain controllers are too busy or the network is too busy. Latency can also be caused by DNS problems as well. So, when latency is occurring within a site, you should check out all of these issues before ever turning to the site replication topology. For intersite replication latency, first look at your schedules and site link costs. You can reduce latency problems by reconfiguring these options instead of manually creating connection objects between sites.

So now that you have observed the warnings, the next question is, "When should I create connection objects?" The following list outlines a few possible scenarios where connection objects could be beneficial:

✦ **You specifically want to connect two domain controllers.** For example, perhaps you need to force replication to occur between two domain controllers in an emergency situation. You can create a connection object between them, force replication, and then remove the connection object.

✦ **You have had a server failure in a remote site and latency is causing problems.** The KCC will automatically fix this situation, but in an emergency, you may need to connect a domain controller in one site with another domain controller in another site so that replication isn't delayed any longer than necessary while the KCC fixes the topology change.

✦ **Within a site, you want to connect two domain controllers to reduce hops.** Remember that at the most, there can be three hops, but perhaps you want only one hop between two domain controllers in order to speed replication. In this case, you can create a direct connection object between the two. Again, consider this issue carefully and make certain you need to reduce hops, and keep in mind that manual connection objects reduce the KCC's effectiveness.

Once again, let me emphasize that manual connection objects should be rarely, if ever, needed. Before creating them, always carefully evaluate your needs and make certain the connection objects you manually create are impacting your replication topology in a positive way. To create a connection object, follow these steps:

1. Click Start ➪ Programs ➪ Active Directory Sites and Services.

2. Expand Sites, expand the desired site, then expand the desired server, and select NTDS Settings.

3. Click the Action menu and then click New Active Directory Connection.

4. The Find Domain Controllers window appears, shown in Figure 13-5. Select the domain controller that you want to create a connection and then click the OK button.

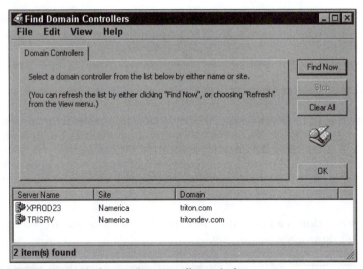

Figure 13-5: Find Domain Controllers window

5. The New Object—Connection window appears with the name of the server you selected, shown in Figure 13-6. Click the OK button.

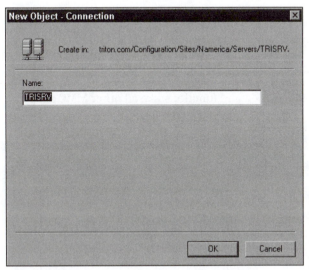

Figure 13-6: New Object—Connection window

Tip   If you want to remove a manually created connection object later, just select it in the right-console pane under NTDS Settings for the server and click Delete.

Using Replication Monitor

Throughout this chapter, I have noted several times that one of the most important things you can do in an Active Directory environment that has multiple sites is to monitor replication traffic. Monitoring replication traffic enables you to examine traffic between sites and determine how effectively replication is occurring in your network. You can use the information you gain from monitoring replication traffic to address replication issues and problems.

Windows 2000 includes a Replication Monitor that is accessible to you once you install the Windows 2000 Support tools.

Cross-Reference   For specific instructions to install the additional Windows 2000 tools, see Appendix C.

Once you have the tools installed, you can access Replication Monitor by clicking Start ➪ Programs ➪ Windows 2000 Support Tools ➪ Tools ➪ Active Directory Replication Monitor. You can also start Replication Monitor by clicking Start ➪ Run and typing *replmon.exe* in the dialog box and clicking OK.

Replication Monitor is a graphical interface tool that enables you to examine Active Directory replication among domain controllers and domains and to perform a number of administrative actions — such as forcing replication between domain controllers, generating a status report about replication, triggering the KCC, viewing intrasite replication topology, and so on. Replication Monitor, shown in Figure 13-7, is an MMC snap-in and functions like all other MMC snap-ins.

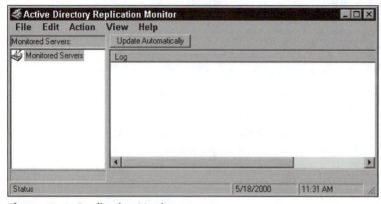

Figure 13-7: Replication Monitor

Replication Monitor is rather intuitive, and you'll find it easy to use once you spend a few minutes using it. The following sections provide you with a Replication Monitor tutorial that shows you how to perform some of the most common Replication Monitor tasks.

Adding a monitored server

To add a server to the console so that it can be monitored, follow these steps:

1. In Replication Monitor, right-click Monitored Servers in the left console pane and click Add Monitored Server.

2. In the Add Monitored Server Wizard, shown in Figure 13-8, select either the "Add server explicitly by name" radio button or the "Search the directory for the server to add" option. If you choose to search the directory for the server, enter the domain name you want to search. For the example, choose to search the directory and click the Next button.

Figure 13-8: Add Monitored Server Wizard

3. In the next window, shown in Figure 13-9, either you select the server from the list if you chose to search a domain or you simply enter the name of the server you want to monitor in the appropriate dialog box. Make your selection and click the Finish button.

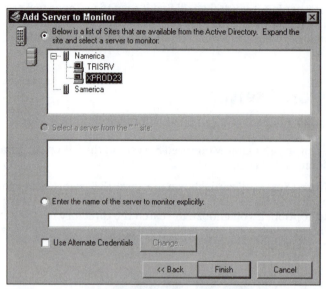

Figure 13-9: Select server

The server now appears in the Replication Monitor. You can see the LDAP informa-tion for the server displayed in the left pane, and you can see the default log file location in the right pane, shown in Figure 13-10.

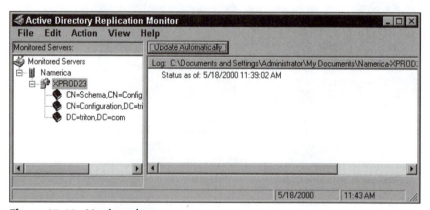

Figure 13-10: Monitored server

Tip

Notice the Update Automatically button above the right pane. If you click this but-ton, a dialog box appears that enables you to enter the number of minutes to wait before the console is automatically updated with new replication information about the selected server. The default is 60 minutes. If you configure this option, the name of the button changes to Cancel Auto Update so you can stop the auto-matic updates if desired.

Domain controller replication errors

Once you have set up a server to monitor, you can check the domain in which the server resides for replication errors among all domain controllers. To perform this action, simple click Action ⇨ Search Domain Controllers for Replication Errors. If replication failures have occurred, a window appears listing them for you.

Server monitoring

If you select the server in the left console pane and click Action ⇨ Server (or just right-click the server icon), you see a list of replication actions you can take concerning the domain controller. The following list explains these options to you and shows you helpful screen prints where useful:

✦ **Update Status (only for this server)** — This option updates your server's replication status in the Replication Monitor.

✦ **Check Replication Topology** — This option triggers the KCC to perform a replication topology check. Use this action to force the KCC to examine the topology. If a server has been taken offline or a new server has been added, the KCC will adjust the topology to accommodate the change.

✦ **Synchronize Each Directory Partition with All Servers** — This option opens the Synchronization window, shown in Figure 13-11. You have three options that you can select by clicking the check box. First, you can disable transitive replication. This setting synchronizes data only with adjacent servers. Next, you can use push mode. By default, pull replication is used in the Active Directory. This option reverses that behavior and enables you to force synchronization to all domain controllers. Finally, you can choose whether or not to cross site boundaries. This option forces synchronization on an enterprise level instead of just a site level.

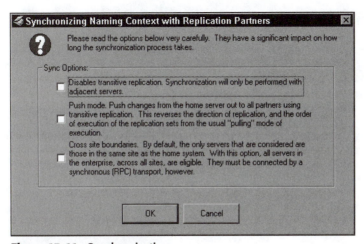

Figure 13-11: Synchronization

Caution

Once you initiate the replication, the Replication Monitor will not be available until the action is complete. This may take some time, depending on the options you selected and the number of domain controllers in your site/enterprise.

✦ **Generate Status Report** — This option enables you to generate a status report. When you click the option, you are prompted to enter a name for the log and then to select a location on your computer to save the log. Then, the Report Options window, shown in Figure 13-12 appears. Use the check boxes to select what items you want to appear in the report. Make your selections and click OK to generate the report. A progress window appears. Click OK when it is finished. You can then open the status report (which is a notepad file) and examine the report information.

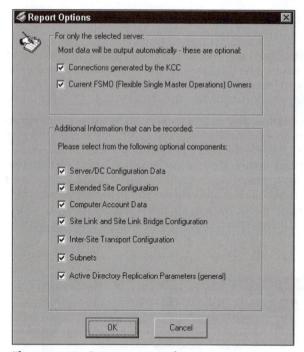

Figure 13-12: Status report options

✦ **Show Domain Controllers in the Domain** — This option opens a window that lists all of the domain controllers in the domain.

✦ **Show Replication Topologies** — This option opens a window where you can see a graphical view of both your intrasite and intersite topologies.

✦ **Show Group Policy object status** — This option opens a window that presents the configured Group Policy objects.

You can learn more about Group Policy in Chapter 15.

✦ **Show Current Performance Data** — This option shows you any performance data you have configured for display. See the "Replication Monitor Options" section toward the end of this chapter to learn more.

✦ **Show Global Catalog Servers in Enterprise** — This option lists all global catalog servers in the enterprise.

✦ **Show Bridgehead Servers** — This option lists all bridgehead servers. You can choose to list them in the server's site or in the entire enterprise.

✦ **Show Trust Relationships** — This option shows trust relationships between domains.

✦ **Show Attribute Meta-Data for Active Directory object** — This option enables you to read the attribute metadata for the server. You need enterprise admin permission to view this data.

You can learn more about attributes and metadata in Chapter 14.

✦ **Clear Log** — This option clears the server's log file in the Replication Monitor console.

✦ **Delete** — This option deletes the server from the Replication Monitor.

✦ **Properties** — This option opens the server's properties sheets for Replication Monitor, which you can learn about in the next section.

Server properties

If you right-click the monitored server in the left console pane and click Properties, you see several tabs relating to replication monitoring. You may find these tabs useful to configure a number of monitoring options. The following sections explain what you can do on each tab.

General tab

The General tab provides you with the server's name, DNS name, computer account LDAP name, and whether or not the server is a preferred bridgehead server. You cannot configure anything on this tab.

Server Flags tab

The Server Flags tab, shown in Figure 13-13, shows you a number of flags that point out specific information about the server. For example, if the server is a global catalog server, a flag is present indicating so. You can't configure anything on this tab, but this is an excellent place to gain a snapshot of the domain controller and information about specific services and functions.

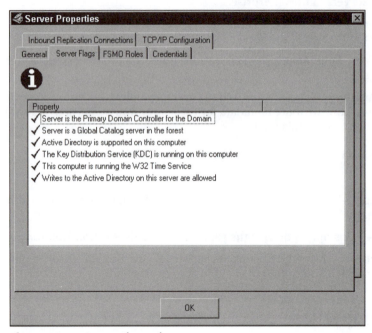

Figure 13-13: Server Flags tab

FSMO roles

Flexible single master operation (FSMO) roles are specific Active Directory roles played by certain domain controllers within the domain and enterprise.

Cross-Reference   You can learn more about master operation roles in Chapters 3 and 7.

The FSMO Roles tab, shown in Figure 13-14, lists the owner of the different master operation roles. You can click the Query button, and Replication Monitor will attempt to resolve, connect, and bind to the server hosting the FSMO role. This is an easy and effective way to make certain all FSMO domain controllers are online and functioning appropriately.

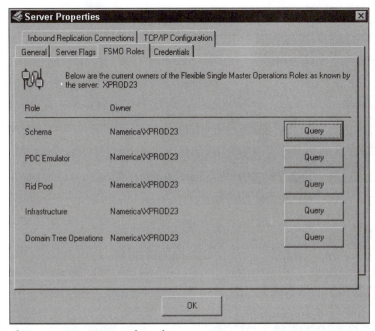

Figure 13-14: FSMO Roles tab

Credentials tab

This tab lists any explicit credentials for access to the particular server. If no credentials were necessary, then the connection is made using your user account.

Inbound Replication Connections tab

This tab, shown in Figure 13-15, gives you a detailed account of the inbound connection objects for the server. You can also read a detailed description of why the connections were established by the KCC. This tab is a good place to gain additional information about the replication topology and how this particular server functions within that topology.

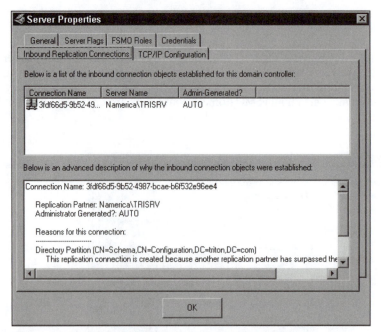

Figure 13-15: Inbound Replication Connections tab

TCP/IP Configuration tab

This tab lists the current TCP/IP configuration for the server, such as IP address, MAC address, subnet mask, DNS server, and so on. You can gain this same information at the command line by typing **ipconfig /all**.

Replication Monitor options

In Replication Monitor, you can click View ➪ Options to enable or disable some options from the Replication Monitor. On the General tab, shown in Figure 13-16, you see a number of check box options. These options are self-explanatory, and they allow you to display certain replication data and configure how the Replication Monitor log file operates.

The Status Logging tab, shown in Figure 13-17, enables you to monitor Group Policy objects and performance statistics. If you choose monitor performance statistics for the server, a dialog box appears where you can enter the desired performance object and counter. You also have the option to log attribute changes, which will log the changes to Update Sequence Numbers (USN). Selecting this option will make the log file larger, but may be helpful for troubleshooting purposes.

Finally, the Cache tab enables you to flush the Replication Monitor cache. Replication Monitor caches data that rarely changes, but you can use this option to force Replication Monitor to recollect any cached data.

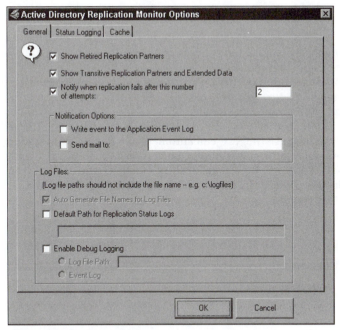

Figure 13-16: General tab

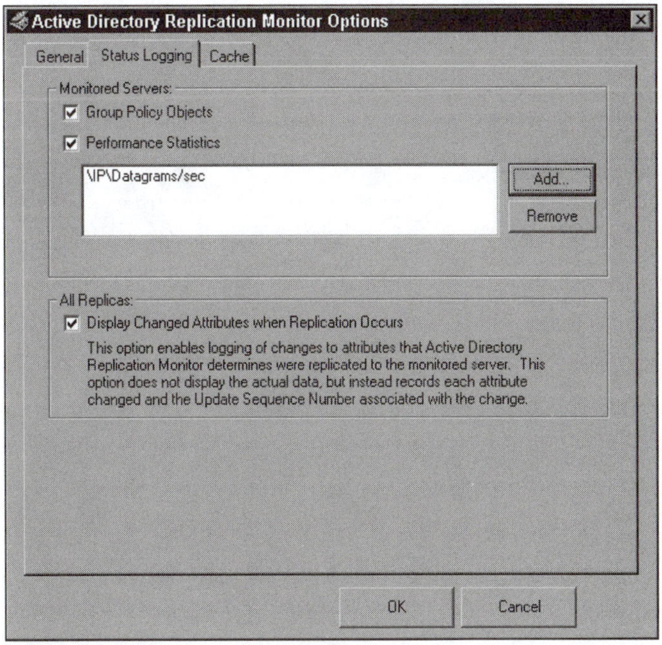

Figure 13-17: Status Logging tab

Summary

This chapter explored the complicated process of Active Directory replication. First, it explored the important replication concepts, and then it examined how Active Directory replication occurs on an intrasite and intersite level. This chapter also explored some tips to make the most of intersite replication through careful planning and configuration of site links. This chapter also looked at connection objects and how you manually create connection objects, although this action should be a rare event because the KCC can automatically handle this task for you. The Active Directory contains a powerful replication design that ensures accurate data and a "hands-off" approach for administrators. However, the Active Directory does include Replication Monitor to enable you to gather detailed information about your replication topology and problems or issues with replication in your enterprise environment.

✦　　✦　　✦

Active Directory Schema

The Active Directory is a complex database, storing and dynamically manipulating objects as the need arises. This complex behavior is based on a list of definitions, or *metadata*, that defines what kind of objects can be placed in the Active Directory, how those objects are defined, and how objects are integrated with one another. This list of definitions is called the Active Directory *schema* — which is simply a schematic or blueprint that defines how Active Directory data will be stored and viewed. This chapter explores the Active Directory schema and how it works and gives you some information about how you extend or change the schema. Let me just offer a big warning here that you will see several times throughout this chapter: Modifying the Active Directory schema is a very serious operation that can have enterprise-wide effects. In fact, incorrect modifications can result in your having to completely reinstall the Active Directory. So, proceed with great caution, and if you are interested in making schema modifications, always begin on a test machine or small test network.

Schema Overview

You can think of the Active Directory schema like a referee at a football game. The referee knows the rules inside and out, and his job is to enforce those rules so all players play the game according to the rules and the game is fair. In the Active Directory world, the schema is the referee, and we, as directory service administrators, are the players. The schema's job is to know the rules of the Active Directory database — to know the definitions that determine what objects can be stored in the database, how they are stored, and how they are defined. The schema keeps the database on a level playing field and makes certain that people (like us!) don't screw it up.

In more technical terms, the schema is made up of a list of definitions about objects and even definitions about the objects' definitions. All of these definitions are simply called metadata, which means "data about data." The metadata determines what is an object and how it is defined. In other words, the metadata knows that user accounts may have qualities of user name, password, physical address, phone number, and so forth—not qualities such as one-sided, staple, color, and sort (which, of course, belong to a printer). The qualities a particular object has are called *attributes*. Each Active Directory object has attributes that define the object, as shown in Figure 14-1. A user object has attributes of user name, password, phone number, and so on, while a printer object has attributes of color, staple, double-sided, and so on. By defining these attributes within the properties sheets for the object, you are essentially entering data into database fields for that object so that it is further identifiable. Attributes either can be mandatory, or required, for the object, or they can be optional. For example, a user account has mandatory attributes of user name and password, but optional attributes of phone number, e-mail address, and so forth.

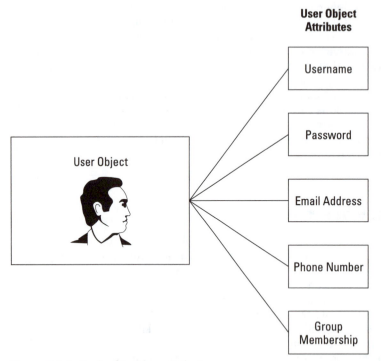

Figure 14-1: Each object has attributes.

Just as each object is defined by attributes, attributes are also defined as well. As you might imagine, each attribute is defined only once so there is consistency among all objects. For example, though both user accounts and computer accounts could have the attribute of "group membership," the group membership attribute is defined only one time in the Active Directory. Each object that uses this attribute must use the same definition for it. This prevents the same attribute from having two conflicting definitions. This definition, referred to as a *syntax,* defines the data type for a particular attribute. You don't see syntaxes in the Active Directory, and you cannot add new syntaxes to the Active Directory.

So, every object has attributes, and every object belongs to a *class* as well. Classes are also a part of the metadata that also help define objects. Each object in the Active Directory must belong to at least one class that further defines the object. For example, user accounts belong to the User class, but a shared folder would not belong to this class. Each object that belongs to a class is considered an *instance* of that class, as shown in Figure 14-2.

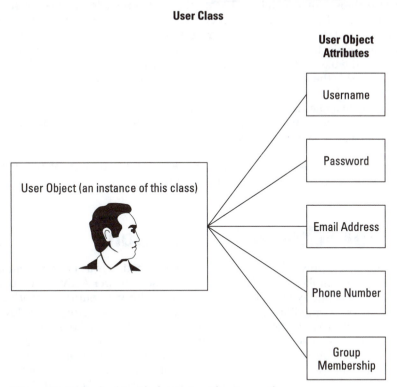

Figure 14-2: Each object belongs to at least one class.

Each object belongs to at least one class, and each class belongs to a specific category of classes, which are as follows:

✦ **Structural** — All directory objects belong to classes that are structural. This means that structural classes can have instances in the class, such as in the User class.

✦ **Abstract** — An abstract class is a template that is used to create new structural classes. Objects do not belong to abstract classes, but abstract classes do contain attributes they provide to other classes.

✦ **Auxiliary** — Auxiliary classes contain lists of attributes and help define structural and abstract classes.

Tip There is also a special 88 class category that is used for backward compatibility for classes that do not fall under one of these three specifications. 88 classes were defined before the 1993 X.500 standards.

Windows 2000 ships with a default, or base, schema that installs when you install the Active Directory. For most Active Directory implementations, the default schema provides all of the classes, objects, and attributes that you need for a highly effective implementation. Objects in the directory are arranged in a Directory Information Tree (DIT), and the base schema configuration is referred to as the *base DIT*. Each domain controller in the forest contains a copy of the schema for that forest.

Note Even the schema has its own set of schema objects and classes, and all schema objects are stored in the Schema container and are found in cn=schema, cn-configuration, dc= <*forest root domainname*>.

Cross-Reference You can find extensive tables in Appendix F that list and cross-reference the default Active Directory classes, attributes, and syntax.

Planning for Schema Modification

As I mentioned in the previous section, schema modification is a serious event that has enterprise-wide implications. There is only one schema per Active Directory forest, so when you modify the schema, you modify it for your entire enterprise. Additionally, incorrect modifications can result in an Active Directory "meltdown" that can require you to completely reinstall the Active Directory from scratch — not a task you want to be faced with. For example, imagine that you create a class or object that conflicts with an existing class or attribute. As this change is replicated among your domain controllers and domains, the database begins to collect consistency errors. Now your metadata is out of consistency, or it is ill-defined. This error can bring down your implementation.

So, with that big warning paragraph said, why would you want to modify the schema? First, remember that the Active Directory is installed with a base DIT, or default schema. Under most circumstances, this base schema is all you will ever need for your implementation. There are almost 200 default classes of objects and hundreds of potential objects and attributes that define them. However, an organization may have a custom object or class they would like to add to the Active Directory. This can be an important and justifiable reason for modifying the Active Directory to include this new object. However, before doing so, the current base DIT should be carefully examined to make certain that a similar object already present cannot meet the needs.

Tip   Don't confuse schema modification with the creation of a new object. When you create a new object, such as a user account, you are simply creating a new instance of an existing class—you are not modifying or extending the schema.

The basic planning strategy for making schema modifications is careful research. Always remember that a bad modification has the potential to cause serious havoc on your entire network, so proceed with great planning and caution.

Begin by examining the proposed need for schema modification. Is the need truly serious enough to justify a schema modification? Also, examine the base schema. Can the base schema actually meet your needs? Consider this last question carefully because quite often, the base schema can, in fact, meet any need you may have. If you determine that the schema does need to be modified, next determine if there is a way to modify an existing class by adding unused attributes. This action does not extend the schema, but simply expands an existing class. If that doesn't work, you may be able to create a subclass of an existing class before actually creating a new class.

Caution   If schema modifications are necessary, always use a test machine first, so you can study the impact of the modification before implementing the modification in a production environment.

Protection process

Fortunately, modifying the schema is not an operation that just any administrator can perform. In order to modify the schema, you *must* be a member of the Schema Admins group. Only a few senior administrators should be members of this group, and if and when schema modifications are necessary, the entire group should meet and work together on the schema modification. So, protect the membership of this group carefully. Also, you must modify the schema on the domain controller that holds the schema master flexible single master operation (FSMO) role. You cannot modify the schema on any other domain controller, and there is only one schema master in the forest. The domain controller that holds this FSMO role should be carefully protected, as you can imagine.

Issues with inheritance

We have explored the concept of inheritance in several chapters throughout the book, and it is a concept you will consider often in a Windows 2000 network. The same is true for schema modifications. If you need to create a new class, inheritance can greatly help you or cause you a lot of problems. Remember that the schema is a Directory Information Tree (DIT), and with the DIT, there are parent classes and child classes. Child classes inherit the properties of the parent, which in this case are the attributes. Mandatory and optional attributes defined for the parent class are automatically inherited by child classes. For example, consider the User class. You want to create a subclass of the User class called Temps to create objects for temporary employees. When you create the Temps subclass, it inherits the attributes from the parent class. Then, all you need do is define additional attributes for the Temps subclass. In this case, inheritance has helped you by providing User class attributes you will need for the Temps subclass. Of course, imagine the reverse. You create a subclass under an inappropriate parent class and attributes are inherited. What if there are mandatory attributes inherited that do not fit with your new class? This situation can be problematic, so once again, planning and careful research is of key importance. As you plan, examine how your new class will fit into the DIT and how inheritance will work.

Schema Modification Tools

You can modify the schema in a couple of ways. First, you can use the Schema Manager console, which is a part of the AdminPak tools found on your Windows 2000 installation CD-ROM. You can also use Active Directory Services Interface (ADSI), which gives you more powerful editing options. Finally, you can make modifications programmatically using such programming languages as Visual Basic and C++. In this section, we explore the use of the Schema Manager and ADSI.

Caution   Once again, as a final warning, you should use these tools only on a test machine until you are ready to make actual schema modifications. Changes in a production environment are replicated to all domain controllers in all domains and may have devastating effects if edits are not correctly performed.

Using the Schema Manager

The Schema Manager is an MMC snap-in tool like your other Active Directory tools. It is not installed by default, but is available once you install the AdminPak tools.

Cross-Reference   See Appendix C for AdminPak installation instructions.

Once the AdminPak tools are installed, you can manually load the Schema Manager by following these steps:

1. On the schema master domain controller, click Start ⇨ Run, type **MMC**, and click OK.

2. Click Console ⇨ Add/Remove snap-in.

3. Click Add in the snap-in window.

4. In the Standalone snap-in window, select Active Directory Schema and then click Add.

5. Click Close on the Standalone snap-in window and then click OK.

6. The Schema Manager snap-in is loaded, as shown in Figure 14-3.

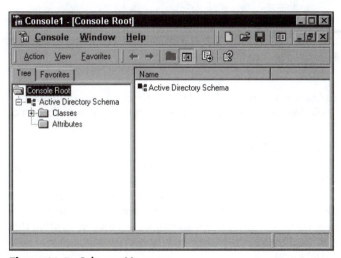

Figure 14-3: Schema Manager

Enabling the console

Once you open the console, schema modification is disabled by default. This is a protection feature so you can use the console without having to worry about actually making a change. To actually enable the console for schema modification, follow these steps:

1. Select Active Directory Schema in the left console pane and then click Action ⇨ Operations Master.

2. Click the check box at the bottom of the window to enable schema modifications, shown in Figure 14-4, and then click the OK button.

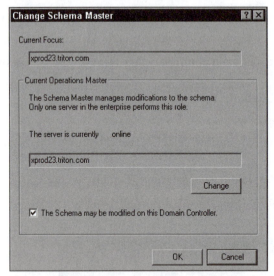

Figure 14-4: Change Schema Master window

Tip

You can change the schema master role to a different domain controller in this same location by clicking the Change button and selecting a different domain controller.

Examining class properties

Notice in the console that you have two containers—one for classes and attributes. If you expand Classes, you can see all of the base default classes. If you select a class in the left console pane, the mandatory and optional attributes for that class appear in the right pane. If you click Action ➪ Properties, you can see the properties sheets for that particular class. The properties sheets for each class contain the same information, and examining the properties sheets for a class can give you more understanding about that class.

In Figure 14-5, you see the General tab for the User class. The General tab contains the following information:

✦ **Description**—This is a description of the class (which you can change).

✦ **Common Name**—This is the CN for the class.

✦ **X.500 OID**—Each class must have a unique Object Identifier (OID). OIDs are controlled by the International Organization for Standardization (ISO). The OID is made up of a branch of numbers. The name registration authority issues the first several digits, such as 1.2.840 in Figure 14-5, and the remaining digits are assigned by the organization that acquires the OID.

✦ **Class Type**—This provides the class type, such as structural, abstract, auxiliary, or 88.

✦ **Category**—This provides a class category. This can be changed for some classes.

✦ **Show objects of this class while browsing**—This is an optional check box that enables you to view the objects in the class.

✦ **Deactivate this class**—You cannot remove a class from the Active Directory, but some classes can be deactivated. As you can see in Figure 14-5, the User class cannot be deactivated.

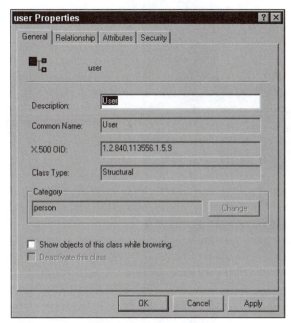

Figure 14-5: General tab

On the Relationship tab, shown in Figure 14-6, you see how the class is related to other classes. For example, in Figure 14-6, you see the parent class, the auxiliary classes, and a list of other possible superior classes. You can use the Add and Remove buttons to change these relationships as needed, but as with all schema modifications, you must be very careful before doing so.

The Attributes tab, shown in Figure 14-7, is like the Relationship tab in that it lists the relationship of attributes with the class. You see a list of mandatory attributes (if there are any) and a list of optional attributes. You cannot change mandatory attributes but you can use the Add and Remove buttons to adjust optional attributes if necessary.

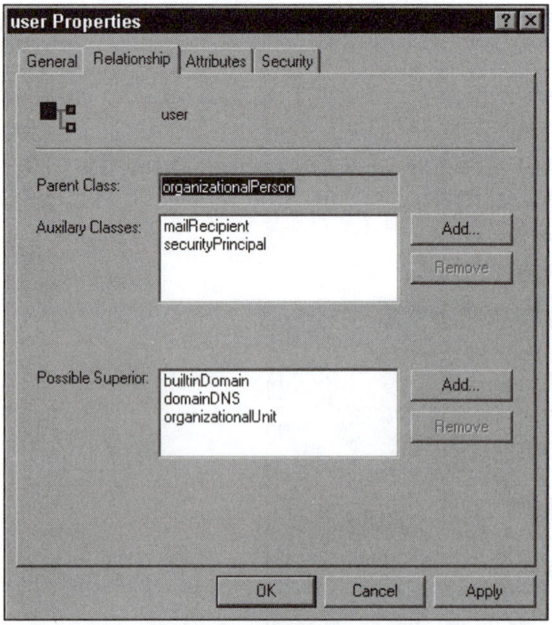

Figure 14-6: Relationship tab

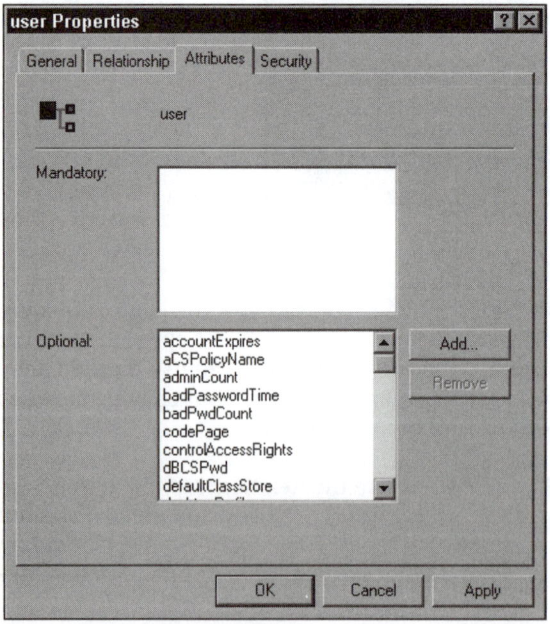

Figure 14-7: Attributes tab

Finally, you see a Security tab that functions just like all other Security tabs in the Active Directory. You can use this tab to set specific security on specific schema classes if necessary. This fine level of control enables you to configure security needs for virtually any desired configuration.

Cross-Reference See Chapter 11 for more information about the Security tab.

Examining attribute properties

Just as you can access a particular class's properties sheets, you can also click the Attributes container in the left pane, select a desired attribute in the right pane, and then click Action ➪ Properties. There is a single General tab for attribute properties, shown in Figure 14-8.

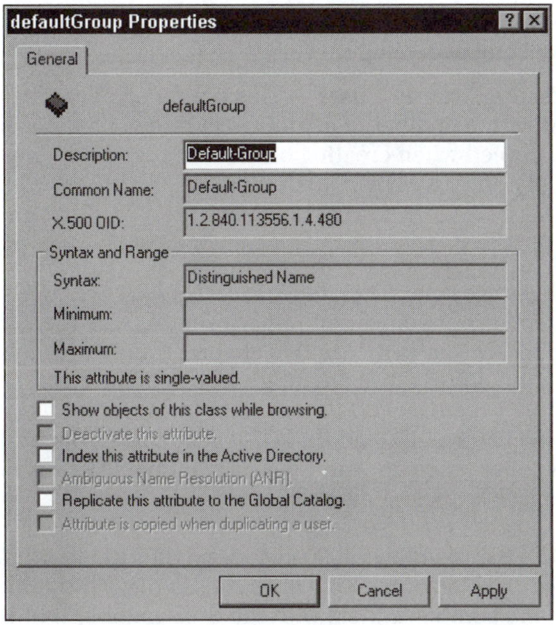

defaultGroup Properties ? X

General

⬦   defaultGroup

Description:	Default-Group
Common Name:	Default-Group
X.500 OID:	1.2.840.113556.1.4.480

Syntax and Range

Syntax:	Distinguished Name
Minimum:	
Maximum:	

This attribute is single-valued.

☐ Show objects of this class while browsing.
☐ Deactivate this attribute.
☐ Index this attribute in the Active Directory.
☐ Ambiguous Name Resolution (ANR).
☐ Replicate this attribute to the Global Catalog.
☐ Attribute is copied when duplicating a user.

OK   Cancel   Apply

Figure 14-8: Attribute properties

You see the same kind of information displayed for attributes as classes, such as description, common name, and X.500 OID. You also see syntax information. Each attribute has a syntax attribute that enables the attribute to function in the Active Directory appropriately and adhere to various naming standards to ensure that the Active Directory provides standardized naming schemes. You cannot change the syntax for an attribute, and you cannot add any new syntax to the Active Directory. Each attribute contains one exact syntax.

At the bottom of the window, you see several check boxes, some of which may be grayed out, depending on which attribute you are examining. The following list explains these options:

✦ **Show objects of this class while browsing** — This option enables you to see objects of the class while browsing.

✦ **Deactivate this attribute** — Some attributes can be deactivated, although none of them can be deleted from the schema.

✦ **Index this attribute in the Active Directory** — The option allows the attribute to be indexed in the Active Directory so it can be searched upon.

✦ **Ambiguous Name Resolution (ANR)** — This option enables ANR, which is a helpful feature in locating attributes not known. For example, if a client searches for Karen Smith, but the directory knows the name of Smith, Karen, ANR enables the search to be completed.

✦ **Replicate this attribute to the Global Catalog** — This option enables the attribute to replicate to all global catalog servers.

✦ **Attribute is copied when duplicating a user** — This option enables you to configure a user account with a number of attributes and then have those attributes automatically copied when creating other user accounts. This option will obviously apply only to certain attributes.

Creating a class

You can use the Schema Manager console to create a new class. The Schema Manager must be enabled for schema modification to perform this task (see the "Using the Schema Manager" section earlier in this chapter), and as always, great care and planning should be done before creating a new schema class. Before creating a class, you must obtain an OID for the class from an issuing agency. Each class must have a custom OID, and that OID must come from a naming authority. You should never make up your own OID numbers because they may conflict with existing schema class numbers.

You have two ways to get OIDs. First, Windows 2000 includes a utility called OIDGEN, which is found on the Windows 2000 Resource Kit. OIDGEN uses the OID numbers already assigned to Microsoft and combines them with the GUID number that is generated when you run OIDGEN. You can then register this new OID for the new class with Microsoft.

A better way to obtain an OID is to request one from the ISO for your area. There is, of course, a fee, but this method makes certain you obtain a registered OID instead of a generated one. If you are inside the United States, visit `http://www.ansi.org/ public/services/reg_org.html`. If you are outside the United States, visit `http://www.iso.ch/members`. You can then learn how to fill out a request form and pay the appropriate fee.

Once you have the OID and you have thoroughly studied the need for the new class and the inheritance issues for this new class, you are then ready to create the new class. Follow these steps:

1. In the Schema Manager console, select the Classes container and then click Action ➪ Create Class.

2. A warning message appears telling you that this is a permanent operation for the enterprise. Click Continue.

3. In the Create New Schema Class window, enter the common name, LDAP display name, OID, parent class, and class type, as shown in Figure 14-9. Click Next.

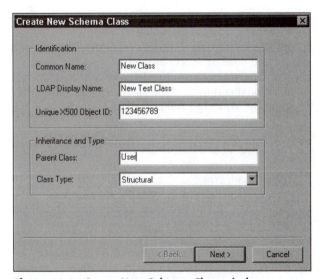

Figure 14-9: Create New Schema Class window

4. In the next window, use the Add and Remove buttons to create a list of mandatory and optional attributes for this class and then click the Finish button.

Caution   Carefully consider which mandatory attributes you assign. This cannot be changed later.

Creating new attributes

You can also use the Schema Manager console to add new attributes. Adding attributes is also a serious operation; however, it is not as difficult as adding a class because you do not have to worry about inheritance or about where the attribute fits into the hierarchy. To create an attribute, follow these steps:

1. In the Schema Manager console, select the Attributes container and then click Action ➪ Create Attribute.

2. A warning message appears telling you this is a permanent operation that has enterprise-wide consequences. Click Continue.

3. Enter the common name, LDAP display name, OID, syntax, and any minimum or maximum variables that may apply. You also see a check box for Multi-valued. This means that the attribute can have more than one value in the Active Directory schema.

Using ADSI

Active Directory Services Interface (ADSI) Editor is an Active Directory editor that enables you to add, move, and delete objects as well as view and manage attributes for objects. ADSI is also used to query the Active Directory and define query scopes. ADSI is available as an additional administrative tool once you install the Windows 2000 Resource Kit, found on the Windows 2000 CD-ROM.

See Appendix C for more information about the Active Directory tools available on the Windows 2000 Resource Kit and the AdminPak.

Once the Resource Kit is installed, you can then manually load the ADSI Edit snap-in into an empty MMC, or you can just access it from the Resource Kit Tools menu. The ADSI Editor loads the current domain schema information and presents it as domain, configuration, and schema containers, as shown in Figure 14-10.

You can expand each category and explore the objects, such as users, computers, OUs, and so forth. You can move them, rename them, and delete them, and you can access properties for the objects to view their attributes, such as in Figure 14-11.

You can use the ADSI Editor to create new objects in desired containers and query various portions of the schema. The ADSI Editor is very straightforward and easy to use, but it is a powerful tool because you can create objects, edit object attributes, and delete objects as well. So, do take great care when using the ADSI Editor.

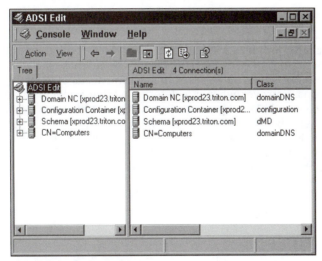

Figure 14-10: ADSI Edit

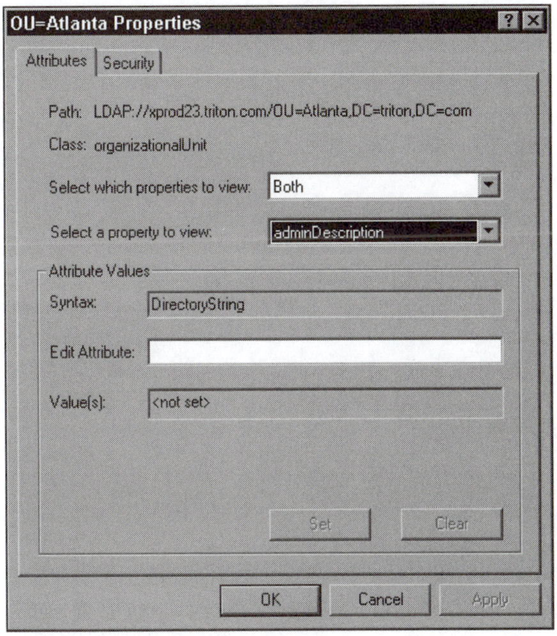

Figure 14-11: OU properties

Summary

The Active Directory schema provides a list of rules and definitions that gives the Active Directory its structure. Windows 2000 ships with a default base schema that provides plenty of objects, attribute, and classes to meet the needs of most Active Directory implementations. However, when it is determined that a schema modification is needed, great care and planning must occur before modification. Always carefully explore the schema before planning a modification, and if a modification is necessary, determine the least invasive method first. The Active Directory can be viewed and modified programmatically or through either the Schema Manager or ADSI Editor, both of which are found in the Windows 2000 Resource Kit.

✦   ✦   ✦

Integrating Supporting Technologies

In the final portion of this book you explore related Active Directory technologies and how those technologies can be used to meet the needs of your organization. First, you explore IntelliMirror and Group Policy. These tools provide client management and control features that are essential to large organizations.

Next, you examine Windows 2000's Distributed File System and Indexing Service. You learn how to set up and configure these services to make your network more user-friendly and easier to use.

In this part of the book you also explore Microsoft Exchange Server 2000 and how it can be implemented with the Active Directory. In addition, in this part you also examine Microsoft DNS, learning about DNS concepts and how to configure DNS for the Active Directory.

Implementing IntelliMirror and Group Policy

◆ ◆ ◆ ◆

In This Chapter

Exploring IntelliMirror technologies

Implementing Group Policy

Configuring a Group Policy

◆ ◆ ◆ ◆

Indirectly, all Active Directory configuration supports network clients in some way or the other. After all, making client computers function more efficiently so that users can find needed resources is one of the major goals of the Active Directory. However, Microsoft has designed the Active Directory so that it does not exist as an island. In fact, several technologies natively work with the Active Directory to provide better client desktop configuration and control. This chapter explores two of those technologies—IntelliMirror and Group Policy.

Understanding IntelliMirror

IntelliMirror is a marketing tool used to collectively group a number of Windows 2000 technologies together. The name IntelliMirror is derived from the concept of intelligently mirroring a user's computer desktop and files—regardless of where the user is on the network or what computer the user accesses. IntelliMirror encompasses a number of technologies that can be used to accomplish that purpose. You can implement all of the IntelliMirror technologies, implement only a few, or slowly implement them over time. In fact, most of the technologies described in IntelliMirror can be implemented using Group Policy, which is explored in this chapter as well.

So, IntelliMirror is a collection of technologies designed to support Windows 2000 Professional clients. (Sorry, only native Windows 2000 clients can use all of IntelliMirror's features—Windows 9x clients need not apply.) In reality, these technologies are designed to enable network administrators to enforce system policies and profiles in order to manage user desktops and implement a standardized configuration on the network. Why would anyone want to do that? The answer is simple. When users configure their own desktop, system settings, and applications, there are configuration errors that require help desk support. This wastes time and costs companies a lot of money. Aside from this fact, many companies do not want employees installing unauthorized applications and games. Although all of this sounds like Big Brother, the reality is that client computer management is very important in terms of time and cost for most large companies.

With all of that said, the following list tells you the technologies that actually make up IntelliMirror and what you can do with them:

✦ **Active Directory** — Of course, the Active Directory is considered a part of IntelliMirror because it directly affects users (as well as Group Policy).

✦ **Group Policy** — Group Policy is a powerful tool that enables administrators to configure and control client computer systems. The bulk of IntelliMirror configuration is performed through Group Policy.

✦ **Offline Files** — Offline files enable the storage of files and even applications on a network server. Users can cache those files and applications and continue to work with them on their local desktops when not connected to the network.

✦ **Synchronization Manager** — Synchronization Manager handles the synchronization of offline files and with the server's copies of the files.

✦ **Disk Quotas** — Disk quotas enable you to manage a user's server disk space usage. For example, you can specify a certain megabyte limit and prohibit the user from saving more files to the server once the limit has been reached.

✦ **Roaming User Profiles** — Roaming user profiles follow the user so that the user can log on to any workstation and receive the same system and desktop settings. You can use Group Policy to implement roaming user profiles.

✦ **Windows Installer** — You can use IntelliMirror with Windows Installer to remotely install, remove, and modify client software installations.

✦ **Remote Installation Services** — You can use Remote Installation Services to remotely install Windows 2000 Professional on client computers.

Once again, all of these technologies are bundled together and labeled IntelliMirror. Obviously, several of them are not new, but you can certainly use them in conjunction with the Active Directory to manage all aspects of the user's computer system.

Consider an example. A new employee, Tim Phillips, has just joined Triton, Inc. Using Remote Installation Services, an administrator installs Windows 2000 Professional on Tim's new desktop system, and the administrator also creates a user account for Tim in a desired OU. Tim's user account automatically becomes part of a Group Policy, depending on where in the enterprise his account is placed (site, domain, and OU). When Tim logs on for the first time, he receives a standardized desktop and system configuration that is just right for his work environment. Files and folders that Tim needs are automatically downloaded to his computer, and software he needs is automatically installed. Without lifting a finger, Tim has a complete system that is configured appropriately and has the files and software he needs. However, Tim is left-handed, so he changes the mouse properties in Control Panel for left-handed use. This setting is permitted under the Group Policy, saved, and reapplied at each logon. At a later time, Tim logs on to a different workstation. He still receives the same settings, files, applications, and left-handed mouse, just as though he were sitting at his original desktop. This same process occurs even when Tim is traveling and logs onto a computer in a remote site.

As you can see, the possibilities IntelliMirror brings are quite powerful. The following sections explore these technologies in more detail, with the exception of Group Policy and roaming user profiles; the second half of this chapter explores these two items in detail.

Offline files

Offline files in Windows 2000 enable your computer to locally store files that reside on a server. If the network connection becomes unavailable, you can continue working on those files with no interruption — in other words, the files are available to you *offline* or when you are not connected. Offline files are very easy to use and configure and are helpful in reducing lost user work time due to problematic network conditions.

Any shared folders and files on a Microsoft network can be made available offline. Also, any computer that supports Server Message Block (SMB)–based file and printer sharing can use offline files. For example, Windows 2000, NT, and 9*x* can all use offline files.

To configure a folder for offline use, access the shared folder's properties sheets, click the Sharing Tab, and then click the Caching button. The Caching Settings window appears, shown in Figure 15-1.

Figure 15-1: Caching Settings window

Click the "Allow caching of files in this shared folder" check box to enable caching for the files in that folder. You can then choose the kind of caching you want to use from the Settings drop-down menu. You have the following options:

✦ **Manual Caching for Documents**—This setting can be used for folders containing user documents. The user must decide which files they want downloaded for offline use.

✦ **Automatic Caching for Documents**—This setting can also be used for folders containing user documents. When this setting is selected, files the user opens are automatically cached on the client computer. Although the automatic feature is effective, give some thought before using automatic caching. Excessive use of this caching feature will generate more network traffic and cause client computers to have to store more documents.

✦ **Automatic Caching for Programs**—This setting is used for folders that contain over-the-network applications or read-only data. With this feature, over-the-network applications are automatically cached as well as all read-only data accessed in the folder that has this setting applied.

Synchronization Manager

Synchronization Manager works with offline files to ensure that a cached copy of a file is synchronized with the server's copy when the user reconnects to the network. Synchronization Manager can be set to run manually or automatically so that synchronization always occurs when a user reconnects.

For example, suppose that a user named Tim uses a file offline. Tim makes several changes to the file. When he reconnects to the network, Tim's file is synchronized with the server so that the server's copy is updated to reflect Tim's changes. However, as you can imagine, there is the possibility for synchronization conflicts because another user could make changes to the same file. If this happens, you are given the choice of either keeping your version, the one that exists on the network, or you can keep them both by giving your cached file a new file name and saving it. As you can see, the synchronization of offline files is *very* important to ensure that changes are saved to the server and that a user is always working with the most current file.

Using Synchronization Manager, you can schedule synchronization to occur at specific times, when you log on or off, when your compute is idle, as well as a number of other options and combinations.

Synchronization Manager is easy to set up and configure. The following steps give you an example and show you the available options.

1. To start Synchronization Manager, click Start ➪ Programs ➪ Accessories ➪ Synchronize.

2. The Items to Synchronize window appears, shown in Figure 15-2. Click the check box next to any items that you want to synchronize and then click the Synchronize button. You will see a progress bar as synchronization occurs.

3. You can also click the Setup button to configure Synchronization Manager. When you click this button, three tabs appear — Logon/Logoff, On Idle, and Scheduled, shown in Figure 15-3. Use each tab to configure how and when Synchronization Manager should automatically run.

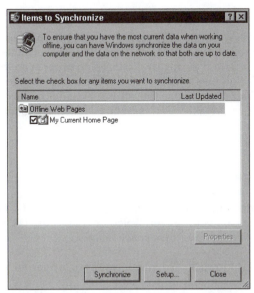

Figure 15-2: Items to Synchronize window

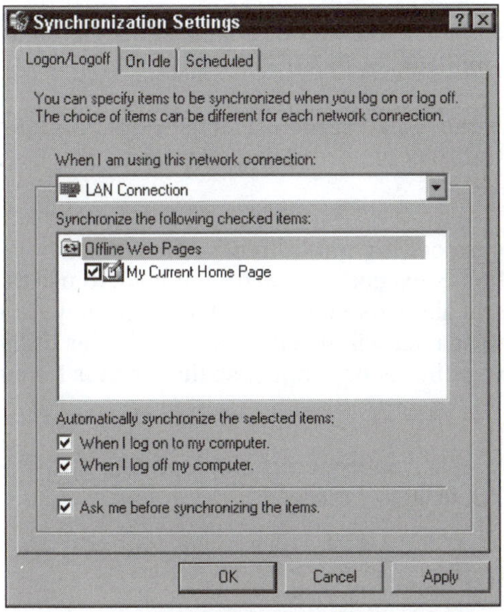

Figure 15-3: Synchronization Manager setup

4. Note that on the Scheduled tab, you can click the Add button to create a schedule of the days and time that synchronization should occur. When you click Add, a wizard appears to help you configure the schedule. The wizard is self-explanatory, so I'll not delve into it here.

Windows Installer

Windows Installer, a part of the Windows 2000 operating system, enables you to remotely install and manage software on user desktops. Windows Installer works by creating setup rules that are followed during the installation process so that software installation is *hands-off*. Windows Installer uses .msi package files to deliver software to client desktops. You can also use the software configuration portion of Group Policy to access Windows Installer, so this issue is addressed in more detail later in the chapter.

Disk quotas

When users are given storage space on a server, it has been traditionally difficult for administrators to track and control disk space usage. After all, you do not want users storing megabytes of junk on your server. Welcome to disk quotas, which enable you to both control and track user disk space usage.

Disk quotas are available on Windows 2000 dynamic volumes formatted with NTFS. Disk quotas are easy to set up and maintain. To enable disk quotas on an NTFS dynamic volume, access the volume's properties sheets (either in My Computer or in the Disk Management console). Click the Quota tab and then click the "Enable quota management" check box, shown in Figure 15-4.

Tip
If you don't see a Quota tab, then you are not a member of the Administrators group or the volume is not formatted with NTFS.

Once you enable quotas on this tab, you can then select several check boxes and radio buttons on this tab in order to configure disk quota usage. You have the following options:

✦ **Deny disk space to users exceeding quota limit** — This check box denies storage space once the limit is exceeded. You do not have to use this option. In other words, you can still allow users to save data once they have exceeded their storage space limit (the user will receive warnings). This option enables you to either enforce storage limits or simply use disk quotas for auditing and control purposes.

Caution
When you use the deny disk space option, users may lose data since they will be unable to save it once the quota limit is exceeded.

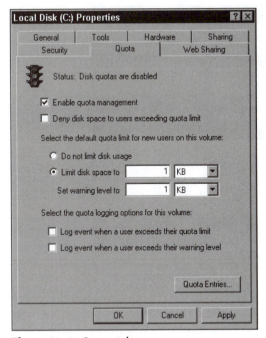

Figure 15-4: Quota tab

✦ **Do not limit disk space or limit disk space to**—You have two radio buttons where you can configure the quota limit. First, you simply select to not limit disk usage, or alternately, you can select to limit disk usage based on a value that you enter. For example, suppose you give each user 5MB of storage space to use on the server. Enter the 5MB value and then set a warning level limit. The warning level limit tells the system when to issue warnings to the user who is getting close to exceeding his or her limit. For example, for the 5MB value, I could set a warning limit to 4MB. Once the user exceeded 4MB of storage, the user would begin receiving warnings about storage space running low.

✦ **Log event when a user exceeds their quota limit**—This check box tells the system to log an event when a user exceeds their quota limit. This option creates a track record for you to examine.

✦ **Log event when a user exceeds their warning level**—Finally, you can also choose to log an event when a user exceeds his or her warning level as well.

At the bottom of the Quota tab, you see a Quota Entries button. When you configure disk quotas, new users are automatically tracked in the quota system, but existing users already connected to the volume are not. You can use the Quota Entries dialog box to add new quota entries for specific users, shown in Figure 15-5.

Quota Entries for Local Disk (C:)

Status	Name	Logon Name	Amount Used	Quota Limit	Warning Level
⊕ OK	Dan...	dcompton@t...	0 bytes	5 MB	4 MB
⊕ OK	Bec...	bsmith@trito...	0 bytes	5 MB	4 MB
⊕ OK	Tom...	tfreeman@trit...	0 bytes	5 MB	4 MB
⊕ OK	Kar...	kjohnson@tri...	0 bytes	5 MB	4 MB
⊕ OK		BUILTIN\Ad...	1.15 GB	No Limit	No Limit
⊕ OK		NT AUTHO...	1.19 MB	5 MB	4 MB

6 total item(s), 1 selected.

Figure 15-5: Quota Entries dialog box

To add a new Quota entry, click Quota ➪ New Quota Entry and then select the user from the list that appears. A dialog box, shown in Figure 15-6, appears so you can enter the desired quota limit and warning level. This feature is quite useful because you can override your default settings. For example, if you wanted one user to have more or less disk space, you can configure it here in order to change the default setting you specified on the Quota tab.

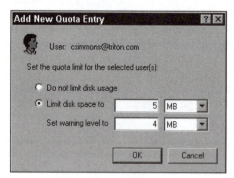

Figure 15-6: Add New Quota Entry dialog box

You can also easily manage any of the quota entries in the list by right-clicking the entry and clicking Properties. This presents you with essentially the same dialog box seen in Figure 15-6, where you can change the default quota limit and warning values. You can also use the Quota menu to import and export quota entries to and from other servers.

Tip   It is important to keep in mind that the big picture for disk quotas is user storage management. You can either deny disk space or simply warn users who are using too much disk space with disk quotas. This technology enables you to conserve storage space by forcing users to be conservative as well.

Remote Installation Services

Remote Installation Services, also considered an IntelliMirror technology, enables you to remotely install Windows 2000 Professional on client computers. Remote Installation Services is a chapter on its own (and quite a long one at that) so I'm not going to go into all of the details here. However, I do want to show you how it works and point out several configuration issues.

Tip   You can find an excellent step-by-step RIS usage document at www.microsoft. com/WINDOWS2000/library/planning/management/remotesteps.asp.

Remote Installation Services (RIS) enables you to remotely install Windows 2000 Professional on networked computers without having to actually visit the client computer (which certainly saves wear and tear on your feet). It's designed to help administrators who must install Professional on a bunch of client computers to do so quickly and from one location.

However, all is not as simple as it sounds. First, Remote Installation Services works only in a Windows 2000 environment, and it will remotely install only Windows 2000 Professional. Also, you have to ensure that DNS, DHCP, and the Active Directory are installed and functioning on your network. RIS uses these network services to communicate with the client computer. There is also an issue of getting your client computers to communicate with the RIS server. This can be done in two ways. First, client computers that are equipped with the Preboot Execution Protocol (PXE) located in the computer's BIOS can automatically access the network upon boot and locate a DHCP server to find a DNS server, which then locates the RIS server. From there, installation can begin. So PXE-enabled computers work great with RIS because all you have to do is connect them to the network and turn them on. If you do not have PXE-enabled client computers, then you have to use a RIS boot disk to get them started (which I'll show you how to make later in this section). This is more of a pain because you have to use the floppy disk on each client to get it started, but the boot disk is a good workaround for computers that do not support PXE. Now, here's the trick. The client's network adapter card must support the use of the RIS boot disk. This sounds easy, but at present, only 25 PCI network adapters are supported. If your client does not support PXE and if it does not have one of these 25 adapters, you're simply out of luck.

Tip   You can see a list of network adapters when you create a RIS boot disk, explained in an upcoming section.

Installing RIS

RIS is not installed on Windows 2000 Servers by default, but you can easily install it using Add/Remove Programs in Control Panel. To install RIS, follow these steps:

1. Click Start ➪ Settings ➪ Control Panel.

2. Double-click Add/Remove Programs and then click the Add/Remove Windows Components button.

3. In the Windows Components Wizard, click the Remote Installation Services check box, shown in Figure 15-7 and then click the Next button.

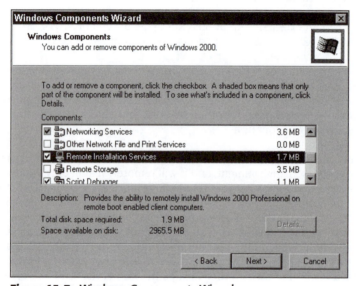

Figure 15-7: Windows Components Wizard

4. Windows 2000 installs RIS. Click the Finish button when prompted, and you will need to reboot the server.

Caution The RIS server must have a second volume available. RIS will not store its installation images on the boot volume or the volume containing your operating system. The volume must be large enough to hold RIS images. A typical RIS image (including applications) takes up about 500MB.

Setting up RIS

Once you have installed RIS and rebooted the server, you will need to complete a few other actions to make RIS work. First, RIS servers must be authorized by the Active Directory to participate on the network. If you have installed and configured DHCP in an Active Directory environment, you have performed this operation before. The authorization process is a security feature designed to prevent unauthorized persons from installing and using unauthorized RIS servers in your environment. The odd thing about authorizing a RIS server is that it must be performed through DHCP. This action essentially authorizes the RIS server to use DHCP for RIS clients. To authorize the RIS server, follow these steps:

1. On a DHCP server, click Start ⇨ Programs ⇨ Administrative Tools ⇨ DHCP.

2. Click Action ⇨ Manage Authorized Servers.

3. In the Manage Authorized Servers window, click the Authorize button. Enter the name or IP address of the RIS server in the dialog box and click OK. Click Yes to the confirmation message that appears.

4. The RIS server now appears in the authorized servers list, shown in Figure 15-8. Click the Close button and then close DHCP Manager.

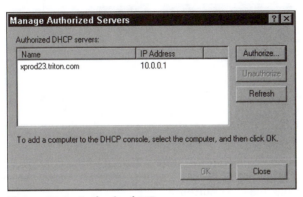

Figure 15-8: Authorized RIS server

Once the RIS server is authorized to participate on the network, you next need to access the RIS Setup Wizard to configure it. To set up the RIS server, follow these steps:

1. Click Start ⇨ Run. Type **risetup** in the dialog box and click OK.

2. The RIS Setup Wizard appears. Click Next on the Welcome screen.

Note　Note the message on the Welcome screen telling you that a DHCP and DNS server must be available to complete setup. You will also need a Windows 2000 Professional installation CD-ROM or the location of a network share that holds the Professional setup files.

3. The Remote Installation Folder Location window appears, as shown in Figure 15-9. Specify the location for the RIS folder by entering a path or using the Browse button to select one. Remember, your drive must not be the same drive as the system drive, must be formatted with Windows 2000 NTFS, and must contain enough disk space. Also note that the folder name should remain "RemoteInstall." Click the Next button.

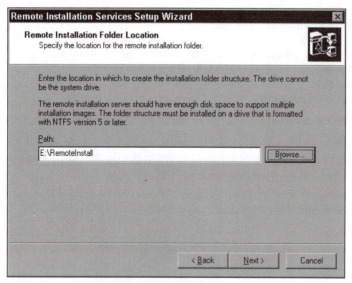

Figure 15-9: RIS Installation Folder Location window

4. In the Initial Settings window, you can choose either to respond immediately to client computer requests when setup is finished or not. By default, RIS does not respond to client computer service requests until you configure it to do so after setup. Make your selection and then click the Next button.

5. In the Source File Location window, enter the path to the Windows 2000 Professional image source files, such as your CD-ROM drive or a network share location. Click the Next button.

6. Enter a folder name for the folder to which the files will be copied. The default name is win2000.pro, but you can change it as desired. Click the Next button.

7. Enter a friendly description and any desired help text. Click the Next button.

8. Review your settings and then click the Finish button. The file copy process begins.

RIS server properties

Once you have set up the RIS server, you can select some further configuration options by accessing the RIS server's computer account properties in the Active Directory. Notice that a Remote Install tab now appears, shown in Figure 15-10.

You have a few configuration options here. First, if you did not specify for the RIS server to begin servicing clients after setup completed, you can do so now by clicking the "Respond to client computers requesting service" check box. You also see a Verify Server button. If you are experiencing problems with the RIS server, click this button to start a wizard that checks the system.

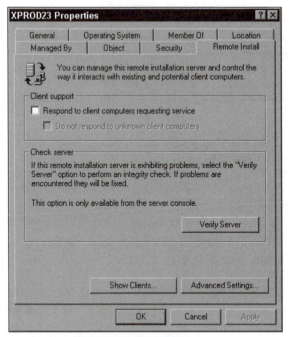

Figure 15-10: Remote Install tab

At the bottom of the Remote Install tab, you also see a Show Clients button and an Advanced Settings button. The Show Clients button opens a search window that lists all RIS, or managed, clients in the Active Directory. If you click Advanced Settings, a new properties sheet opens that contains New Clients, Images, Tools, Object, and Security tabs. The Object and Security tabs are like all others for Active Directory objects, so I'll not cover those here. However, I do want to point out what is available on the New Clients, Images, and Tools tabs.

The New Clients tab enables you to configure how RIS generates a name for the new client computer and where in the Active Directory the computer account is created. For the computer name, you can click a drop-down menu so that you can select a variety of options, such as a combination of the user name and numbers, MAC address, and so forth.

The Images tab displays a list of your current installation images. You can use this tab to view the properties of an existing installation image, to remove the image, or to create a new one.

Finally, the Tools tab provides you with a list of additional tools you may have installed on your server that can support RIS.

Prestaging RIS clients

Before you can identify and install software on client computers, you must perform some actions that prepare the clients for RIS installation. This process is called *prestaging*, and it essentially ensures that particular clients use a particular RIS server and that proper permissions are in place to use RIS. Prestaging helps you, as the administrator, control what clients can access a RIS server, so this is an effective security feature.

You use the Active Directory Users and Computers console to prestage RIS clients. To perform the process, follow these steps:

1. Click Start ➪ Programs ➪ Administrative Tools ➪ Active Directory Users and Computers.

2. Select the OU or container where the new computer account should be stored and then click Action ➪ New ➪ Computer.

3. In the New Object — Computer window, enter a desired computer name and click the Next button.

4. Click the "This is a managed computer" check box, shown in Figure 15-11. You will need to enter the Globally Unique Identifier (GUID) number for the client computer account. You can get the GUID from the system BIOS, or it may be posted on the computer's case. Enter this information and click Next.

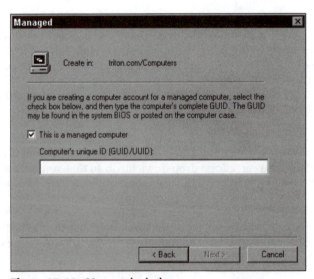

Figure 15-11: Managed window

5. Select the RIS server you want to service the needs of this client or allow any RIS server to service the needs of the client.

Users who access a RIS computer must log on for the installation to begin. Once you have the client computer account prestaged, you also need to set permissions for the user or group that will have access to the computer account for RIS installation purposes. To set the permissions, just access the client computer's account in the Active Directory and then access the Security tab on the properties sheets. Click the Add button and select the desired users or groups that have permission to access the computer account. Then click OK.

Creating a client boot floppy

As I mentioned earlier, clients that support PXE can automatically boot and locate a RIS server. Clients that do not support PXE must have a RIS boot disk and use a supported network adapter card. Creating a RIS boot disk is easy—just follow these steps:

1. On the RIS server, navigate to the Remoteinstall\Admin\I386 directory. You will see a utility called RBFG.EXE. Double-click the icon.

2. The Boot Disk Generator window appears, shown in Figure 15-12. Click the Adapter List button to view a list of supported adapters. Place a blank, formatted floppy disk into the drive and then click Create Disk.

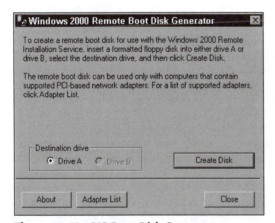

Figure 15-12: RIS Boot Disk Generator

Tip   If the client computer does not contain one of the supported network adapter cards, the RIS boot disk will not work on the client.

Once you have the boot disk, you can boot the client using the disk so that the RIS server can be contacted. I should also note that you can create a number of different images to use for installation. Although RIS supports only Windows 2000 Professional, you could create different images that have different applications installed. Also, you can use a tool called RIPrep found on your RIS drive under

RemoteInstall\Admin\I3867\Riprep. This tool enables you to install Windows 2000 Professional on a client, configure the desired settings and applications, and then take a snapshot image of the system. You can then install this image on other computers as desired.

All in all, RIS is an effective tool, provided you have client computers that can support it, and it is an important part of the IntelliMirror technologies.

Group Policy

Now I want to turn my attention to Group Policy, which is also considered an important part of IntelliMirror. Group Policy basically replaces system policies in a Windows 2000 network, and Group Policy provides you with some powerful features for desktop management. With Group Policy, you can enforce a standardized desktop and system setting configuration, install software, download documents to a client computer, and even configure Internet settings. Group Policy is designed to lower the Total Cost of Ownership (TCO) by giving administrators more control over user desktops. With Group Policy, you can then enforce company policy regarding configuration and use of client computers.

Group Policy basics

Before exploring Group Policy, it is very important that you understand Group Policy inheritance behavior. Once you understand how Group Policy is applied, you can then begin to plan a Group Policy implementation for your Active Directory infrastructure. Group Policy can be applied at the site, domain, or OU level. The inheritance structure is site to domain, then domain to OU. In other words, inheritance works from the top down.

Tip   In actuality, you can configure a local Group Policy that applies to your specific computer. In this case, the processing order is local policy, site policy, domain policy, and then OU policy.

Suppose that you want to configure a single Group Policy that applies to all users and groups in your entire enterprise. You can create the Group Policy and then implement the policy at the site level. Due to inheritance, the policy will be applied to all domains and OUs within the enterprise. Or, you may possibly have different Group Policies that are applied to domains. Domain A has a different Group Policy than Domain B. You create the Group Policy, implement it in the desired domain, and all users, groups, and computers in the domain receive the policy. You can perform the same process on individual OUs if necessary. So inheritance is in effect from the site level down to the domain and OU levels. Therefore, what happens if there is a site policy, then a domain policy, and an OU policy?

Not to be confused with inheritance, override is also in effect by default. This simply means that if a site policy is in place, it is applied to all domains, unless a domain has its own Group Policy. In that case, the domain Group Policy overrides the site policy. If an OU in that domain also has a Group Policy, it overrides the domain policy. Here's the key — the policy closest to the user is one that will get applied. There may be a site policy, but if there is an OU policy for a particular OU in which a user or computer resides, the OU policy is the one that will be used. Figure 15-13 helps illustrate this process.

Note   The term *Group Policy* may seem like a misnomer because you can't actually apply a Group Policy to a user or group of users. You can apply it only to a site, a domain, or an OU — those are the only three levels of application.

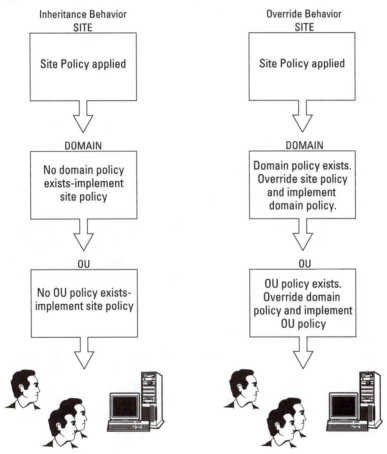

Figure 15-13: Inheritance and override behavior

Now here's the tricky and ridiculously confusing part. While it is true that the policy closest to the user is applied, this does not mean that no components of the higher policy get applied. What this means is that if a site policy says remove the Run command and a domain policy says use the Run command, then the Run command is used. If however, a domain policy has "not configured" on a number of possible policies and a site policy has a configured setting, then it is still applied at the domain level. The override behavior overrides conflicting policies. So, to completely stop a higher-level policy from becoming effective, you must block inheritance. For example, suppose a domain policy is in place, but a particular OU has its own policy. You don't want the OU to receive any of the domain policy, so you can choose to block the domain policy at the OU level. This way, only the OU policy is applied. However, to keep the chain of command straight, a domain administrator can also configure "no override" so that a policy cannot be blocked. In this case, the no override *overrides* block inheritance. As you can imagine, this can quickly become a big, configuring mess. As with all configurations in the Active Directory, simplicity is always best. Strive for only one or just a few Group Policies that can be applied at the highest levels possible. This reduces conflict problems and can help you avoid confusing Group Policy configurations.

Group Policy objects

There are three major components of Group Policy — Group Policy Objects, Group Policy Containers, and Group Policy Templates. The first is Group Policy objects (GPOs), which contain the actual setting configuration that is applied to user and groups within the Active Directory. When you create a Group Policy, you are in essence creating a GPO. GPOs are like all other objects in the Active Directory, and you apply the GPO to the site, domain, or OU where you want to implement the policy. The GPO stores its configuration information in a Group Policy Container (GPC), as well as in Group Policy Templates (GPTs). Like GPOs, GPCs and GPTs are Active Directory objects, but they also reside in the SYSVOL folder of domain controllers. This is a good place for them because you don't have to worry about replication. Windows 2000's File Replication Service (FRS) replicates them among domain controllers for you.

Accessing a Group Policy

You can access the Group Policy console, an MMC snap-in, in two different ways. You can access it from the site, domain, or OU properties sheets within the Active Directory. For example, suppose you want to implement a site level Group Policy. In Active Directory Sites and Services, expand the Sites container and then select the desired site. Click Action ⇨ Properties, and you'll see a Group Policy tab on the properties sheets, shown in Figure 15-14.

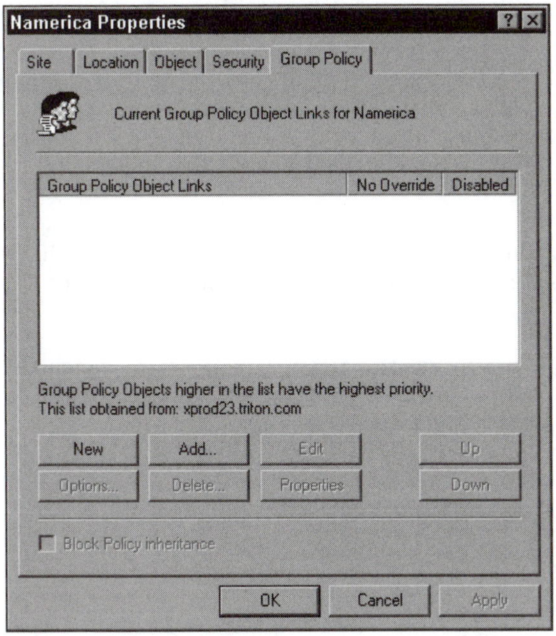

Figure 15-14: Group Policy tab

You'll see the same tab if you access your domain and OU properties sheets as well. Click the New Button to create a new policy. You see the new Group Policy Object Link called New Group Policy Object appear in the window (you can rename it). If you select the Group Policy object and click the Options button, a window appears, shown in Figure 15-15, that enables you to select the "No Override" option or the "Disabled" option, with which you can disable the Group Policy. Also notice that the "Block Policy inheritance" check box is available at the bottom of the Group Policy tab, as shown in Figure 15-14.

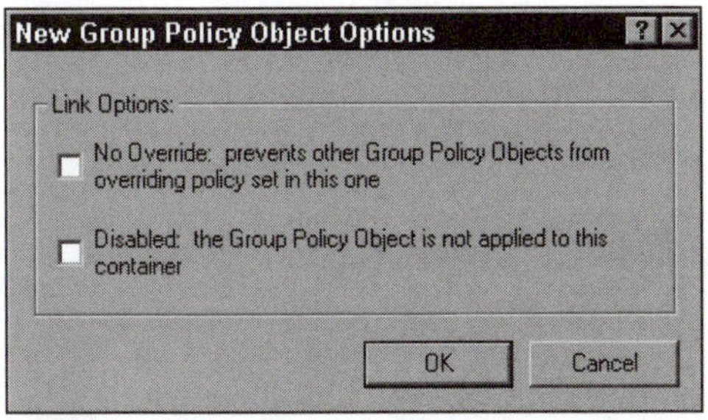

Figure 15-15: Group Policy object options

If you click the Properties button, you see a General, Links, and Security tab. The Links and Security tabs are standard object tabs, but do notice on the General tab that you can choose to disable the computer configuration or the user configuration portion of a Group Policy. This is an effective option because you could have a Group Policy where you configure only the user portion and not the computer portion. You could then disable the computer portion to speed the policy application process.

You can also click the Add button to add a different GPO to the console. This feature opens a window that enables you to select an existing site, domain, or OU policy you can add and use.

Finally, the Edit button opens the Group Policy MMC console, shown in Figure 15-16, where you can actually configure the Group Policy. Notice that you have two categories — User Configuration and Computer Configuration.

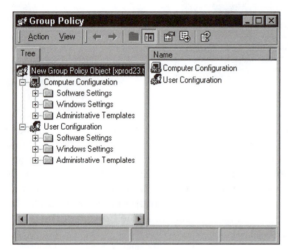

Figure 15-16: Group Policy MMC console

Aside from accessing the Group Policy from the site, domain, or OU properties, you can also manually open the Group Policy snap-in. To open the GPO in this manner, follow these steps:

1. Click Start ➪ Run, type **MMC**, and then click OK.

2. Click Console ➪ Add/Remove snap-in.

3. On the Add/Remove Snap-in window, click the Add button.

4. From the snap-in list that appears, select Group Policy and click OK.

5. The Select Group Policy Object window appears, shown in Figure 15-17.

   Thus, by default the Group Policy is focused on the local computer. You can change this focus by clicking the Browse button.

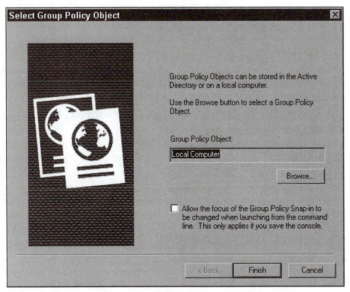

Figure 15-17: Select Group Policy Object window

6. The Browse for a Group Policy Object window opens, shown in Figure 15-18. You see tabs for Domain/OUs, Sites, Computers, or All. You can browse the tabs, open the desired policy, and then click OK.

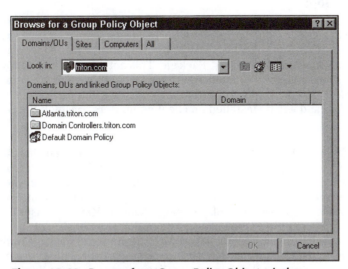

Figure 15-18: Browse for a Group Policy Object window

7. Click the Finish button, then click Close on the Add Standalone Snap-in window, and then click OK to open the snap-in.

Configuring a Group Policy

Once you open a Group Policy, either by using the site, domain, or OU properties sheets or by manually opening the console, you can then configure the Group Policy object as desired. You can configure either the user object or computer object (or both, of course) by clicking on the icon in the left pane to expand it. You'll see that the categories are the same for the user and computer objects, and you'll even find that many of the policies overlap.

> **Tip**   When the policy is applied, if the user policy and computer policy conflict, the user policy is applied.

Configuration is easy for the most part, but you do have quite a few options. The following two sections examine the Computer and User Configurations separately.

> **Note**   To create a Group Policy, you must be a member of the Administrators group or the Group Policy Creator Owners group.

Computer Configuration

If you expand Computer Configuration in the Group Policy console, you see that you have three containers: Software Settings, Windows Settings, and Administrative Templates. The following sections consider what is available in each of these.

Software Settings

The Software Settings container contains a software installation icon. If you select the icon, you can see any configured software packages displayed in the right pane. You can also create a new software package by selecting Software Installation in the left pane and clicking Action ➪ New ➪ Package. This action opens a window where you can browse for a Windows Installer package (.msi) that you have previously created. Any installer packages you add to the console will then become a part of the Group Policy and will be installed on client computers to which the policy applies.

If you select Software Installation in the left console pane and then click Action ➪ Properties, you see the properties sheet for software installation. On the General tab, you have a few basic options to control how installation behaves when it is being deployed. For example, you can choose to display a Deployment Software dialog box, and you can choose to display either a Basic or Maximum user interface while installation is occurring. You also see an option to publish. This means that you want the new package to be published with the standard package options. As you can see in Figure 15-19, the Publish option is grayed out. This is because you can only publish to users, not to computers. If you were to access this sheet from a user object, this option would be available. You can also see that you can assign software with the Assign option, which means that you have assigned a software package to any user or computer with standard properties. You also have an "Advanced published or assigned" option. This feature enables you to configure the publication options at the time of deployment. You can also choose to uninstall any applications when they fall out of the scope of management.

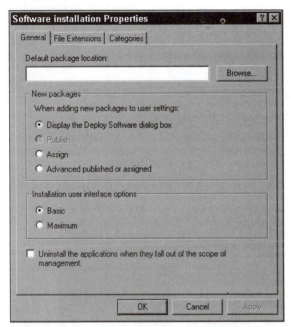

Figure 15-19: Software installation Properties

The File Extensions tab enables you to associate all extensions with particular applications. This option is useful for custom applications so that correct files can be associated with them. The Categories tab enables you to add custom categories to Add/Remove Programs on the user's computer. These custom categories can store corporate software applications.

Windows Settings

If you expand Windows Settings, you see two categories: Scripts and Security Settings. If you select Scripts in the left pane, you see Startup and Shutdown Options appear in the right pane. If you select one of the options and then click Action ⇨ Properties, you can choose to use a desired script or you can add one as needed. When you add scripts, or remove them for that matter, the scripts become part of the Group Policy and will be run when the user boots the computer or shuts down.

If you expand the Security Settings container, you see a number of subcontainers that house different kinds of security policies. For example, if you select account policies in the left pane, the password policy and account lockout policy containers appear in the right pane. If you double-click one of the policy containers, you see a list of actual policies. For example, under password policy, you see such policies as enforce password history, maximum password age, minimum password length, and so on. If you double-click one of the policies, a simple dialog box appears where you can define a policy. For example in Figure 15-20, you see the "Enforce password history" policy. To define the policy, simply click the check box and enter the number of passwords a computer should remember. Then click the OK button.

Figure 15-20: Security Policy Setting

Tip

You will notice that, by default, most policies are not defined. This is a big design issue because you need only access and define the policies you want to implement. You have many policies available to you, but you will not use all of them for your implementation. Therefore you need only access the ones you want to implement since, by default, the policies are not defined anyway.

So, to configure the policies you want, simply move through the different containers, and access the desired policy container, then the desired policy. You may have to spend some time wading around to find the exact policy you want, but the following bulleted list reviews what is available in the Security Settings container.

✦ **Account Policies** — Contains subcontainers for password policy and account lockout policy.

✦ **Local Policies** — Contains subcontainers for audit policy, user rights assignment, and security options.

✦ **Event Log** — Contains policy settings for the Event Log.

✦ **Restricted Groups** — Contains security access policies for restricted group access.

✦ **System Services** — Contains security policies for system services on the computer, such as DHCP Client, FRS, and so on. This feature enables you to set security on various system services to prevent user tampering.

✦ **Registry** — Contains security policies for registry access and editing.

✦ **File System** — Contains security policies for file system configuration.

✦ **Public Key Policies** — Contains subcontainers for encrypted data recovery agents, automatic certificate request settings, trusted root certification authorities, and enterprise trusts.

✦ **IP Security Policies** — When IP Security (IPSec) is in effect, these policies define security settings client and server IP traffic.

Administrative Templates

The Administrative Templates container contains a number of templates and different categories that you can use to configure various system components. You can also import other templates as desired. Fortunately, policy templates all look basically the same. When you double-click the template, you have Policy and Explain tabs. On the Policy tab, shown in Figure 15-21, you can choose to enable or disable the policy or to keep the policy not configured.

Caution

Keeping the policy not configured simply means "I don't care — use the default setting." Enabling and disabling both invoke registry changes. If you do not care whether a setting is enabled or not, always leave the "Not Configured" radio button selected.

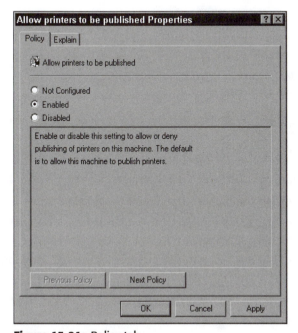

Figure 15-21: Policy tab

The Explain tab, shown in Figure 15-22, gives you additional information about the setting and what will happen if you enable or disable the policy.

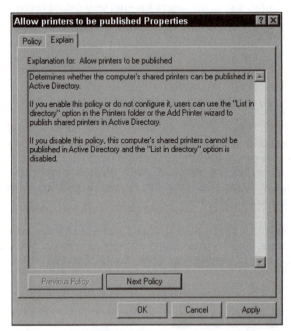

Figure 15-22: Explain tab

 Tip

When using policy templates, you can use the Previous Policy and Next Policy buttons to navigate easily through a long list.

For Computer Configuration, there are quite a number of helpful administrative templates. I'm obviously not going to list them all here, but the following list gives you an overview of the template categories available to you.

✦ Under Windows Components, you have the following:

- **NetMeeting** — Contains templates to configure NetMeeting.

- **Internet Explorer** — Contains templates to configure Internet Explore and Internet connectivity settings.

- **Task Scheduler** — Contains templates to manage task usage and modification.

- **Windows Installer** — Contains templates to prevent or control the use of Windows Installer.

✦ Under System, you have the following:

- **Logon** — Contains templates to configure logon processes.

- **Disk Quotas** — Contains templates to enforce disk quota settings.

- **DNS Client** — Contains templates for DNS communication.

- **Group Policy** — Contains templates to control the configuration of a local Group Policy.

- **Windows File Protection** — Contains templates to control the use of Windows File Protection.

✦ Under Network, you have the following:

- **Offline Files** — Contains templates to control and configure offline file usage.

- **Network and Dial-up Connections** — Contains templates to configure connection sharing.

✦ Under Printers, you have a number of templates that determine what users can do with a local printer when logged onto the computer.

User Configuration

As you can guess, Group Policy User Configuration places management restrictions or permissions on items directly associated with the user/group account. You have the same Software Settings, Windows Settings, and Administrative Templates containers as you saw in the previous sections, so I'm going to point out only information that is different in User Configuration.

First, under Windows Settings, you have a few additional categories, which are as follows:

✦ **Internet Explorer Maintenance** — This category contains policies which enable you to configure a number of custom Internet Explorer options, such as a custom title bar, shown in Figure 15-23. You can also use animated bitmaps, custom logos, preconfigured connection settings, preconfigured URLs, security settings, and program settings.

✦ **Remote Installation Services** — This category gives you a Choice Options icon that presents you with a simple window so you can define the level of user interaction during a remote installation, such as using custom setup, and so on.

✦ **Folder Redirection** — Folder redirection enables a user to log on to any workstation and receive his or her files and folders. You can choose the target location on the user's computer to redirect the folders.

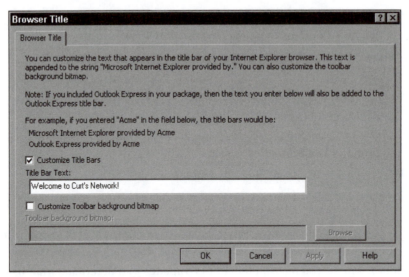

Figure 15-23: Custom title bar

Under Administrative Templates, you also have categories for the following:

✦ **Start Menu & Task Bar** — This enables you to configure Start Menu and taskbar items.

✦ **Desktop** — This enables you to control desktop settings including the Active Desktop as well as Active Directory searches.

✦ **Control Panel** — This enables you to manage and control Control Panel items.

Summary

This chapter explored Microsoft's approach to computer and user management in Windows 2000 through IntelliMirror and specifically through the Active Directory. In order to reduce the TCO, organizations must control user and computer settings in order to create the most productive work environment and avoid help desk trouble tickets. IntelliMirror technologies can provide highly customized management configuration, including remote installation and software deployment. These features enable network and system streamlining that can enforce and implement company policies.

✦   ✦   ✦

Implementing Distributed File System and Indexing Service

When the concept of networking first came onto the scene, networks were rather small in terms of servers, workstations, and geographic area. Network users could more easily locate resources because network size or server number was not a hindrance. In today's large distributed networks, where it is not uncommon for a network to span multiple geographic locations around the world and contain thousands of users and servers, users often struggle when attempting to locate a particular resource. The Active Directory is designed to reduce this problem by giving users powerful query capabilities and removing the network topology from the users' view. There are two other technologies, Distributed File System and Indexing Service, that also further the Active Directory's cause by making shared folders more easy to locate and improving user text searches. This chapter explores these two technologies and how they can be useful in your Active Directory environment.

Understanding Distributed File System (Dfs)

Picture this scenario: A network user needs to find a shared folder that contains a group of spreadsheet templates. The user knows the folder exists, but does not know the name of the shared folder or the computer on which the shared folder resides. What can the user do? Before the Active Directory and Dfs, the user could only begin browsing the network and hope he or she found the right folder. In a large network, this task is essentially overwhelming.

Distributed File System is a server service that attempts to take the mystery out of finding shared folders and is a system that I believe is quite good. It is easy to set up and configure, and it greatly simplifies the work of an end user.

Distributed File System works by having one or more servers configured for Dfs. You set up shared folder "links" in a hierarchy fashion on the server. The shared folders themselves still reside on other computers and servers, but the Dfs server provides an internal link to the real network location. When users view the Dfs hierarchy, they simply see an organized list of shared folders—as if the entire network's shared folders reside on one server. In reality, when a user opens a shared folder in the Dfs hierarchy, the user is actually redirected to the server that physically holds the shared folder. That server determines if the user has appropriate permissions to access the folder and returns the share results to the user. So, in essence, the Dfs acts as a server that provides an organized view of the shared folders and an internal link to the actual server that holds the actual folder. All of this is invisible to the end user who simply sees the shared folders as if they physically reside in one location. Figure 16-1 gives you a graphical view of this discussion.

In Figure 16-1, you see a folder hierarchy called "Sales." Within Sales, you see a number of shared folders pertaining to the Sales department. Users simply see Sales and all of its shared folders. In reality, the shared folders exist on three different servers. With Dfs, users do not have to keep track of the actual location of the shared folders or which server holds which shared folder. Of course, keeping track of 3 servers would not be hard in the real world, but suppose there were 40 sales folders spread out over 25 servers in different network sites.

In conjunction with Figure 16-1, now is a good time to introduce some Dfs terms to you. First, a Dfs starts with a *root*. In Figure 16-1, the Sales folder is the root and what is initially visible to network users. When users open the root share, they see the other shared folders available. In your Dfs implementation, you can have as many Dfs roots as you desire, but the trick is that each Dfs server can hold only one Dfs root. You'll see some examples of this in upcoming sections in this chapter.

Under each Dfs root, you have *Dfs links*. In Figure 16-1, each of the sales folders is actually a Dfs link to the actual server that holds the share. Figure 16-2 redraws the figure to show the root and Dfs links. In Figure 16-2, the links are shown as UNC paths to the correct server and share for discussion's sake. In reality, the link would be the full DNS name in a pure Windows 2000 network.

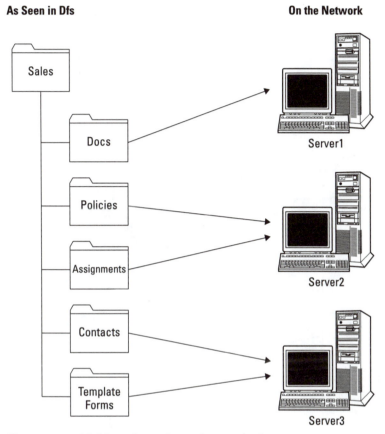

As Seen in Dfs

On the Network

Sales

Docs → Server1

Policies

Assignments → Server2

Contacts

Template Forms → Server3

Figure 16-1: Dfs hierarchy and actual network placement

Tip   At present, you can assign up to 1000 Dfs links to a single Dfs root. You can think of a Dfs link like a hyperlink in a Web page. You click the hyperlink, and you are redirected to the actual Web site or Web page. A Dfs link is the same. The user clicks the Dfs link and is redirected to the actual server and shared folder.

Aside from the Dfs root and Dfs links, you can also have a *replica*, which can refer to either a root or a link. A replica is just that — a copy of a share. Suppose you have two of the same share on different servers, or perhaps in different sites. The two shares can be combined on the same Dfs link as Dfs replica members. In the same manner, you can have a replica of an existing Dfs root, such as one that exists in a foreign site. When you configure Dfs replica members, then the Windows 2000 File Replication Service (FRS) keeps the replica members synchronized.

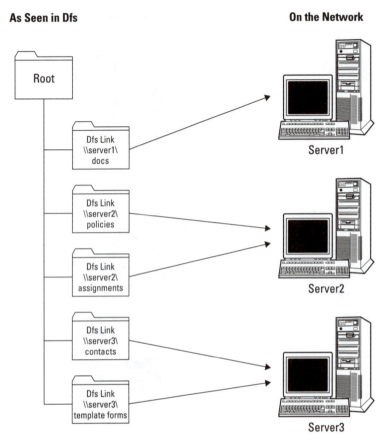

As Seen in Dfs

On the Network

Figure 16-2: Dfs root and Dfs links

Now that you have a handle on the basic concept and terminology, I want to consider why a network might want to use Dfs. Consider the following bulleted list as you decide whether Dfs is right for your environment:

✦ Dfs is designed for large distributed networks and is best used in these environments. In smaller environments that have only one site, Dfs usually isn't necessary.

✦ Your users access many different shared folders on a regular basis. In other words, the use of shared folders is very important for your business.

✦ You use an intranet or Internet for shared folders as well as shared folders on servers throughout your network.

There are two types of Dfs you can implement — a standalone Dfs and an Active Directory integrated Dfs. The following sections explore both of these, and Table 16-1 is provided as a quick reference for the clients that use both standalone and Active Directory integrated Dfs.

Table 16-1		
Dfs Clients		
Client	**Standalone**	**Active Directory Integrated**
DOS	No	No
Windows 3.x	No	No
WFW	No	No
Windows 95	Yes, with Dfs 4.x client download	Yes, with Dfs 5.0 client download
Windows 98	Yes	Yes, with Dfs 5.0 client download

Note   Windows NT server 4.0 with Service Pack 3 can host a standalone Dfs root. Only Windows 2000 servers can host a domain-based Dfs root.

Standalone Dfs

A standalone Dfs is configured on a single server designated as the root Dfs server. A standalone Dfs does not function directly with the Active Directory, and the Dfs hierarchy, or topology, is stored locally on the server. When clients want to use Dfs, the single root server is contacted. If the root server becomes unavailable, then Dfs is not available to clients. As such, Dfs is not fault tolerant in terms of network availability.

However, if the Active Directory has not yet been implemented, you can choose to use the standalone Dfs in order to begin using the technology. Other than this situation, however, you should implement an Active Directory integrated Dfs if the Active Directory is configured.

You can access the Dfs console by clicking Start ➪ Administrative Tools ➪ Distributed File System. The Dfs console, which is an MMC snap-in, appears, as shown in Figure 16-3.

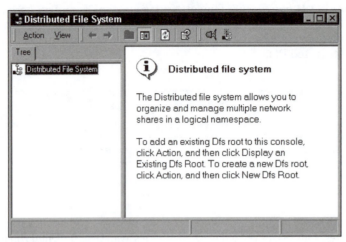

Figure 16-3: Dfs console

Once the console is open, you can use the Action menu either to display an existing Dfs root or to create a new one. If you want to open an existing Dfs root, click the option on the Action menu. A window appears where you can enter the name of the Dfs root or the host server on which is resides. The trusting domains in your network are also displayed, shown in Figure 16-4.

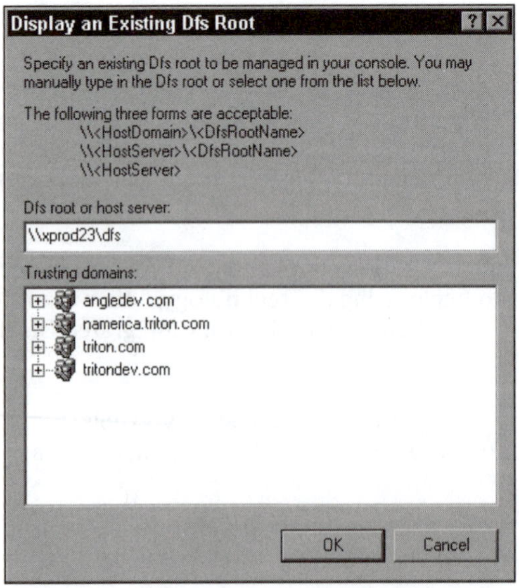

Figure 16-4: Display an existing Dfs root

To create a new standalone Dfs root, follow these steps:

1. In the Dfs console, click Action ⇨ New Dfs Root.

2. The Dfs Root Wizard begins. Click Next on the Welcome screen.

3. In the Select the Dfs Root Type window, you have two selection options. Choose the "Create a standalone Dfs root" radio button, shown in Figure 16-5, and then click the Next button.

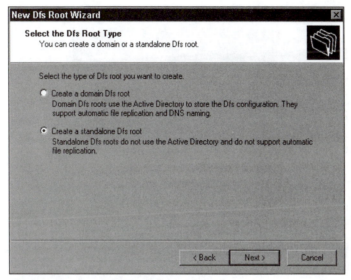

Figure 16-5: Create a standalone Dfs

4. Enter the name of host server for the standalone Dfs root or use the Browse button to select the desired server. Click the Next button.

5. The Specify the Dfs Root Share window appears. Remember from our earlier discussion that the Dfs root is simply a shared folder. In this window, shown in Figure 16-6, you can select an existing shared folder to become the Dfs root, or you can create a new Dfs share by entering the path to the share and the share name. Make your selection and click the Next button.

6. The Dfs Root Name window appears showing path and name of the Dfs root share. You can enter a comment if desired. Click the Next button.

7. The Summary window appears. Review your selections and then click the Finish button.

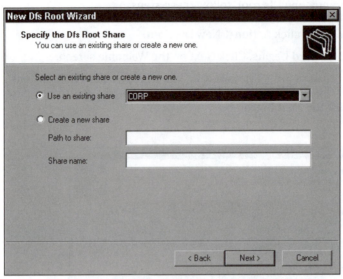

Figure 16-6: Choose the Desired Share Option

Adding Dfs links

Once you have configured the Dfs root, you can begin setting up your Dfs by adding Dfs links. Remember that Dfs links are like hyperlinks — they appear as folders to users but they transparently redirect the user to the actual server that holds the shared folder.

To create a Dfs link, follow these steps:

1. In the Dfs console, select the Dfs root and click Action ➪ New Dfs Link (or you can just click the icon that appears in the MMC).

2. In the Create a New Dfs Link window, enter the link name as you want it to appear in Dfs, the network path to the actual share, and a comment if desired. Also notice that link caching is in effect for clients, with a default setting of 1800 seconds (30 minutes). This is the period of time the link can be cached on the user's computer before it has to be updated from Dfs. You can raise or lower this value if necessary. Figure 16-7 shows you a properly configured window. Enter the link information and then click OK. The new link will now appear in the Dfs console.

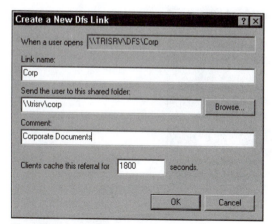

Figure 16-7: Create a New Dfs Link window

Creating a replica

A replica points the way to a different location on the network for a shared folder. For example, if you had two identical folders in two different locations on the network, the replica enables you to point to the alternate shared folder. To create a replica, follow these steps:

1. In the Dfs console, select the Dfs link for which you want to specify a replica.

2. Click Action ⇨ New Replica.

3. The Add New Replica window appears. Enter path to the shared folder for which you want to redirect the users and then click OK, as shown in Figure 16-8.

Notice that the Replication Policy options are grayed out. Since this is a standalone Dfs, replication policies cannot be used.

Once you create your Dfs links and any desired replicas, your job is basically done except for maintenance. As you use the console, notice that you can perform other actions, such as check the status of the root and links, remove links, and so forth. These actions are all self explanatory, so I'll not address them here.

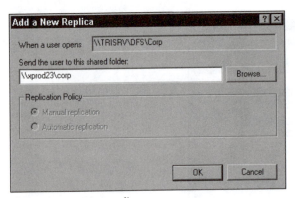

Figure 16-8: New replica

Active Directory Integrated Dfs

Under most circumstances, you will choose to implement an Active Directory integrated Dfs, also called a domain-based Dfs. With a domain-based Dfs, the Dfs topology is stored in the Active Directory and the Dfs information is available from a number of different servers. Because the Dfs topology is stored in the Active Directory, the Dfs is inherently fault tolerant. Additionally, with a domain-based Dfs, you can choose to replicate your Dfs roots and Dfs shared folders so that they will always be available. For example, suppose you have a shared folder called "Corp" that is accessed by many users every day. You can choose to replicate this folder so that it is physically available on several servers. If one server goes offline, the other servers that hold the replica can service the needs of clients. Finally, a domain-based Dfs provides load balancing among Dfs servers. The Dfs root can support multiple Dfs shared folders. This way, if one folder is accessed heavily, Dfs can ensure that the load is balanced among all of the servers instead of taxing one server. All of these features are transparent to end users.

Concerning configuration, the Active Directory integrated Dfs is configured in the same manner as a standalone Dfs, so refer to the previous section for specific steps.

Tip When you install Dfs, choose "Active Directory integrated" when you run the wizard.

There is one task I would like to point out that is different in the domain-based Dfs. You configure Dfs links and replicas in the same manner, but you can determine replication for the Dfs replicas. Right-click the child node with multiple members and choose Replication Policy. The Replication Policy window opens, shown in Figure 16-9.

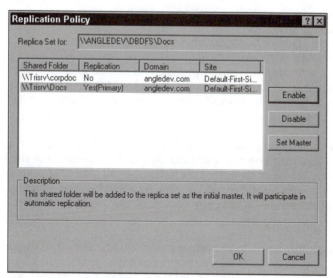

Figure 16-9: Replication Policy window

In the dialog box, you see each member of the replica set. Select the desired primary master and click the Set Master button. The primary master is the share from which all other replicas will be set. You can also use the console to enable or disable members as necessary.

Indexing Service

Though not a part of the Active Directory itself, Microsoft Indexing Service enables end users to locate particular documents on your computer by performing text searches. This service makes your computer act like a library catalog to users so they can search for words, phrases, or even authors. Users can search either through the Start menu's search feature or from a Web browser.

Let me make a categorical statement here — Indexing Service is a per machine service. It is not used with the Active Directory or integrated with the Active Directory. The purpose of Indexing Service is to index a local drive and enable users to search for particular documents on that computer. I have included Indexing Service in this chapter because its goal is the same as many goals of Dfs and the Active Directory — to help end users find what they need.

Consider an example. Suppose you have a Windows 2000 member server that is being used as a file server. The server has hundreds of documents in a number of different shared folders. Many of those documents are research white papers and other scholarly documents. With Indexing Service in use, a user can connect to your server, search for a particular word or phrase, and find all matching documents. The user does not have to roam through your shared folders or peruse hundreds of documents to find the desired information. Obviously, this saves the user a lot of time and aggravation.

Note   Indexing Service is fully compliant with NTFS permissions. When performing a search, the user is returned only document matches for documents he or she has permissions to view. However, do not put the indexing catalog on a FAT volume, or users will be able to view the entire catalog. Also, note that Indexing Service does not index encrypted documents, and any document that is encrypted after it is indexed is removed from the index.

Indexing Service takes information from certain kinds of documents and organizes that information so it can be used to answer user search queries. The Indexing Service can index both the entire document and the document's parameters, such as title, author, date of creation, and so forth. By indexing the document and the parameters, the Indexing Service gives users more search options and more chances to locate the actual documents they need. Users can find material based on keywords, phrases, titles, author's name, and so forth.

The Indexing Service is capable of reading a document and indexing it through the use of a *filter*. The filter enables the Indexing Service to scan the document and extract the necessary information for indexing. Indexing Service can scan and index the following documents:

- ✦ Text
- ✦ Hypertext Markup Language (HTML) files
- ✦ Microsoft Office 95 or later documents
- ✦ Internet mail and news (requires Internet Information Service to be installed) files

Additionally, Indexing Service can index any document for which you obtain a filter. Filters can be custom created using the Microsoft Platform Software Development Kit.

Installing Indexing Service

Indexing Service is not difficult to install, but before doing so, you should make certain that your server meet the needs of Indexing Service and your users. Indexing Service's installation requirements are the same as a typical server installation. If you have a low to moderate number of queries, your system should be able to handle indexing, but in large environments with many, many queries, your server may need more RAM and a more powerful CPU to service clients. So, take a look at both your server and your environment before proceeding.

To install Indexing Service, follow these steps:

1. Open Control Panel and double-click Add/Remove Programs.

2. In the Add/Remove Programs window, click the Add/Remove Windows Components button.

3. In the Windows Components list, click the check box next to Indexing Service, shown in Figure 16-10, and then click the Next button.

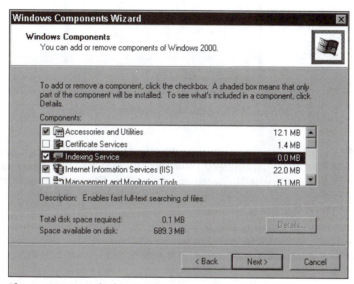

Figure 16-10: Indexing Service

4. The service is installed on your system. Click Finish.

The Indexing Service interface is located in the Computer Management console. Click Start ➪ Programs ➪ Administrative Tools ➪ Computer Management. In the left pane, expand the Services and Applications note and select Indexing Service, shown in Figure 16-11.

Indexing Service catalogs

When you install Indexing Service, a catalog is automatically created, and all of your documents that can be indexed are automatically indexed. This catalog, called the System catalog, scans and indexes all of your fixed or permanent hard disks. If Internet Information Server (IIS) is installed, a Web catalog is also created. You can see both of these catalogs in Figure 16-11.

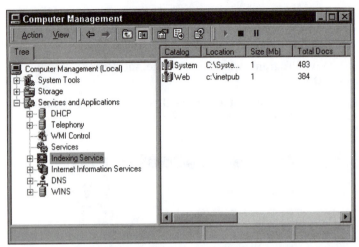

Figure 16-11: Indexing Service in Computer Management console

When the Indexing Service scans documents, it indexes all of the documents' contents along with their parameters. However, the Indexing Service does not include any words that are on the word exception list. The word exception list is called Noise.*xxx* where *xxx* is an extension indicating the word list language, such as Noise.eng. The Noise file is located by default in C:\WINNT\System32, and you can open it and edit it with any text editor such as Notepad. You can see the default file in Figure 16-12, and it includes common words and articles, such as *because*, *been*, *before*, and other words, symbols, and numbers.

Figure 16-12: Noise.eng file

You can choose to include or exclude any desired directory on your computer from the index list. This feature allows you to manage what is and what is not included in the catalog. To add a new directory to the catalog, follow these steps:

1. In the Indexing Service console in Computer Management, right click either System or Web catalog as desired, point to New, and then click Directory.

2. In the Add Directory dialog box, shown in Figure 16-13, enter the path to the new directory you want to add and include an alias if desired. If the directory you want to add is located on a different computer, you enter a valid user name and password.

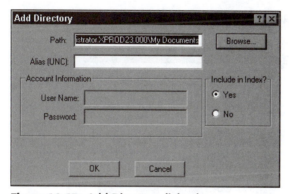

Figure 16-13: Add Directory dialog box

3. Click the Include in Index "Yes" radio button and then click OK.

You can prevent a directory from being indexed in the catalog in the same manner. Just locate the directory, then choose the Include in Index "No" radio button, and click OK. For directories or files stored on NTFS volumes, you can also select the directory or file, right-click it, and choose Properties. On the General tab, click the Advanced button and then clear the "Index Contents for Fast File Searching" check box. This prevents the directory or file from being indexed.

Tip

In addition to adding or removing a directory, you can also right-click the desired catalog, point to All Tasks, and then choose to stop, start, or pause a catalog if necessary. You can also use this menu to merge two catalogs together. Generally, you would not want to merge catalogs together, but in terms of indexing organization, this feature may be helpful on file servers that index many documents.

Finally, there are two other points I would like to mention concerning catalogs. In the Computer Management console, you can select Indexing Service in the left pane, and then click Action ➪ New ➪ Catalog to create a custom catalog. You don't need to do this under most circumstances, but depending on your needs, you may choose to create several catalogs for organizational needs and purposes.

Also, it is possible that you may need to cache some document properties. Remember that properties are additional document attributes, such as author name, date of creation, and so forth. These properties are indexed along with the document, but some properties cannot be directly indexed and must be stored in the property cache so the Indexing Service can use them. A common example is meta tags in an HTML document. To use meta tags, you would need to manually cache them.

To perform this action, expand Indexing Service in the left pane and click the Properties folder. A list of properties appears in the right pane, shown in Figure 16-14.

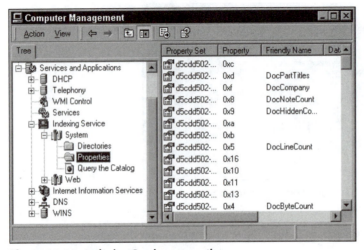

Figure 16-14: Indexing Service properties

To cache a desired property, right-click the property in the right pane and click Properties. On the Property tab, simply click the Cached check box.

Caution You should not cache properties unless you are certain there is a need. Some cached properties can cause a performance problem with the Indexing Service.

Managing the Indexing Service

Fortunately, managing the Indexing Service is very easy. Once you have the Indexing Service up and running, it takes care of itself by automatically rescanning documents and incorporating changes into the index. In a nutshell, there shouldn't be much you need to do, but I'll point out a few possible housekeeping tasks.

If you select the Indexing Service in the left pane and click the Action menu (or just right-click it), you can access the service's properties sheets. You see a Generation and a Tracking tab. By default, the Indexing Service indexes files with unknown extensions, and it generates abstracts, with a maximum abstract character size of 320. You can change these features on the Generation tab if you like, but as a general rule, the default settings work well. The Tracking tab simply tells you that the inheritable setting of "Add Network Share alias automatically" is enabled, and it should remain enabled so that aliases are indexed as well. The settings configured on these tabs are automatically inherited by your catalogs, but you can change this by accessing a catalog's properties sheets and manually changing the settings.

As mentioned previously, Indexing Service scans documents automatically and updates catalogs automatically. However, you can manually rescan a directory if you feel there may be errors or you want the changes immediately updated. To perform this action, simply select the Directories folder in the left pane, then right-click the desired directory in the left pane, point to All Tasks, and choose either Rescan (Full) or Rescan (Incremental). A full scan completely reexamines the directory while an incremental scan looks only for changes in the directory.

Finally, if you are having problems with Indexing Service, there is an Indexing Service object in Performance Monitor you can use to attempt to isolate the cause of performance problems. Also, you'll find a list of error code messages for Indexing Service in the Windows 2000 Help files.

Summary

This chapter explored two Active Directory–supporting technologies—Distributed File System and Indexing Service. Dfs makes the network transparent to your users by creating a shared folder hierarchy that users can use to view and locate the desired shared folder. Users are transparently redirected to the actual server and shared folder so that knowledge of the network topology is not necessary. Dfs supports both standalone and Active Directory integrated options. Also, you can use the Indexing Service to index files and folders on your local machine or Web directories. The Indexing Service enables users to perform full text searches in order to locate desired files.

✦   ✦   ✦

Connecting Exchange Server and the Active Directory

Exchange Server is Microsoft's enterprise messaging and groupware product. Through Exchange Server, enterprise environments can implement corporate e-mail and a number of related services, such as newsgroups. As the newest version of Exchange Server, Exchange 2000 works natively with the Active Directory. In this chapter, we explore both Exchange 5.5 and Exchange 2000 and how these two products can integrate with the Active Directory. This chapter focuses on connecting the two products together, so I assume you have some previous Exchange knowledge. If you have an existing NT network running Exchange 5.5, you'll find the information in this chapter most helpful, and if you are considering implementing Exchange 2000, you learn how it integrates with the Active Directory.

Exchange and the Active Directory

Exchange and the Active Directory are both directories. Both store information about real network objects, such as users, phone numbers, e-mail addresses, mailbox locations, and so forth. However, managing two different directories on the same network can be time consuming and cost more in terms of administrative burden. An integrated directory service is always best, and Exchange and the Active Directory can make this integration happen.

Interestingly enough, the Active Directory was initially built on the Exchange Server database model, but the development of the Active Directory left most of the Exchange concepts seen in Exchange 5.5 and earlier behind. However, the Active Directory provides a way to synchronize and connect Exchange 5.5 networks with the Active Directory, and as you'll soon find out, Exchange 2000 and the Active Directory are integrated from the very start.

Exchange 5.5 and the Active Directory

As you might guess, Exchange Server 5.5 does not natively integrate with the Active Directory. However, Microsoft provides a way to connect Exchange 5.5 to the Active Directory through the Active Directory Connector (ADC). The ADC enables the two directories to *synchronize* with each other. Synchronization means that the two directories are equivalent, though not necessarily identical, to each other. With the ADC, you can manage two different directories more seamlessly.

Tip   The ADC is a Windows 2000 service that is displayed as MSADC in Task Manager. You can install a GUI MMC interface to manage it, however, which is explored later in this chapter.

For example, suppose you modify an attribute in Johnny Smith's user account. Through the ADC, replication ensures that Exchange's mailbox for Johnny Smith is synchronized with the attribute change you just made. This synchronization occurs through the ADC by way of a *connection agreement (CA)*. CA's contain the following properties:

✦ Server names (Active Directory domain controller to Exchange Server)

✦ Objects that can be synchronized

✦ Synchronization containers (Active Directory containers/OUs and Exchange site recipient containers)

✦ A schedule

The CA enables an Active Directory container or OU to synchronize with an Exchange site recipient container. You manually create the CA in order to connect the two containers together that hold like information.

As you might guess you use multiple CAs to make the connections you need for synchronization. You synchronize multiple Active Directory containers to a single Exchange recipient container and vice versa — basically whatever you need to make synchronization effective in your environment.

So, if you can do all of this with Exchange 5.5, why would you want Exchange 2000? As you will see in the next section, ADC is provided to help you upgrade to Exchange 2000 — which with an Active Directory implementation is certainly something you will want to do.

Exchange 2000 and the Active Directory

Exchange 2000 is the first version of Exchange Server that does not have its own directory—Exchange 2000 uses the Active Directory to store Exchange data. You may be thinking, "Wait a minute! If I don't implement the Active Directory, I cannot upgrade to Exchange 2000?" That's right. Microsoft expects (demands?) that you upgrade to Windows 2000 and implement the Active Directory in order to implement Exchange 2000.

The good news is that if you upgrade to the Active Directory and install Exchange Server 2000, you have a completely integrated, enterprise mail system that works within your existing directory service. And, it is not just integrated in terms of how it operates, but it is integrated through the management tools as well. How would you like to configure user mailboxes using Active Directory Users and Computers? Well, in Exchange 2000, that is exactly what you do. The following list points out some of the other major features and issues:

✦ Exchange 2000 is limited to a single Active Directory forest in terms of implementation. This is due to the Global Address List generation by the Active Directory's global catalog, which is limited to a single forest. For practical purposes, this is not a serious issue because virtually all Active Directory implementations are limited to a single forest configuration on an enterprise scale. While it is possible to connect two Active Directory forests together, this configuration is not recommended on a permanent basis.

See Chapter 3 for more information about multiple forest configurations.

✦ In earlier versions of Exchange, users find other users within the Exchange environment through the Global Address List. In Exchange 2000, the Active Directory's global catalog creates the Global Address List. Because the global catalog holds a partial replica of all objects in the entire Active Directory forest, the Global Address List is pulled from the global catalog (and is also part of the reason why the Exchange 2000 is limited to a single forest). Because the Global Address List is pulled from the global catalog, Windows 9x or NT users are able to access the Global Address List as well.

For the sake of further explanation, I would like to point out that a single Exchange implementation is not limited to the forest because of domains. In Windows NT, your Exchange organization could span multiple domains because the domain security had no effect on Exchange. In the Active Directory, all domains and security between them are integrated within the forest. So, the domain structure is not the problem, but the limitations of the global catalog, which is limited to the forest, serves as a Global Address List boundary for Exchange server.

✦ In addition to the forest limitation and the use of the global catalog for the Global Address List, Exchange 2000 requires a DNS implementation. This is basically a moot point since you cannot integrate the Active Directory without DNS and you cannot implement Exchange 2000 without the Active Directory. Thus, DNS is required.

✦ Upon installation, Exchange 2000 extends the Active Directory's current schema. This feature enables schema modification to include Exchange messaging components. This process occurs automatically during installation and does not require any configuration from you.

✦ Replication functions through the use of Active Directory. In previous versions of Exchange, replication occurred with mail servers through object replication. In the Active Directory, only attribute changes are replicated instead of the entire object. This is a better design because it conserves network bandwidth by replicating not entire objects, but only the attributes that have changed. Exchange 2000 uses the Active Directory's replication process.

✦ Do you need quick Internet mail access? No problem. Because the SMTP service is installed by default when you install Windows 2000, you can begin using SMTP mail as soon as you install Exchange 2000. (The Active Directory can even use it for replication.) SMTP is used as the primary messaging protocol in Exchange 2000.

✦ Exchange 2000 uses your existing Active Directory infrastructure, using Active Directory sites for communication purposes. In other words, you don't have to create a separate Exchange infrastructure (which is obviously great news).

✦ Finally, Exchange 2000 further integrates with the Active Directory by using the same terminology describing Active Directory objects with Exchange objects. This may seem like a minor point, but the name changes in Exchange can cause a little confusion. Those changes are as follows:

- **User**—In Exchange 2000, a user is the same as a *mailbox* in earlier versions of Exchange.

- **Contact**—In Exchange 2000, a contact is the same as a *custom recipient* in earlier versions of Exchange.

- **Group**—In Exchange 2000, a group is the same as a *distribution list* in earlier versions of Exchange.

Tip   Users, Contacts, and Groups in Exchange are referred to as mail-enabled and/or mailbox-enabled. Mail-enabled means that an object has an e-mail address. If the object were only mail-enabled, it would not have an Exchange mailbox, but could send and receive mail using another messaging system. Mailbox-enabled means that an object has an Exchange mailbox association as well. Only a User can have a mailbox. Mailbox-enabled objects are automatically mail-enabled.

Installing the Active Directory Connector

As you have discovered so far, Exchange 5.5 is the end of the road for Windows NT networks. In order to install and implement Exchange 2000, you must have Windows 2000 installed and the Active Directory configured. As part of that process, Windows 2000 expects that you will install the Active Directory and then at some point in the future install Exchange 2000. During the interim, you can use the Active Directory Connector to synchronize Exchange 5.5 and Active Directory.

There is, however, another reason for using the ADC. Once your Active Directory installation is in place, you can install and use the ADC to migrate objects into the Active Directory from the Exchange directory. This process enables you to replicate user object information from Exchange into the Active Directory, which can help decrease your implementation time since you will not have to manually enter that information.

 Note Aside from synchronization and implementation assistance, a practical reason to use the ADC is to enable you to manage your Active Directory and Exchange directory from one administrative tool. Using the Exchange 5.5 console and Active Directory tools, you can perform administrative tasks from a single location instead of having to travel from server to server.

But aside from assisting with implementation, the ADC enables you to continue to use Exchange server without the hassle of maintaining two independent directories. In order to implement the ADC, you'll need to install the service on a Windows 2000 server in an Active Directory network. Note that the server does not have to be a domain controller. In fact, in large environments, there can be a lot of synchronization traffic that could drain resource availability on domain controllers, so using the ADC on a member server may be a better option. Also, ADC uses LDAP to exchange information between Exchange and the Active Directory among the CAs that are configured. This should not be a problem considering the wide use of LDAP in the Active Directory, but for informational purposes, be aware that the ADC must use LDAP. Exchange 5.5 supports LDAP, so there is no additional configuration that must be performed on the server for use with the ADC.

The ADC is found on your Windows 2000 Server installation CD-ROM in the Valueadd folder. Open the MSFT folder, then open the Mgmt folder, then open the ADC folder, and then double-click Setup.exe. Exchange 2000 also provides an enhanced version of the ADC that you should install upon the upgrade to Exchange 2000.

The following steps show you how to install the ADC:

1. After clicking Setup.exe, a Welcome screen appears, shown in Figure 17-1. Note that you cannot install system files or update shared files if any are currently in use. Click Next to continue.

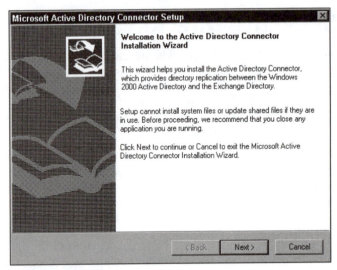

Figure 17-1: Welcome screen

2. In the Component Selection window, shown in Figure 17-2, select the ADC and the ADC management components check boxes and then click Next.

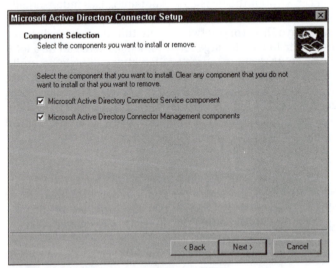

Figure 17-2: Component Selection window

3. In the Install Location window, shown in Figure 17-3, select a location for setup to install the ADC, which is C:\Program Files\MSADC by default. You can enter the name of an alternate location or click the browse button to locate it. Click the Next button when you're done.

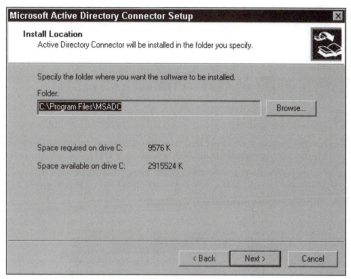

Figure 17-3: Install Location window

4. Installation requires a service account in order to install the service, shown in Figure 17-4. Typically, you would choose to use an administrator account. Once installation is complete, this account will also be assigned the Logon As Service, Restore Files and Directories, Act as Part of the Operating System, and Audit Permissions rights. Select an account, enter a valid password, and click Next.

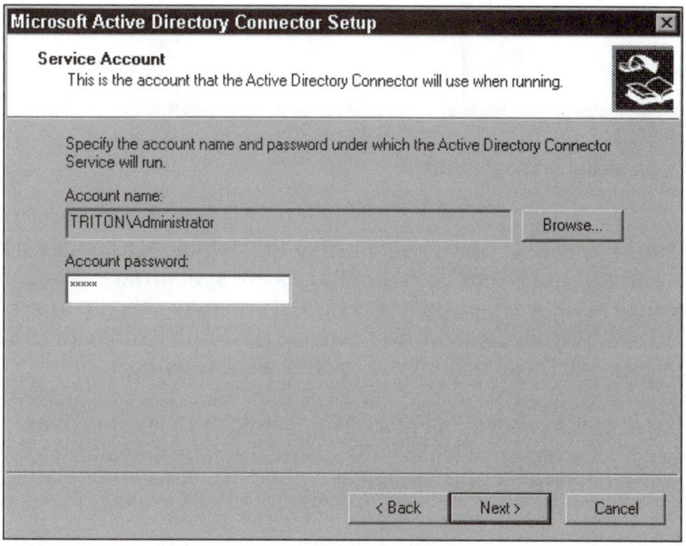

Microsoft Active Directory Connector Setup

Service Account
This is the account that the Active Directory Connector will use when running.

Specify the account name and password under which the Active Directory Connector Service will run.

Account name:

TRITON\Administrator

Account password:

`*****`

< Back   Next >   Cancel

Figure 17-4: Service Account window

5. Setup installs the ADC by copying the files, modifying the registry, and modifying the Active Directory schema. Click Finish when prompted.

Configuring Connector Management Properties

Once you have installed the ADC and the management console, you can manually load the ADC snap-in into an MMC (refer to Appendix B), or you can access it in Administrative Tools. As you can see in Figure 17-5, you have an Active Directory Connector Management. If you select the object and then click Action ➪ Properties, you have a few important configuration options.

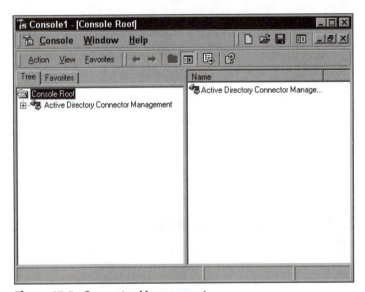

Figure 17-5: Connector Management

The General tab simply tells that you are using the default ADC policy. The default policy is that all attributes from both directories are synchronized with each other. However, because of network or business needs, you may select certain attributes that you do not want synchronized. You can use the From Exchange and From Windows tabs to make these default ADC policy adjustments.

The From Exchange tab, shown in Figure 17-6, displays all attributes available to be replicated from Exchange preselected. Clear the check beside any attribute you do not want replicated to the Active Directory.

You can also customize attribute matching rules. By default, Exchange and the Active Directory attempt to match each other's directory data. This, however, may not always be possible, due to customized schema configurations you may have in place. You can customize any relationships necessary by clicking the Add button and selecting which Exchange attribute you want to match with which Windows attribute.

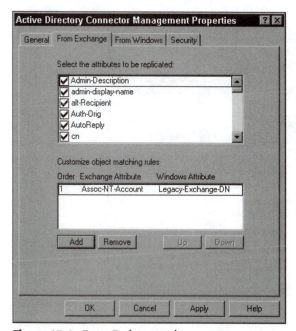

Figure 17-6: From Exchange tab

The From Windows tab looks and behaves in the same manner. The difference is that you select Windows attributes you do not want replicated to Exchange. The customize attribute matching option also functions in the same manner.

Creating and Configuring Connection Agreements

A connection agreement creates a connection between an Exchange server and a Windows 2000 server. The connection agreement determines how data between the two servers will be synchronized. You can have any number of connection agreements as needed for your environment. Typically, you need a connection agreement between each Active Directory domain and each Exchange site. As previously mentioned, a single container from the Active Directory can be configured to replicate to several Exchange containers, and vice versa.

If you expand Active Directory Connector Management in the console, you see the ADC for the server, which you installed. If you select the ADC and then click Action ➪ New ➪ Connection Agreement, you can create a new CA, shown in Figure 17-7.

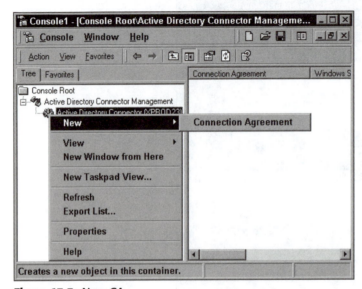

Figure 17-7: New CA

You create and configure a CA at the same time, which is somewhat different than the typical object creation windows you are used to seeing in the Active Directory. On the General tab, shown in Figure 17-8, give the CA a name and then select the direction for replication by clicking the desired radio button.

You have three replication direction options:

✦ **Two-way** — Using this option, changes in either the Active Directory or Exchange directory can trigger replication. If you are managing the Active Directory and Exchange on their own servers, use this option.

✦ **From Exchange to Windows** — Using this option, replication occurs from Exchange to Windows. Use this option if all object administration changes are performed on the Exchange side.

✦ **From Windows to Exchange** — Using this option, replication occurs from Windows to Exchange. Use this option if all object administration changes are performed on the Active Directory side.

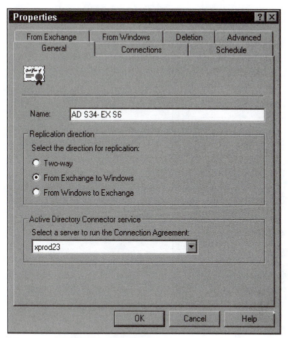

Figure 17-8: General tab

Finally, you can use the drop-down menu at the bottom of the window to select a server to run the CA. The server on which it was installed is selected by default.

Next, you see a Connections tab. The Connections tab enables you to configure a bridgehead server for both the Active Directory and Exchange environments. A bridgehead server is one that receives replication data and then passes that data onto other servers within the domain/site. For a Windows 2000 domain, the bridgehead server must be a domain controller. The changes sent to and from the Exchange environment must go to a domain controller so they can be replicated to all other domain controllers. While it is true that the CA does not have to reside on a domain controller, but can reside on a member server, the CA must send changes to a domain controller for replication throughout the domain to occur. On the Exchange side, the bridgehead server can be any Exchange server.

To configure the bridgehead server, enter the server name, authentication type, and an account to connect with for both the Windows 2000 server and the Exchange server, shown in Figure 17-9.

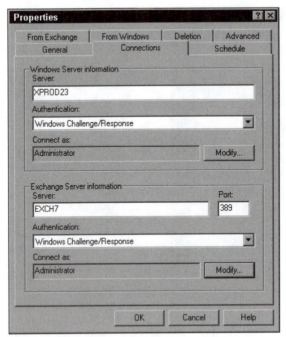

Figure 17-9: Connections tab

Tip   The permissions account you assign will need at least write permission if you will be writing changes to the directory on that particular side. For example, in a two-way configuration, both Windows and Exchange need write permission. In Windows to Exchange, only Exchange needs write permission, and vice versa.

Next, you see a Schedule tab. The Schedule tab determines when synchronization can take place between the Windows 2000 server and the Exchange server. Polling for directory changes takes place every 5 seconds during the scheduled times that you specify. As you can see in Figure 17-10, you can choose to never synchronize, always synchronize, or use the schedule, in which case you click the desired grid blocks to mark the time that you want synchronization to occur.

Also notice at the bottom of the Schedule tab, you see a "Replicate the entire direc-tory the next time the agreement is run" check box option. This feature enables you to force complete synchronization if you feel the action is needed.

I should note here that excessive polling and replication may, of course, present you with some traffic issue problems. Replication and synchronization are always a trade-off in terms of data consistency and bandwidth usage, so you will have to find the balance that works best for your environment.

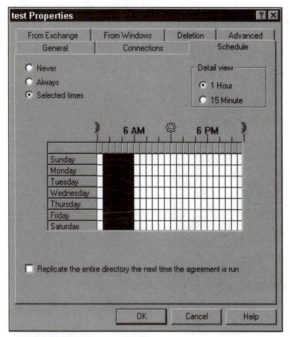

Figure 17-10: Schedule tab

Tip The 5-second polling frequency can be manually changed in the registry by accessing HKEY_LOCAL_MACHINE\System\CurrentControlSet\Services\MSADC\Parameters. Under Name, you see Sync Sleep Delay (Secs) and under Type you see DWORD. Under data, enter the polling value (default of 5) to the number of seconds you want the system to wait between cycles. This can reduce the frequency of polling and help reduce both server and network load.

Next, you see From Exchange and From Windows tabs. These two tabs look and function in exactly the same way, so I'll address them together. The From Exchange and From Windows tabs enable you to determine the source and destination containers from each directory. You use these tabs to determine which containers are polled for changes, where changes are to be written, and the types of items you want to replicate. In addition to these items, the From Windows tab enables you to replicate secured Active Directory objects to Exchange. Just check the box at the bottom of the tab to enable this feature. As you can see in Figure 17-11, just use the Add and Remove buttons and check box options to determine which containers should be replicated and which objects should be replicated.

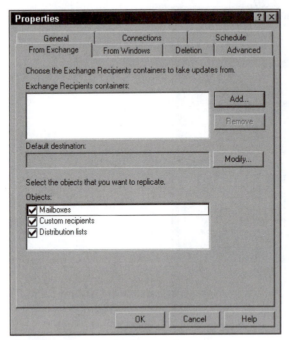

Figure 17-11: From Exchange tab

On the Deletion tab, shown in Figure 17-12, you have four radio button options affecting object deletions. For example, you delete a user account in the Active Directory. By default, that account on the Exchange directory is not deleted, but a record of the deletion is kept instead. This tab enables you to continue using deleted records (CSV files in Exchange and LDF files in Active Directory) or to actually delete the item from the partner directory when deletion occurs on the other side. The trick with using the delete both sides option is you may have data deleted that you do not want deleted. For example, if you delete a user account in the Active Directory and specify for it to also be deleted in Exchange, then the user account's mailbox, custom recipients, and distribution lists will also be deleted. In the same manner, if you delete a mailbox in Exchange, then the user account in the Active Directory will be deleted. As you can see, there can be some serious consequences to using the delete option, so think through the process carefully before using it.

Finally, you see an Advanced tab, shown in Figure 17-13. First, the Advanced tab enables you to set Paged results. The settings for Windows and Exchange, which you can change, are 20 by default. This specifies how many entries exist per page for synchronization purposes. Moving this setting to zero prevents synchronization and moving the setting too high puts a drain on system memory. The default setting of 20 is the best setting for most environments.

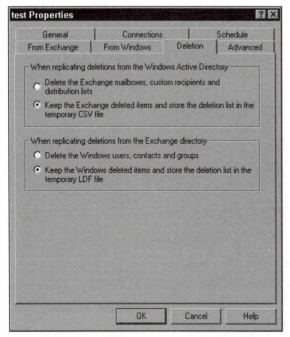

Figure 17-12: Deletion tab

Next, you see two check box options:

✦ **This is a primary Connection Agreement for the connected Exchange organization** — When you select this option, you are telling the ADC that this is a primary CA that should synchronize new Active Directory objects that are mail enabled (such as user accounts) but do not have corresponding Exchange mailboxes. This feature enables synchronization between the two directories without Exchange having to create new objects. This option is selected by default, and you do not need to change it unless you have more than one CA, in which case you should select which CA should be the primary CA.

✦ **This is a primary Connection Agreement for the connected Windows Domain** — This selection specifies which CA is primary for the Windows domain. This CA synchronizes new Exchange objects with the Active Directory (like new mailboxes, distribution lists, and so on). With this check box selected, the CA will create new Active Directory objects in order to synchronize with the Exchange directory.

Finally, you also see a drop-down menu to select an option for a Windows account. When Exchange creates a mailbox for which there is no primary Windows user account, the drop-down menu enables you to determine which action synchronization should take. You have the option to create a new Windows account, a new disabled Windows account, or a new contact.

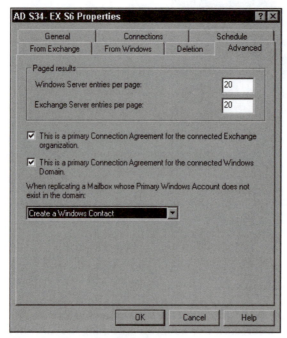

Figure 17-13: Advanced tab

Once all of this is done, the new CA appears in console. You can create additional CAs in the same way, and you can use the console to add and remove then as necessary.

ADC Properties

In the Connector Management Console, you can also right-click Active Directory Connector and access a properties sheet as well. This properties sheet functions as overall settings for the ADC. You have General, Diagnostic Logging, and Security tabs. The General tab simply tells you which server is the ADC server (home server), and the Security tab is like all other Security tabs in the Active Directory. I do want to call attention to the Diagnostic Logging tab because you may find it helpful.

In Figure 17-14, you see different categories and the Logging level. You can change the Logging level by selecting none, minimum, medium, or maximum at the bottom of the window, depending on the detail of information you want written to the Windows Event Log. The ADC provides the following logging options:

✦ **Replication** — Events generated during replication

✦ **Account Management** — Events that occurred when write or delete attempts were in progress

✦ **Attribute Mapping** — Events that occurred while attributes were being mapped between Active Directory and Exchange

✦ **Service Controller** — Events that occurred while the ADC service was stopped or started

✦ **LDAP Operations** — Events that occurred while using LDAP

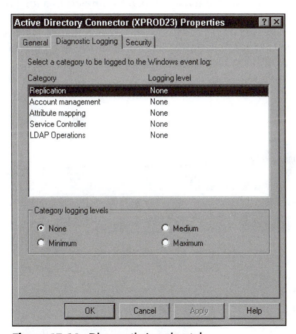

Figure 17-14: Diagnostic Logging tab

Using Multiple ADC Servers

Depending on the nature of your network and the number of CAs that need to be made, you could possibly need more than one ADC Server. In fact, Microsoft recommends that each ADC server host no more than 75 CAs due to performance reasons. If you need excessive numbers of CAs due to complex site structures, you may need to deploy several ADC servers to manage the CA load.

When you deploy multiple ADC servers, you must configure the CAs to replicate different sets of objects for each server. Administration overhead can be assisted with multiple ADC servers because systems administrators can manage the ADC servers remotely due to the design of the Active Directory.

Synchronizaton with the ADC

As a final word to this chapter, remember that the ADC is designed to provide you synchronization capabilities between the Active Directory and Exchange 5.5. This is meant to be a temporary solution until you upgrade your Exchange environment to Exchange 2000, which is designed to natively work with the Active Directory. Although you can use the ADC and Exchange 5.5 connector as long as needed, you should make certain you install Exchange 2000's version of the ADC, which is enhanced to provide greater operability. The ADC for Exchange 2000 is available on the Exchange 2000 Server installation CD-ROM, shown in Figure 17-15, and should be deployed along with Exchange 2000.

Figure 17-15: Exchange 2000 ADC

Summary

This chapter gave you an overview of connecting Exchange Server with the Active Directory. Exchange 5.5 can be connected with the Active Directory through the Windows 2000 Active Directory Connector service, included with Windows 2000. The ADC enables the Exchange 5.5 directory to connect and synchronize with the Active Directory so that administrators do not have to separately manage two different directory services. Exchange 2000 ships with its own version of the ADC, and Exchange 2000 is designed to work natively with the Active Directory, using the Active Directory's database for complete integration. This integration feature enables you to use a powerful messaging system directly with your Active Directory enterprise.

✦　　✦　　✦

Implementing Microsoft DNS

Domain Name System (DNS) is a name resolution strategy that enables domain names to be resolved to TCP/IP addresses. As you know, humans use language to communicate with one another while computers use binary math. In a TCP/IP network, each computer has a unique TCP/IP address, subnet mask, and possibly even a default gateway. Computers use the IP address to exchange information with one another. So, in a network where language-based names are used, the names must be resolved to an IP address. The Active Directory functions by using DNS as a naming and resolution strategy. In fact, you cannot implement the Active Directory without DNS. This chapter explores Microsoft DNS and shows you how to configure a DNS server. As you can imagine, this chapter is not comprehensive since entire books are devoted to the subject of DNS, but this chapter will help you see how DNS and the Active Directory work together and how to perform standard DNS server configuration.

Understanding DNS

DNS is a logical naming system that enables computers on your network to resolve domain names to IP addresses. As I mentioned in this chapter's introduction, DNS is required for a Windows 2000 implementation, and if you have installed the Active Directory, you know that the Installation Wizard will prompt you to install DNS if no DNS server is available.

Before Windows 2000, all Windows networks used NetBIOS, which required you to use Windows Internet Name Service (WINS) to resolve NetBIOS computer names to IP addresses. Windows 2000 abandons NetBIOS and uses DNS as its primary naming strategy. In fact, if your network uses only Windows 2000 computers, you don't need WINS at all, but WINS is still supported for backward compatibility with downlevel Windows clients.

Cross-Reference   You can learn all about Active Directory installation in Chapters 6 and 7.

So, DNS is required in Windows 2000, and you must use it to build a Windows 2000 network. Why did Microsoft choose DNS? DNS was built for use on the Internet, and it is highly scalable. This simply means that DNS works just fine in a network of only a few or thousands of computers. Because DNS is virtually unlimited (it makes up the entire Internet), it is a wise choice for the Active Directory because the scalability of DNS does not limit an Active Directory implementation. Another reason for using DNS is that the DNS network implementation makes your local network more seamless with the Internet. Triton.com can be a company name in your local network, and it can also be an Internet name. Ksmith@triton.com is both a user name on the local network and an e-mail address. With this approach, company Web sites and company Web presence is less divided between the Internet and the local network. This, of course, does not mean that lower network security standards must be used, but it does enable your network to be more integrated with the Internet.

As I have mentioned, DNS resolves host names to IP addresses. For example, suppose you want to visit www.idgbooks.com. In order to access the IDG Books Web site with your Internet browser, the host name www.idgbooks.com must be resolved to a TCP/IP address. Remember that computers always communicate with a numerical address — not a language-based name — so the host name must be resolved. Your computer queries DNS servers to resolve the name to an IP address, and then your computer can use the IP address to communicate with the server(s) that hosts www.idgbooks.com.

All of that sounds easy, but remember, there are millions of computers on the Internet. How does a DNS server keep track of all of them? In truth, a single DNS server does not. Typically, several DNS servers are used to resolve a host name to IP address. This is performed through domains, or the DNS namespace.

The DNS namespace

Although I explored the DNS naming hierarchy in Chapter 2 in the context of planning an Active Directory namespace, I'll expand on that information because you need to firmly understand the hierarchical nature of DNS in order to accurately plan and implement it.

DNS is based on a hierarchy of domains referred to as the DNS namespace. Each domain is an individual, yet contiguous part of the namespace that can be resolved. So, it is important to understand that when a computer needs to resolve www.idgbooks.com, it may use several servers who have authority over various parts of the namespace in order to resolve the address. I'll explore that resolution process in the next section, but I first want to consider the actual hierarchy.

The DNS hierarchy is built on resolvable domains. At the top of the hierarchy is a DNS root, which is represented by a period. Next is the first-level domain, which is a large domain division such as com, net, org, mil, gov, or so on. Next is the second-level domain, which is a representative, or friendly name, of the entity hosting the site, such as idgbooks, Microsoft, ATT, and so forth. Typically, the second-level domain is descriptive enough so you know where you are visiting, such as www.idgbooks.com. Next, the third-level domain either represents the type of service, such as www, ftp, and so forth, or it can further divide the second-level domain, such as acct.idgbooks.com. These domains can be further subdivided into other child domains as necessary. Resolution always occurs by beginning at the Internet root and resolving the name by first-level domain, second-level domain, and so forth. For example, in Figure 18-1, you see the hierarchy for server12.acct.idgbooks.com. When resolution reaches a host computer, such as in Figure 18-1, then the DNS name is said to be a Fully Qualified Domain Name (FQDN).

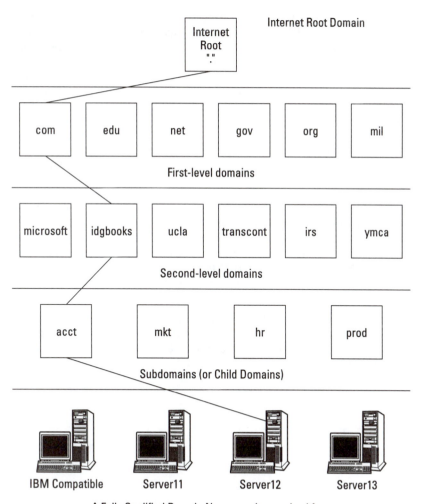

A Fully Qualified Domain Name can be resolved from
the top of the tree down to the host computer.

Figure 18-1: The DNS hierarchy

A common comparison of the DNS namespace is the postal system. When you send a letter, you include a person's name, mailing address, city, state, and zip code. This information must be *resolved* in order to deliver the mail to the correct address. The resolution process begins with the zip code, city, and state. Once the mail arrives in the correct city and state, the mailing address is next used to route the mail to a particular carrier. The person's name is then used to verify the mailing address. DNS resolution begins at the top-level domain and works its way down the hierarchy until it reaches the correct server IP address for which the DNS name represents.

How name resolution works

The DNS hierarchy provides a contiguous, yet scalable, naming structure so that domain names can be resolved to IP addresses. As previously mentioned, this resolution strategy requires a DNS server to resolve each portion of the DNS namespace in order to reach the actual server for the address. For example, a typical resolution process may include an Internet root server, a first-level domain sever, a second-level domain server, and so forth in order to actually resolve the names. Each DNS server queries its DNS database to determine if it has the requested information. If not, the DNS server knows to forward the request to another DNS server that can fulfill it.

The easiest way to get the resolution concept in your mind is to consider an example. The following steps outline a resolution process and are accompanied by a number of figures to make the process easier to explore.

1. First, a computer requests a resolution for a FQDN, for example, `server12.acct.idgbooks.com`. The client sends the request to a local DNS server for resolution. If the DNS server does not have authority over the domain `idgbooks.com`, then it has to go through a resolution process with other servers, beginning with an Internet root server. The DNS server asks the Internet root server for the IP address of a COM server to begin the resolution process, as shown in Figure 18-2.

2. The Internet root returns the IP address of a COM server, and then the DNS server contacts this server for the IP address of an idgbooks DNS server, as shown in Figure 18-3. The COM server checks its database and returns the IP address of an idgbooks DNS server.

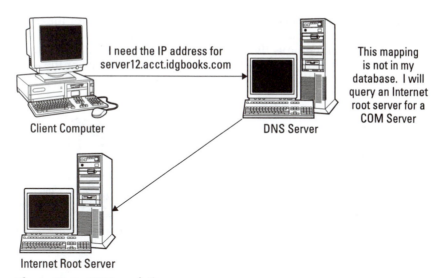

Figure 18-2: COM resolution

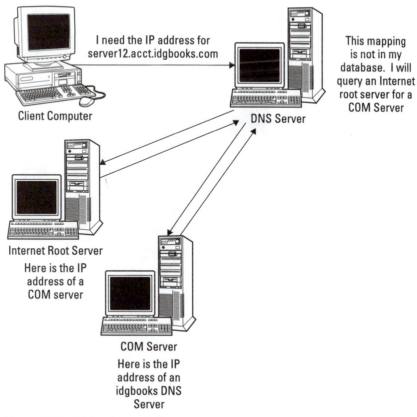

Figure 18-3: idgbooks resolution

3. The DNS server then queries the idgbooks DNS server for the IP address of an Acct DNS server, as shown in Figure 18-4. The idgbooks DNS server checks its database and returns the IP address to the DNS server. In reality, the idgbooks server may have direct authority over the acct domain, or the acct domain may be its own zone (which is discussed later in this chapter).

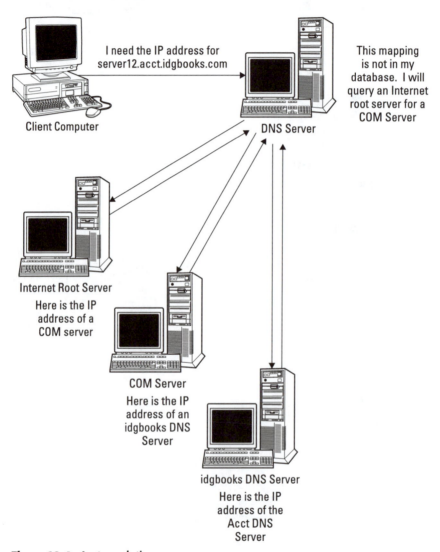

Figure 18-4: Acct resolution

4. The DNS server then queries the Acct DNS server for the IP address of server12, as shown in Figure 18-5. The Acct DNS server checks its database and returns the IP address of server12 to the DNS server.

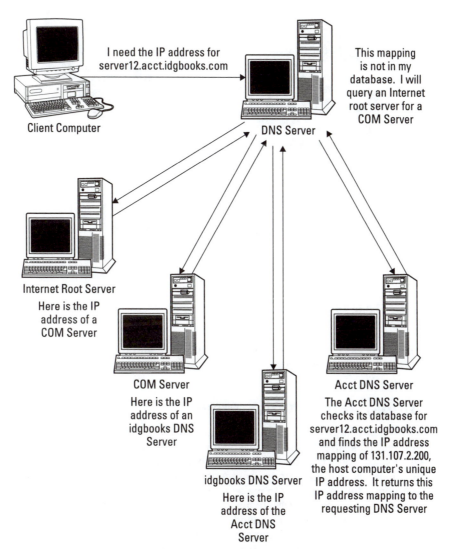

I need the IP address for
server12.acct.idgbooks.com

This mapping
is not in my
database. I will
query an Internet
root server for a
COM Server

Client Computer

DNS Server

Internet Root Server

Here is the IP
address of a
COM Server

COM Server

Here is the IP
address of an
idgbooks DNS
Server

idgbooks DNS Server

Here is the IP
address of the
Acct DNS
Server

Acct DNS Server

The Acct DNS Server
checks its database for
server12.acct.idgbooks.com
and finds the IP address
mapping of 131.107.2.200,
the host computer's unique
IP address. It returns this
IP address mapping to the
requesting DNS Server

Figure 18-5: Host computer resolution

5. The DNS server then returns the IP address mapping to the client computer, as shown in Figure 18-6. The client computer can now establish a TCP/IP communication session with server12 using the server's IP address.

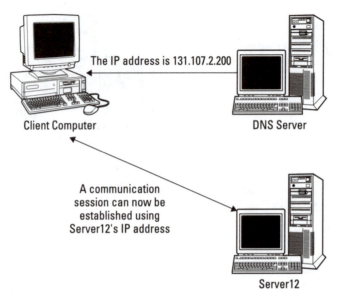

Figure 18-6: IP resolution

This process can be used to resolve any FQDN, and the entire process is invisible to the user and very fast.

Understanding DNS zones

Within any large network, there is generally a need to partition administrative duties. This, after all, is one reason for domains and OUs in the Active Directory. The same holds true for DNS. After all, you may need different administrators to manage DNS within your environment. You can use DNS zones to segment your DNS implementation in order to make it more manageable. A zone is a discreet and contiguous portion of the DNS namespace that enables you to segment the namespace so it can be more easily managed. For example, suppose you have a root domain of triton.com and two child domains of namerica.triton.com and samerica.triton.com. Triton.com is physically located in Canada while the namerica domain is located in Dallas and the samerica domain is located in Venezuela. DNS zones can be used to partition the network implementation of DNS so that administrators can more easily manage each physical site, shown in Figure 18-7. Once the zones are established, the DNS servers in each zone are authoritative over that zone and can query each other for name resolution outside of their zones.

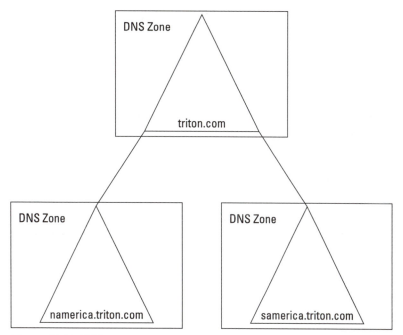

Figure 18-7: DNS zones

Within the zone, you can have more than one DNS server. This provides load balancing and fault tolerance. However, only one DNS server is authoritative for the zone. This means that one DNS server has a writable copy of the DNS zone database while all other DNS servers in the zone have a read-only copy. The writable copy of the zone database file is called the *primary zone database file* while all copies are called *secondary zone database files.* When updates or changes to the DNS database need to be made, they are made on the primary zone database file and replicated to all other DNS servers in the zone through a process called *zone transfer.* Secondary zone servers can process query requests just like the primary server, but only the primary server can write zone changes to the database and transfer those changes to the other DNS servers.

Understanding Dynamic DNS

During the pre-release days of Windows 2000, you heard a lot about Dynamic DNS (DDNS). In fact, Windows 2000 DNS is dynamic. This simply means that a Windows 2000 DNS server has the capability to update its database on the fly. That may not sound like much, but prior to this, an administrator had to physically sit down and update the DNS HOSTS file. For example, suppose that computer12's IP address changed. You had to manually change the entry in the DNS database. In a Windows

2000 network where DNS is the name resolution strategy this simply would not work. In previous versions of Microsoft DNS, DNS did not talk to other server services to get any updates. For example, if a client's IP address changed due to a DHCP lease, then you would have to manually enter the change. Dynamic DNS first appeared on the scene in 1997 as described in RFC 2136, which enabled DNS to dynamically receive updates from DHCP and even other DNS servers. A Windows 2000 network is dependant on this dynamic ability, and that characteristic is one of the major reasons for choosing to implement Microsoft DNS over other DNS versions that may not support the necessary features expected by the Active Directory.

Installing DNS

Now that I have explored the basics of DNS, how it works, and why it is used by the Active Directory, I want to turn my attention to configuring the DNS server, and I want to begin by installing DNS. You install DNS on a Windows 2000 server just like you install any other server service or component by using Add/Remove Windows Components.

 Tip You do not have to install DNS manually on a domain controller. When you install the Active Directory, DNS will be automatically installed.

To install DNS on a Windows 2000 server, follow these steps:

1. Open Control Panel and double-click Add/Remove Programs.

2. Click the Add/Remove Windows Components button.

3. When the wizard appears, click the Next button.

4. In the list that appears, click the Networking Services check box and click the Details button.

5. Click the check box for Domain Name System (DNS), click OK, and then click the Next button.

6. The system installs DNS. When prompted, click the Finish button. You do not need to reboot your computer.

Once DNS is installed, you can access the DNS console, an MMC snap-in shown in Figure 18-8, by clicking Start ➪ Programs ➪ Administrative Tools ➪ DNS.

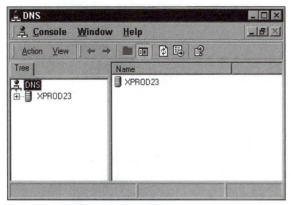

Figure 18-8: DNS console

Creating Forward and Reverse Lookup Zones

Once you have DNS installed, you can expand your server name in the console by clicking the plus (+) sign next to it. You see a Forward Lookup Zones and Reverse Lookup Zones container. I'll explore both of these zones in the next two sections.

Creating a new forward lookup zone

Once you have expanded the server name in the DNS console by clicking the plus sign next to it, you see a Forward Lookup Zone container. If you select Forward Lookup Zones and then click Action ➪ New Zone, you can create a new forward lookup zone with the help of the wizard.

Note If you're an expert, I'm sorry to say there is no "wizard workaround" — you must use the wizard to create the zone.

The following steps show you how to use the wizard to create the new forward lookup zone.

1. In the New Zone Wizard, click Next on the Welcome screen.

2. In the Zone Type window, shown in Figure 18-9, select the type of zone that you want to create. Microsoft DNS enables you to create standard primary or standard secondary zones in a non–Active Directory environment. In an Active Directory environment, you should choose to create an Active Directory integrated zone, which stores all zone data in the Active Directory. (If you are working from a standalone server, this option will be grayed out.) Select the Active Directory–integrated zone radio button and then click Next.

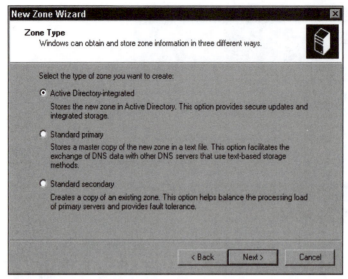

Figure 18-9: Zone Type window

3. In the Zone Name window, shown in Figure 18-10, enter the DNS name of the zone.

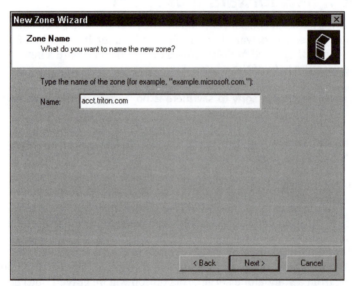

Figure 18-10: Zone Name window

4. Click the Finish button to complete the installation of the new zone.

Creating a reverse lookup zone

As I have discussed, DNS resolves a host name to an IP address. However, DNS can also provide a reverse service that resolves an IP address to a host name. You can use the reverse zone to create pointer records, which you learn about later in this chapter, in order to point to the host name of the IP address. You don't necessarily have to configure a reverse lookup zone, but many networks find that they increase performance, so do consider how they should be used in your DNS implementation.

To create a reverse lookup zone, follow these steps:

1. Select the Reverse Lookup Zone container in the DNS console and then click Action ➪ New Zone.

2. Click Next on the Welcome screen.

3. Select the Active Directory–integrated radio button on the Zone Type window and then click Next.

4. In the Reverse Lookup Zone window, shown in Figure 18-11, enter the network ID or name of the reverse lookup zone. The number construction is somewhat confusing. To enter the network number, take the IP address and remove the digits you control, leaving only the digits assigned to you by a naming authority. For example, in a Class A network, you might have 5.0.0.0. You control the last three numbers, so after dropping them, you are left with a network ID of 5.in-addr.arpa (which is added by DNS). In a class B network, such as 132.107.0.0, you would drop the two numbers you control and then *reverse* the remaining two numbers (107.132.in-addr.arpa). Enter your ID or name and then click the Next button.

5. Click the Finish button to complete the reverse lookup zone configuration.

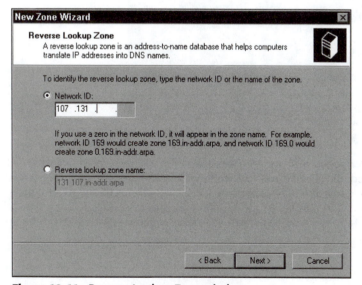

Figure 18-11: Reverse Lookup Zone window

Managing the DNS Server

If you select the DNS Server icon in the left pane of the DNS console and then click the Action menu, you see several tasks you perform on the DNS Server. The following list explores the tasks that appear to you on the Action menu:

✦ **Set Aging/Scavenging for all zones**—When you select this option, a window appears, shown in Figure 18-12, that enables you to set values in order to manage the cleaning, or scavenging, of old records in the database so that all database records are correct. The properties window presents you with a no-refresh and refresh interval, both of which are set to 7 days by default. The no-refresh interval is the time between the most recent refresh of a record timestamp and the time when it can be refreshed. The refresh interval is the time between the earliest moment when a record timestamp can be refreshed and when the record can be scavenged.

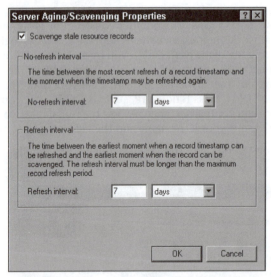

Figure 18-12: Server Aging/Scavenging Properties window

✦ **Scavenge Stale Resource Records**—The Aging/Scavenging properties presented above enable DNS to remove and update records automatically. If you choose to scavenge stale resource records from the menu, you are simply choosing to manually run the scavenge process. This could be useful in circumstances where you know several resource records need to be updated.

✦ **Update Server Data Files**—This option enables you to manually update the server's database files, which normally occurs when the server is shut down and at predefined intervals. You do not need to manually update the server data files under normal circumstances, but you can choose this option to force the DNS server to write all changes to the zone data files immediately.

✦ **Clear Cache**—The DNS server maintains a cache of resolved host names to IP addresses. You can clear the cache with this option.

Aside from these tasks, you can also start, stop, or pause the DNS service on the server, and you can access the DNS server properties sheets. You see several tabs, and the following sections explore your configuration options on each tab.

Interfaces tab

For servers that have multiple IP addresses, you can restrict which IP addresses are used to listen for DNS client query requests on the Interfaces tab, shown in Figure 18-13. By default, the server listens on all IP addresses, but you can restrict this behavior by clicking the "Only the following IP addresses" radio button, then entering the desired IP address(es), and clicking the Add button. You can manage the list with the Remove button if necessary.

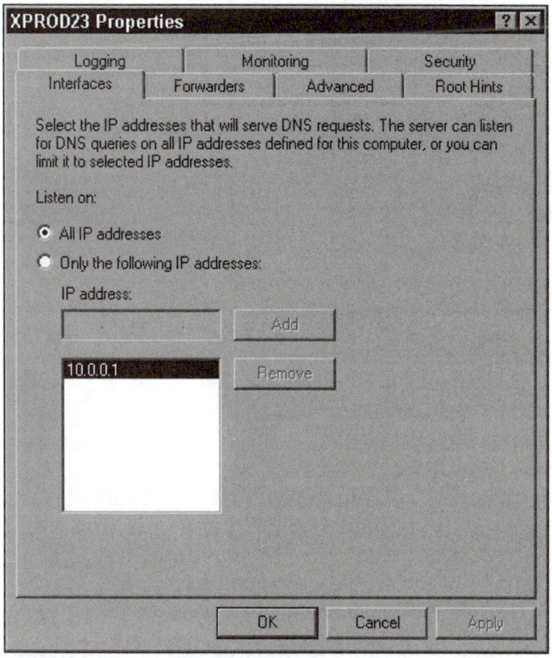

Figure 18-13: Interfaces tab

Forwarders tab

The Forwarders tab, shown in Figure 18-14, enables you to enter the IP address of DNS servers that are higher in the naming hierarchy that can be queried for name resolution. This feature enables a DNS server to forward a query request that it cannot solve. To enable this option, click the "Enable forwarders" check box, enter the IP address of the forwarder, and click the Add button.

Tip   If your server is a root server, such as the one shown in Figure 18-14, the "Enable forwarders" option is not available since the root server is already at the top of the hierarchy.

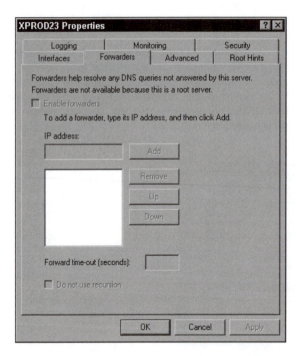

Figure 18-14: Forwarders tab

Advanced tab

You have several configuration options available on the Advanced tab, shown in Figure 18-15. You see the server version number displayed and a section with several check boxes you can choose to select:

✦ **Disable recursion** — This option prevents recursive queries on this server.

✦ **BIND secondaries** — This option is enabled by default and is used to bind your server to secondary servers.

✦ **Fail on load if bad zone data** — This option ensures that if zone data is determined to be corrupt, the server service fails on loading the data.

✦ **Enable round robin** — This option is enabled by default and is used to combine several DNS servers to process queries in a round-robin approach.

✦ **Enable netmask ordering** — This option is enabled by default and is used to combine the IP address/subnet mask of resolutions into a netmask.

✦ **Secure cache against pollution** — This option provides additional cache protection.

You also see a Name checking drop-down menu with the following options:

✦ **Strict RFC** — This option strictly enforces the use of RFC complaint names. Any names not RFC compliant are regarded as errors.

✦ **Non RFC** — This option allows the use of non-RFC names

✦ **Multibyte (UTF8)** — Selected by default, this option uses the Unicode 8-bit translation encoding scheme, which is now supported in Windows 2000 DNS.

✦ **All Names** — This option allows any names to be used.

You can also use the "Load zone data on startup" drop-down menu to select a way to load zone data. For Active Directory integrated zones, zone data is loaded from the Active Directory and the registry. For non–Active Directory integrated zones, you can also select to load the data from the registry only or from a file. You can also choose to automatically scavenge zone data (the default is every 7 days).

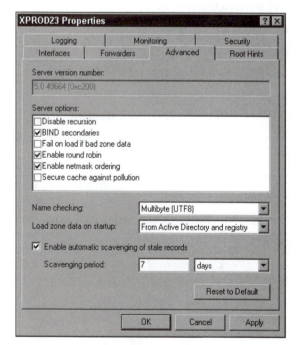

Figure 18-15: Advanced tab

Root Hints tab

Root hints are provided to help the DNS server find and use other DNS servers higher in the DNS hierarchy. This feature enables the server to find authoritative servers that can help process queries. Use the Add, Edit, and Remove buttons to create and manage the list as desired. Of course, if your server is a root server, you cannot add any entries on this tab since your server is already at the top of hierarchy.

Tip When you configure the Root Hints tab, you are actually editing the Cache.dns file.

Logging tab

The Logging tab, shown in Figure 18-16, enables you to configure logging options so you can determine what debug logging options you want to record. By default, none of the options are selected, and you should make certain you have a specific reason for logging any of the events in order to preserve disk space. You have the following selectable options:

✦ **Query**—logs all queries received by the DNS service from clients

✦ **Notify**—logs notification messages received from other servers

✦ **Update**—logs all dynamic updates received

✦ **Questions**—logs the question portion of a DNS query

✦ **Answers**—logs the answer portion of a DNS query

✦ **Send**—logs the number of DNS query messages sent

✦ **Receive**—logs the number of DNS query messages received

✦ **UDP**—logs the number of DNS requests received on a UDP port

✦ **TCP**—logs the number of DNS requests received on a TCP port

✦ **Full packets**—logs the number of full packets written and sent

✦ **Write through**—logs the number of write-through packets back through the zone

Monitoring tab

The Monitoring tab, shown in Figure 18-17, provides you with a simple way to test a query or recursive query against the DNS server. This can be performed to test your DNS server for operability. You can also configure automatic testing to be performed at desired intervals. Simply select the desired check boxes and click the Test Now button or click the automatic testing check box and enter a desired value.

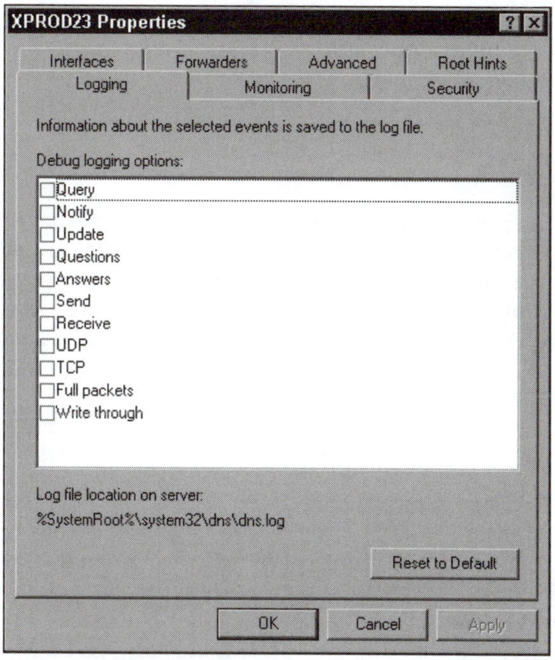

Figure 18-16: Logging tab

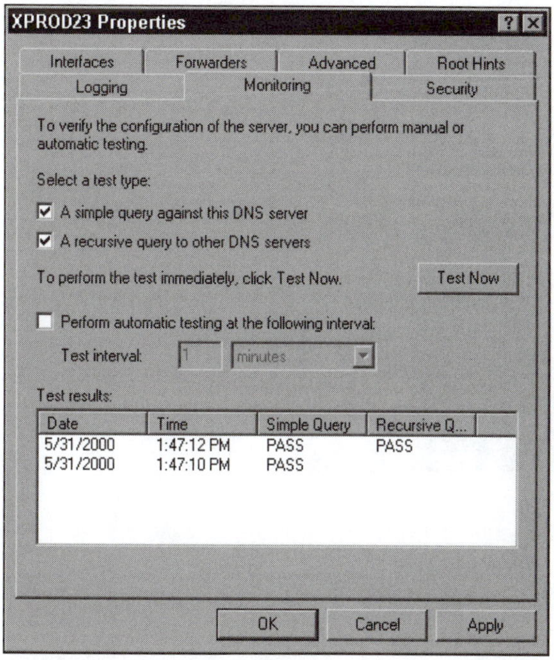

Figure 18-17: Monitoring tab

Note   You also see a Security tab, which functions like all other Security tabs in Windows 2000. See Chapter 11 to learn more about security.

Managing DNS Zones

Just as you can select the DNS server and click the Action menu to see a list of management options, you can also do the same with a desired zone. If you select a desired zone and then click the Action menu, you can choose to reload the zone database file, and you see a list of resource records you can create. You'll need to know a thing or two about using resource records, so the following sections explain each of them.

Host records

A Host record, also called an A record, simply lists the IP address and host name for a particular host. The GUI interface refers to this record as a Host record but is stored as an A record in the actual database. Your server will contain many Host records, as you can imagine. If you click New Host on the Action menu, you can manually add a new Host record to the zone database file. Enter the name of the host and the IP address in the window that appears, shown in Figure 18-18. Notice that you can also create an associated pointer record for the host by clicking the check box.

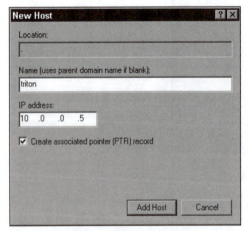

Figure 18-18: New Host window

Alias records

An Alias record, also called a CNAME or canonical name record, enables to you configure a host so that it responds to more than one name. This feature can be useful in a variety of scenarios. For example, suppose you want a particular DNS server to respond to queries at www.triton.com, but you also want the same server to respond to queries directed at prod.triton.com. You create an Alias record so that your server has more than one name it responds to. On the Action menu, click New Alias and then enter the alias name and the actual FQDN for the host, shown in Figure 18-19.

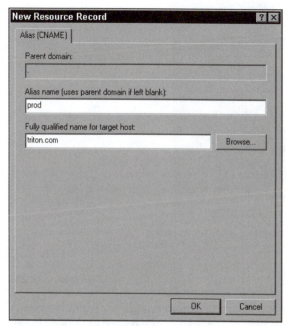

Figure 18-19: Alias (CNAME)

Mail Exchanger records

Mail Exchanger (MX) records point to the mail server in an environment. For example, if you send an e-mail message to curt_simmons@hotmail.com, the MX record defines which servers are actually mail servers at hotmail.com. Without MX records, it would be impossible to tell which servers handle the mail. Click New Mail Exchanger on the Action menu and then in the window shown in Figure 18-20 simply enter the host or domain, the mail server, and set a priority. The default priority setting is 10, and this feature enables you to use several mail servers and set priority for each. For example, your primary mail server could have a priority of 10 while the backup mail server could have a priority of 20. Lower priority numbers are favored over higher priority numbers.

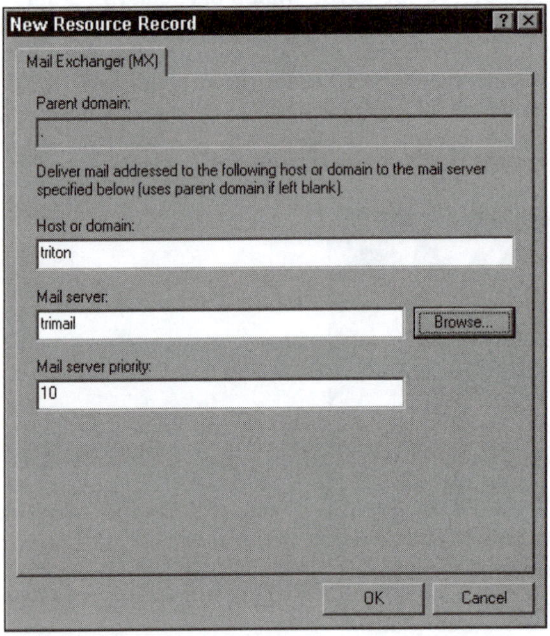

Figure 18-20: Mail Exchanger

Other records

A, CNAME, and MX are common records, but there are quite a few others supported by the Active Directory. Most of these resource records are used for specific purposes. If you click Action ➪ Other New Records, you see a window, shown in Figure 18-21, where you can select a type of resource record and then click the Create Record button. When you click Create Record, a window appears where you enter the information needed to create that particular record.

As I mentioned, you'll need to create these records only under specific circumstances, but it is helpful to know they are available. Table 18-1 gives you a succinct look at each record type and its definition for quick reference purposes.

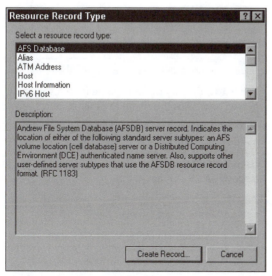

Figure 18-21: Other records

Table 18-1
Other DNS Resource Records

Resource Record	Description
AFS Database (AFSDB)	Used to support Andrew File System Database
ATM Address (ATMA)	Maps a DNS domain name to an ATM address
Host Information (HINFO)	Used by special application protocols, like FTP, for communication with specific operating systems
IPv6 Host (AAAA)	Maps a DNS domain name to an IPv6 address
ISDN	Integrated Services Digital Network (ISDN) mapping to a DNS domain name
Mail Group (MG)	Creates mailbox group records in the DNS zone
Mailbox (MB)	Maps a domain mailbox to a specific host within the domain
Mailbox Information (MINFO)	Points to a domain mailbox that can be contacted
Pointer (PRT)	Used to perform reverse lookups

Continued

Table 18-1 *(continued)*	
Resource Record	**Description**
Renamed Mailbox (MR)	Used as a forwarder to a different mailbox
Responsible Person (RP)	Points to a domain mailbox name for a responsible person and maps the name to other resource records
Route Through (RT)	Provides a binding for internal DNS hosts that do have a direct WAN address
Text (TXT)	Used with RP records and used as descriptive text for a specific DNS domain name
Well Known Services (WKS)	Describes the well known TCP/IP services supported by a certain protocol on a certain IP address
X.25	Maps a DNS domain name to an X.25 address

There are two final records I want to mention that we have not discussed so far. Both of these are very important to the Active Directory and Microsoft DNS. The first is Service Location or SRV records (RFC 2052). SRV records are used to identify DNS servers and can be used in a variety of ways, such as mapping several severs to a single domain name or moving IP services from one host to another. Dynamic DNS automatically generates SRV records for all DNS servers, domain controllers, and global catalog servers, and thus, SRV records are required by the Active Directory.

Tip   If you do not use Microsoft DNS in your Active Directory implementation, the DNS you do choose to use must support SRV records.

Finally, I also want to mention the Start of Authority (SOA) record. The SOA record tells which server is the primary DNS server for a domain. Every domain controller maintains an SOA in order to point to the primary DNS server. There are some configuration options you can perform concerning the SOA, which are addressed in the next section.

Zone properties

A final management task for zones is the possible configuration options found on the zone's properties sheets. If you select the desired zone in the left pane of the console and then click Action ➪ Properties, the properties sheets for that zone appear.

On the General tab, shown in Figure 18-22, you have a few options. First, you can pause the zone on the server by clicking the Pause button. This enables you to perform troubleshooting or maintenance, but of course, prevents the server from servicing query requests. You can also change the type of zone, such as from Active Directory integrated to standard, by clicking the Change button.

A very important part of this tab is the dynamic updates drop-down menu. Remember that Windows 2000 DNS is dynamic, and the Active Directory assumes you implement DNS (whether Microsoft or not) that can perform dynamic updates. The drop-down menu enables you to allow or not allow dynamic updates (or use only secure updates). You need to allow dynamic updates in order for DNS to function properly for the Active Directory. Finally, the General tab enables you to set aging/scavenging properties for the zone. If you click the Aging button, you are provided the same zone aging properties (default of 7 days) we explored earlier in the chapter.

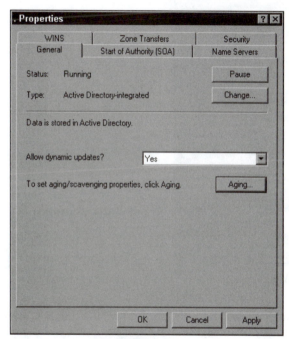

Figure 18-22: General tab

The Start of Authority (SOA) tab enables you to make configuration changes to the SOA record for the zone. Remember that the SOA record defines which server is the primary server for the zone. The SOA tab, shown in Figure 18-23, provides a serial number and the name of the primary server, both of which you can change. The serial number just tells you how many changes have been made to the zone since you first created it. The number will increase each time you make a change to the zone, and this isn't something you need to manually change. It also lists the responsible person for the server, which can also be changed. This information provides that person's e-mail address. The remaining options enable you to change the refresh, retry, and expiration interval for the server's DNS cache. For example, the default value for the refresh interval is every 15 minutes. This tells the secondary servers to query the primary server for zone database changes every 15 minutes and to retry every ten minutes in the case of a transfer failure. You also see a default Time to Live (TTL) value.

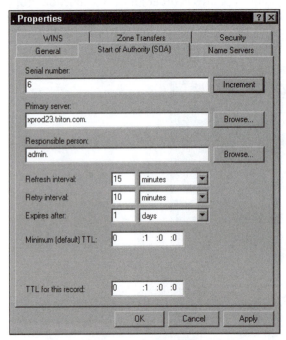

Figure 18-23: Start of Authority tab

The Name Servers tab lists the name servers (NS records) for the domain. You can manually edit the list as necessary by using the Add, Edit, and Remove buttons.

The WINS tab, shown in Figure 18-24, allows you to enable the DNS server to access the WINS database for name resolution if the name is not found in DNS. In environments where WINS is used (which will be in any environment that is not pure Windows 2000), this feature enables DNS to interact with WINS to determine a NetBIOS name to IP address mapping. To enable this feature, click the "Use WINS forward lookup" check box, enter the IP address of the WINS server(s), and click the Add button. You also have the option to not replicate the record to other DNS servers.

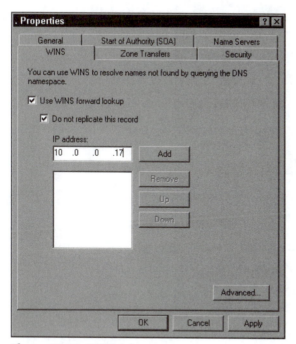

Figure 18-24: WINS tab

The Zone Transfers tab, shown in Figure 18-25, allows you to adjust how zone transfers occur. Remember that within a zone, there is one primary server that holds the primary zone database file, while there may be many secondary servers that hold secondary zone database files. Changes are made only to the primary zone database file, so all secondary zone database files must be updated through a process called zone transfer. By default, the primary server can send zone transfer data to any DNS server in the zone. You can modify this behavior by choosing to send zone transfer data to only the servers that appear on the Name Servers tab, or you can generate a specific list. You can also click the Notify button so that all servers are notified of coming zone transfers. As a general rule, you need to allow zone transfers to all DNS servers in the zone. However, the restriction options are provided to help you secure the DNS zone against unauthorized servers. For example, you can specify the "authorized" DNS servers on this tab so that if a disgruntled employee brings another DNS server online without permission, zone transfer would not occur since you have not included that server in the "OK" list.

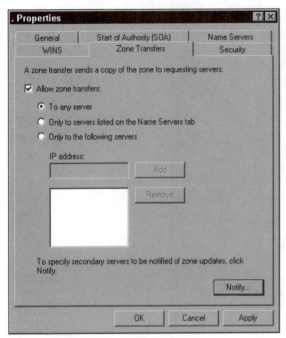

Figure 18-25: Zone Transfers tab

Final DNS Tips

As I mentioned in the introduction, this chapter does not provide an exhaustive examination of DNS since entire books are devoted to that topic. This chapter has, however, explored the foundation DNS concepts and standard configuration issues using the DNS Manager. It is important to remember that DNS is required for an Active Directory installation. Upon installation, the Active Directory Installation Wizard will search for a DNS server, and if one is not available, it will prompt you to install DNS. You do not have to use Microsoft DNS with your Active Directory implementation. However, the Active Directory makes certain assumptions about your DNS implementation, and several DNS components are required. So, as with all implementations, the importance of planning cannot be overstated. You can learn more about planning a namespace and DNS requirements in Chapter 2, but I do want to conclude this chapter with a quick list of DNS requirements. If you do not plan on implementing Microsoft DNS, make certain that your DNS implementation supports the following:

✦ **Dynamic Updates (RFC 2136)** — Technically, dynamic updates are not required for an Active Directory implementation, but in practical terms, they are. Your DNS servers should support RFC 2136 and be able to dynamically update the DNS database when changes occur; otherwise, you're in for a serious headache.

✦ **SRV Records**—SRV records are required for an Active Directory implementation—no excuses. If your DNS service does not support SRV records, it will not work with the Active Directory.

✦ **Dynamic DHCP Updates**—Windows 2000 DHCP can dynamically update DNS records when IP address leases change. Your DNS implementation needs to support this feature.

✦ **RFC 1995**—Although not required, RFC 1995 enables incremental zone transfers, which enables the primary server to send only incremental zone transfer data to other DNS servers instead of the entire database. This feature helps reduce network bandwidth usage.

Your easiest implementation option is to use Microsoft DNS. This will ensure compatibility and most likely avoid problems with other versions of DNS and the Active Directory. Of course, that solution may not be practical from a financial and management standpoint, so when using other DNS versions, you will need to perform some extensive testing to make certain all of your DNS requirements are met before implementing the Active Directory.

Summary

This chapter gave you an overview of Microsoft DNS by exploring how DNS works and the basic configuration options in the DNS Manager. DNS is a name resolution strategy that resolves domain names to IP addresses. DNS is fully integrated in Windows 2000 and is required by the Active Directory. In fact, pure Windows 2000 networks no longer need WINS. Upon Active Directory installation, the wizard searches for a DNS server, and if one is not found, you are prompted to install DNS. With DNS support in the Active Directory, you are provided with a highly scalable naming system that can meet the needs of your growing network.

✦   ✦   ✦

What's on the CD-ROM

This Active Directory Bible contains a CD-ROM with several useful features to help you study, plan, and implement an Active Directory infrastructure. The CD-ROM will run under any Windows operating system (95 and above). The following sections give you a brief overview of the CD-ROM's contents.

Electronic Book

The entire text of this book is found on the CD-ROM. You can use the PDF reader to open the electronic version of this book and perform keyword searches. This tool is an excellent way to quickly locate everything in the book about a specific topic. For example, if you want to find every reference to "replication," just search on the word to find all incidents of it.

Adobe Acrobat Reader 4.0

The Adobe Acrobat reader trial version 4.0 is included on your CD-ROM so you can easily access and use the electronic version of this book.

IP Subnet Calculator

If you are planning an Active Directory infrastructure and need to spend some time planning or examining your IP subnets, you may find this handy IP subnet calculator very useful.

◆   ◆   ◆

Microsoft Management Console Tutorial

The Microsoft Management Console (MMC) is a GUI interface that first came onto the scene with a few Microsoft
BackOffice products like Internet Information Server, Proxy
Server, and Systems Management Server. The MMC provides
a streamlined way to use a variety of administrative tools.
The MMC is fully integrated into Windows 2000 Server and
the Active Directory, and this appendix gives you an overview of the MMC and shows you how to master its use.

What Is the MMC?

The Microsoft Management Console (MMC) is a stripped-down
GUI interface that looks similar to an Explorer window. The
MMC is just a simple console that enables you to control various administrative tools. Administrative tools are called *snap-
ins* — they snap into the MMC. Without any snap-ins, the MMC
has no functionality. In other words, the purpose of the MMC is
to enable you to use administrative tools. The MMC does not
do anything on its own. The MMC provides you the controls to
manage the snap-in.

I like to think of the MMC and snap-ins as a car and a motor.
The inside of the cab is the MMC — you have a steering wheel,
brake, gearshift, headlights, and so forth. The snap-in is the
car's motor. Without the motor, the steering wheel, brake, and
so on do not have any purpose. Those components enable
you to control the car's motor. The same is true for the MMC.
The purpose of the MMC is to enable you to control and use
snap-ins.

All tools in Windows 2000 Server are MMC snap-ins. This includes all of the Active Directory tools as well as the tools found in your Administrative Tools folder. When you launch one of these tools, the MMC is opened, and the appropriate snap-in is loaded. For example, if you click Start ⇨ Programs ⇨ Administrative Tools ⇨ DHCP, the MMC is opened, and the DHCP snap-in is automatically loaded as well.

However, you can manually load snap-ins and create custom consoles that you can save and use later. You can open an empty MMC by clicking Start ⇨ Run and then typing **mmc** in the dialog box, and clicking OK. Figure B-1 shows you an empty MMC with no snap-in loaded. As you can see, there really isn't anything you can do without a snap-in.

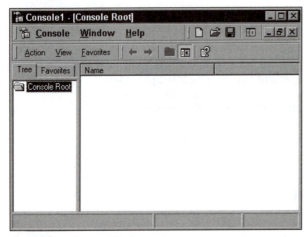

Figure B-1: Empty MMC

So, now that you understand the basic purpose of the MMC and the snap-ins you might ask, "Why?" Why did Microsoft integrate the MMC with Windows 2000 so heavily? The answer lies in an attempt by Microsoft to reduce administrative overhead, learning, and general aggravation. In Windows NT Server 4.0, for example, each administrative tool had its own GUI interface with its own menus and commands. The DHCP interface looked a lot different than the WINS interface, which looked a lot different from the Disk Administrator interface, which ... you get the picture. Learning a different interface for each administrative tool made administration more difficult than necessary. With the MMC, all administrative tools *look* exactly the same and have the same menus and basic functionality. This feature makes the administrative learning curve much easier to master. Another great benefit of the MMC is that you can build your own custom consoles that contain the tools you most commonly use. For example, let's say you are the primary DHCP administrator for a domain, but there are several DHCP servers. You can create a custom MMC console that connects to all DHCP servers and displays them in one console for you. You can then save this console and perform your administrative tasks from one simple interface. Or, suppose you primarily work with the Active Directory snap-ins and the DNS Manager. You can load all of these into one MMC and save it so your most common tools are always together in one window. As you can see, the possibilities are endless, and the MMC can make your administrative tasks easier. Finally, another benefit of the MMC is that third-party companies can build snap-ins for the Windows environment. For example, suppose you want to deploy a third-party technology on a server. That company can develop a snap-in for that technology that fits in with all of your other administrative tools. The key word in all of this is *streamlining*, which to busy administrators is a great word for the ears.

An MMC Tutorial

So, now that I have sold you on the importance and benefits of the MMC (hopefully), you can use this section to master the MMC. Fortunately, the MMC is quite easy to use, but I'm going to show you several tips and tricks that you can apply in your daily use of the MMC. I've organized this section by topics so you can quickly work through it or immediately find the topic that you need help with. Also, whenever possible, I have organized information in a step-by-step format for easy reference.

Loading snap-ins

To manually load a snap-in or several snap-ins into an empty MMC, follow these steps:

1. Click Start ➪ Run. Type *mmc* in the dialog box and click OK. The empty console appears.

2. In the MMC, click Console ➪ Add/Remove Snap-in.

3. The Add/Remove Snap-in window appears.

4. A list of standalone snap-ins appears, which is shown in Figure B-2. Select the desired snap-in, then click the Add button. Repeat this step to load additional snap-ins. When you are finished, click Close.

Tip

If you're unsure about a particular snap-in, select it. A description of the snap-in will appear in the second half of the window.

Depending on the snap-in you select, a Connect to Computer dialog box may appear, as shown in Figure B-3. In this dialog box, select whether the snap-in will manage the local computer or manage another computer, in which case you enter the name of the computer you want to manage.

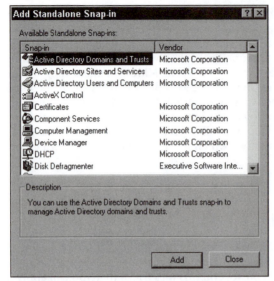

Figure B-2: Adding a standalone snap-in

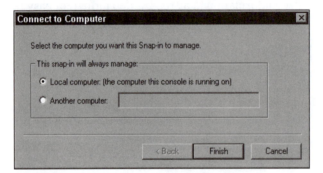

Figure B-3: Connect to Computer dialog box

5. Once you click Close, you are returned to the Add/Remove Snap-in list, shown in Figure B-4. You see the snap-ins you selected displayed. If you made a mistake, just select the snap-in you do not want to use and click the Remove button. You can also click the About ... button to learn more about the snap-in. Click OK when you're done.

Also notice that there is an Extensions tab, shown in Figure B-5. On the Standalone tab, select the desired snap-in and then click the Extensions tab. The Extensions tab lists other snap-ins that are dependent on the selected snap-in. For example, in Figure B-5, you see the Computer Management snap-in, which contains a number of extensions, such as Device Manager, Disk Defragmenter, and so on.

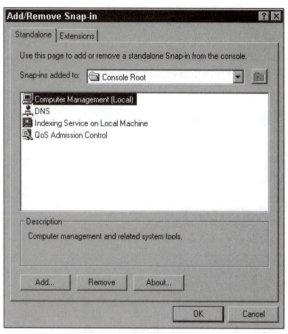

Figure B-4: Add/Remove Snap-in list

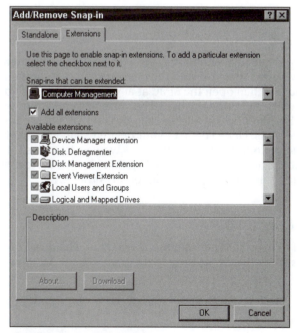

Figure B-5: Extensions tab

Note   By default, all extensions for a snap-in are automatically loaded as well.

Once you have loaded the snap-ins, you see that they now appear in the console and are ready for you to use, as shown in Figure B-6.

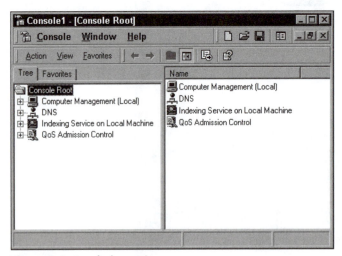

Figure B-6: Loaded snap-ins

Saving a console

The primary reason for manually loading snap-ins is to enable you to create a custom MMC. This simply means that you load the desired snap-ins and then save the MMC. Once saved, you can then open the MMC at any time and access your snap-ins. Administrators find this feature very useful because you can group your most commonly used snap-ins into one console and simply use that single console for your administrative tasks. Once you load your desired snap-ins, simply click Console ➪ Save As to save your console. MMCs are saved as .msc files (MMC). You can give the console a name and select the location on your system where you want to save the console, just as you would for any other file.

Opening a new window

The MMC enables you to open several windows at one time. The question you might ask is, "Why?" The answer is that you can open the same console window in several instances to make your work easier. For example, in Figure B-7, I have two windows open. The windows show the same console, but you can see in Window 1 that I have DNS open and in Window 2 I have the Indexing Service open. This feature enables me to work with several different snap-ins at one time by keeping them organized in their own windows. To open a new window, just click Window ➪ New Window. If you have several windows open at one time, you can easily adjust how they appear in the console. Just click the Window menu and select either cascade or tile horizontally. Also, you can drag each window around inside of the console and place it in a manner that is easy for you to use.

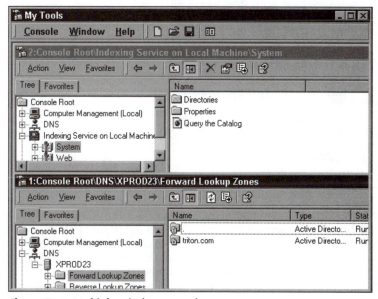

Figure B-7: Multiple window console

Configuring console options

In order to give you different levels of control, the MMC provides you, as the author of the MMC, with some options you can choose to implement. Click Console ➪ Options. You see a single Options window, shown in Figure B-8, which enables you to perform a few different actions.

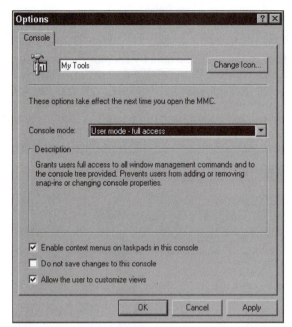

Figure B-8: MMC Options window

First, you have the option to change the default icon for the console by clicking the Change Icon button. This action enables you to select a different icon or use one of your own. More importantly, you have the option to configure a console mode for the MMC. A console mode either enables or denies the user from certain console rights. For example, let's say you are a senior administrator. You create a custom console containing DNS and DHCP for certain administrators. Once you have created the console, you can then change the console mode so that other administrators cannot make certain changes to the console. This feature enables you to create the console and then have others use the console without fear of configuration changes being made. There are several modes from which you can choose:

✦ **Author Mode** — This is your current mode. In author mode, you have full MMC functionality. You can add or remove snap-ins, create taskpad views (explained later in this appendix), and perform any other function within the console.

✦ **User Mode: Full Access** — This mode gives users full access to all console and window commands, but the user cannot add or remove snap-ins or change the console's properties.

✦ **User Mode: Limited Access; Multiple Window** — This mode gives users access rights only to the console areas that were visible when the console was saved. Users can create new windows but cannot close existing windows.

✦ **User Mode: Limited Access; Single Window** — This mode gives the user access only to all areas that were visible when the console was saved. However, the user cannot open new windows.

Note Any changes you make to the MMC mode take effect the next time the console is opened.

For all three user mode options, you also see three check boxes at the bottom of the window, which you can select or deselect. The three options are the following:

✦ **Enable context menus on taskpads in this console** — This feature enables context menus for taskpad views. You can learn more about taskpad views later in this appendix.

✦ **Do not save changes to this console** — The user cannot save any changes made to the console.

✦ **Allow the user to customize views** — This enables the user to customize the window view.

Using the Action menu

The Action menu is the primary menu you use to manage snap-ins and their components. In a console that contains more than one snap-in, use your mouse and select the snap-in you want to use. From that point, most of your configuration and usage of snap-in is accomplished through the Action menu. Click the plus sign next to the snap-in to expand it and then select any desired components and use the Action menu again. You'll notice that the contents in the Action menu change according to what you have selected.

Tip Instead of using the Action menu, you can just right-click with your mouse. Right-clicking on any snap-in or snap-in component gives you the same list of options found on the Action menu.

Using the View menu

The View menu enables you to make changes for the appearance of the console and your snap-ins. You have the following options:

✦ **Choose Columns** — This feature enables you to change the column labels that appear in the right-pane. For example, in the DNS snap-in, you can expand the DNS server and select a desired DNS zone. The zones appear in the right-pane giving you the name, type, and status. I can use the Choose Columns option to change which columns are displayed for the snap-in.

✦ **Large Icons** — This feature provides large icons in the details pane of the console.

✦ **Small Icons**—This feature provides small icons in the details pane of the console.

✦ **List**—This feature provides small icons in a list format in the details pane of the console.

✦ **Detail**—This feature provides the list with column information.

✦ **Advanced**—This feature turns on the advanced information features of the console. The Advanced option makes certain information, such as security, available in some snap-ins that have advanced features.

✦ **Filter**—Some snap-ins have a Filter option that appears in the View menu. For example, DNS has the feature. Filter enables you to filter certain names so that you are not overwhelmed with console information. In other words, the filter helps you to display only information you want.

✦ **Customize**—The Customize option gives you a Customize View window, shown in Figure B-9. You can use these check boxes to customize the console appearance as desired.

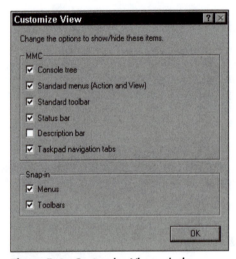

Figure B-9: Customize View window

Using favorites

You see a Favorites menu and a Favorites tab in the MMC. This is a takeoff of Internet Explorer's favorites list, which you create as you bookmark Web sites you like. In a similar manner, you can add items to a favorites list in a console. For example, let's say that I like to check my system's interrupt request lines (IRQs) on a regular basis. (Hey, this is just an example.) I have the Computer Management snap-in loaded. I can examine those pesky IRQs by expanding Computer Management, expanding System Tools, expanding Hardware Resources, and then selecting IRQs—or I can just add

IRQs to my favorites list, click the Favorites tab, and see them easily whenever I want, as shown in Figure B-10.

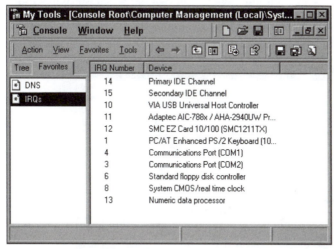

Figure B-10: Favorites list

You can manage your favorites by using the Favorites menu. You have two options here. First, you can choose to add an item to your favorites list. Just select the desired item in the console and click Favorites ⇨ Add to Favorites. In a likewise manner, you click Favorites ⇨ Organize Favorites to open a simple organization window. Here, you can delete items, rename then, move them to various folders, and even create folders within your favorites list.

Creating taskpad views

The MMC includes an important feature that you can use to greatly simplify difficult administrative tasks, or one that you can use to make things easier for inexperienced personnel. That feature is taskpad views. Taskpad views enable to you to create a custom view of the details pane of the console or generate icons that enable you to start certain functions with only a double-click (like a shortcut). You have a number of options with taskpad views, and as I think you will see, you can use them for a variety of situations. The following steps show you how to create a new taskpad view:

1. Select the desired snap-in in the console and then click Action ⇨ New Taskpad View.

2. The New TaskPad View Wizard appears. Click Next on the Welcome screen.

3. In the Taskpad Display window, shown in Figure B-11, select a style for the Taskpad by clicking the Vertical List, Horizontal List, or No List radio button.

The graphic in the right part of the window shows you how the display will appear. At the bottom of the window, select a style by clicking either the Text or InfoTip radio button. The Text option makes explanatory text appear next to the icon. The InfoTip option enables the text to be displayed in a pop-out form. You can use the drop-down menu to change the size of the lists. Click the Next button once you have made your selections.

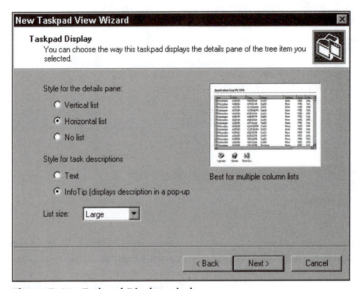

Figure B-11: Taskpad Display window

4. In the Taskpad Target window, shown in Figure B-12, select the desired radio button to determine if the taskpad view applies to the current tree item only or to all tree items of this type. Make your selection and click the Next button.

5. In the Name and Description window, enter a desired name for the taskpad view and a description. Click the Next button.

6. The summary window appears. Notice that a check box appears so you can start the New Task Wizard. Leave this check box selected and then click the Finish button.

7. The New Task Wizard begins. Click Next on the Welcome screen.

8. On the Command Type window you have three radio button options, shown in Figure B-13 and defined in the following list:

   • **Menu Command** — Enables you to configure a task that runs a menu command within the MMC.

- **Shell Command** — Enables you to configure a task that automatically runs a script, starts a program, opens a Web page, or runs some other shell command.

- **Navigation** — Enables you to configure a task that automatically navigates to a selected view in your Favorites list.

Figure B-12: Taskpad Target window

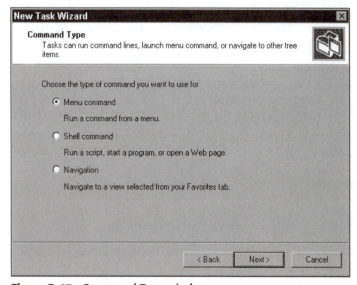

Figure B-13: Command Type window

For the example here, I will configure a Menu Command. You can experiment with Shell Commands and Navigation, and you will discover that they are self-explanatory. Select Menu Command and click the Next button.

9. The Shortcut Menu Command window appears, shown in Figure B-14. You see a Command Source drop-down menu, which contains a tree item task and list in details pane task. Select the desired option. For a tree command, you see the console tree items and available commands. Note, as shown in Figure B-14, that the commands available are simply menu commands for the item selected, such as Action ⇨ All Tasks ⇨ Connect to Another Domain Controller, Action ⇨ Properties, and so forth. Make your desired selection and click the Next button.

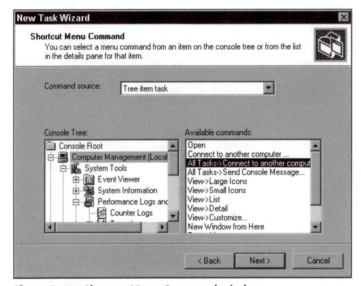

Figure B-14: Shortcut Menu Command window

10. The Name and Description window appears. The text you enter appears either as text in the console or as InfoTip text, depending on what option you select. Make your entries and click the Next button.

11. In the Task Icon window, shown in Figure B-15, select a desired icon for this task and click Next.

Tip   Try to select an icon that visually describes the task.

12. Click the Finish button to complete the wizard.

Note   If you want to create additional tasks, click the Run this Wizard Again check box before clicking Finish.

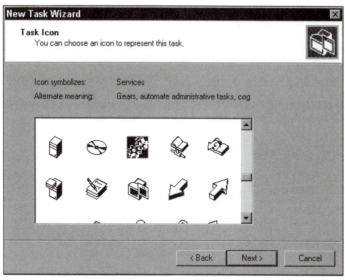

Figure B-15: Icon selection

Once you complete the wizard, you see your taskpad view and any tasks you have created in the details pane, shown in Figure B-16.

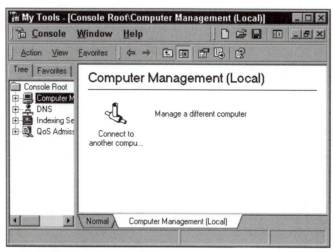

Figure B-16: Taskpad view

You can easily create new tasks, delete them, or alter your taskpad view by clicking Action ⇨ Edit Taskpad View.

Summary

This appendix gave you an overview of the Microsoft Management Console, and then gave you a tutorial to show you how to use the MMC. The MMC provides a streamlined approach to Windows 2000 administrative tools and eases the learning curve for both new and seasoned IT professionals. You can expect much more in the development of the MMC in coming years as well as more snap-in support and functionality.

✦   ✦   ✦

Additional Administrative Tools

Windows 2000 Server includes some additional tools that enable you to manage the Active Directory and perform specific functions. You can install these additional tools by installing the Resource Kit and the AdminPak. Once you install the Resource Kit and the AdminPak, you can then explore these tools and see how they can be useful to you during your Active Directory implementation. This appendix shows you how to install the Resource Kit and the AdminPak and then reviews the Active Directory tools that are installed.

Installing the Windows 2000 Resource Kit

The Windows 2000 Resource Kit is found on your installation CD-ROM. To install the Resource Kit, follow these steps:

1. Insert your Windows 2000 Server CD-ROM into your CD-ROM drive. When the splash screen appears, choose the Browse This CD option.

2. Double-click the Support folder and then double-click the Tools folder.

3. Double-click the Setup icon.

4. The Windows 2000 Support Tools Setup Wizard appears. The message tells you to close any running programs and then click the Next button.

5. Enter your name and organization, if desired. Then click the Next button.

6. Next, you can choose either the Typical installation or Custom installation. A typical installation installs the common components while a custom installation enables you to choose components. The typical installation is all you need. Choose Typical, and then click the Next button.

7. Click the Next button to begin the installation.

8. Files are copied and installed to your system. Click the Finish button to complete the installation.

Installing the AdminPak

The AdminPak is found on your Windows 2000 Server installation CD-ROM. Installing the AdminPak is easy—just follow these steps:

1. Insert your Windows 2000 Server installation CD-ROM into your CD-ROM drive. When the splash screen appears, choose Browse This CD.

2. Double-click the I386 folder and scroll down until you see the AdminPak icon, shown in Figure C-1.

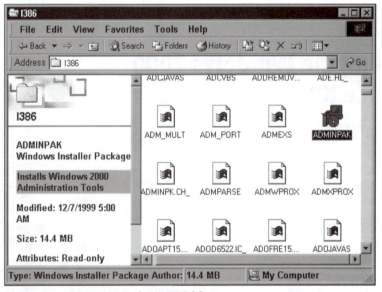

Figure C-1: AdminPak in the I386 folder

3. Double-click the AdminPak icon to start the installation. Windows presents you with a Windows 2000 Administration Tools Setup Wizard. Click Next.

4. Windows installs the components. When installation is complete, click the Finish button.

Once the Resource Kit and AdminPak are installed, you have access. Click Start ➪ Programs ➪ Windows 2000 Support Tools to see your options. Note that you can access a Tools Help page from this location where you can learn about all tools that were installed.

Active Directory Support Tools

The Resource Kit and AdminPak install a number of helpful tools. This appendix explores only those tools that are used for Active Directory implementation or management, but you can learn about all of the tools by clicking Start ➪ Programs ➪ Windows 2000 Support Tools ➪ Tools Help.

The following sections give you an overview of the Active Directory tools and how those tools may be useful to you.

SIDWalker

SIDWalker (security identifier) refers to a collection of administrative tools that help you access control policies for both Windows 2000 and NT Servers. With SIDWalker, you can modify access control lists (ACLs). This is no small task. The process of changing ACLs requires careful planning and analysis. So, why would SIDWalker be useful? Primarily, you can use SIDWalker to clean up ACLs of merged groups and migrated groups in an interforest migration. The process of integrating two forests is not a simple task because new SIDs must be assigned to the merged or migrated groups. Fortunately, SIDWalker can be used to aid in this complicated task.

SIDWalker is made up of three tools, two of which are command-line utilities and the third is an MMC snap-in. Let's look at the three tools that collectively make up SIDWalker.

Showaccs.exe

Showaccs.exe is a command-line tool, shown in Figure C-2, that enables you to examine ACLs and memberships in local groups. Using showaccs.exe, you can examine the following:

✦ Specific file system directories

✦ The registry

✦ An entire system

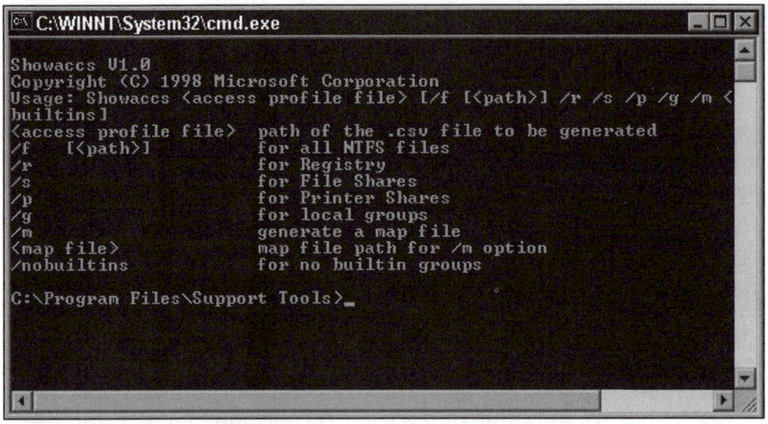

Figure C-2: Showaccs.exe

Showaccs.exe creates a text file as a comma separator file (.csv), which is called the Access Profile File. This file shows the ACLs on your system for specific objects. Table C-1 shows the command-line syntax for showaccs.exe.

```
showaccs access_profile_file [/f [path]] [/r] [/s] [/p] [/g]
[/m [map_file_path]] [/nobuiltins] [/?]
```

Table C-1
Showaccs.exe Command-line Reference

Parameters	Explanation
access_profile_file	Specifies the path of the .csv file to be generated.
/f [path]	Shows access rights for all NTFS files or, optionally, for those in the directory tree of the specified path.
/r	Shows access rights for the registry.
/s	Shows access rights for file shares.
/p	Shows access rights for printer shares.
/g	Shows access rights for local groups.
/m [map_file_path]	Generates a map file, optionally in the directory specified by map_file_path.
/nobuiltins	Omits access rights for built-in groups.
/? (or with no switch)	Displays a usage screen.

SIDWalk.exe

SIDWalk.exe, shown in Figure C-3, is the second command-line utility that makes up SIDWalker. SIDWalk takes a mapping file and scans all ACLs in the registry, the file system, shares, and local group memberships. Then, SIDWalk uses the ACL scan to replace every instance of the old file's SID with the new file's SID—thus the name SIDWalk.

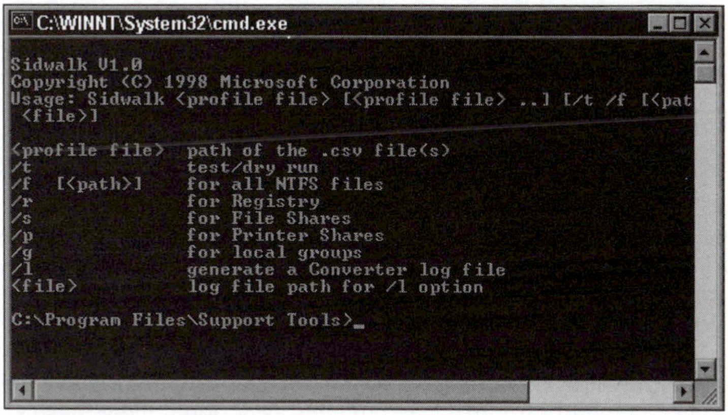

```
C:\WINNT\System32\cmd.exe                                          _ □ X

Sidwalk V1.0
Copyright (C) 1998 Microsoft Corporation
Usage: Sidwalk <profile file> [<profile file> ..] [/t /f [<pat
<file>]

<profile file>   path of the .csv file(s)
/t               test/dry run
/f   [<path>]    for all NTFS files
/r               for Registry
/s               for File Shares
/p               for Printer Shares
/g               for local groups
/l               generate a Converter log file
<file>           log file path for /l option

C:\Program Files\Support Tools>_
```

Figure C-3: SIDWalk.exe

Table C-2 shows you the command-line syntax for SIDWalk.exe:

```
sidwalk profile_file [profile_file ...] [/t] [/f [path]] [/r]
[/s] [/p] [/g] [/l file] [/?]
```

Table C-2
SIDWalk.exe Command-line Reference

Parameters	Explanation
profile_file	Specifies the path and filename of one or more .csv mapping files to be used for input.
/t	Conducts a test run.
/f [path]	Scans all NTFS file system files or only those on the directory tree of the specified path.
/r	Scans the registry.
/s	Scans file shares.

Continued

Table C-2 *(continued)*	
Parameters	**Explanation**
/p	Scans printer shares.
/g	Scans local groups.
/l file	Generates a Converter log file with file as the filename and path.
/? (or with no switch)	Displays a usage screen.

Security Migration Editor (Sidwalk.msc)

The Security Migration Editor (Sidwalk.msc) is an MMC snap-in that enables you to map old SIDs created by the Showaccs.exe file to the new SIDs. The Security Migration Editor is the third tool that makes up SIDWalker, and you use this graphical snap-in to complete the migration to the new SIDs so that SIDWalk.exe can read the updates to the mapping file for the actual SID conversion.

Sidwalk.msc requires the Sidwkr.dll file, and before you can use it, you have to initialize the file at the command prompt. To complete this action, follow these steps:

1. Click Start ⇨ Run and type **cmd** in the dialog box. Click OK.

2. At the command prompt, type **regsvr32 sidwkr.dll** and press Enter.

3. Click OK to the message that appears. Then type **exit** and press Enter.

To use the Security Migration Editor snap-in, manually load the snap-in into an MMC, or from the command line, type **sidwalk.msc** and press enter.

Cross-Reference   For instructions on loading the snap-in into an MMC, see Appendix B.

The Security Migration Editor appears, shown in Figure C-4. The snap-in works like all other MMCs where you can use the Console menu to map accounts. Use the Help menu for more information about the Security Migration Editor.

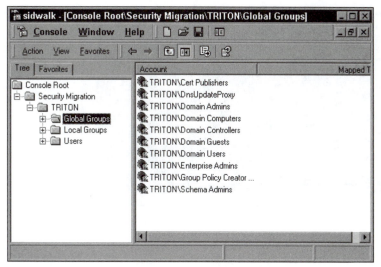

Figure C-4: Security Migration Editor

Acldiag.exe

ACL Diagnostics is a command-line tool that helps you solve problems with objects in the Active Directory. Acldiag takes an ACL, reads the security attributes, and then produces output in a tab-delimited or readable format. ACL Diagnostics performs three major functions:

✦ You can examine the ACL on an object and compare the ACL to the permissions defined in the schema defaults.

✦ You can clean up or fix problems with delegation of control assignment made using the Delegation of Control Wizard.

✦ You can grant permissions to specific users or groups that show up in the ACL.

Tip　ACL Diagnostics cannot be used on Group Policy objects (GPOs) because GPOs do not have a distinguished name (DN).

All in all, Acldiag.exe is easy to use. Figure C-5 shows you the utility, and Table C-3 gives the command-line syntax.

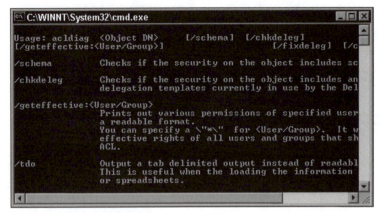

Figure C-5: Acldiag.exe

```
acldiag "ObjectDN" [/chkdeleg] [/fixdeleg] [/geteffective:{User
| Group}] [/schema] [/skip] [/tdo]
```

Table C-3
Acldiag.exe Command-line Reference

Parameters	Explanation
ObjectDN	Specifies the distinguished name of a valid Active Directory object. Must be enclosed in quotation marks.
/chkdeleg	Checks whether the security on the object includes any of the delegation templates currently in use by the Delegation of Control Wizard.
/fixdeleg	Causes the tool to fix any delegations that have been applied to the object by the Delegation of Control Wizard.
/geteffective:{user | group}	Prints out permissions of the specified user or group in a readable format. If you specify "*" for user or group, it prints the effective rights of all users and groups that show up on the ACL.
/schema	Checks whether the security on the object includes schema defaults.
/skip	Does not display the security description.
/tdo	Writes tab-delimited output for use in databases or spreadsheets instead of readable format output.

Dcdiag.exe

Domain Controller Diagnostics is a command-line utility that enables you to gain important information about the status of domain controllers in a forest. Dcdiag.exe can be a useful troubleshooting tool when you are experiencing DC problems. From this tool, you can gain useful information about connectivity, intersite health, role check, replication, trust relationship verification, your topology, and so forth. Figure C-6 shows you the command-line utility, and Table C-4 gives you the command-line syntax.

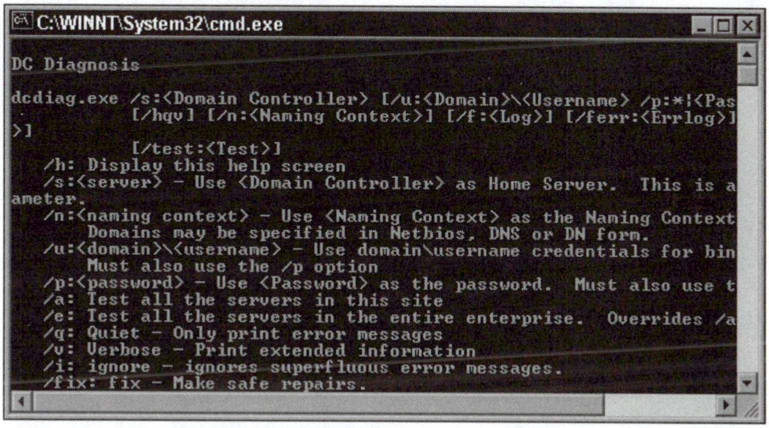

Figure C-6: Dcdiag.exe

```
dcdiag /s:DomainController [/n:NamingContext]
[/u:Domain\Username /p:{* | Password | ""}] [{/a | /e}] [{/q |
/v}] [/i] [/f:LogFile] [/ferr:ErrLog] [/c [/skip:Test]]
[/test:Test] [{/h | /?}]
```

Table C-4
Dcdiag.exe Command-line Reference

Parameters	Explanation
/s:	DomainController. Uses DomainController as home server. This is a required parameter.
/n:	NamingContext. Uses NamingContext as the naming context to test. Domains may be specified in NetBIOS, DNS, or DN form.

Continued

Table C-4 (continued)

Parameters	Explanation
/u:Domain\Username /p:{* | Password | ""}	Uses Domain\Username credentials for binding, with Password as the password. "" is an empty or null password. * prompts for the password.
/a	Tests all the servers on this site.
/e	Tests all the servers in the entire enterprise. Overrides /a.
/q	(Quiet) Prints only error messages.
/v	(Verbose) Prints extended information.
/i	Ignores superfluous error messages.
/f:LogFile	Redirects all output to LogFile. /f: operates independently of /ferr:.
/ferr:ErrLog	Redirects fatal error output to a separate file ErrLog. /ferr: operates independently of /f:.
/c	(Comprehensive) Runs all tests, including nondefault tests. Optionally, can be used with /skip to skip specified tests. The Topology, CutoffServers, and OuboundSecureChannels tests are not run by default.
/skip:Test	Skips the specified test. Must be used with /c. Should not be run in the same command line with /test. The only test that cannot be skipped is Connectivity.
/test:Test	Runs only this test. The nonskippable test Connectivity is also run. Should not be run in the same command line with /skip.
{/h | /?}	Displays a syntax screen at the command prompt.

Table C-5 explains valid Dcdiag.exe tests.

Table C-5
Valid Dcdiag.exe Tests

Tests	Explanation
Connectivity	Tests whether domain controllers are DNS registered, can be pinged, and have LDAP/RPC connectivity.
Replications	Checks for timely replication between domain controllers.
Topology	Checks that the generated topology is fully connected for all domain controllers.
CutoffServers	Checks for servers that won't receive replications because their partners are down.
NCSecDesc	Checks that the security descriptors on the naming context heads have appropriate permissions for replication.
NetLogons	Checks that the appropriate logon privileges allow replication to proceed.
LocatorGetDc	Checks whether each domain controller is advertising itself in the roles it should be capable of.
Intersite	Checks for failures that would prevent or temporarily hold up intersite replication.
RolesHeld	Checks that global role holders are known, can be located, and are responding.
RidManager	Checks to see if RID master is accessible and to see if it contains the proper information.
MachineAccount	Checks to see if the machine account has the proper information.
Services	Checks to see if appropriate domain controller services are running.
OutboundSecureChannels	Checks that secure channels exist from all of the domain controllers in the domain to the domains specified by /testdomain:. /nositerestriction prevents the test from being limited to the domain controllers in the site.
ObjectsReplicated	Checks that machine account and DSA objects have replicated. Use /objectdn:dn with /n:nc to specify additional objects to check.

Netdiag.exe

The Network Connectivity Tester is not an Active Directory tool per se, but is an important and easy to use networking command-line utility. So, I thought it deserved inclusion here. With Netdiag, you can perform diagnostic tests on your network to help isolate problems with your network clients. The command-line syntax is very straightforward, and there are quite a few networking tests you can perform. Figure C-7 shows you the utility, and Tables C-6 and C-7 give you the command-line syntax and test references you need.

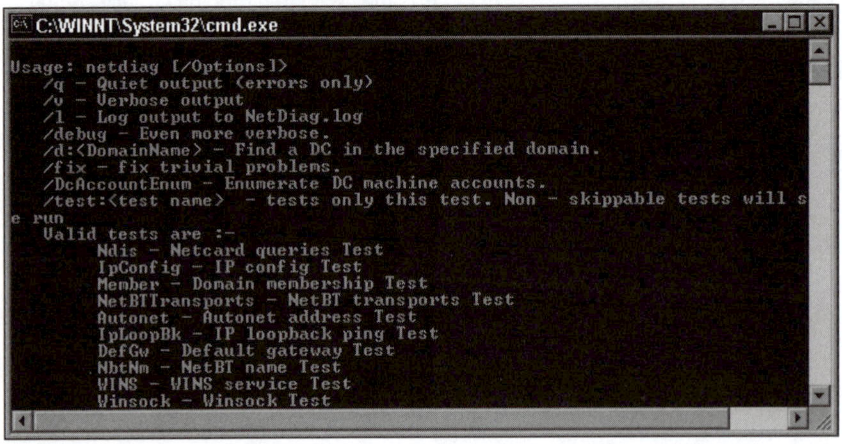

```
C:\WINNT\System32\cmd.exe                                    _ □ X

Usage: netdiag [/Options]>
      /q - Quiet output (errors only>
      /v - Verbose output
      /l - Log output to NetDiag.log.
      /debug - Even more verbose.
      /d:<DomainName> - Find a DC in the specified domain.
      /fix - fix trivial problems.
      /DcAccountEnum - Enumerate DC machine accounts.
      /test:<test name>  - tests only this test. Non - skippable tests will s
e run
      Valid tests are :-
          Ndis - Netcard queries Test
          IpConfig - IP config Test
          Member - Domain membership Test
          NetBTTransports - NetBT transports Test
          Autonet - Autonet address Test
          IpLoopBk - IP loopback ping Test
          DefGw - Default gateway Test
          NbtNm - NetBT name Test
          WINS - WINS service Test
          Winsock - Winsock Test
```

Figure C-7: Netdiag.exe

```
netdiag [/q] [/v] [/l] [/debug] [/d:DomainName] [/fix]
[/DcAccountEnum] [/test:testname] [/skip:testname]
```

Table C-6
Netdiag.exe Command-line Reference

Parameters	Explanation
/q	Specifies quiet output (errors only).
/v	Specifies verbose output.
/l	Sends output to NetDiag.log; the log file is created in the same directory where netdiag.exe was run.
/debug	Specifies even more verbose output; may take a few minutes to complete.
/d:DomainName	Finds a domain controller in the specified domain.

Parameters	Explanation
/fix	Fixes minor problems.
/DcAccountEnum	Enumerates domain controller computer accounts.
/test:*TestName*	Executes only listed test or tests. TCP/IP must be bound to one or more adapters before running any of the tests. Nonskippable tests will still be run.
/skip:*TestName*	Skips the named test.

Table C-7 gives you the test references you need.

Table C-7
Valid Netdiag.exe Tests

Tests	Explanation
Autonet	Automatic Private IP Addressing (APIPA) address test
Bindings	Bindings test
Browser	Redir and Browser test
DcList	Domain controller list test
DefGw	Default gateway test
DNS	DNS test
DsGetDc	Domain controller discovery test
IpConfig	IP address configuration test
IpLoopBk	IP address loopback ping test
IPX	IPX test
Kerberos	Kerberos test
Ldap	LDAP test
Member	Domain membership test
Modem	Modem diagnostics test
NbtNm	NetBT name test
Ndis	Netcard queries test
NetBTTransports	NetBT transports test

Continued

Table C-7 *(continued)*	
Tests	**Explanation**
Netstat	Netstat information test
Netware	Netware test
Route	Routing table test
Trust	Trust relationship test
WAN	WAN configuration test
WINS	WINS service test
Winsock	Winsock test

Dfsutil.exe

Distributed File System utility is a command-line tool that enables you to troubleshoot problems with a Distributed File System (Dfs).

 Cross-Reference   Chapter 16 explores the Distributed File System.

The Dfsutil.exe utility is included in this appendix because Dfs can be integrated with the Active Directory (and typically is integrated). Dfsutil can be used to check Dfs servers and locate Dfs hierarchy problems. Figure C-8 shows you the command-line utility, and Table C-8 gives you the command-line syntax.

```
C:\WINNT\System32\cmd.exe                                    _ □ ×

Microsoft(R) Windows(TM) Dfs Utility Version 1.1.1
Copyright (C) Microsoft Corporation 1991-2000. All Rights Reserved.

Dfsutil performs maintenance of a dfs root, and cleaning up of
metadata left behind by orphaning or abandoning Domain-based dfs
roots.

Usage: dfsutil [/OPTIONS]

    /HELP - This help
    /? - Same as /HELP
    /SCRIPTHELP - Scripting help
    /ADDROOT:<DomDfsName> /SERVER:<ServerName> /SHARE:<ShareName>
        /COMMENT:<Comment>  Create a Standalone or DomDfs root
    /REMROOT:<DomDfsName> /SERVER:<ServerName> /SHARE:<ShareName>
        Remove a Standalone or DomDfs root
    /LIST:<Domain> - List the DomDfs's in <Domain>
        /DCNAME:<DcName> - Use the DS on a specific DC.
    /VERIFY:<\\dfsname\dfsshare> - Verify the metadata in \\dfsname\d
        /DCNAME:<DcName> - Use the DS on a specific DC.
        /LEVEL:<Level> - High level -> more checks (good for NT4 Dfs
    /VIEW:<\\dfsname\dfsshare> - View the metadata in <\\dfsname\dfss
        /DCNAME:<DcName> - Use the DS on a specific DC.
    ◄                                                          ►
```

Figure C-8: Dfsutil.exe

    dfsutil [options]

Table C-8
Dfsutil.exe Command-line Reference

Options Parameters	Explanation
/list:*Domain* [/dcname:*DcName*]	Lists the Domain Distributed File Systems in the Domain or a specific domain controller. This command displays the root or roots hosted on the computer or domain.
/view:*dfsname**dfsshare* [/dcname:*DcName*] [/level:*Level*]	Views the metadata in \\dfsname\dfsshare. You can pipe the output with the |more command or send it to a text file for large Dfs configurations. When specified with the optional [*MachineName*] parameter, DFSGETBLOB is useful for *walking* a specific domain controller's view of the Dfs configuration to check for inconsistencies in the Dfs namespace due to latency in Active Directory replication. The /dcname:*DcName* parameter uses the directory service on a specific domain controller. The /level:*Level* specifies a level of viewing. A higher level shows more detail.
/verify:*dfsname**dfsshare* [/dcname:*DcName*] [/level:*Level*]	Verifies the metadata in *dfsname**dfsshare*.
/reinit:*ServerName*	Reinitializes the Dfs root *ServerName*.
/whatis:*ServerName*	Reports what kind of root *ServerName* is.
/dfsalt:*UNCPath*	Resolves the UNC path to a *server**share*. This lists the currently selected server to which a client is connected when a folder is backed by more than one server.
/unmap:*dfsname**dfsshare* / root:*server**share*	Removes *server**share* from Dfs.
/clean:*ServerName*	Updates the registry of *ServerName* so that it is not a Dfs root. This cleans out Dfs-related entries.
/dclist:*Domain*	Lists the domain controllers in Domain.
/dcname:*DcName*	Uses the directory service on a specific domain controller.
/trusts:*Domain*	Lists the Windows 2000 trusted domains of Domain.
/dcname:*DcName*	Uses the directory service on a specific domain controller.
/all	Lists all trusted domains regardless of type (Windows 2000 or Windows NT 4.0).

Continued

Table C-8 *(continued)*	
Options Parameters	**Explanation**
/? or /help	Displays this syntax at the command line.
/pktinfo [/dfs] [/level:Level]	This syntax is for client-side only. It shows the parts of the Dfs namespace cached by the client, the names of the servers participating in the Dfs share, the clients' randomization order of the participating servers, and the current go to server.
/pktflush[:EntryToFlush]	This syntax is for client-side only. It flushes the local Partition Knowledge Table (PKT) cached by the client. If EntryToFlush is specified, it flushes just the specified local PKT entry.
/spcinfo [/all]	Dumps the SPC table.
/spcflush[:EntrytoFlush]	Flushes the local SPC table. If EntryToFlush is specified, it flushes just the specified SPC table entry.
/readreg	Makes Mup.sys reread the registry.
/dfs	Makes Dfs.sys reread the registry.

ADSI Edit

The Active Directory Services Interface Editor is a lower-level editor for the Active Directory. Using ADSI Edit, you can perform all kinds of tasks, such as add, delete, and move Active Directory objects as well as add, remove, and view attributes of objects.

Caution   As with the Schema Manager console, great care must be taken when using ADSI Edit. Editing should be performed only by experienced administrators or programmers. Incorrect edits can bring an Active Directory environment to a halt and result in the Active Directory having to be reinstalled.

ADSI Edit is an MMC snap-in that you manually open (see Appendix B for instructions). As shown in Figure C-9, you see a Domain NC, Configuration Container, and a Schema container. The ADSI Edit snap-in functions like all other snap-ins.

Cross-Reference   See Chapter 14 to learn more about ADSI Editor and schema modifications.

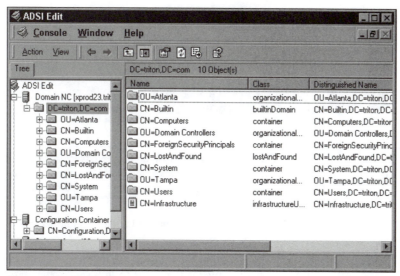

Figure C-9: ADSI Edit

Dsacls.exe

Directory Service Access Control Lists (ACLs) is a command-line utility that enables you to both query and manipulate ACLs on Active Directory objects. Dsacls.exe is the same as using the GUI Security tab found in the Properties of most Active Directory objects in the various Active Directory consoles. Figure C-10 shows you Dsacls.exe, and Table C-9 gives you the command-line syntax.

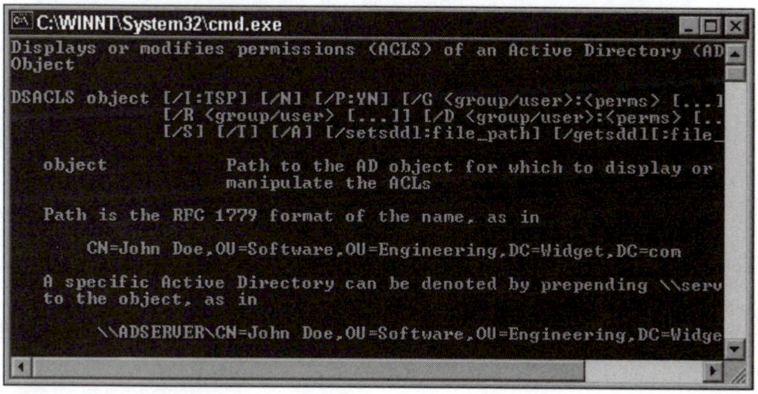

Figure C-10: Dsacls.exe

```
dsacls object [/a] [/d {user | group}:permissions [...]] [/g
{user | group}:permissions [...]] [/i:{p | s | t}] [/n] [/p:{y
| n}] [/r {user | group} [...]] [/s [/t]] [/?]
```

<table>
<tr><td colspan="2" align="center">Table C-9
Dsacls.exe Command-line Reference</td></tr>
<tr><td>Parameters</td><td>Explanation</td></tr>
<tr><td>dsacls object</td><td>Displays the security on an object. Object is the path to the directory services object on which to display or manipulate the ACLs. This path must be a distinguished name.</td></tr>
<tr><td>/a</td><td>Displays the ownership and auditing information as well as the permissions.</td></tr>
<tr><td>/d {user | group}:permissions</td><td>Denies specified permissions to user or group. You can specify more than one user or group in a command.</td></tr>
<tr><td>/g {user | group}:permissions</td><td>Grants specified permissions to user or group. You can specify more than one user or group in a command.</td></tr>
<tr><td>/i:{c | o | i | p}</td><td>Specifies one of the inheritance flags, which are p = Propagate inheritable permissions one level only, s = Subobjects only, and t = This object and subobjects.</td></tr>
<tr><td>/n</td><td>Replaces the current access on the object instead of editing it.</td></tr>
<tr><td>/p</td><td>Marks the object as protected (y = yes) or not protected (n = no). If the /p option is not present, the current protection flag is maintained.</td></tr>
<tr><td>/r {user | group}</td><td>Removes all permissions for the specified user or group. You can specify more than one user or group in a command.</td></tr>
<tr><td>/s</td><td>Restores the security on the object to the default for that object class as defined in Active Directory schema.</td></tr>
<tr><td>/t</td><td>Restores the security on the tree of objects to the default for each object class. This switch is valid only with the /s option.</td></tr>
<tr><td>/?</td><td>Displays this syntax listing.</td></tr>
</table>

Syntax for {<i>user</i> | <i>group</i>} must be expressed in one of the following ways:

✦ user@domain or domain\user

✦ group@domain or domain\group

Note More than one user or group can be specified in a command.

Syntax for permissions must be expressed in the following form:

`[PermissionBits];[{Object | Property}];[InheritedObjectType]`

Table C-10 lists the *PermissionBits* values that can be used.

	Table C-10
	PermissionsBits Values

PermissionBits	Explanation
GR	Generic Read
GE	Generic Execute
GW	Generic Write
GA	Generic All
SD	Delete
DT	Delete an object and all of its children
RC	Read security information
WD	Change security information
WO	Change owner information
LC	List the children of an object
CC	Create a child object
DC	Delete a child object
WS	Write to self object
RP	Read property
WP	Write property
CA	Control access right
LO	List the object access

Dsastat.exe

DSA Statistics is a command-line diagnostic tool that compares and detects differences between naming contexts on domain controllers. You can use Dsastat.exe to compare two directory trees within the same domain or through the global catalog server in an across-domain format. Dsastat.exe gathers statistics that help you determine if domain controllers have an accurate image of the objects in their own domain, and it is a great tool to determine if domain controllers within a domain are up-to-date with one another or if global catalog servers are up-to-date across domains. Figure C-11 shows you Dsastat.exe, and Table C-11 gives you the command-line syntax.

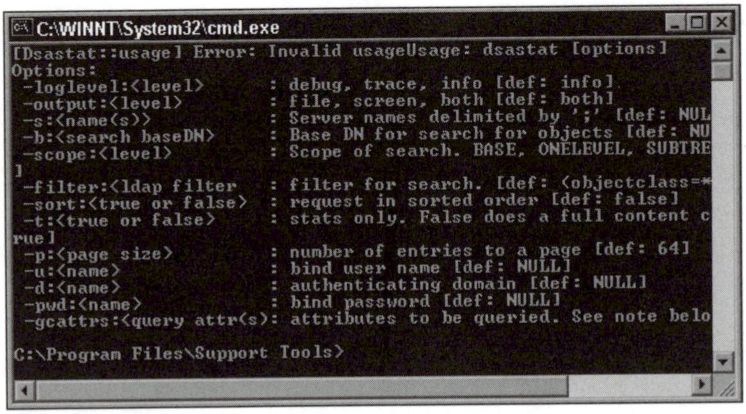

Figure C-11: Dsastat.exe

```
dsastat [/?] [-loglevel:option] [-output:option] [-f:filename]
[-s:servername[portnumber][;servername[portnumber];...]] [-
t:option] [-sort:option] [-p:entrynumber] [-b:searchpath] [-
filter:ldapfilter] [-gcattrs:option[;option;...]]
```

<table>
<tr><td colspan="2" align="center">Table C-11
Dsastat.exe Command-line Reference</td></tr>
<tr><td>*Parameters*</td><td>*Explanation*</td></tr>
<tr><td>/?</td><td>Displays help for Dsastat, along with the default options and parameter values.</td></tr>
<tr><td>-loglevel:option</td><td>Specifies the extent of logging that is performed during execution. Valid option values are INFO, TRACE, and DEBUG. The default option is INFO.</td></tr>
<tr><td>-output:option</td><td>Specifies where the results of Dsastat are displayed. Valid options are SCREEN, FILE, or BOTH. If FILE is selected the output is saved to a file named Dsastat.log.nnnnn. The default option is SCREEN.</td></tr>
</table>

Parameters	Explanation
-f:*filename*	Specifies the name of an initialization file to use for parameters if user does not specify the parameters on the command line.
-s:*servername*[*portnumber*] [;*servername*[*portnumber*];...]	Specifies the names of the servers on which the comparison will be performed. If the port number is :3268, the comparison will be performed against the global catalog of that server. The default port number is the default LDAP port (389).
-t:*option*	Specifies whether to perform a statistics comparison or a full-content comparison. Valid option values are TRUE (perform a statistical comparison) or FALSE (perform a full-content comparison). The default option is TRUE.
-sort:*option*	Determines whether the search operations are performed with sorting based on object GUID. Valid option values are TRUE (perform sorted queries) or FALSE (do not perform sorted queries). The default value is FALSE.
-p:*entrynumber*	Sets page size for *ldap_search* operation. The valid range for *entrynumber* is from 1 to 999. The default value is 64. The number indicates the number of entries to be returned per page.
-b:*searchpath*	Sets the distinguished name of the base search path. This allows Dsastat to perform the comparison against any subtree of the directory.
-filter:*ldapfilter*	Sets LDAP filter used in the LDAP search operation. The filter must conform to LDAP search syntax as specified in RFC 2254. The default filter is (objectclass=*).
-gcattrs:*option*[;*option*;...]	Specifies attributes to be returned from search. This option is used only if the comparison option -t is set to FALSE. Valid option values are any LDAP attribute, *objectclass* when no attributes are requested, *auto* if only those attributes that are replicated to the Global Catalog are requested, and *all* when you want all attributes contained in an object to be retrieved.

Ldp.exe

Ldp.exe is an Active Directory administration tool that enables you to perform Lightweight Directory Access Protocol (LDAP) operations and view objects in the Active Directory with their metadata. Ldp.exe can be useful in troubleshooting objects by examining the metadata, and you can perform LDAP operations using this tool, such as add, delete, search, connect, and so forth. Shown in Figure C-12, Ldp.exe is a graphical tool and is easy to use and intuitive.

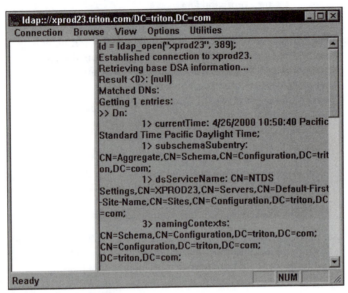

Figure C-12: Ldp.exe

Movetree.exe

The Movetree command-line utility enables you to relocate Active Directory Organizational Units (OUs) and objects to a different tree in the same forest. For example, if you wanted to move an OU named Atlanta and all of the objects in Atlanta from the triton.com domain tree to the tritonau.com domain tree, then you can use Movetree.exe.

> **Note** Group Policy objects are moved with the OU. However, the GPO continues to be the same GPO used in the old domain. Review your Group Policy objects before using Movetree to define a strategy to update the GPO settings once the objects are moved to the new domain.

Although Movetree is an effective tool, there are a few issues you should be aware of and have plans in place to resolve before moving the objects:

+ Most objects can be moved using Movetree. However, some objects internal to the Active Directory cannot be moved. Any information related to an object that exists outside of the Active Directory also cannot be moved.

✦ Computer objects are not moved during a Movetree operation. You can use Netdom.exe, explained in the next section, to move computer objects between domains.

✦ Users' personal data, logon scripts, policies, and so forth are not moved using Movetree.

✦ Local and Domain Global groups are not moved and all user accounts and groups maintain their security identities. ACLs are not reset. Universal groups are moved during a Movetree operation.

✦ The following objects cannot be moved: system objects, objects in the configuration or schema naming contexts, domain controllers, any object whose parent is a domain controller, any object with an identical name as an object in the new domain, and all objects in special containers (Builtin, ForeignSecurityPrincipal, System, and LostAndFound).

Caution If a Movetree operation is paused or aborted, any objects that have not yet been moved but were targeted for the move are placed in an Orphan container found in the LostAndFound container. See Chapter 12 to learn more about the LostAndFound container.

Figure C-13 shows you the Movetree tool, and Table C-12 gives you the command-line syntax.

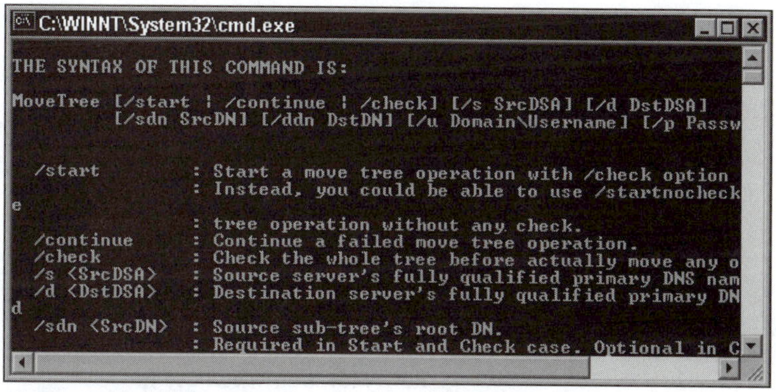

```
⌧ C:\WINNT\System32\cmd.exe                                  _□×

THE SYNTAX OF THIS COMMAND IS:

MoveTree [/start : /continue : /check] [/s SrcDSA] [/d DstDSA]
        [/sdn SrcDN] [/ddn DstDN] [/u Domain\Username] [/p Passw


   /start        : Start a move tree operation with /check option
                 : Instead, you could be able to use /startnocheck
e
                 : tree operation without any check.
   /continue     : Continue a failed move tree operation.
   /check        : Check the whole tree before actually move any o
   /s <SrcDSA>   : Source server's fully qualified primary DNS nam
   /d <DstDSA>   : Destination server's fully qualified primary DN
d
   /sdn <SrcDN>  : Source sub-tree's root DN.
                 : Required in Start and Check case. Optional in C
```

Figure C-13: Movetree.exe

```
movetree {/start | /startnocheck | /continue | /check} /s
SrcDSA /d DstDSA /sdn SrcDN /ddn DstDN [/u [Domain\]Username /p
Password] [/verbose] [{/? | /help}]
```

Table C-12
Movetree.exe Command-line Reference

Parameters	Explanation
/start	Starts a Movetree operation. This command includes a /check operation by default.
/startnocheck	Starts a Movetree operation with no /check.
/continue	Continues the execution of a previously paused or failed Movetree operation.
/check	Performs a test of the Movetree operation, checking the whole tree without moving any objects. An error message occurs if necessary permissions are not met, the destination server does not have enough disk space, an RDN conflict exists, a sameAccountName conflict occurs, or nonmovable objects exist (see previous bulleted list).
/s SrcDSA	Specifies the fully qualified primary DNS name of the source server in the domain from which the objects are being moved.
/d DstDSA	Specifies the fully qualified primary DNS name of the destination server in the domain to which the objects are being moved.
/sdn SrcDN	Specifies the distinguished name of the source subtree to which the object is being moved.
/ddn DstDN	Specifies the distinguished name of the destination subtree to which the object is being moved.
/u [Domain\]Username /p Password	Runs Movetree under the credentials of a valid user name and password.
/verbose	Runs Movetree in verbose mode.
/? or /help	Displays the command-line syntax.

When using Movetree, you may receive error level code. The following bulleted list defines those error levels:

✦ 0 — No error

✦ 1 — Command-line syntax error

✦ 2 — Directory conflict, such as a duplicate name

✦ 3 — Network error, such as an unavailable domain controller

✦ 4 — System resource error, such as low disk space

✦ 5 — Internal processing error

Netdom.exe

Netdom.exe is a command-line utility designed to help you manage network domains. With Netdom you manage domains and trust relationships between domains, and you can perform a number of specific tasks, such as joining a computer to a domain and managing computer accounts for both member servers and workstations. You can create trust relationships between domains and manage those trust relationships as well. Figure C-14 shows you the Netdom.exe tool, and Table C-13 gives you the command-line syntax.

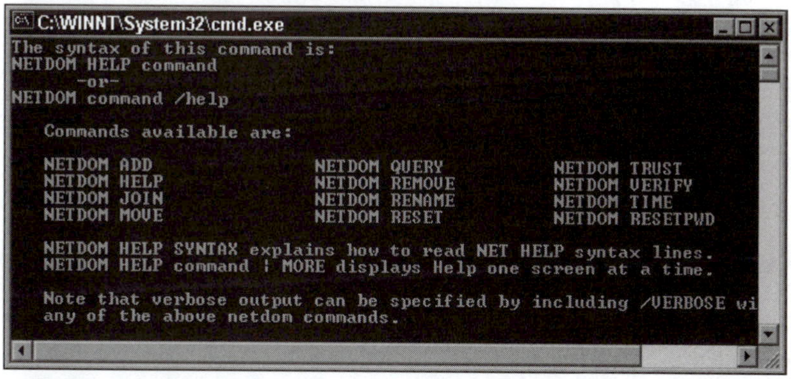

```
C:\WINNT\System32\cmd.exe                                    _ □ X
The syntax of this command is:
NETDOM HELP command
         -or-
NETDOM command /help

   Commands available are:

   NETDOM ADD              NETDOM QUERY         NETDOM TRUST
   NETDOM HELP             NETDOM REMOVE        NETDOM VERIFY
   NETDOM JOIN             NETDOM RENAME        NETDOM TIME
   NETDOM MOVE             NETDOM RESET         NETDOM RESETPWD

   NETDOM HELP SYNTAX explains how to read NET HELP syntax lines.
   NETDOM HELP command : MORE displays Help one screen at a time.

   Note that verbose output can be specified by including /VERBOSE wi
   any of the above netdom commands.
```

Figure C-14: Netdom.exe

```
netdom command object [/D:domain] [options]
```

Note   Parameters and commands for Netdom.exe are case sensitive.

Table C-13
Netdom.exe Command-line Reference

Command Parameters	Explanation
ADD computer /D:*domain* [/Ud:*User* /Pd:{*Password* | *}][/S:*Server*] [/OU:*ou_path*] [/DC]	This is a workstation or server command that adds a workstation or server account to the domain.
HELP	Displays a command-line syntax screen.
HELP *command*	Displays a more detailed command-line syntax screen for a particular command.
command | MORE	Displays the detailed command-line syntax screen for command one screen at a time.
HELP SYNTAX	Explains how to interpret the notation used in the syntax screens.
JOIN computer /D:*domain* [/OU:*ou_path*] [/Ud:*User* /Pd:{*Password* | *}] [/Uo:*User* / Po:{*Password* | *}] [/Reboot[:*time_in_seconds*]]	Joins a workstation or member server (computer) to a domain.
MOVE computer /D:*domain* [/OU:*ou_path*] [/Ud:*User* /Pd: {*Password* | *}] [/Uo:*User* /Po: {*Password* | *}] [/Reboot[:*time_in_seconds*]]	Moves a workstation or member server (computer) to a new domain.
REMOVE computer /D:*domain* [/Ud:*User* /Pd:{*Password* | *}] [/Uo:*User* /Po:{*Password* | *}] [/Reboot[:*time_in_seconds*]]	Removes a workstation or member server (computer) from a domain.
RENAME computer [/D:*domain*] [/Reboot[:*time_in_seconds*]]	Renames a Windows NT 4.0 backup domain controller (computer).
RESET computer /D:*domain* [/S:*Server*] [/Uo:*User* /Po:{*Password* | *}]	Resets the secure connection between a workstation and a domain controller.
VERIFY computer /D:*domain* [/Uo:*User* /Po:{*Password* | *}]	Verifies the secure connection between a workstation and a domain controller.

Command Parameters	Explanation
QUERY /D:*domain* [/S:*Server*] [/Ud:*User* /Pd:{*Password*	*}] [/Verify] [/Reset] [/Direct] {WORKSTATION	SERVER	DC	OU	PDC	FSMO	TRUST}	Retrieves membership, trust, and other information from a domain.
TIME computer /D:*domain* [/Ud:*User* / Pd:{*Password*	*}] [/Uo:*User* /Po: {*Password*	*}] [/Verify] [/Reset] [WORKSTATION] [SERVER]	Verifies or resets and synchronizes time within a domain.
TRUST *trusting_domain_name* / D:*trusted_domain_name* [/Ud:*User*] [/Pd:{*Password*	*}] [Uo:*User*] [/Po:{*Password*	*}] [/Verify] [/Reset] [/PasswordT:*new_realm_trust_password*] [/Add] [/Remove [/Force]] [/Twoway] [/Kerberos] [/Transitive[:{yes	no}]]	Establishes, verifies, or resets a trust relationship between domains.

Repadmin.exe

Repadmin.exe is a command-line replication diagnostics tool that enables you to examine and troubleshoot replication problems between domain controllers in the Active Directory. You can use Repadmin to examine each domain controller in order to see the replication topology from that domain controller's viewpoint. The Knowledge Consistency Checker (KCC) generates and maintains the replication topology within a site, but you can use Repadmin to manually make changes to the topology. This feature, however, should not be necessary under normal circumstances. The best use of this tool is the monitoring of replication between servers or between servers connected with unreliable WAN connections.

Caution

You do not need to manually manipulate an Active Directory site's replication topology under normal circumstances, and incorrectly doing so may cause replication problems or failure. See Chapter 13 for more information about how the KCC functions in the Active Directory.

Figure C-15 shows the Repadmin tool, and Table C-14 gives you the command-line parameters and arguments.

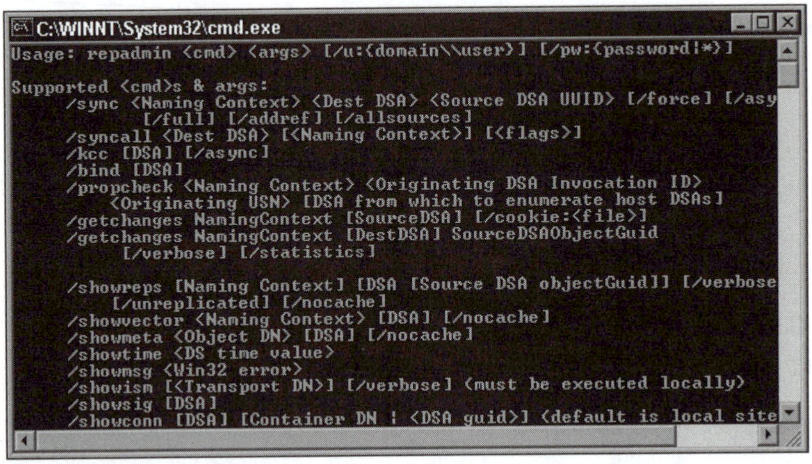

Figure C-15: Repadmin.exe

```
repadmin command arguments [/u:[domain\]user /pw:{password|*}]
```

Table C-14
Repadmin.exe Command-line Reference

Commands and Arguments	Explanation
/u:[domain\]user	Specifies an optional user (from an optional domain) as the administrator. If the user name and password are not specified, Repadmin uses the credentials of the currently logged-on user.
/pw:{password|*}	Specifies the password of the user specified by the /u: switch. If the user name and password are not specified, Repadmin uses the credentials of the currently logged-on user.
/sync Naming_Context Destination_DSA Source_DSA_UUID [/force] [/async][/full] [/addref] [/allsources]	Starts a replication event for the specified naming context between the source and destination domain controllers. The source DSA UUID can be determined when viewing the replication partners with the repadmin /showreps command.
/force	Overrides the normal replication schedule.
/async	Starts the replication event, but Repadmin does not wait for the replication event to complete.

Commands and Arguments	Explanation
/full	Forces a full replication of all objects from the destination DSA.
/syncall Destination_DSA [Naming_Context] [Flags]/kcc [DSA] [/async] /async	Repadmin does not wait for the replication event to complete.
/bind [DSA]	Binds the Directory System Agent (DSA).
/propcheck Naming_Context Originating_DSA_Invocation_ID Originating_USN [DSA_from_which_to_enumerate_host_DSAs]	Checks USN of DSA.
/getchanges Naming_Context [Source_DSA] [/cookie:file]	Checks for DSA naming context changes.
/showreps [Naming_Context] [DSA [Source_DSA_UUID]] [/verbose] [/unreplicated] [/nocache]	Displays the replication partners (RepsFrom and RepsTo) for each naming context that is held on the specified domain controller. The output also indicates whether or not the domain controller is also a Global Catalog server.
/showvector Naming_Context [DSA] [/nocache]	For a specified naming context, shows the up-to-date information.
/showmeta Object_DN [DSA] [/nocache]	Displays the replication metadata for any object stored in Active Directory such as attribute ID, version number, originating and local Update Sequence Number (USN), and originating DSA's GUID and date/time stamp.
/showtime [Windows_2000_Directory_Service_Time_Value] format and string format.	With no arguments, this command displays the current system time in both the directory service
/showmsg Win32_error_number	Takes as an argument the Win32 error number and displays the Win32 error text.
/showism [Transport_DN] [/verbose]	Must be executed locally.
/showsig [DSA]	DSA signature.
/showconn [DSA] [{Container_DN | DSA_UUID}]	DSA connection.
/showcert [DSA]	DSA connection
/showctx [DSA] [/nocache]	DSA connection.
/queue [DSA]	DSA connection.
/failcache [DSA]	DSA connection.

Replmon.exe

Replication Monitor is a graphical interface tool that enables you to examine Active Directory replication among domain controllers and domains and to perform a number of administrative actions, such as force replication between domain controllers, generate a status report about replication, trigger the KCC, and view intra-site replication topology. Replication Monitor is an MMC snap-in and functions like all other MMC snap-ins. Figure C-16 shows you Replication Monitor.

 Cross-Reference   You can learn more about using Replication Monitor in Chapter 13.

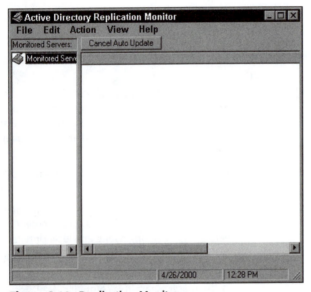

Figure C-16: Replication Monitor

Sdcheck.exe

Sdcheck.exe is a command-line tool that checks the security descriptor for any object in the Active Directory. Remember that the security descriptor contains the ACLs that determine permissions for that object. Figure C-17 shows you the Sdcheck tool, and Table C-15 gives you the command-line syntax.

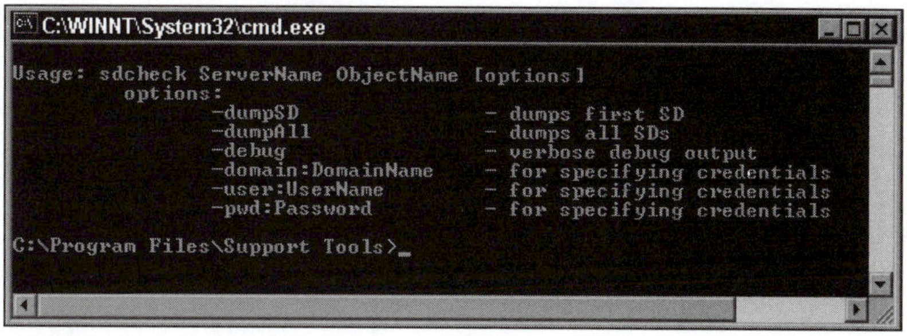

Figure C-17: Sdcheck.exe

```
sdcheck Server Object [-dumpSD] [-dumpAll] [-debug] [[-domain:
DomainName] -user: UserName -password: Password] [/?]
```

Table C-15
Sdcheck.exe Command-line Reference

Parameters	Explanation
Server	Specifies the name of the domain controller on which to perform the query. You can provide either the DNS or UPN name.
Object	Specifies the name of the object on which you want to determine the ACL entries. The name can be the logon name, DN, or UPN.
-dumpSD	Displays only the security descriptor for the selected object.
-dumpALL	Displays the security descriptor for the selected object along with all security descriptors inherited from parent containers.
-debug	Displays internal debugging information for Sdcheck.exe.
-domain: *DomainName*	Specifies the domain name of *UserName* in either DNS or NetBIOS format.
-user: *UserName*	Specifies the name of a user other than the current one, in the form of either the logon name or user principal name.
-password: *Password*	Specifies the name of *UserName*. Used to specify credentials other than the current user's name.
/?	Displays syntax on the command line.

Summary

Aside from the primary Active Directory tools installed during an Active Directory implementation, the Windows 2000 Resource Kit and the AdminPak tools provide you with several administrative tools that are beneficial in your Active Directory deployment and troubleshooting. Use this appendix to reference the tools and appropriate command-line syntax.

✦   ✦   ✦

PDC and BDC Upgrade Reference

APPENDIX

D

◆ ◆ ◆ ◆

In This Appendix

Upgrading a
PDC or BDC to
Windows 2000

Upgrading a PDC
or BDC to Active
Directory

◆ ◆ ◆ ◆

As I have said throughout this book, the odds are quite good that you are implementing the Active Directory as an upgrade to an existing NT network. During your planning process, you have to make a lot of decisions about what you will do with existing domains and how you will consolidate some or most of your NT domains into the new Active Directory networking model.

With that said, you will be doing a lot of NT Server upgrades to Windows 2000. In domains that you choose to keep, or at least choose to maintain the user accounts, you will need to upgrade your primary domain controller (PDC) first to establish the domain and retain your user accounts. Then, you can upgrade your backup domain controllers (BDCs) so they become supporting domain controllers in the Active Directory environment.

This appendix is designed to be a handy installation reference tool for upgrading Windows NT PDCs and BDCs to Windows 2000. Before you upgrade to Windows 2000, you should check your PDC and BDC hardware to ensure that all hardware is compatible with Windows 2000. You should also perform a full backup of your data—just in case things do not go well during the installation.

Upgrading a PDC or BDC to Windows 2000

For the most part, Windows 2000 and Active Directory upgrades are easy to perform and trouble free. The following steps show how to upgrade a PDC or BDC to Windows 2000 Server:

1. Insert the Windows 2000 Server installation CD-ROM into the PDC's or BDC's CD-ROM drive.

2. A message appears telling you that your operating system is running an older version of Windows and asking you if you would like to upgrade, as shown in Figure D-1. Click the Yes button.

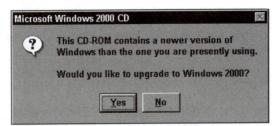

Figure D-1: Click Yes to start the upgrade.

3. The Welcome to Windows Setup Wizard appears. You are presented with two radio buttons with which you can choose either to upgrade to Windows 2000 or to install a new copy. Since you want setup to retain all of your settings and accounts, select the upgrade radio button and then click the Next radio button, shown in Figure D-2.

4. Read the licensing agreement that appears and then click the "I accept this agreement" radio button. You must accept the licensing agreement for setup to continue. Now, click the Next button, shown in Figure D-3.

5. The product key window appears, shown in Figure D-4. Enter the product key found on the back of your Windows 2000 CD case and then click Next.

6. Setup checks your system and reports any compatibility problems, as shown in Figure D-5. Click Next to continue.

7. Setup copies files from your CD for the installation and then automatically restarts your computer.

8. After the computer restart, the text-based portion of setup begins. Setup loads files necessary for the Windows 2000 installation. This process takes several minutes to perform. At this point, no input is needed from you for several minutes (half an hour or longer).

Figure D-2: Select the Upgrade option.

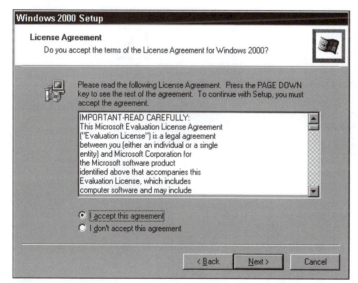

Figure D-3: Click the "I accept this agreement" radio button.

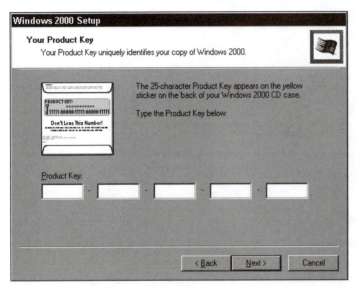

Figure D-4: Enter your product ID number.

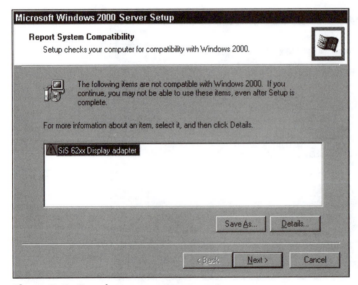

Figure D-5: Examine your system report.

9. Setup restarts your computer, and you see the Windows 2000 Server splash screen for the first time. Setup continues with hardware detection. During this time, your screen may flicker, and hardware detection may take several minutes to perform.

10. Once hardware detection is complete, Windows 2000 installs and configures networking components. No input is required from you.

11. Setup continues by installing components, which also takes several minutes.

12. Finally, setup installs Start Menu items, registers components, saves settings, and removes temporary files used during installation. Once installation is complete, setup restarts your computer.

13. Windows 2000 Server boots for the first time.

Upgrading a PDC or BDC to Active Directory

Before the first boot is complete, the Active Directory Installation Wizard appears so you can complete the upgrade of the PDC or BDC to a domain controller. The following steps show you the upgrade options to select for the PDC:

1. **Welcome Screen** — The welcome screen tells you that the upgrade process must install the Active Directory in order to be complete. Click Next to continue.

2. **Appropriate Forest** — A window, shown in Figure D-6, with two radio button options appears. You can either install the domain controller for a new domain or for an existing Active Directory domain. If you are upgrading an NT domain, you may already have a forest in place from previously upgrading other NT domains, so you will need to make decisions here about what you will do. The remainder of these steps assumes you are creating a new forest. Click the "Create a new domain tree" radio button and then click the Next button.

3. **Forest Option** — You see two radio button options in the next window, as shown in Figure D-7. You have the option either to create a new forest of trees or to join your new tree to an existing forest. This step-by-step process assumes you do not currently have other Active Directory forests, so choose the "Create a new forest of domain trees" radio button. Then click the Next button.

4. **Root Domain Name** — The domain name window appears, shown in Figure D-8. Enter the desired DNS name of your Active Directory root in this window. Throughout the rest of the book, my example root domain is tritondev.com, a fictitious company. Type the name into the box and click the Next button.

5. **Database and Log File Storage** — You see a window with default storage locations for the Active Directory database and the log files, which is C:\WINNT\ NTDS by default. You can change this default location by using the browse button. Make any desired changes and click Next, as shown in Figure D-9.

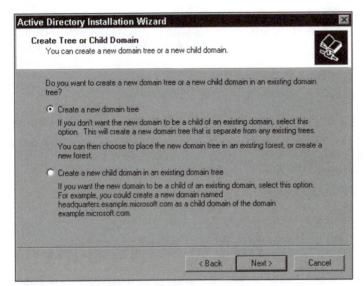

Figure D-6: Select the appropriate forest option.

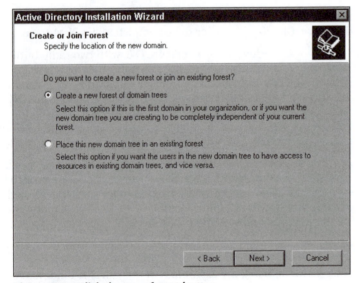

Figure D-7: Click the new forest button.

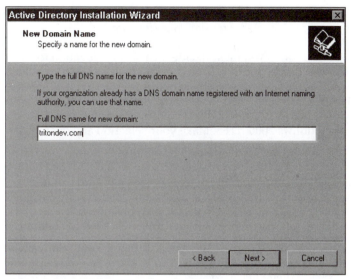

Figure D-8: Enter the root domain name.

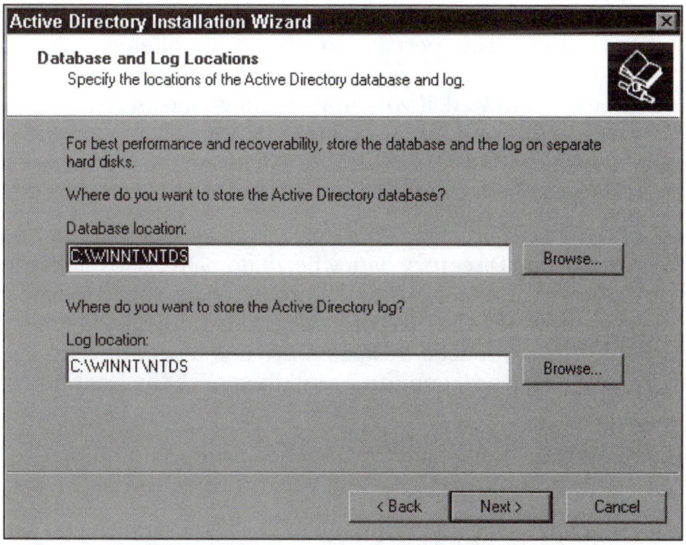

Figure D-9: Adjust database and log file locations and click Next.

Tip   Microsoft recommends that you store the database and log files on a hard disk separate from your boot volume for maximum performance.

6. **SYSVOL Folder Storage** — You must decide on a storage location for the SYSVOL folder, which is C:\WINNT\SYSVOL by default. All Windows 2000 servers have a SYSVOL folder, but domain controllers' SYSVOL folders contain Active Directory information. As with database and log files, you may want to store the SYSVOL on a different disk or volume, but it must be formatted with Windows 2000 NTFS. Make your selection and click Next.

7. **DNS Server** — If you did not configure DNS on another Windows 2000 Server, then a message appears telling you that a DNS server could not be contacted. If a DNS Server could be contacted, the Active Directory Wizard would query the DNS Server to make certain that it supports dynamic updates. By clicking OK to the message, you tell Windows 2000 to install and configure DNS automatically with the Active Directory on this domain controller. Click OK to continue.

8. **Automatic DNS** — You can either let the Active Directory automatically set up DNS or install it yourself. Select the Yes button to allow the Active Directory to configure DNS and then click Next.

9. **Permissions Window** — You have two options. You can choose to use either permissions compatible with Windows NT Server or permissions compatible with Windows 2000 Servers in Windows 2000 domains only. If you use Windows NT permissions, you are using weaker permissions than those offered in Windows 2000. Specifically, in Windows NT, anonymous users can read domain information if anonymous logon is allowed. If your upgrade to Windows 2000 will take time, use the NT permissions options. If you are upgrading all at once and you have no intention of using NT Servers in the future, choose the Windows 2000 permissions radio button. Make your selection and click the Next button.

10. **Restore Mode** — The Active Directory contains a Restore Mode option that allows you to restore Active Directory data when a domain controller failure occurs. The use of Restore Mode is password protected as a security measure. The Restore Mode window asks you to enter a Restore Mode password and confirm the password. You will need this password if you ever have to use Restore Mode. Enter a password, confirm it, and then click the Next button.

11. **Summary** — A summary window appears. Review your selections and use the Back button if you need to change anything. If the information is correct, click the Next button.

12. **Configuration** — Setup begins configuring the Active Directory, as you see in Chapter 6, Figure 6-17. Configuration may take several minutes. Once the installation is complete, you are prompted to reboot the server. Once the reboot takes place, the installation is complete, and your former member server is now an Active Directory domain controller for the root domain.

The process of upgrading a BDC to a domain controller is simple. When the Active Directory Wizard appears after the server installation, choose to become an additional domain controller for an existing domain. The remaining options in the wizard are very similar to the previous steps, and you can see a complete walk-through in Chapter 7.

Summary

In this appendix, you explored a PDC/BDC upgrade reference so that primary domain controllers and backup domain controllers in Windows NT can be upgraded to the Active Directory. Upgrading your existing domains does not have to be a difficult task, but like all upgrades, make certain you have backed up your data, you have an upgrade plan in place, and you can recover from the upgrade should you experience problems along the way.

✦　　✦　　✦

Windows 2000 Deployment Strategies

If you've read the title of this appendix, you might think, "Why talk about deployment in an Active Directory book?" It is important to remember that Microsoft views the Active Directory as a total network solution, and in your Windows 2000 network, you will often use tools and strategies that are not directly related to the Active Directory. However, as the old saying goes, "all roads lead home."

This appendix is designed to give you helpful information and appropriate steps for using the Windows 2000 tools that can help you deploy both server and client software on your network. As a part of the Active Directory's network management, deploying Windows 2000 is major component of that management strategy.

When networks were smaller, deployment did not receive the attention that it does today. IT professionals could handle the deployment of both servers and clients by physically running setup on the desired computers. That solution, commonly called the "Sneaker Net," is not very practical in distributed networks today where different locations within the same company or organization may contain thousands and thousands of computers. IT professionals need tools to help them deploy computers automatically and centrally from one location. Windows 2000 Server provides some helpful tools for you; some of them are great, some need to mature a little, but this appendix will help you get your feet on solid ground with these technologies.

Remote Installation Service

Remote Installation Service (RIS) is a Windows 2000 Server service that enables you to install Windows 2000 Professional automatically over the network. RIS functions like an unattended installation (which you can learn more about later in this chapter), but RIS is designed to be a *total* solution—especially a total, *hands-off* solution.

RIS functions by storing the Windows 2000 Professional setup files on the RIS server and then deploying those setup files to clients over the network. The RIS server can also hold a complete drive image of a Windows 2000 Professional computer, including all settings and applications, and deploy that image to network clients. This feature enables you to configure a single Windows 2000 computer and roll out that standardized installation to all clients.

I must note here that RIS is not perfect, and I believe it still needs a little maturing. First, you can use RIS only to install Windows 2000 Professional to clients. Second, RIS works only with certain types of network cards, which you can learn about later in this section. Nevertheless, RIS is a great technology and one you should become familiar with. If your network needs and current hardware meet the requirements, RIS can save you a lot of time and aggravation as you deploy Windows 2000 Professional. The following sections show you how to set up and use RIS on your network.

Installing the RIS server

RIS is not installed by default on a Windows 2000 server. Before installing RIS, you need to check out a few installation requirements to make certain that the Windows 2000 server has the requirements to become a RIS server. First, the typical Windows 2000 server hardware requirements apply, so if your server can run Windows 2000, it can run RIS. However, in order to function as a RIS server, the Windows 2000 server needs a second drive. This means that the Windows 2000 Professional setup files cannot be stored on the RIS server's boot volume or the volume containing the operating system. So, in a perfect world, RIS is best installed on a server that has a second disk that can be used to store RIS images. A single RIS image typically requires about 500MB of disk space, which includes any applications. You may choose to use several different images depending on your network deployment needs, and if you do, then you'll need quite a bit more room. Any volume or disk you choose to use must be formatted with NTFS.

 Tip   RIS uses Single Instance Store (SIS) technology to reduce the server storage space by storing files only one time among images. However, even with SIS, plan on needing several gigabytes of storage space if you have several images that are quite different from each other.

The final RIS requirement is, as you might guess, the Active Directory. Your RIS server must be connected to the network so that it can access the Active Directory. Also, your network must use DNS and DHCP in order to use RIS.

So, if you meet those requirements, your next step is to turn your Windows 2000 server into a RIS server. The following steps walk you through the installation of RIS:

1. In Windows 2000 Server, choose Start ➪ Settings ➪ Control Panel.

2. Double-click Add/Remove Programs and then click the Add/Remove Windows Components button.

3. In the Windows Components window, select the Remote Installation Services check box, shown in Figure E-1, and then click the Next button.

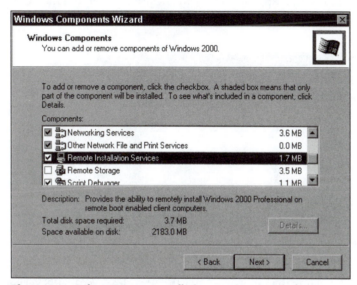

Figure E-1: Select Remote Installation Services in Windows Components window.

4. The RIS components are installed on the system.

5. Click Finish and reboot your computer.

Authorizing a RIS server

Once the installation has taken place and you have rebooted the RIS server, the RIS server must be authorized by the Active Directory to function on the network. If you have installed DHCP, you know that in Windows 2000, the DHCP server must be authorized by the Active Directory to participate on the network. This process prevents unauthorized, or *rogue*, DHCP servers from issuing bad IP addresses to clients on the network.

For a RIS server, the same security holds true. The RIS server must be authorized before it can be used. However, to authorize a RIS server, you indirectly use the Active Directory by authorizing the RIS server on a DHCP server. If you installed RIS on a DHCP server, then authorization takes place automatically and you don't have to worry about manually performing the authorization. If not, then you need to authorize the RIS server with a DHCP server. Just follow these steps:

1. On a DHCP server, choose Start ⇨ Programs ⇨ Administrative Tools ⇨ DHCP.

2. Choose the Action menu and then choose Manage Authorized servers.

3. In the window that appears, select the desired server and then click the Authorize button, shown in Figure E-2.

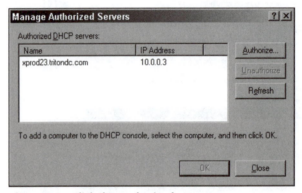

Figure E-2: Click the Authorize button.

4. In the dialog box that appears, enter the IP address of the RIS server.

5. The RIS server is authorized, and the IP address now appears in the "Authorized DHCP servers" list window. Click Close and then close DHCP Manager.

RIS server setup

Now that your server has the RIS setup files and has been authorized by DHCP, you finally get to set up the RIS server. As you can probably guess, Windows 2000 gives you a wizard to walk you through the setup process. Keep in mind that this wizard is going to configure your drive or volume for RIS storage, so make certain you have a drive ready for that purpose. Also, setup will configure a default Windows 2000 Professional image, so you will need a Windows 2000 Professional CD-ROM or access to the installation source files on the network in order to complete the setup. The following steps walk you through the wizard:

1. Click Start ⇨ Run and then type **risetup** in the dialog box. Click OK.

2. The Remote Installation Services Setup Wizard appears. Note that the wizard will need an active DHCP and DHS server on the network. Click Next.

3. The Remote Installation Folder Location window appears. Enter the location where you want to store the RIS installation folder, which cannot be your system drive (boot partition/volume). The drive must be formatted with Windows 2000's version of NTFS. Use the Browse button to change the drive as necessary, but do keep the default name of "RemoteInstall," shown in Figure E-3. Click Next.

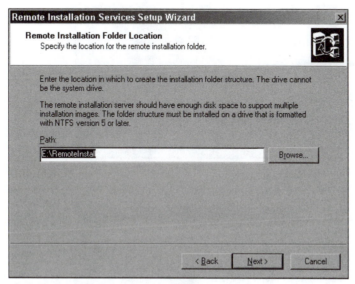

Figure E-3: Select a storage location.

4. The Initial Settings window appears next. By default, the server does not begin responding to clients until you configure it to do so once setup is complete. This prevents the RIS server from servicing a client before you have the image(s) configured as desired. If you want the RIS server to begin responding immediately, just check the check box. You can also use this box to tell the RIS server not to respond to any unknown client computers, as shown in Figure E-4. Make your selection (if any) and click Next.

5. Next, setup wants to know the location of the Windows 2000 Professional installation files, which can be your CD-ROM drive, a network location, or even another location on your computer. Enter the location or use the Browse button and then click Next.

6. Enter a folder name for the image. By default, this name is win2000.pro. You can use a different name, but it should be one that is as descriptive as possible (especially if you plan on using several different images). Click Next.

7. Enter a friendly description of the image and insert additional help text as desired, as shown in Figure E-5. Then click Next.

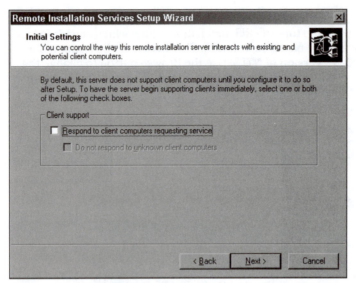

Figure E-4: Initial Settings options

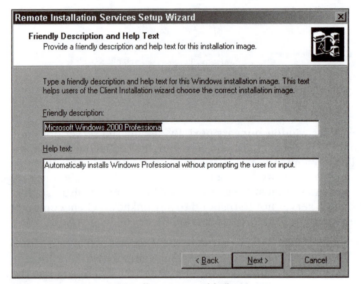

Figure E-5: Insert a friendly name and help text.

8. A Review Settings window appears. Check your selections and then click Next. The RIS server begins copying the files, as shown in Figure E-6. Click the Done button when setup completes.

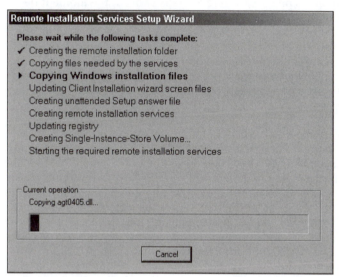

Figure E-6: RIS setup

Image Descriptions

Depending on the requirements of your environment, you may need several different images. For example, the marketing department may need a specific image that automatically installs a number of applications used by its employees. Likewise, the accounting department may need a completely different configuration. Keep in mind that you can store as many images for which you have storage space, and SIS helps keep those storage sizes to a minimum.

With several images, you should use image titles and help texts that are as descriptive as possible. This action helps other IT professionals determine which image should be used for a particular need. You will find help text that describes the application or configuration features of an image to be very useful.

RIS clients

In order to begin a Windows 2000 Professional client installation automatically, a client computer must be able to contact the RIS server so that installation can begin. This contact is one area where RIS falls short at the moment because clients must meet some very restrictive requirements in order to communicate with the RIS server, and those requirements leave many network client computers out of the RIS picture. If you are purchasing new client hardware, you can use these requirements to make certain the hardware supports RIS. However, if you are using existing hardware, you'll find that many of your client computers cannot use RIS without upgrading their network adapter card (which may not be too practical in a wide deployment scenario).

There are two different ways client computers can contact the RIS server. First, any computer that has a Preboot Execution (PXE) ROM network adapter card can contact the RIS server. With a PXE ROM, a client computer can be started, and the PXE ROM will display a message asking if you want to start the computer from the network. After choosing to do so, the PXE ROM will obtain an IP address from the DHCP server, and then it will contact the DNS server to locate the RIS server. Once the RIS server is found, then RIS can begin the installation of the desired Windows 2000 Professional image. Before beginning the installation, the RIS server contacts the Active Directory using Boot Information Negotiation Layer (BINL) to see if the client is a "known" client in the Active Directory, which is a computer client that has a computer object in the Active Directory, and if installation can occur. If the client is a known client, then RIS begins the installation. All of this occurs without any input from an administrator.

Note   Personal computers that conform to the PC98 specification have the PXE capability.

This is all great, of course, but what happens if your client computers do not support PXE? In this case, Windows 2000 includes a RIS PXE boot emulator disk creator. This feature enables you to create a boot disk to boot nonPXE clients so they can contact the RIS server using the boot disk. However, things are not as simple as they seem. The boot disk works only on clients that have certain network adapters installed. Not just any network adapter will do, and all of the network adapters supported are PCI, leaving out most laptop computers. There's hope that more network adapter cards will be supported in the not too distant future, but right now only the following network adapters are supported:

  ✦ 3Com 3c900B-Combo

  ✦ 3Com 3c900B-FL

  ✦ 3Com 3c900B-TPC

✦ 3Com 3c900B-TPO

✦ 3Com 3c900-Combo

✦ 3Com 3c900-TPO

✦ 3Com 3c905B-Combo

✦ 3Com 3c905B-FX

✦ 3Com 3c905B-TX

✦ 3Com 3c905C-TX

✦ 3Com 3c905-T4

✦ 3Com 3c905-TX

✦ AMD PCnet Adapters

✦ Compaq NetFlex 100

✦ Compaq NetFlex 110

✦ Compaq NetFlex 3

✦ DEC DE450

✦ DEC DE500

✦ HP DeskDirect 10/100 TX

✦ Intel Pro 10+

✦ Intel Pro 100+

✦ Intel Pro 100B

✦ SMC 8432

✦ SMC 9332

✦ SMC 9432

So, if the network adapter card in the client computer is not PXE compliant or if one of these network adapter cards is not installed, you're simply out of luck (unless you want to start installing new network adapter cards). If, however, you do use one of the supported network adapter cards, then you can make the PXE boot disk. Just follow these steps:

1. On the RIS server, right-click My Computer and choose Explore.

2. Locate the volume that contains the RIS folder and then navigate to the Remoteinstall\Admin\I386 directory. You see a utility called RBFG.EXE, as shown in Figure E-7.

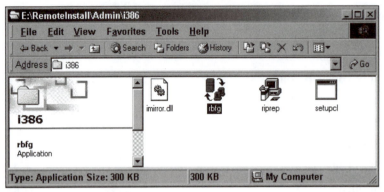

Figure E-7: RBFG.EXE

3. Double-click the RBFG.EXE icon. A Boot Disk Generator window appears, as shown in Figure E-8. You can click the Adapter List button to view the supported adapters.

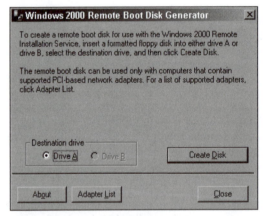

Figure E-8: Boot Disk Generator

4. Insert a blank, formatted floppy disk into the A drive and then click the Create Disk button on the Boot Disk Generator window.

5. The disk is created. Click No when asked if you want to create another disk. Then click Close.

Assigning permission to create computer objects

Before a client computer can use RIS to install Windows 2000 Professional, a computer object must be created in the Active Directory. Remember that this object creation is necessary because the RIS server will check for this object to determine if the client is a "known" computer.

You don't want just anyone to be able to create computer objects, so you need to establish the permission for particular users or groups. In order to enable users or IT professionals the ability to create computer accounts, you use the Delegation of Control Wizard in the Active Directory. When you use the Delegation of Control Wizard, you assign the right to "Create Computer Objects." To assign this permission to users or groups, you must be a member of the Domain Admins group for the domain where the users or groups will be installing Windows 2000 Professional.

Follow these steps to assign the Create Computer Objects permission:

1. On a domain controller, log on with an enterprise admin account.

2. Click Start ➪ Programs ➪ Administrative Tools ➪ Active Directory Users and Computers.

3. Right-click the desired domain and choose Delegate Control from the menu that appears.

4. Click the Next button on the Welcome screen.

5. In the Users or Groups screen, click the Add button.

6. In the Users, Groups, and Computers dialog box that appears, select the desired user or group and then click the Add button. Repeat this process to add other users or groups. Click OK when you're done and then click Next.

7. In the Tasks to Delegate screen, shown in Figure E-9, select the Join a Computer to the Domain check box and then click Next.

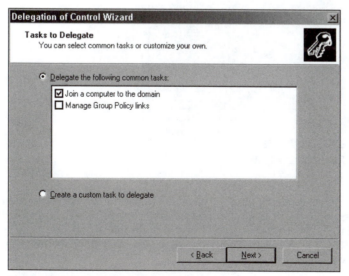

Figure E-9: Tasks to Delegate window

8. Click Finish. The desired users or groups now have the right to create computer objects in the Active Directory.

Enabling the RIS server

During RIS server setup, you had the option to enable the server to begin responding to clients immediately. If you didn't choose to enable this option, you need to do so now so that the RIS server can begin servicing clients. If at any time in the future you want to stop the RIS server from servicing clients, you can also easily disable the server. Both of the actions are performed using the Active Directory Users and Computers console.

In Active Directory Users and Computers, open the folder or OU that holds the RIS server's computer account. Right-click the server icon and choose Properties. You see a Remote Install tab on the properties sheets, shown in Figure E-10.

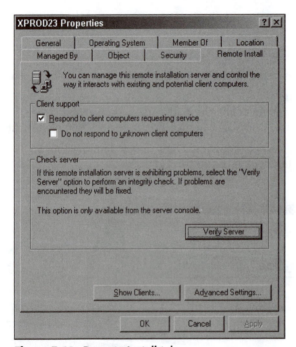

Figure E-10: Remote Install tab

Notice on the Remote Install tab that you can enable the RIS server by simply checking the "Respond to client computers requesting service" check box as well as "Do not respond to unknown computers." Keep in mind that if you select the second check box, the RIS server will check the Active Directory to see if the client computer is known or not.

You also see a Verify Server button on this tab as well. The Verify Server option opens a wizard that checks the integrity of the RIS server and resolves any problems, if they exist.

If you click the Show Clients button, you see a list of RIS clients who have accessed the RIS server for installation. If you are just starting to use RIS, there will, of course, be no listing here, but for future reference, this is an easy place to examine clients.

The Advanced Settings button opens advanced setting features, shown in Figure E-11.

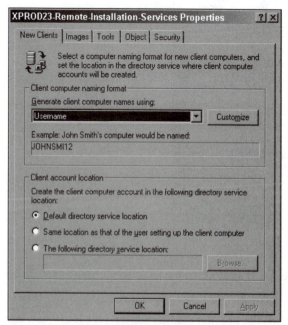

Figure E-11: RIS advanced settings

On the New Clients tab, you can determine how client computer names are generated. By default, the user name is used to generate the client computer name, but this may not be your best option. You can use the drop-down menu and select a different naming scheme, such as first initial, last name, and NP plus MAC, or you can click the Customize button and select a custom name generating setting.

In the second part of the window, you can determine where the client computer account is created, such as in the default directory service location, in the same location as that of the user setting up the client computer, or in a specific location in the Active Directory.

The Images tab, shown in Figure E-12, provides a list of your current images and enables you to manage them using the Add, Remove, or Properties buttons.

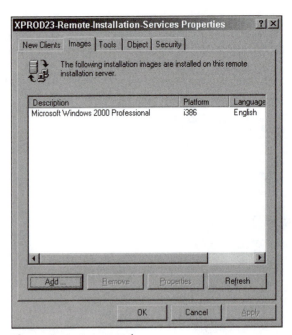

Figure E-12: Images tab

You can use this tab to create new answer files for images in order to automate the setup process completely.

The Tools, Object, and Security tabs provide standard interfaces for RIS server management.

RIS and Group Policy

It is important to remember that RIS is not an island, and other client management tools, such as Group Policy, apply as well. You can actually manage some RIS setup options within Group Policy by opening the Group Policy console for the desired GPO (at the site, domain, or OU level).

Under User Configuration, expand Windows Settings and double-click on the Remote Installation Service icon. You then see the policy for the Remote Installation Service. Beyond this basic option, do keep in mind that Group Policy is applied to RIS clients, just as it would be to any other clients for any GPOs configured for the site, domain, and OU in which the new computer object resides.

Working with RIS images

RIS supports two different types of images — CD-based and Remote Installation Preparation Wizard (RIPrep) images. The basic difference is that the CD-based image is copied from the Windows 2000 Professional installation CD-ROM. You can create multiple CD-based images and assign different answer files to them for particular installation needs. RIPrep images copy an installed Windows 2000 Professional computer's hard drive and store the image on the server. This feature enables you to make an exact copy of a computer that configured as desired and has desired applications installed. RIS can then copy this drive to another computer so your computers have an exact configuration and applications already installed. The following two sections explore both of these options in more detail.

Creating new CD-based images

When you installed RIS, a CD-based image was created. This is a default Windows 2000 Professional image. You can create additional CD-based images by accessing the Image tab of the RIS server properties as described in the previous section. You might ask, "Why would I want additional CD-based images?" In reality, when you create additional CD-based images, you are creating different answer files for the same image. For example, suppose you have a marketing group and an administrative group. The marketing group needs different setup options configured when Windows 2000 Professional is installed than the administrative group does. The solution to this dilemma is to create different answer files for each group in order to meet the installation needs. You learn how to create answer files later in this chapter, but for now, you simply need to know that you can apply different answer files to the same CD-based image.

However, you can also create a new CD-based image as well. This feature is particularly useful if you need to make different language versions of Windows 2000 Professional available and will be useful in the future with different client releases of Windows that support RIS.

To assign a different answer file to an image, just follow these steps:

1. In Active Directory Users and Computers, access the RIS server icon.
2. Right-click the icon and choose Properties.
3. Click the Remote Install tab and then click the Advanced Settings button.
4. Select the Images tab.
5. Click the Add button. A window appears, as shown in Figure E-13, that allows you to associate a new answer file with an existing image or to create a new image.

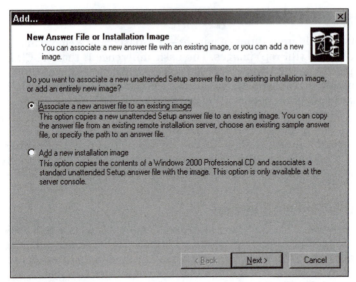

Figure E-13: Associate an answer file or create a new image.

Note If you are not running the Active Directory Users and Computers console on the RIS server, the option to create a new image will not appear. Install the AdminPak found on the Windows 2000 Server installation CD-ROM to use the Active Directory Users and Computers console on the RIS server.

6. If you choose to install a new CD-based image, just follow the wizard. If you choose to associate a new answer file, you can choose to use one of the RIS sample answer files, an answer file on another RIS server, or an answer file you have created in an alternate location.

Tip Answer files used with RIS must end in a *.sif* extension. Typical *unattended.txt* answer files will not work.

7. Depending on the selection you made, specify the answer file that you want to use and then specify which image you want to associate with the answer file.

8. Enter the friendly description and help text.

9. Review your settings and then click Finish.

Creating RIPrep images

As mentioned, RIPrep enables you to configure a particular Windows 2000 Professional computer, install desired applications, and then copy the computer's hard drive. This copy can then be imaged to RIS clients. As you can imagine, this option is quite powerful because you can install thousands of identical computers, complete with desired settings and applications, automatically.

RIPrep is a lot like Sysprep, which you can learn about later in this appendix. RIPrep, however, is easier to work with because client computers do not have to have the exact same hardware configuration in order to receive a RIPrep image. However, as you can imagine, problems can occur when trying to use RIPrep with very different client computers. Ideally, all of the computers should be the same in terms of hardware, or at least very similar.

It is also important to note that you cannot have all RIPrep images. You must keep at least one CD-based image of Windows 2000 Professional so that a driver can be extracted if necessary. The point is simply not to delete all CD-based images if you plan on using only RIPrep images.

To create a RIPrep image, first install and configure the Windows 2000 Professional computer as desired. This includes all settings and applications. Once you have completed the installation, you should spend some time testing the new computer to make certain the configuration is what is needed — after all, this is the image that will copied to the new target clients.

Tip   When installing the master computer, make sure you install Windows 2000 Professional in the C drive. RIPrep will copy only the contents of the C drive.

To create a RIPrep image, follow these steps:

1. On the Windows 2000 Professional master computer log on with a domain administrator account. Access the RIS server by mapping to or using My Network Places to browse.

2. The RIS server has a share called REMINST. Navigate to REMINST\Admin\ I386\. You see the RIPrep icon, shown in Figure E-14.

Figure E-14: RIPrep icon

3. Double-click the RIPrep icon and then click Next on the Welcome screen.

4. In the Server Name window, enter the RIS server name to which the master computer will copy the image and then click Next.

5. In the Folder Name window, type the name of a folder you want to use to store the image. If the folder does not exist, it will be created. Enter the folder name and then click Next.

6. Enter a friendly description and any help text for the image and then click Next.

7. A "Programs or Services are Running" window appears. Any running applications and/or services are listed in the window, shown in Figure E-15. Close these applications and services and then click Next.

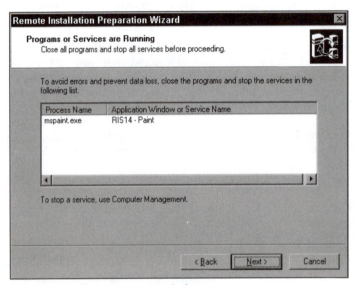

Figure E-15: Close Programs window

8. A review settings window appears. Double-check your settings and then click Next.

9. A window appears telling you that the image will be prepared and replicated to the server, and then the workstation will shut down. Once the workstation reboots, mini-setup will run. Click Next to begin the image copy.

10. Once the files are copied and the workstation reboots, then a mini-setup program runs that appears as though Windows 2000 Professional is reinstalling. RIPrep takes out the user-specific settings and the computer's SID, so when the computer reboots, mini-setup allows you to reenter the necessary information, such as user name, organization, time zone, and so forth. Mini-setup does not have to go through hardware detection and all that — it simply needs user setting information, so the process does not take much time.

Prestaging client computers

Client computers can be prestaged, which simply means you configure a computer account for them and determine which RIS server will service which client. Prestaged computers are referred to as "managed" computers in the Active Directory, and this feature helps you control load balancing between RIS servers. Prestaging is quite easy—just follow these steps:

1. On a Windows 2000 domain controller, open Active Directory Users and Computers.

2. Right-click the OU or container that will contain the new client computer object and then point to New and select Computer.

3. In the New Object—Computer window, enter a desired name for the new computer object.

4. Click the "This is a managed computer" check box, as shown in Figure E-16. Enter the Globally Unique Identifier (GUID), which is found in the computer's BIOS or on the computer case.

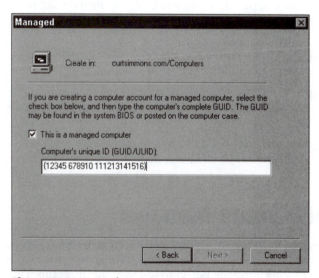

Figure E-16: Enter the computer's GUID.

5. In the next window, select "any RIS server" or specify the RIS server you want the computer to use.

Tip Once you have prestaged client computers, you also need to set permissions for the users or groups that will access the RIS client accounts in order to run the installation. These users and groups need to have read, write, reset password, and change password permissions for the computer object. Just right-click the computer object and choose Properties. Then select the Security tab to configure the permissions.

Running a RIS installation

Now that you have learned how to set up RIS and create both CD-based and RIPrep images, your final step is simply to run installations for your client computers. For PXE clients, just turn on the computer and choose the "boot from network" option that appears. For other clients that have a supported network adapter card, use the PXE boot disk to access the RIS server. Either way, you will be prompted to press F12 once the RIS server is contacted so that installation can begin. Follow these steps:

1. Start the client computer and press y to boot from the network. Then, press F12 to begin the installation.

2. A Welcome message appears, telling you that you need a valid logon name and password to install RIS. When prompted, enter a valid user name and password.

3. Depending on how Group Policy is configured, options may appear (such as automatic, custom, and so on).

4. The Operating System Choice screen appears. Select the appropriate image. A caution window appears telling you the client computer's hard disk will be formatted.

5. The summary window appears, and then the installation of Windows 2000 Server begins. If an answer file is in use, no further interaction is required.

Windows 2000 Setup Manager

If you read the previous section, and if you have any experience deploying Windows clients, you have most likely heard of an answer file. An answer file is a simple file that answers the questions normally posed to the user during setup. This feature removes the need for a person to physically sit at the machine during installation and enables the automation of installation. As you can see, an answer file can be very helpful in mass deployment scenarios.

Answer files are not new, but Windows 2000 includes a wizard called Setup Manager designed to easily help you create answer files. Setup Manager is very easy to use, and the following sections will show you how.

Installing Setup Manager

Setup Manager is not installed by default with a Windows 2000 installation, but it is found, along with some other tools, in Deploy.cab on your Windows 2000 Server installation CD-ROM. To install Setup Manager, you need to create a folder where the cabinet files can be extracted. You might simply want to create a "Deployment" folder for this purpose. Once you have created a folder, just follow these steps:

1. Insert your Windows 2000 Server installation CD-ROM into your CD-ROM drive and then choose the Browse This CD option from the menu that appears.

2. Open the Support folder and then open the Tools folder.

3. Right-click Deploy.cab and click Explore. The files in Deploy.cab appear in an Explorer window, shown in Figure E-17.

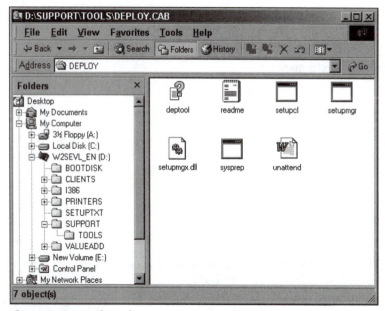

Figure E-17: Deploy.cab

4. Choose the Edit menu and then choose Select All. Right-click on the content and choose Extract. A browse for folder window appears. Select the folder where you want the items extracted and click OK.

5. The items are extracted and placed in the destination folder. The deployment tools are now ready to use, as shown in Figure E-18.

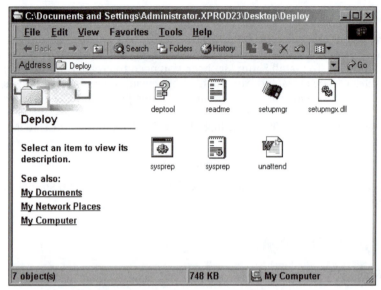

Figure E-18: Deployment tools

Using Setup Manager

Once Setup Manager is installed, you can then use Setup Manager to create answer files as they are needed. The following steps walk you through the Setup Manager Wizard and discuss the options available.

1. Locate the folder where you extracted Deploy.cab.

2. Double-click setupmgr.

3. The Setup Manager Wizard begins. Click Next on the Welcome Screen.

4. The New or Existing Answer File window appears. You have three radio button options, shown in Figure E-19:

   • **Create a new answer file** — This option creates a new answer file by leading you through the wizard to answer setup questions.

   • **Create an answer file that duplicates this computer's configuration** — This option allows the wizard to create an answer file that copies your computer configuration.

   • **Modify an existing answer file** — This option allows you to open an existing answer file and make changes to it.

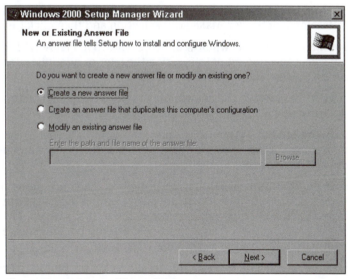

Figure E-19: Answer file options

5. The Product to Install window appears, shown in Figure E-20. You have the option of selecting Windows 2000 Unattended Installation, Sysprep Install, or Remote Installation Services. Select Windows 2000 Unattended Installation and then click Next.

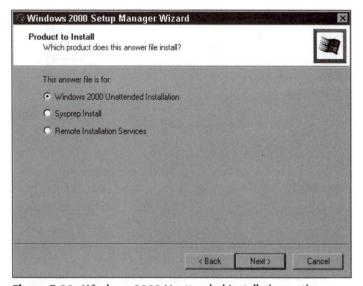

Figure E-20: Windows 2000 Unattended Installation option

6. Select the platform the answer file installs. You can choose either Windows 2000 Professional or Server. Make your selection and then click Next.

7. The User Interaction Level window appears, shown in Figure E-21. In this window, you select the amount of interaction the user or administrator must perform during the installation. You have the following options:

- **Provide defaults**—The answer file provides the default setup answers, and the user has to accept the defaults or make changes.

- **Fully automated**—The user has no interaction with setup. All of the answers are provided in the answer file, and the user cannot intervene and make changes.

- **Hide pages**—Typical setup pages, where the user ordinarily provides information, are hidden if they are answered in the answer file. Those pages that are not answered appear to the user to answer. This feature allows you to automate some portions of setup but collect specific information from the user as necessary.

- **Read only**—In Read-only mode, the pages are presented to the user, but the user cannot make any changes to the pages.

- **GUI attended**—The GUI attended option automates only the text-based portion of setup. The graphical phase of setup functions like a normal install where the user enters setup information.

Make your selection by clicking the appropriate radio button and then click Next.

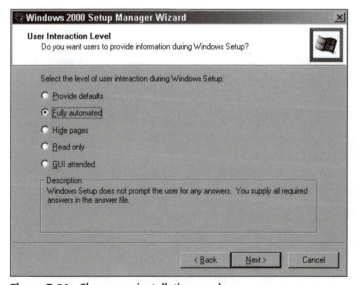

Figure E-21: Choose an installation mode.

8. Enter the default name and organization and then click Next.

9. Depending on whether you selected the Server or Professional option, the next several windows ask you the same questions you would see during a Server or Professional installation. Answer the questions as desired, keeping in mind these will be the default answers provided during installation.

10. Once you have responded to the answer file questions, Setup Manager needs to know whether you will create a distribution folder for the setup files or whether you will use the CD to run the installs. Typically, you will want to use a distribution folder for the over-the-network installations. This option keeps all of your files, drivers, and other setup information in one location. If you want to create the folder, click the Yes radio button. If you do not want to create the folder, click No. Then click Next.

11. The Distribution Folder window, shown in Figure E-22, allows you to either create a new distribution folder or modify an existing one. By default, new distribution folders are named win2000dist and shared with the same name. Make your selection and then click Next.

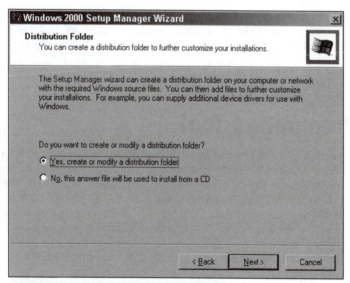

Figure E-22: Create a distribution folder.

12. The Additional Mass Storage Drivers window appears. You can use the Browse button to select the driver files for any mass storage devices that may exist on your computers. If you do not have any additional devices to select or once you have selected the drivers, simply click Next.

13. The Hardware Abstraction Layer window appears. You can use this window to replace the default HAL with one of your choice by using the Browse button. Make desired changes or simply click Next.

14. The Additional Commands window appears. This window allows you to enter additional commands to run scripts at the end of unattended setup. You can run any command that does not require you to be logged on. Click Next.

15. The OEM Branding window appears. This window allows you to add OEM branding, such as logos or custom background bitmaps, to setup. Use the Browse button to select the desired bitmap files if necessary and then click Next.

16. The Additional Files or Folders window appears. Use this window to copy files and folders after install. This feature is useful to copy documents, drivers, and other data to the computer you are installing. Select the desired folder location and then use the Add Files and Remove Files buttons to manage the list. Click Next.

17. The Answer File Name window appears. By default, the file is called unattended.txt, but you can change it if desired. Click Next.

18. Next, specify the location of the installation files. You can choose to copy the files either from the CD-ROM or from a specified location. Make your selection and then click Next. The files are copied to the distribution folder.

19. Setup Manager completes. Click Finish.

System Preparation Tool

System Preparation (Sysprep.exe) is an additional deployment tool found in the Deploy.cab folder. Sysprep is designed to help produce drive images. At first glance, this option may not seem any different than RIPrep images, and in fact, the two are quite similar. However, Sysprep is designed for mass installations and is often used by original equipment manufacturers (OEMs) to mass-produce drive installations. The Sysprep tool copies a complete drive image and then runs a mini-setup routine where user specific information is gathered from the user. This information replaces the Sysprep generic user information and assigns the computer an SID. The end result is a copy of the same machine with individual user data.

A common example of Sysprep technology is a typical home PC. Most users purchase a desired PC from a computer store. When they turn on the PC, a mini-setup routine runs that gathers user information, assigns an SID, and makes the PC all their own. The reality is that each machine sold has exactly the same drive data, but the mini-setup routine customizes the computer to the desires of the user.

Sysprep.exe isn't a Microsoft idea, and there are many third-party programs that provide similar drive copy functions. The problem with Sysprep is that it can be used *only* to copy Windows 2000 Professional and Server computers (but not domain controllers). Also, Windows 2000 does not include the ability to physically duplicate a computer's disk—it just includes the software to prepare a disk for duplication. You *must* use a third-party imaging utility to actually copy the computer hard disk. System Preparation does just as it sounds—it prepares the system for drive imaging.

Before using Sysprep, you should spend a considerable amount of time preparing the master computer. The master computer is the computer whose hard drive will be copied. Since an exact copy of this hard drive is distributed to all other machines, it is critical that you configure the system as desired and correctly install desired application and system components. The following list provides some guidelines on what you should and should not do when configuring your system:

✦ Install only applications that are necessary.

✦ Do not map any network drives or create network places.

✦ Do not configure Internet connections or Internet Explorer favorites.

✦ Be sure to configure any desired desktop and system settings.

✦ Do not install printers or other peripherals.

✦ Remember, anything you do on the master computer will be copied and installed on the duplicated drives.

Also, Sysprep is a little more stubborn about computer hardware than RIS. The client computers need to have essentially the same basic system components as the master computer. Some of the specific components you should examine are in the following list:

✦ The master and target computers must use identical mass storage controllers.

✦ Hard disk sizes on the master and target should be the same.

✦ The master and target must use the same hardware abstraction layer (HAL).

✦ Standard hardware should be close to the same. It doesn't have to be identical, but you should have drivers available if it is not identical.

Remember, the idea behind Sysprep is to create clones of the same machine. By keeping the computers physically the same, you greatly reduce the possibility of problems.

Once your master computer is ready to go, you will most likely want to create a sysprep.inf file, which is essentially an answer file that enables you to automate the mini-setup portion of installation. Create the sysprep.inf file and then create a folder in the C drive on the master computer called "Sysprep." To create the sysprep.inf file, just follow these steps:

1. Launch Setup Manager and click Next on the Welcome screen.

2. In the New or Existing Answer File window, select the Create a new answer file radio button and then click Next.

3. In the Product to Install window, select the Sysprep Install radio button and then click Next.

4. Select the Windows 2000 Professional button and then click Next.

5. You can accept the end user license agreement (EULA) for the user, or you can allow the user to accept the agreement. If you do not want the user involved in the process at all, click the Yes button. If you want the users to have to read and accept the agreement, click the No button. After making your choice, click Next, as shown in Figure E-23.

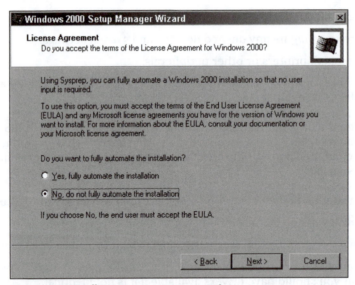

Figure E-23: Fully automate process options

6. Enter a default user name and organization and then click Next.

7. Enter a default computer name and click Next.

8. In the Administrator Password window, provide a password or choose the "prompt the user for an Administrator password" option. Make your selection and click Next.

9. In Display Settings window, use the drop-down menu to select the desired display settings or simply accept the Windows default settings by clicking Next.

10. In the Network Settings window, select either the typical settings radio button or the custom settings radio button and then click Next. If you select custom settings, you will be prompted to select the networking components you want to install.

11. In the Workgroup or Domain window, select either a workgroup or domain the computer will join. You can also specify a computer account and automatically create a user account for the user by selecting the check box and entering the information, as shown in Figure E-24.

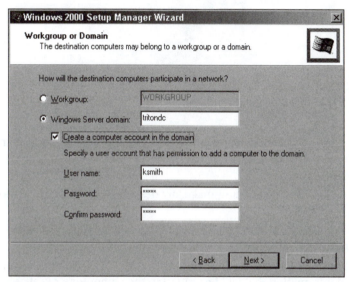

Figure E-24: Join workgroup or domain.

12. In the Time Zone window, specify a time zone if desired by using the drop-down menu. Click Next.

13. In the Additional Settings window, you can choose to edit additional Windows settings or not. If you choose to edit additional settings, other windows appear asking to configure various Windows components. Make your selection and click Next.

14. The Sysprep Folder window appears, shown in Figure E-25. This window allows you to create a Sysprep folder where the system can store your Sysprep files. You should choose to create this folder. Click Yes and then click Next.

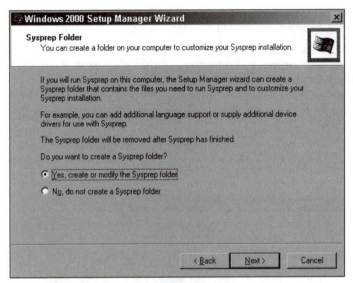

Figure E-25: Sysprep Folder window

15. In the Additional Commands window, you can specify additional commands or scripts that should run at the end of setup. Make any desired selections and click Next.

16. In the OEM Branding window, make any desired OEM bitmap selections and then click Next.

17. In the Additional Files and folders window, select any desired files or folders you would like to be copied. Click Next.

18. The OEM Duplicator String window appears. This window allows you to enter Sysprep information that will be written to the computer's registry. This allows you to track the Sysprep installation version or installation as desired. Enter information you desire and then click Next.

19. Provide an answer file name. By default, this file is named "sysprep.inf." The file must be stored in C:\Sysprep of the master computer, or it will not be read. Click Next.

20. Click Finish.

If you do not create a sysprep.inf file, you still need to do a little work on the master computer so that Sysprep.exe can use it. First, you still need to create a folder named Sysprep in drive C on the master computer. Once this is done, locate your Deploy.cab folder and copy setupcl.exe and sysprep.exe to the C:\Sysprep folder. Sysprep needs these files to operate and assumes they will be located in C:\Sysprep.

In order to run Sysprep on the master computer, simply access the command prompt, type **cd sysprep,** and press Enter. Then type **sysprep** and press enter. This action opens the Sysprep folder and then begins the Sysprep utility. There are some command-line options you can learn about by typing **sysprep /?** and pressing Enter. Follow additional instructions that may appear. Once Sysprep has run, you can then use a third-party drive imaging software to duplicate the disk.

Summary

In this appendix, you explored the deployment features of Windows 2000. Because deployment can be a rather intensive proposition, Windows 2000 includes tools to help you prepare and complete deployment in a way that saves administrative time and frustration. Working in conjunction with the Active Directory, Remote Installation Service can be used to easily and effectively roll out Windows 2000 Professional, and you can use Setup Manager to create appropriate answer files needed for unattended installations. Likewise, Sysprep can also be used to prepare master computers for drive duplication, although the actual drive duplication must be performed by a third-party utility.

✦   ✦   ✦

APPENDIX

In This Appendix

Schema classes and
related attributes

Default schema
attributes

Schema Class
and Attribute
Reference

The Active Directory is built using a schema, or schematic,
that defines the objects that can be stored in the Active
Directory and the attributes that define those objects. In this
appendix, you find a table listing all of the schema classes and
the attributes that belong to each class. Then, you find a list
of all default schema attributes.

Cross-Reference You can learn more about the Active Directory Schema in
Chapter 14.

Schema Classes and
Related Attributes

Table F-1 is a reference table that lists every default schema
class, the type of class, and all mandatory and optional attributes for each class. Use this table as a handy reference tool.

Table F-1
Schema Classes and Related Attributes

Class	Class Type	Mandatory & Optional Attributes
ACSPolicy	Structural	aCSAggregateTokenRatePerUser aCSDirection aCSIdentityName aCSMaxAggregatePeakRatePerUser aCSMaxDurationPerFlow aCSMaximumSDUSize aCSMaxPeakBandwidthPerFlow aCSMaxTokenBucketPerFlow aCSMaxTokenRatePerFlow aCSMinimumDelayVariation aCSMinimumLatency aCSMinimumPolicedSize aCSPermissionsBits aCSServiceType aCSTimeOfDay aCSTotalNoOfFlows
aCSResourceLimits	Structural	aCSAllocableRSVPBandwidth aCSMaxPeakBandwidth aCSMaxPeakBandwithdPerFlow aCSMaxTokenRatePerFlow aCSServiceType
aCSSubnet	Structural	aCSAllocableRSVPBandwidth aCSCacheTimeout aCSDSBMDeadTime aCSDSBMPriority aCSDSBMRefresh aCSEnableACSService aCSEnableRSVPAccounting aCSEnableRSVPMessageLoggin aCSEventLogLevel aCSMaxDurationPerFlow aCSMaxNoOfAccountFiles aCSMaxNoOfLogFiles aCSMaxPeakBandwidth aCSMaxPeakBandwidthPerFlow aCSMaxSizeOfRSVPAccountFile aCSMaxSizeOfRSVPLogFile aCSMaxTokenRateFlow aCSNonReservedMaxSDUSize aCSNonRerservedMinPolicedSize aCSNonReservedPeakRate aCSNonReservedTokenSize

Class	Class Type	Mandatory & Optional Attributes
		aCSNonReservedTxLimit aCSNonReservedTxSize aCSRSVPAccountFilesLocation aCSRSVPLogFilesLocation aCSServerList
addressBookContainer	Structural	displayName purportedSearch
addressTemplate	Structural	displayName addressSyntax addressType perMsgDialogDisplayTable perRecipDialogDisplayTable proxyGenerationEnabled
applicationEntity	Structural	cn presentationAddress l o ou SeeAlso SupportedApplicationContext
applicationProcess	Structural	cn l ou seeAlso
applicationSettings	Abstract	applicationName notificationList
applicationSiteSettings	Abstract	applicationName notificationList
attributeSchema	Structural	attributeID attributeSyntax cn isSingleValued IDAPDisplayName oMSyntax schemaDGUID attributeSecurityGUID classDisplayName extendedCharsAllowed isDefunct isEphemeral isMemberOfPartialAttributeSet linkID

Continued

Table F-1 *(continued)*		
Class	*Class Type*	*Mandatory & Optional Attributes*
attributeSchema	Structural	mAPIID oMObjectClass rangeLower rangeUpper schemaFlagsEx searchFlags systemOnly
builtinDomain	Structural	{none}
categoryRegistration	Structural	categoryId localeID localizedDescription managedBy
certificationAuthority	Structural	authorityRevocationList cACertifcate certifcateRevocationList cn cACertifcateDN cAConnect cAUsages cAWEBURL certificateTemplates cRLObject crossCertificatePair currentParentCA deltaRevocationList dNSHostName domainID domainPolicyObject enrollmentProviders parentCA parentCACertificateChain pendingCACertificates pendingParentCA previousCACertificates previousParentCA searchGuides signatureAlgorithms supportedApplicationContext teletexTerminalIdentifier

Class	Class Type	Mandatory & Optional Attributes
classRegistration	Structural	cOMCLSID cOMInterfaceID cOMOtherProgId cOMProgID cOMTreatAsClassId implementedCategories managedBy requiredCategories
classSchema	Structural	cn defaultObjectCategory governsID objectClassCategory schemaIDGUID subClassOf auxiliaryClass classDisplayName defaultHidingValue defaultSecurityDescriptor isDefunct lDAPDisplayName mayContain mustContain possSuperiors rDNAttID schemaFlagsEx systemAuxiliaryClass systemMayContain systemMustContain systemOnly systemPossSuperiors
classStore	Structural	appSchemaVersion lastUpdateSequence nextLevelStore versionNumber
comConnectionPoint	Structural	cn marshalledInterface moniker monikerDisplayName

Continued

Table F-1 *(continued)*		
Class	*Class Type*	*Mandatory & Optional Attributes*
computer	Structural	catalogs
		cn
		defaultLocalPolicyObject
		dNSHostName
		localPolicyFlags
		location
		machineRole
		managedBy
		netbootGUID
		netbootinitialization
		netbootMachineFilePath
		netbootMirrorDataFile
		netbootSIFFile
		networkAddress
		operatingSystem
		operatingSystemHotfix
		operatingSystemServicePack
		operatingSystemVersion
		physicalLocationObject
		rIDSetReferences
		siteGUID
		volumeCount
configuration	Structural	cn
connectionPoint	Abstract	cn
		keywords
		managedBy
contact	Structural	cn
		notes
container	Structural	cn
		defaultClassStore
		schemaVersion
controlAccessRight	Structural	appliesTo
		localizationDisplayId
		rightsGuid
		validAccesses
country	Abstract	c
		co
		searchGuide

Class	Class Type	Mandatory & Optional Attributes
cRLDistirbutionPoint	Structural	cn authorityRevocationList certificateAuthorityObject certificateRevocationList cRLPartitionedRevocationList deltaRevocationList
crossRef	Structural	cn dnsRoot nCName Enabled nETBIOSName rootTrust superiorDNSROOT trustParent
crossRefContainer	Structural	uPNSuffixes
device	Abstract	cn l o ou owner seeAlso serialNumber
dfsConfiguration	Structural	{none}
dHCPClass	Structural	dhcpFlags dhcpIdentification dhcpType dhcpUniqueKey dhcpClasses dhcpMask dhcpMaxKey dhcpObjDescription dhcpObjName dhcpOptions dhcpProperties dhcpRanges dhcpReservations dhcpServers dhcpSites dhcpState dhcpSubnets dhcpUpdateTime mscopeId

Continued

Table F-1 *(continued)*

Class	Class Type	Mandatory & Optional Attributes
dHCPClass	Structural	networkAddress optionDescription optionsLocation superScopeDescription superScopes
displaySpecifier	Structural	adminContexMenu adminPropertyPages attributeDisplayNames classDisplayName contextMenu createDialog createWizardExt creationWizard iconPath queryFilter scopeFlags shellContextMenu shellPropertyPages treatAsLeaf
displayTemplate	Structural	cn addressEntryDisplayTable addressEntryDisplayTableMSDOS helpData16 helpDate32 helpFileName originalDisplayTable originalDisplayTableMSDOS
dMD	Structural	cn dmdName prefixMap schemaInfo schemaUpdate
dnsNode	Structural	dc dNSProperty dnsRecord dNSTombstoned
dnsZone	Structural	dc dnsAllowDynamic dnsAllowXFR dnsNotifySecondaries dnsProperty dnsSecureSecondaries managedBy

Class	Class Type	Mandatory & Optional Attributes
domain	Abstract	dc
domainDNS	Structural	managedBy
domainPolicy	Structural	authenticationOptions defaultLocalPolicyObject domainCAs domainPolicyReference domainWidePolicy eFSPolicy forceLogoff ipsecPolicyReference lockoutDuration lockOutObservationWindow lockoutThreshold managedBy maxPwdAge maxRenewAge maxTicketAge minPwdAge minPwdLength minTicketAge proxyLifetime publicKeyPolicy pwdHistoryLength pwdProperties qualityOfService
dSA	Structural	knowledgeInformation
dSUISetting	Structural	dSUIAdminMaximum dSUIAdminNotification dSUIShellMaximum
fileLinkTracking	Structural	{none}
fileLinkTrackingEntry	Structural	{none}
foreignSecurityPrincipal	Structural	objectSid foreignIdentifier
fTDfs	Structural	pKT pKTGuid remoterServerName
group	Structural	groupType adminCount controlAccessRights desktopProfile groupAttributes

Continued

Table F-1 *(continued)*		
Class	*Class Type*	*Mandatory & Optional Attributes*
group	Structural	groupMemebershipSAM mail managedBy member nonSecurityMember nTGroupMembers operatorCount primaryGroupToken
groupOfNames	Abstract	cn member businessCategory o ou owner seeAlso
groupPolicyContainer	Structural	flags gPCFileSysPath gPCFunctionalityVersion gPCMachineExtensionNames gPCUserExtensionNames versionNumber
indexServerCatalog	Structural	creator friendlyNames indexedScopes queryPoint uNCName
infrastructureUpdate	Structural	dnReferenceUpdate
intellimirrorGroup	Structural	{none}
intellimirrorSCP	Structural	netbootAllowNewClients netbootAnswerOnlyValidClients netbootAnswerRequests netbootCurrentClientCount netbootIntelMirrorOSes netbootLimitClients netbootLocallyInstalledOSes netbootMachineFilePath netbootMaxClients netbootNewMachineNamingPolicy netbootNewMachineOU netbootServer netbootTools

Class	Class Type	Mandatory & Optional Attributes
interSiteTransport	Structural	transportAddressAttribute transportDLLName options repInterval
interSiteTransportContainer	Structural	{none}
ipsecBase	Abstract	ipsecData ipsecDataType ipsecID ipsecName ipsecOwnersReference
ipsecFilter	Structural	{none}
ipsecISAKMPPolicy	Structural	{none}
ipsecNegotiationPolicy	Structural	iPSECNegotiationPolicyAction iPSECNegotiationPolicyType
ipsecNFA	Structural	ipsecFilterReference ipsecNegotiationPolicyReference
ipsecPolicy	Structural	ipsecISAKMPRefernce ipsecNFAReference
leaf	Abstract	{none}
licensingSiteSettings	Structural	siteServer
linkTrackObjectMoveTa	Structural	{none}
linkTrackOMTEntry	Structural	birthLocation currentLocation oMTGuid oMTIndxGuid timeRefresh
linkTrackVolEntry	Structural	currMachineId linkTrackSecret objectCount seqNotification timeRefresh timeVolChange volTableChange volTabledxGUID
linkTrackVolumeTable	Structural	{none}

Continued

	Table F-1 *(continued)*	
Class	*Class Type*	*Mandatory & Optional Attributes*
locality	Structural	l searchGuide seeAlso st street
lostAndFound	Structural	moveTreeState
mailRecipient	Auxiliary	cn garbageCollPeriod info legacyExchangeDN showInAddressBook telephoneNumber textEncodedORAddress userCert userCertificate userSMIMECertificate
meeting	Structural	meetingName meetingAdvertiseScope meetingApplication meetingBandwidth meetingBlob meetingContactInfo meetingDescription meetingEndTime meetingID meetingIP meetingIsEncrypted meetingKeyword meetingLanguage meetingLocation meetingMaxParticipants meetingOriginator meetingOwner meetingProtocol meetingRating meetingRecurrence meetingScope meetingStartTime meetingType meetingURL

Class	Class Type	Mandatory & Optional Attributes
msExchConfigurationContainer	Structural	addressBookRoots globalAddressList templateRoots
mSMQConfiguration	Structural	mSMQComputerType mSMQComputerTypeEx mSMQDependentClientServices mSMQDsServices mSMQEncryptKey mSMQForeign mSMQInRoutingServers mSMQJournalQuota mSMQOSType mSMQOutRoutingServers mSMQOwnerID mSMQQuota mSMQRoutingServices mSMQServiceType mSMQSignKey mSMQSites
mSMQEnterpriseSettings	Structural	mSMQCSPName mSMQInterval1 mSMQInterval2 mSMQLongLived mSMQNameStyle mSMQVersion
mSMQMigratedUser	Structural	mSMQDigests mSMQDigestsMig mSMQSignCertificates mSMQSignCertificatesMig mSMQUserSid objectSid
mSMQQueue	Structural	mSMQAuthenticate mSMQBasePriority mSMQJournal mSMQLabel mSMQLabelEx mSMQOwnerID mSMQPrivacyLevel mSMQQueueJournalQuota mSMQQueueNameExt mSMQQueueQuota mSMQQueueType mSMQTransactional

Continued

Table F-1 (continued)		
Class	**Class Type**	**Mandatory & Optional Attributes**
mSMQSettings	Structural	mSMQDependentClientService mSMQDsService mSMQMigrated mSMQNt4Flags mSMQOwnerID mSMQQMID mSMQRoutingService mSMQServices mSMQSiteName mSMQSiteNameEx
mSMQSiteLink	Structural	mSMQCost mSMQSite1 mSMQSite2 mSMQSiteGates mSMQSiteGatesMig
mS-SQL-OLAPCube	Structural	mS-SQL-Contact mS-SQL-Description mS-SQL-InformationURL mS-SQL-Keywords mS-SQL-LastUpdatedDate mS-SQL-Name mS-SQL-PublicationURL mS-SQL-Size mS-SQL-Status
mS-SQL-OLAPDatabase	Structural	mS-SQL-Applications mS-SQL-ConnectionURL mS-SQL-Contact mS-SQL-Description mS-SQL-InformationURL mS-SQL-Keywords mS-SQL-LastBackupDate mS-SQL-LastUpdatedDate mS-SQL-Name mS-SQL-PublicationURL mS-SQL-Size mS-SQL-Status mS-SQL-Type
mS-SQL-OLAPServer	Structural	mS-SQL-Build mS-SQL-Contact mS-SQL-InformationURL mS-SQL-Keywords mS-SQL-Language mS-SQL-Name

Class	Class Type	Mandatory & Optional Attributes
		mS-SQL-PublicationURL
		mS-SQL-RegisteredOwner
		mS-SQL-ServiceAccount
		mS-SQL-Status
		mS-SQL-Version
mS-SQL-SQLDatabase	Structural	mS-SQL-Alias
		mS-SQL-Applications
		mS-SQL-Contact
		mS-SQL-CreationDate
		mS-SQL-Description
		mS-SQL-InformationURL
		mS-SQL-Keywords
		mS-SQL-LastBackupDate
		mS-SQL-LastDiagnosticDate
		mS-SQL-Name
		mS-SQL-Size
		mS-SQL-Status
mS-SQL-SQLPublication	Structural	mS-SQL-AllowAnonymousSub...
		mS-SQL-AllowImmediateUpda...
		mS-SQL-AllowKnownPullSub...
		mS-SQL-AllowQueuedUpdating...
		mS-SQL-AllowSnapshotFileFT...
		mS-SQL-Database
		mS-SQL-Description
		mS-SQL-Name
		mS-SQL-Publisher
		mS-SQL-Status
		mS-SQL-ThirdParty
		mS-SQL-Type
mS-SQL-SQLRepository	Structural	mS-SQL-Build
		mS-SQL-Contact
		mS-SQL-Description
		mS-SQL-InformationDirectory
		mS-SQL-Name
		mS-SQL-Status
		mS-SQL-Version
mS-SQL-SQLServer	Structural	mS-SQL-AppleTalk
		mS-SQL-Build
		mS-SQL-CharacterSet
		mS-SQL-Clustered
		mS-SQL-Contact
		mS-SQL-GPSHeight
		mS-SQL-GPSLatitude

Continued

Table F-1 *(continued)*

Class	Class Type	Mandatory & Optional Attributes
mS-SQL-SQLServer	Structural	mS-SQL-GPSLongitude mS-SQL-InformationURL mS-SQL-Keywords mS-SQL-LastUpdatedDate mS-SQL-Location mS-SQL-Memory mS-SQL-MultiProtocol mS-SQL-Name mS-SQL-NamedPipe mS-SQL-RegisteredOwner mS-SQL-ServiceAccount mS-SQL-SortOrder mS-SQL-SPX mS-SQL-Status mS-SQL-TCPIP mS-SQL-UnicodeSortOrder mS-SQL-Vines
nTDSConnection	Structural	enabledConnection fromServer options generatedConnection mS-DS-ReplicatesNCReason schedule transportType
nTDSDSA	Structural	dMDLocation fRSRootPath hasMasterNCs hasPartialReplicaNCs invocationId lastBackupRestorationTime managedBy networkAddress options queryPolicyObject retiredRepIDSASignatures serverReference
nTDSService	Structural	gSHeuristics garbageCollPeriod replTopologyStayOfExecution sPNMappings tombstoneLifetime

Class	Class Type	Mandatory & Optional Attributes
nTDSSiteSettings	Structural	interSiteTopologyFailover interSiteTopologyGenerator interSiteTopologyRenew managedBy options queryPolicyObject schedule
nTFRSMember	Structural	frsComputerReference fRSControlDataCreation fRSControlInboundBacklog fRSControlOutboundBacklog fRSExtensions fRSFlags fRSPartnerAuthLevel fRSRootSecurity fRSServiceCommand fRSUpdateTimeout serverReference
nTFRSReplicaSet	Structural	fRSDirectoryFilter fRSDSPoll fRSExtensions fRSFileFilter fRSFlags fRSLevelLimit fRSPartnerAuthLevel fRSPrimaryMember fRSReplicaSetGUID fRSReplicaSetType fRSRootSecurity fRSServiceCommand fRSVersionGUID managedBy schedule
nTFRSSettings	Structural	fRSExtensions managedBy
nTFRSSubscriber	Structural	fRSRootPath fRSStagingPath fRSExtensions fRSFaultCondition fRSFlags fRSMemberReference fRSServiceCommand fRSServiceCommandStatus

Continued

Table F-1 (continued)		
Class	**Class Type**	**Mandatory & Optional Attributes**
nTFRSSubscriber	Structural	fRSTimeLastCommand fRSTimeLastConfigChange fRSUpdateTimeout schedule
nTFRSSubscriptions	Structural	fRSExtensions fRSVersion fRSWorkingPath
organization	Structural	o businessCategory destinationIndicator facsimileTelephoneNumber internationalISDNNumber l physicalDeliveryOfficeName postalAddress postalCode postOfficeBox preferredDeliveryMethod registeredAddress searchGuide seeAlso st street telephoneNumber teletexTerminalIdentifier telexNumber userPassword x121Address
organizationalPerson	Abstract	assistant c co comment company countryCode department destinationIndicator division employeeID facsimileTelephoneNumber generationQualifier givenName homePhone homePostalAddress

Class	Class Type	Mandatory & Optional Attributes
		initials
		internationalISDNNumber
		ipPhone
		l
		mail
		manager
		mhsORAddress
		middleName
		mobile
		o
		otherFacsimileTelephoneNumber
		otherHomePhone
		otherIpPhone
		otherMailbox
		otherMobile
		otherPager
		otherTelephone
		ou
		pager
		personalTitle
		physicalDeliveryOfficeName
		postalAddress
		postalCode
		postalOfficeBox
		preferredDeliveryMethod
		primaryInternationalISDNNumber
		primaryTelexNumber
		registeredAddress
		st
		street
		streetAddress
		teletexTerminalIdentifier
		telexNumber
		thumbnailLogo
		thumbnailPhoto
		title
		x121Address
organizationalRole	Structural	cn
		destinationIndicator
		facsimileTelephoneNumber
		internationalISDNNumber
		l
		ou
		physicalDeliveryOfficeName
		postalAddress

Continued

Table F-1 *(continued)*		
Class	*Class Type*	*Mandatory & Optional Attributes*
organizationalRole	Structural	postalCode postOfficeBox preferredDeliveryMethod registeredAddress roleOccupant seeAlso st street telephoneNumber teletexTerminalIdentifier telexNumber x121Address
organizationalUnit	Structural	ou businessCategory c co countryCode defaultGroup desktopProfile destinationIndicator facsimileTelephoneNumber gPLink gPOptions internationalISDNNumber l managedBy physicalDeliveryOfficeName postalAddress postalCode postOfficeBox preferredDeliveryMethod registeredAddress searchGuide seeAlso st street telephoneNumber teletexTerminalIdentifier telexNumber thumbnailLogo uPNSuffixes userPassword x121Address

Class	Class Type	Mandatory & Optional Attributes
packageRegistration	Structural	canUpgradeScript
		categories
		cOMClassID
		cOMInterfaceID
		cOMProgID
		cOMTypeLibId
		fileExtPriority
		iconPath
		installUiLevel
		lastUpdateSequence
		localeID
		machineArchitecture
		managedBy
		msiFileList
		msiScript
		msiScriptName
		msiScriptPath
		msiScriptSize
		packageFlags
		packageName
		packageType
		productCode
		setupCommand
		upgradeProductCode
		vendor
		versionNumberHi
		versionNumberLo
person	Abstract	cn
		seeAlso
		sn
		telephoneNumber
		userPassword
physicalLocation	Structural	managedBy
pKICertificateTemplate	Structural	displayName
		flags
		pKICriticalExtensions
		pKIDefaultCSPs
		pKIDefaultKeySpec
		pKIEnrollmontAccess
		pKIExpirationPeriod
		pKIExtendedKeyUsage
		pKIKeyUsage
		pKIMaxIssuingDepth
		pKIOverlapPeriod

Continued

Table F-1 *(continued)*		
Class	*Class Type*	*Mandatory & Optional Attributes*
pKIEnrollmentService	Structural	cACertificate cACertificateDN certificateTemplates dNSHostName enrollmentProviders signatureAlgorithms
printQueue	Structural	printerName serverName shortServerName uNCName versionNumber assettNumber bytesPerMinute defaultPriority driverName driverVersion location operatingSystem operatingSystemHotfix operatingSystemServicePack operatingSystemVersion physicalLocationObject portName printAttributes printBinNames printCollate printColor printDuplexSupported printEndTime printFormName printKeepPrintedJobs printLanguage printMACAddress printMaxCopies printMaxResolutionSupported printMaxXExtent printMaxYExtent printMediaReady printMediaSupported printMemory printMinXExtent printMinYExtent printNetworkAddress printNotify

Class	Class Type	Mandatory & Optional Attributes
		printNumberUp printOrientationsSupported printOwner printPagesPerMinute printRate printRateUnit printSeparatorFile printShareNae printSpooling printStaplingSupported printStartTime printStatus priority
queryPolicy	Structural	IDAPAdminLimits IDAPIPDenyList
remoteMailRecipient	Structural	managedBy remoteSource remoteSourceType
remoteStorageServicePo	Structural	remoteStorageGUID
residentialPerson	Structural	businessCategory destinationIndicator facsimileTelephoneNumber internationalISDNNumber l ou physicalDeliveryOfficeName postalAddress postalCode postOfficeBox preferredDeliveryMethod registeredAddress st street teletexTerminalIdentifier telexNumber title x121Address
rIDManager	Structural	rIDAvailablePool
rIDSet	Structural	rIDAllocationPool rIDNextRID rIDPReviousAllocationPool rIDUsedPool

Continued

Table F-1 *(continued)*

Class	Class Type	Mandatory & Optional Attributes
rpcContainer	Structural	nameServiceFlags
rpcEntry	Abstract	{none}
rpcGroup	Structural	rpcNsGroup rpcNsObjectID
rpcProfile	Structural	{none}
rpcProfileElement	Structural	rpcNsInterfaceID rpcNsPriority rpcNsAnnotation rpcNsProfileEntry
rpcServer	Structural	rpcNsCodeset rpcNsEntryFlags rpcNsObjectID
rpcServerElement	Structural	rpcNsBindings rpcNsInterfaceID rpcNsTransferSyntax
rRASAdministrationConn	Structural	msRRASAttribute
rRASAdministrationDictio	Structural	msRRASVendorAttributeEntry
samDomain	Auxiliary	auditingPolicy builtinCreationTime builtinModifiedCount cACertificate controlAccessRights creationTime defaultLocalPolicyObject description desktopProfile domainPolicyObject eFSPolicy gPLink gPOptions lockoutDuration lockoutObservationWindow lockoutThreshold lSACreationTime lSAModifiedCount maxPwdAge minPwdAge minPwdLength modifiedCountAtLastProm nETBIOSName

Class	Class Type	Mandatory & Optional Attributes
		nextRid nTmixedDomain pekKeyChangeInterval pekList privateKey pwdHistoryLength pwdProperties replicaSource rIDManagerReference treename
samDomainBase	Auxiliary	creationTime domainReplica forceLogoff lockoutDuration lockoutObservationWindow lockoutThreshold maxPwdAge minPwdAge minPwdLength modifiedCount modifiedCountAtLastProm nextRid nTSecurityDescriptor objectSid oEMInformation pwdHistoryLength pwdProperties revision serverRole serverState uASCompat
samServer	Structural	{none}
secret	Structural	currentValue lastSetTime priorSetTime priorValue
securityObject	Abstract	cn
securityPrincipal	Auxiliary	objectSid sAMAccountName accountNameHistory altSecurityIdentities nTSecurityDescriptor rid

Continued

Table F-1 *(continued)*		
Class	*Class Type*	*Mandatory & Optional Attributes*
securityPrincipal	Auxiliary	sAMAccountType securityIdentifier sIDHistory supplementalCredentials tokenGroups tokenGroupsGlobalAndUniversal tokenGroupsNoGCAcceptable
server	Structural	bridgeheadTransportList dNSHostName mailAddress managedBy serialNumber serverReference
serversContainer	Structural	{none}
serviceAdministrationPoint	Structural	{none}
serviceClass	Structural	displayName serviceClassID serviceClassInfo
serviceConnectionPoint	Structural	serviceBindingInformation serviceClassName serviceDNSName serviceDNSNameType
serviceInstance	Structural	displayName serviceClassID serviceInstanceVersion winsockAddresses
site	Structural	gPLink gPOptions location managedBy mSMQInterval1 mSMQInterval2 mSMQNt4Stub mSMQSiteForeign mSMQSiteID notificationList
siteLink	Structural	siteList cost options replInterval schedule

Class	Class Type	Mandatory & Optional Attributes
siteLinkBridge	Structural	siteLinkList
sitesContainer	Structural	{none}
storage	Structural	iconPath moniker monikerDisplayName
subnet	Structural	location physicalLocationObject siteObject
subnetContainer	Structural	{none}
subSchema	Structural	attributeTypes dITContentRules extendedAttributeInfo extendedClassInfo modifyTimeStamp objectClasses
top	Abstract	instanceType nTSecurityDescriptor objectCategory objectClass adminDescription adminDisplayName allowedAttributes allowedAttributesEffective allowedChildClasses allowedChildClassesEffective bridgeheadServerListBL canonicalName cn createTimeStamp description directReports displayName displayNamePrintable distinguishedName dSASignature dSCorePropagationData extensionName flags fromEntry frsComputerReferenceBL frsMemberReferenceBL fSMORoleOwner isCriticalSystemObject

Continued

Table F-1 *(continued)*

Class	Class Type	Mandatory & Optional Attributes
top	Abstract	isDeleted
		isPrivilegeHolder
		lastKnownParent
		managedObjects
		masteredBy
		memberOf
		modifyTimeStamp
		mS-DS-ConsistencyChildCount
		mS-DS-ConsistencyGuid
		name
		netbootSCPBL
		nonSecurityMemberBL
		objectGUID
		objectVersion
		otherWellKnownObjects
		partialAttributeDeletionList
		partialAttibuteSet
		possibleInferiors
		proxiedObjectName
		proxyAddresses
		queryPolicyBL
		replPropertyMetaData
		replUpToDateVector
		repsFrom
		repsTo
		revision
		sDRightsEffective
		serverReferenceBL
		showInAdvancedViewOnly
		siteObjectBL
		subRefs
		subSchemaSubEntry
		systemFlags
		url
		uSNChanged
		uSNCreated
		uSNDSALastObjRemoved
		uSNIntersite
		uSNLastObjRem
		uSNSource
		wbemPath
		wellKnownObjects
		whenChanged
		whenCreated
		wWWHomePage

Class	Class Type	Mandatory & Optional Attributes
trustedDomain	Structural	additionalTrustedServiceNames domainCrossRef domainIdentifier flatName intialAuthIncoming intialAuthOutgoing securityIdentifier trustAttributes trustAuthIncoming trustAuthOutgoing trustDirection trustPartner trustPosixOffset trustType
typeLibrary	Structural	cOMClassID cOMInterfaceID cOMUniqueLIBID
user	Structural	accountExpires aCSPolicyName adminCount badPasswordTime badPwdCount codePage controlAccessRights dBCSPwd defaultClassStore desktopProfile dynamicLDAPServer groupMembershipSAM groupPriority groupsToIgnore homeDirectory homeDrive lastLogoff lastLogon lmPwdHistory localeID lockoutTime logonCount logonHours logonWorkstation maxStorage mS-DS-CreatorSID mSMQDigests

Continued

Table F-1 (continued)		
Class	**Class Type**	**Mandatory & Optional Attributes**
user	Structural	mSMQDigestsMig
		mSMQSignCertificates
		mSMQSignCertificatesMig
		msNPAllowDialin
		msNPCallingStationID
		msNPSavedCallingStationID
		msRADIUSCallbackNumber
		msRADIUSFramedIPAddress
		msRADIUSFramedRoute
		msRADIUSServiceType
		msRASSavedCallbackNumber
		msRASSavedFramedIPAddress
		msRASSavedFramedRoute
		networkAddress
		ntPwdHistory
		operatorCount
		otherLoginWorkstations
		preferredOU
		primaryGroupID
		profilePath
		pwdLastSet
		scriptPath
		servicePrincipalName
		terminalServer
		unicodePwd
		userAccountControl
		userCertificate
		userParameters
		userPrincipalName
		userSharedFolder
		userSharedFolderOther
		userWorkstations
volume	Structural	uNCName
		contentIndexingAllowed
		lastContentIndexed

Default Attribute Reference

In Table F-2, you'll find every default attribute in the Active Directory schema that ships from Microsoft. I've also included the syntax type for each attribute. Use this table as a quick and easy reference tool.

<table>
<tr><td colspan="2" align="center">Table F-2
Default Attribute Reference</td></tr>
<tr><td>*Attribute*</td><td>*Syntax*</td></tr>
<tr><td>accountExpires</td><td>Large Integer</td></tr>
<tr><td>accountNameHistory</td><td>Unicode String</td></tr>
<tr><td>aCSAggregateTokenRatePerUser</td><td>Large Integer</td></tr>
<tr><td>aCSAllocableRSVPBandwidth</td><td>Large Integer</td></tr>
<tr><td>aCSCacheTimeout</td><td>Integer</td></tr>
<tr><td>aCSDirection</td><td>Integer</td></tr>
<tr><td>aCSDSBMDeadTime</td><td>Integer</td></tr>
<tr><td>aCSDSBMPriority</td><td>Integer</td></tr>
<tr><td>aCSDSBMRefresh</td><td>Integer</td></tr>
<tr><td>aCSEnableACSService</td><td>Boolean</td></tr>
<tr><td>aCSEnableRSVPAccounting</td><td>Boolean</td></tr>
<tr><td>aCSEnableRSVPMessageLogging</td><td>Boolean</td></tr>
<tr><td>aCSEventLogLevel</td><td>Integer</td></tr>
<tr><td>aCSIdentityName</td><td>Unicode String</td></tr>
<tr><td>aCSMaxAggregatePeakRatePerUser</td><td>Large Integer</td></tr>
<tr><td>aCSMaxDurationPerFlow</td><td>Integer</td></tr>
<tr><td>aCSMaximumSDUSize</td><td>Large Integer</td></tr>
<tr><td>aCSMaxNoOfAccountFiles</td><td>Integer</td></tr>
<tr><td>aCSMaxNoOfLogFiles</td><td>Integer</td></tr>
<tr><td>aCSMaxPeakBandwidth</td><td>Large Integer</td></tr>
<tr><td>aCSMaxPeakBandwidthPerFlow</td><td>Large Integer</td></tr>
<tr><td>aCXMaxSizeOfRSVPAccountFile</td><td>Integer</td></tr>
<tr><td>aCSMaxSizeOfRSVPLogFile</td><td>Integer</td></tr>
<tr><td>aCSMaxTokenBucketPerFlow</td><td>Large Integer</td></tr>
<tr><td>aCSMaxTokenRatePerFlow</td><td>Large Integer</td></tr>
<tr><td>aCSMinimumDelayVariation</td><td>Large Integer</td></tr>
<tr><td>aCSMinimumLatency</td><td>Large Integer</td></tr>
<tr><td>aCSMinimumPolicedSize</td><td>Large Integer</td></tr>
<tr><td>aCSNonReservedMaxSDUSize</td><td>Large Integer</td></tr>
</table>

Continued

Table F-2 *(continued)*	
Attribute	**Syntax**
aCSNonReservedMinPolicedSize	Large Integer
aCSNonReservedPeakRate	Large Integer
aCSNonReservedTokenSize	Large Integer
aCSNonReservedTxLimit	Large Integer
aCSNonReservedTxSize	Large Integer
aCSPermissionBits	Large Integer
aCSPolicyName	Unicode String
aCSPriority	Integer
aCSRSVPAccountFilesLocation	Unicode String
aCSRSVPLogFilesLocation	Unicode String
aCSServerList	Unicode String
aCSServiceType	Integer
aCSTimeOfDay	Unicode String
aCSTotalNoOfFlows	Integer
additionalTrustedServiceNames	Unicode String
addressBookRoots	Distinguished Name
addressEntryDisplayTable	Octet String
addressEntryDisplayTableMSDOS	Octet String
addressSyntax	Octet String
addressType	Case Insensitive String
adminContextMenu	Unicode String
adminCount	Integer
adminDescription	Unicode String
adminDisplayName	Unicode String
adminPropertyPages	Unicode String
allowedAttributes	Object Identifier
allowedAttributesEffective	Object Identifier
allowedChildClasses	Object Identifier
allowedChildClassesEffective	Object Identifier
altSecurityIdentities	Unicode String
aNR	Unicode String

Attribute	Syntax
applicationName	Unicode String
appliesTo	Unicode String
appSchemaVersion	Integer
assetNumber	Unicode String
assistant	Distinguished Name
assocNTAccount	Octet String
attributeDisplayNames	Unicode String
attributeID	Object Identifier
attributeSecurityGUID	Octet String
attributeSyntax	Object Identifier
attributeTypes	Unicode String
auditingPolicy	Octet String
authenticationOptions	Integer
authorityRevocationList	Octet String
auxiliaryClass	Object Identifier
badPasswordTime	Large Integer
badPwdCount	Integer
birthLocation	Octet String
bridgeheadServerListBL	Distinguished Name
bridgeheadTransportList	Distinguished Name
builtinCreationTime	Large Integer
builtinModifiedCount	Large Integer
businessCategory	Unicode String
bytesPerMinute	Integer
c	Unicode String
cACertificate	Octet String
cACertificateDN	Unicode String
cAConnect	Unicode String
canonicalName	Unicode String
canUpgradeScript	Unicode String
catalogs	Unicode String

Continued

Table F-2 (continued)	
Attribute	**Syntax**
categories	Unicode String
categoryID	Octet String
cAUsages	Unicode String
cAWEBURL	Unicode String
certificateRevocationList	Distinguished Name
certificateRevocationList	Octet String
certificateTemplates	Unicode String
classDisplayName	Unicode String
cn	Unicode String
co	Unicode String
codePage	Integer
cOMClassID	Unicode String
cOMCLSID	Unicode String
cOMInterfaceID	Unicode String
comment	Unicode String
cOMOtherProgId	Unicode String
company	Unicode String
cOMProgID	Unicode String
cOMTreatAsCLassId	Unicode String
cOMTypelibId	Unicode String
cOMUniqueLIBID	Unicode String
contextIndexingAllowed	Boolean
contextMenu	Unicode String
controlAccessRights	Octet String
cost	Integer
countryCode	Integer
createDialog	Unicode String
createTimeStamp	Generalized Time
createWizardExt	Unicode String
creationTime	Large Integer
creationWizrd	Unicode String

Attribute	Syntax
creator	Unicode String
cRLObject	Distinguished Name
cRLPartitionedRevocationList	Octet String
crossCertificatePair	Octet String
currentLocation	Octet String
currentParentCA	DistinguishedName
currentValue	Octet String
currentMachineId	Octet String
dBCSPwd	Octet String
dc	Unicode String
defaultClassStore	Distinguished Name
defaultGroup	Distinguished Name
defaultHidingValue	Boolean
defaultLocalPolicyObject	Distinguished Name
defaultObjectCategory	Distinguished Name
defaultPriority	Integer
defaultSecurityDescriptor	Unicode String
deltaRevocationList	Octet String
department	Unicode String
description	Unicode String
desktopProfile	Unicode String
destinationIndicator	Print Case String
dhcpClasses	Octet String
dhcpFlags	Large Integer
dhcpIdentification	Unicode String
dhcpMask	Print Case String
dhcpMaxKey	Large Integer
dhcpObjDescription	Unicode String
dhcpObjName	Unicode String
dhcpOptions	Octet String
dhcpProperties	Octet String

Continued

Table F-2 *(continued)*	
Attribute	*Syntax*
dhcpRanges	Print Case String
dhcpReservations	Print Case String
dhcpServers	Print Case String
dhcpSites	Print Case String
dhcpState	Print Case String
dhcpSubnets	Print Case String
dhcpType	Integer
dhcpUniqueKey	Large Integer
dhcpUpdateTime	Large Integer
directReports	Distinguished Name
displayName	Unicode String
displayNamePrintable	Print Case String
distinguishedName	Distinguished Name
dITContentRules	Unicode String
division	Unicode String
dMDLocation	Distinguished Name
dmdName	Unicode String
dNReferenceUpdate	Distinguished Name
dnsAllowDynamic	Boolean
dnsAllowXFR	Boolean
dNSHostName	Unicode String
dnsNotifySecondaries	Integer
dNSProperty	Octet String
dnsRecord	Octet String
dnsRoot	Unicode String
dnsSecureSecondaries	Integer
dNSTombstoned	Boolean
domainCAs	Distinguished Name
domainCrossRef	Distinguished Name
domainID	Distinguished Name
domainIdentifier	Integer

Attribute	Syntax
domainPolicyObject	Distinguished Name
domainPolicyReference	Distinguished Name
domainReplica	Unicode String
domainWidePolicy	Octet String
driverName	Unicode String
driverVersion	Integer
dSASignature	Octet String
dSCorePropagationData	Generalized Time
dSHeuristics	Unicode String
dSUIAdminMaximum	Integer
dSUIAdminNotication	Unicode String
dSUIShellMaximum	Integer
dynamicLDAPServer	Distinguished Name
eFSPolicy	Octet String
employeeID	Unicode String
employeeNumber	Unicode String
employeeType	Unicode String
enabled	Boolean
enabledConnection	Boolean
enrollmentProviders	Unicode String
extendedAttributeInfo	Unicode String
extendedCharsAllowed	Boolean
extendedClassInfo	Unicode String
extensionName	Unicode String
facximileTelephoneNumber	Unicode String
fileExtPriority	Unicode String
flags	Integer
flatName	Unicode String
forceLogoff	Large Integer
foreignIdentifier	Octet String
friendlyNames	Unicode String

Continued

Table F-2 *(continued)*

Attribute	Syntax
fromEntry	Boolean
fromServer	Distinguished Name
fRSComputerReference	Distinguished Name
fRSComputerReferenceBL	Distinguished Name
fRSControlDataCreation	Unicode String
fRSControlInboundBacklog	Unicode String
fRSControlOutboundBacklog	Unicode String
fRSDirectoryFilter	Unicode String
fRSDSPoll	Integer
fRSExtensions	Octet String
fRSFaultCondition	Unicode String
fRSFileFilter	Unicode String
fRSFlags	Integer
fRSLevelLimit	Integer
fRSMemberReference	Distinguished Name
fRSMemberReferenceBL	Distinguished Name
fRSPartnerAuthLevel	Integer
fRSPrimaryMember	Distinguished Name
fRSReplicaSetGUID	Octet String
fRSReplicaSetType	Integer
fRSRootPath	Unicode String
fRSRootSecurity	NT Security Descriptor
fRSServiceCommand	Unicode String
fRSServiceCommandStatus	Unicode String
fRSStagingPath	Unicode String
fRSTimeLastCommand	UTC Coded Time
fRSTimeLastConfigChange	UTC Coded Time
fRSUpdateTimeout	Integer
fRSVersion	Unicode String
fRSVersionGUID	Octet String
fRSWorkingPath	Unicode String

Attribute	Syntax
fSMORoleOwner	Distinguished Name
garbageCollPeriod	Integer
generatedConnection	Boolean
generationQualifier	Unicode String
givenName	Unicode String
globalAddressList	Distinguished Name
governsID	Object Identifier
gPCFileSysPath	Unicode String
gPCFunctionalityVersion	Integer
gPCMachineExtensionNames	Unicode String
gPCUserExtensionNames	Unicode String
gPLink	Unicode String
gPOptions	Integer
groupAttributes	Integer
groupMembershipSAM	Octet String
groupPriority	Unicode String
groupsToIgnore	Unicode String
groupType	Integer
hasMasterNCs	Distinguished Name
hasPartialReplicaNCs	Distinguished Name
helpData16	Octet String
helpData32	Octet String
helpFileName	Unicode String
homeDirectory	Unicode String
homeDrive	Unicode String
homePhone	Unicode String
homePostalAddress	Unicode String
iconPath	Unicode String
implementedCategories	Octet String
indexedScopes	Unicode String
info	Unicode String

Continued

Table F-2 (continued)	
Attribute	**Syntax**
initialAuthIncoming	Unicode String
initialAuthOutgoing	Unicode String
initials	Unicode String
installUiLevel	Integer
instanceType	Integer
internationalISDNNumber	Numerical String
interSiteTopologyFailover	Integer
intersiteTopologyGenerator	Distinguished Name
interSiteTopologyRenew	Integer
invocationId	Octet String
ipPhone	Unicode String
ipsecData	Octet String
ipsecDataType	Integer
ipsecFilterReference	Distinguished Name
ipsecID	Unicode String
ipsecISAKMPReference	Distinguished Name
ipsecName	Unicode String
iPSECNegotiationPolicyAction	Unicode String
iPSECNegotiationPolicyReference	Distinguished Name
iPSECNegotiationPolicyType	Unicode String
ipsecNFAReference	Distinguished Name
ipsecOwnersReference	Distinguished Name
ipsecPolicyReference	Distinguished Name
isCriticalSystemObject	Boolean
isDefunct	Boolean
isDeleted	Boolean
isEphemeral	Boolean
isMemberOfPartialAttributeSet	Boolean
isPrivilegeHolder	Distinguished Name
isSingleValued	Boolean
keywords	Unicode String

Attribute	Syntax
knowledgeInformation	Case Insensitive String
l	Unicode String
lastBackupRestorationTime	Large Integer
lastContentIndexed	Large Integer
lastKnownparent	Distinguished Name
lastLogoff	Large Integer
lastLogon	Large Integer
lastSetTime	Large Integer
lastUpdateSequence	Unicode String
LDAPAdminLimits	Unicode String
LDAPDisplayName	Unicode String
LDAPIPDenyList	Octet String
legacyExchangeDN	Case Insensitive String
linkID	Integer
linkTrackSecret	Octet String
lmPwdHistory	Octet String
localeID	Integer
localizationDisplayId	Integer
localizedDescription	Unicode String
localPolicyFlags	Integer
localPolicyReference	Distinguished Name
location	Unicode String
lockoutDuration	Large Integer
lockoutObservationWindow	Large Integer
lockoutThreshold	Integer
lockoutTime	Large Integer
logonCount	Integer
logonHours	Octet String
logonWorkstation	Octet String
LSACreationTime	Large Integer
LSAModifiedCount	Large Integer

Continued

Table F-2 *(continued)*	
Attribute	**Syntax**
machineArchitecture	Enumeration
machinePasswordChangeInterval	Large Integer
machineRole	Enumeration
machineWidePolicy	Octet String
mail	Unicode String
mailAddress	Unicode String
managedBy	Distinguished Name
managedObjects	Distinguished Name
manager	Distinguished Name
mAPIID	Integer
marshalledInterface	Octet String
masteredBy	Distinguished Name
maxPwdAge	Large Integer
maxRenewAge	Large Integer
maxStorage	Large Integer
maxTicketAge	Large Integer
mayContain	Object Identifier
meetingAdvertiseScope	Unicode String
meetingApplication	Unicode String
meetingBandwidth	Integer
meetingBlob	Octet String
meetingContactInfo	Unicode String
meetingDescription	Unicode String
meetingEndTime	UTC Coded Time
meetingID	Unicode String
meetingIP	Unicode String
meetingIsEncrypted	Unicode String
meetingKeyword	Unicode String
meetingLanguage	Unicode String
meetingLocation	Unicode String
meetingMaxParticipants	Integer

Attribute	Syntax
meetingName	Unicode String
meetingOriginator	Unicode String
meetingOwner	Unicode String
meetingProtocol	Unicode String
meetingRating	Unicode String
meetingRecurrence	Unicode String
meetingScope	Unicode String
meetingStartTime	UTC Coded Time
meetingType	Unicode String
meetingURL	Unicode String
member	Distinguished Name
memberOf	Distinguished Name
mhsORAddress	Unicode String
middleName	Unicode String
minPwdAge	Large Integer
minPwdLength	Integer
minTicketAge	Large Integer
mobile	Unicode String
modifiedCount	Large Integer
modifiedCountAtLastProm	Large Integer
modifyTimeStamp	Generalized Time
moniker	Octet String
monikerDisplayName	Unicode String
moveTreeState	Octet String
mscopeId	Prince Case String
mS-DS-ConsistencyChildCount	Integer
mS-DS-ConsistencyGuid	Octet String
mS-DS-CreatorSID	SID
mS-DS-MachineAccountQuota	Integer
mS-DS-ReplicatesNCReason	DN Binary
msiFileList	Unicode String

Continued

Table F-2 *(continued)*	
Attribute	*Syntax*
msiScript	Octet String
msiScriptName	Unicode String
msiScriptPath	Unicode String
msiScriptSize	Integer
mSMQAuthenticate	Boolean
mSMQBasePriority	Integer
mSMQComputerType	Case Insensitive String
mSMQComputeTypeEx	Unicode String
mSMQCost	Integer
mSMQCSPName	Case Insensitive String
mSMQDependentClientService	Boolean
mSMQDependentClientServices	Boolean
mSMQDigests	Octet String
mSMQDigestsMig	Octet String
mSMQDsService	Boolean
mSMQDsService	Boolean
mSMQEncryptKey	Octet String
mSMQForeign	Boolean
mSMQInRoutingServers	Distinguished Name
mSMQInterval1	Integer
mSMQInterval2	Integer
mSMQJournal	Boolean
mSMQJournalQuota	Integer
mSMQLabel	Case Insensitive String
mSMQLabelEx	Unicode String
mSMQLongLived	Integer
mSMQMigrated	Boolean
mSMQNameStyle	Boolean
mSMQNt4Flags	Integer
mSMQNt4Stub	Integer
mSMQOSType	Integer

Attribute	Syntax
mSMQOutRoutingServers	Distinguished Name
mSMQOwnerID	Octet String
mSMQPrevSiteGates	Distinguished Name
mSMQPrivacyLevel	Enumeration
mSMQQMID	Octet String
mSMQQueueJournalQuota	Integer
mSMQQueueNameExt	Unicode String
mSMQQueueQuota	Integer
mSMQQueueType	Octet String
mSMQQuota	Integer
mSMQRoutingService	Boolean
mSMQRoutingServices	Boolean
mSMQServices	Integer
mSMQServiceType	Integer
mSMQSignCertificates	Octet String
mSMQSignCertificatesMig	Octet String
mSMQSignKey	Octet String
mSMQSite1	Distinguished Name
mSMQSite2	Distinguished Name
mSmQSiteForeign	Boolean
mSMQSiteGates	Distinguished Name
mSMQSiteGatesMig	Distinguished Name
mSMQSiteID	Octet String
mSMQSiteName	Case Insensitive String
mSmQSiteNameEx	Unicode String
mSMQSites	Octet String
mSMQTransactional	Boolean
mSMQUserSid	Octet String
mSMQVersion	Integer
msNPAllowDialin	Boolean
msNPCalledStationID	IA5-String

Continued

Table F-2 *(continued)*	
Attribute	**Syntax**
msNPCallingStationID	IA5-String
msNPSavedCallingStationID	IA5-String
msRADIUSCallbackNumber	IA5-String
msRADIUSFramedIPAddress	Integer
msRADIUSFramedRoute	IA5-String
msRADIUSServiceType	Integer
msRASSavedCallbackNumber	IA5-String
msRASSavedFramedIPAddress	Integer
msRASSavedFramedRoute	IA5-String
msRRASAttribute	Unicode String
msRRASVendorAttributeEntry	Unicode String
mS-SQL-Alias	Unicode String
mS-SQL-AllowAnonymousSubscription	Boolean
mS-SQL-AllowImmediateUpdatingSu...	Boolean
mS-SQL-AllowKnownPullSubcription	Boolean
mS-SQL-AllowQueuedUpdatingSubs...	Boolean
mS-SQL-AllowSnapshotFilesFTPDow...	Boolean
mS-SQL-AppleTalk	Unicode String
mS-SQL-Applications	Unicode String
mS-SQL-Build	Integer
mS-SQL-CharacterSet	Integer
mS-SQL-Clustered	Boolean
mS-SQL-ConnectionURL	Unicode String
mS-SQL-Contact	Unicode String
mS-SQL-CreationDate	Unicode String
mS-SQL-Database	Unicode String
mS-SQL-Description	Unicode String
mS-SQL-GPSHeight	Unicode String
mS-SQL-GPSLatitude	Unicode String
mS-SQL-GPSLongitude	Unicode String
mS-SQL-InformationDirectory	Boolean

Attribute	Syntax
mS-SQL-InformationURL	Unicode String
mS-SQL-Keywords	Unicode String
mS-SQL-Language	Unicode String
mS-SQL-LastBackupDate	Unicode String
mS-SQL-LastDiagnosticDate	Unicode String
mS-SQL-LastUpdatedDate	Unicode String
mS-SQL-Location	Unicode String
mS-SQL-Memory	Large Integer
mS-SQL-MultiProtocol	Unicode String
mS-SQL-Name	Unicode String
mS-SQL-NamedPipe	Unicode String
mS-SQL-PublicationURL	Unicode String
mS-SQL-Publisher	Unicode String
mS-SQL-RegisteredOwner	Unicode String
mS-SQL-ServiceAccount	Unicode String
mS-SQL-Size	Large Integer
mS-SQL-SortOrder	Unicode String
mS-SQL-SPX	Unicode String
mS-SQL-Status	Large Integer
mS-SQL-TCPIP	Unicode String
mS-SQL-ThirdParty	Boolean
mS-SQL-Type	Unicode String
mS-SQL-UnicodeSortOrder	Integer
mS-SQL-Version	Unicode String
mS-SQL-Vines	Unicode String
mustContain	Object Identifier
name	Unicode String
nameServiceFlags	Integer
nCName	Distinguished Name
nETBIOSName	Unicode String
netbootAllowNewClients	Boolean

Continued

Table F-2 *(continued)*	
Attribute	*Syntax*
netbootAnswerOnlyValidClients	Boolean
netbootAnswerRequests	Boolean
netbootCurrentClientCount	Integer
netbootGUID	Octet String
netbootInitialization	Unicode String
netbootIntelliMirrorOSes	Unicode String
netbootLimitClients	Boolean
netbootLocallyInstalledOSes	Unicode String
netbootMachineFilePath	Unicode String
netbootMaxClients	Integer
netbootMirrorDataFile	Unicode String
netbootNewMachineNamingPolicy	Unicode String
netbootNewMachineOU	Distinguished Name
netbootSCPBL	Distinguished Name
netbootServer	Distinguished Name
netbootSIFFile	Unicode String
netbootTools	Unicode String
networkAddress	Case Insensitive String
nextLevelStore	Distinguished Name
nextRid	Integer
nonSecurityMember	Distinguished Name
nonSecurityMemberBL	Distinguished Name
notes	Unicode String
notificationList	Distinguished Name
nTGroupMembers	Octet String
nTMixedDomain	Integer
ntPwdHistory	Octet String
nTSecurityDescriptor	NT Security Descriptor
o	Unicode String
objectCategory	Distinguished Name
objectClass	Object Identifier

Attribute	*Syntax*
objectClassCategory	Enumeration
objectClasses	Unicode String
objectCount	Integer
objectGUID	Octet String
objectSid	SID
objectVersion	Integer
oEMInformation	Unicode String
oMObjectClass	Octet String
oMSnytax	Integer
oMTGuid	Octet String
oMTIndxGuid	Octet String
operatingSystem	Unicode String
operatingSystemHotfix	Unicode String
operatingSystemServicePack	Unicode String
operatingSystemVersion	Unicode String
operatorCount	Integer
optionDescription	Unicode String
options	Integer
optionsLocation	Print Case String
originalDisplayTable	Octet String
originalDisplayTableMSDOS	Octet String
otherFacximileTelephoneNumber	Unicode String
otherHomePhone	Unicode String
otherIpPhone	Unicode String
otherLoginWorkstations	Unicode String
otherMailbox	Unicode String
otherMobile	Unicode String
otherPager	Unicode String
otherTelephone	Unicode String
otherWellKnownObjects	DN Binary
ou	Unicode String

Continued

Table F-2 *(continued)*	
Attribute	**Syntax**
owner	Distinguished Name
packageFlags	Integer
packageName	Unicode String
packageType	Integer
pager	Unicode String
parentCA	Distinguished Name
parentCACertificateChain	Octet String
parentGUID	Octet String
partialAttributeDeletionList	Octet String
partialAttributeSet	Octet String
pekKeyChangeInterval	Large Integer
pekList	Octet String
pendingCACertificates	Octet String
pendingParentCA	Distinguished Name
perMsgDialogDisplayTable	Octet String
perRecipDialogDisplayTable	Octet String
peronalTitle	Unicode String
physicalDeliveryOfficeName	Unicode String
physicalLocationObject	Distinguished Name
pKICriticalExtensions	Unicode String
pKIDefaultCSPs	Unicode String
pKIDefaultKeySpec	Integer
pKIEnrollmentAccess	NT Security Descriptor
pKIExpirationPeriod	Octet String
pKIExtendedKeyUsage	Unicode String
pKIKeyUsage	Octet String
pKIMaxIssuingDepth	Integer
pKIOverlapPeriod	Octet String
pKT	Octet String
pKTGuid	Octet String
policyReplicationFlags	Integer

Attribute	*Syntax*
portName	Unicode String
possibleInferiors	Object Identifier
possSuperiors	Object Identifier
postalAddress	Unicode String
postalCode	Unicode String
postOfficeBox	Unicode String
preferredDeliveryMethod	Enumeration
preferredOU	Distinguished Name
prefixMap	Octet String
presentationAddress	Address
previousCACertificates	Octet String
previousParentCA	Distinguished Name
primaryGroupID	Integer
primaryGroupToken	Integer
primaryInternationalISDNNumber	Unicode String
primaryTelexNumber	Unicode String
printAttributes	Integer
printBinNames	Unicode String
printCollate	Boolean
printColor	Boolean
printDuplexSupported	Boolean
printEndTime	Integer
printerName	Unicode String
printFormName	Unicode String
printKeepPrintedJobs	Boolean
printLanguage	Unicode String
printMACAddress	Unicode String
printMaxCopies	Integer
printMaxResolutionSupported	Integer
printMaxXExtent	Integer
printMaxYExtent	Integer

Continued

| Table F-2 *(continued)* ||
Attribute	*Syntax*
printMediaReady	Unicode String
printMediaSupported	Unicode String
printMemory	Integer
printMinXExtent	Integer
printMinYExtent	Integer
printNetworkAddress	Unicode String
printNotify	Unicode String
printNumberUp	Integer
printOrientationsSupported	Unicode String
printOwner	Unicode String
printPagesPerMinute	Integer
printRate	Integer
printRateUnit	Unicode String
printSeparatorFile	Unicode String
printShareName	Unicode String
printSpooling	Unicode String
printStaplingSupported	Boolean
printStartTime	Integer
printStatus	Unicode String
priority	Integer
priorSetTime	Large Integer
priorValue	Octet String
privateKey	Octet String
privilegeAttributes	Integer
privilegeDisplayName	Unicode String
privilegeHolder	Distinguished Name
privilegeValue	Large Integer
productCode	Octet String
profilePath	Unicode String
proxiedObjectName	DN Binary
proxyAddresses	Unicode String

Attribute	*Syntax*
proxyGenerationEnabled	Boolean
proxyLifetime	Large Integer
publicKeyPolicy	Octet String
purportedSearch	Unicode String
pwdHistoryLength	Integer
pwdLastSet	Large Integer
pwdProperties	Integer
qualityOfService	Integer
queryFilter	Unicode String
queryPoint	Unicode String
queryPolicyBL	Distinguished Name
queryPolicyObject	Distinguish Name
rangeLower	Integer
rangeUpper	Integer
rDNAttID	Object Identifier
registeredAddress	Octet String
remoteServerName	Unicode String
remoteSource	Unicode String
remoteSourceType	Integer
remoteStorageGUID	Unicode String
replicaSource	Unicode String
replInterval	Integer
replPropertyMetaData	Octet String
replTopologyStayOfExecution	Integer
replUpToDateVector	Octet String
repsFrom	Replica Link
repsTo	Replica Link
requiredCategories	Octet String
retiredReplDSASignatures	Octet String
revision	Integer
rid	Integer

Continued

Table F-2 *(continued)*	
Attribute	**Syntax**
rIDAllocationPool	Large Integer
rIDAvailablePool	Large Integer
rIDManagerReference	Distinguished Name
rIDNextRID	Integer
rIDPreviousAllocationPool	Large Integer
rIDSetReferences	Distinguished Name
rIDUsedPool	Large Integer
rightsGuid	Unicode String
roleOccupant	Distinguished Name
rootTrust	Distinguished Name
rpcNsAnnotation	Unicode String
rpcNsBindings	Unicode String
rpcNsCodeset	Unicode String
rpcNsEntryFlags	Integer
rpcNsGroup	Unicode String
rpcNsInterfaceID	Unicode String
rpcNsObjectID	Unicode String
rpcNsPriority	Integer
rpcNsProfileEntry	Unicode String
rpcNsTransfersyntax	Unicode String
sAMAccountName	Unicode String
sAMAccountType	Integer
schedule	Octet String
schemaFlagsEx	Integer
schemaIDGUID	Octet String
schemaInfo	Octet String
schemaUpdate	Generalized Time
schemaVersion	Integer
scopeFlags	Integer
scriptPath	Unicode String
sDRightsEffective	Integer

Attribute	Syntax
searchFlags	Enumeration
searchGuide	Octet String
securityIdentifier	SID
seeAlso	Distinguished Name
seqNotification	Integer
serialNumber	Print Case String
serverName	Unicode String
serverReference	Distinguished Name
serverReferenceBL	Distinguished Name
serverRole	Integer
serverState	Integer
servicebindingInformation	Unicode String
serviceClassID	Octet String
serviceClassInfo	Octet String
serviceClassName	Unicode String
serviceDNSName	Unicode String
serviceDNSNameType	Unicode String
serviceInstanceVersion	Octet String
servicePrincipalName	Unicode String
setupCommand	Unicode String
shellContextMenu	Unicode String
shellPropertyPages	Unicode String
shortServerName	Unicode String
showInAddressBook	Distinguished Name
showInAdvancedViewOnly	Boolean
sIDHistory	SID
signatureAlgorithms	Unicode String
siteGuid	Octet String
siteLinkList	Distinguished Name
siteList	Distinguished Name
siteObject	Distinguished Name

Continued

Table F-2 *(continued)*	
Attribute	**Syntax**
siteServer	Distinguished Name
sn	Unicode String
sPNMappings	Unicode String
st	Unicode String
street	Unicode String
streetAddress	Unicode String
subClassOf	Object Identifier
subRefs	Distinguished Name
subSchemaSubEntry	Distinguished Name
superiorDNSRoot	Unicode String
superScopeDescription	Unicode String
superScopes	Print Case String
supplementalCredentials	Octet String
supportedApplicationContext	Octet String
syncAttributes	Integer
syncMembership	Distinguished Name
syncWithObject	Distinguished Name
syncWithSid	SID
systemAuxiliaryClass	Object Identifier
systemFlags	Integer
systemMayContain	Object Identifier
systemMustContain	Object Identifier
systemOnly	Boolean
systemPossSuperiors	Object Identifier
telephoneNumber	Unicode String
teletexTerminalIdentifier	Octet String
telexNumber	Octet String
templateRoots	Distinguished Name
terminalServer	Octet String
textEncodedORAddress	Unicode String
thumbnailLogo	Octet String

Attribute	Syntax
thumbnailPhoto	Octet String
timeRefresh	Large Integer
timeVolChange	Large Integer
title	Unicode String
tokenGroups	SID
tokenGroupsGlobalAndUniversal	SID
tokenGroupsNOGCAcceptable	SID
tombstoneLifetime	Integer
transportAddressAttribute	Object Identifier
transportDLLName	Unicode String
transportType	Distinguished Name
treatAsLeaf	Boolean
treeName	Unicode String
trustAttributes	Integer
trustAuthIncoming	Octet String
trustAuthOutgoing	Octet String
trustDirection	Integer
trustParent	Distinguished Name
trustPartner	Unicode String
trustPosixOffset	Integer
trustType	Integer
uASCompat	Integer
uNCName	Unicode String
unicodePwd	Octet String
upgradeProductCode	Octect String
uPNSuffixes	Unicode String
url	Unicode String
userAccountControl	Integer
userCert	Octet String
userCertificate	Octet String
userParameters	Unicode String

Continued

Table F-2 (continued)

Attribute	Syntax
userPassword	Octet String
userPrincipalName	Unicode String
userSharedFolder	Unicode String
userSMIMECertificate	Octet String
userWorkstations	Unicode String
uSNChanged	Large Integer
uSNCreated	Large Integer
uSNDSALastObjRemoved	Large Integer
USNIntersite	Integer
uSNLastObjRem	Large Integer
uSNSource	Large Integer
validAccesses	Integer
vendor	Unicode String
versionNumber	Integer
versionNumberHi	Integer
versionNumberLo	Integer
volTableGUID	Octet String
volTabledxGUID	Octet String
volumeCount	Integer
wbemPath	Unicode String
wellKnownObjects	DN Binary
whenChanged	Generalized Time
whenCreated	Generalized Time
winsockAddresses	Octet String
wWWHomePage	Unicode String
x121Address	Numerical String

✦   ✦   ✦

Index